pocket →

PRESCRIPTION for SUCCESS

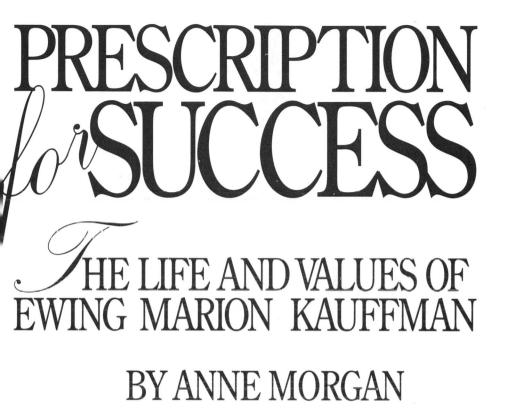

PRESCRIPTION *for* SUCCESS

THE LIFE AND VALUES OF EWING MARION KAUFFMAN

BY ANNE MORGAN

ANDREWS and McMEEL
A Universal Press Syndicate Company
KANSAS CITY

Photos courtesy of the Ewing M. Kauffman Foundation, Sue Kauffman, the Kansas
City Royals, the *Kansas City Star,* Kathy Davison, Chuck Kneyse, and Chris Vleisides.

The Major League Baseball trademarks and copyrights used with permission from
Major League Baseball Properties, Inc.

Library of Congress Cataloging-in-Publication Data
Morgan, Anne Hodges, 1940–
      Prescription for success : the life and values of Ewing Marion Kauffman / by
Anne Hodges Morgan.
            p.   cm.
      Includes bibliographical references.
      ISBN 0-8362-0466-2
      1. Kauffman, Ewing Marion, 1916–1993. 2. Businessmen—United States—Bio-
graphy. 3. Philanthropists—Missouri—Kansas City—Biography. 4. Baseball team
owners—United States—Biography. 5. Pharmaceutical industry—United States—
History. 6. Marion Laboratories—History. 7. Kansas City Royals (Baseball team)—
History. I. Title.
HD9666.95.K38M67   1995
338.7′616151′092—dc20   95-23169
[B]   CIP

CONTENTS

Foreword

Mr. Kauffman's success as an entrepreneur, sportsman, and philanthropist is well documented. With clear values, hard work, careful selection of colleagues, and an aggressive approach, he built a multibillion dollar company from virtually nothing, save a competitive idea and an eye for a marketing niche. Some would say it was genius, many might say it was timing, but all who knew him would have to agree that Mr. Kauffman's greatest talent was his ability to bring out the best in people.

For over forty years, between 1950 and 1993, this leadership philosophy was essential to building first Marion Laboratories, Inc., and later the Kansas City Royals. Today, I witness that legacy in the dedication of my associates at the Kauffman Foundation and their work in meeting clients' needs. Tomorrow, we expect that it will manifest itself in the "graduates" of our youth development programs and the Center for Entrepreneurial Leadership.

Mr. K's fundamental philosophy, to treat others as we would like to be treated, was never considered by him to be simply a religious tenet. Rather, he would say, "It is the happiest principle by which to live and the most intelligent principle by which to do business and make money!" More importantly, it is the way he lived every day.

At Marion, it was common to come across some happy commotion as anniversaries and victories were celebrated. It was vital to Mr. K to build associates' self-esteem and to find public ways to make them feel appreciated. For example, at the end of each quarter we celebrated our successes and reflected on our learnings in an all-associate forum called "Marion on the Move," which he led. This and other communication forums were designed to keep associates well informed about the company's progress and were an essential part of the Marion culture. When I joined Marion in 1975, he led these meetings from the shipping dock with our then-small group of associates gathered around him in the driveway. His last "Marion on the Move" meeting was held at Municipal Auditorium with more than 2,500 associates present. The spirit and warmth of the culture he created prevailed through the forty years he led these associate gatherings.

Mr. K would often remind us that we did not hire employees at Marion to place them in superior-subordinate relationships. Instead, he helped us understand that we appointed *associates* and created an environment of people working with each other in partnership to accomplish agreed-upon goals. Similarly, he focused on leadership rather than management, always saying he would not want to be managed, but he did not mind being led by others. He believed that if associates were treated with dignity and respect, that they, too, would treat others, particularly customers and vendors, the same way, thereby magnifying the effect and enhancing the company's reputation.

Mr. Kauffman's second philosophy, that those who produce should share the rewards, is the foundation of the oft-repeated folklore about Marion Laboratories having created scores of wealthy Americans and at least a dozen philanthropies. All associates at Marion fully participated in a wide range of compensation programs. As a result, many of Marion's early associates dedicated their time and energies to a struggling new company in exchange for Mr. K's promise that eventually they would be rewarded well. It gave him great personal pleasure that the faith of office support staff, production workers, and executives alike eventually paid off handsomely through profit sharing, stock options, and other rewards.

The "Spirit Suggestion Award Program" was a highly successful reward program and a particular favorite of Mr. K's. He directed this program personally and gave great encouragement to all his associates to submit their ideas for improving the company's operating results. All awardees received a plaque describing their contributions, which they proudly displayed in their work areas. They were also recognized at meetings of all associates of the company. More material rewards ranged from dinner for two at local restaurants to a trip around the world for two and large stock awards. All rewards were tied to the value added to the company by implementing the idea submitted. For example, a secretary suggested that we rent an idle school across the street from the company in lieu of more expensive office space miles away. Because of the cost savings, she received a stock award that turned out to be enough to send her two children through college.

Mr. Kauffman identified with associates' individual goals, helped them develop professional goals, and then created an environment in which they were motivated to succeed. He set clear objectives and straightforward methods by which to arrive at them. He led by example to ensure that his philosophies and values were communicated and internalized by all associates. Finally, Mr. K engendered a cooperative attitude among everyone with whom he worked, sharing the joys, frustrations, and the credit among the team.

His key message here, beyond pay for performance, was to make his associates aware of how much he appreciated their contributions. The way to get credit from Mr. K was simply to give credit to others, since he believed that *appreciation* is the greatest motivator after basic needs are met. All associates received a letter from him on their anniversary with the company congratulating them on their individual contributions to the overall success of the company during the past year. He was also known to write letters to the parents of high-achieving associates letting them know what a great child they raised. These little things meant a lot to his associates.

That approach also provides the impetus for Mr. K's third philosophy . . . giving back to the community. Mr. K's doctrine of giving to the community which had provided the fertile environment for his business success not only guided his early philanthropic activities, but also led him to encourage several of his newly affluent associates to establish foundations of their own. That particular piece of Mr. K's vision is alive and well, not only in his foundation, but also through the Community foundation of Greater Kansas City, with whom many of Mr. K's associates have established philanthropic funds that contribute to the resolution of a wide range of social and economic development problems.

These then, are the three fundamental philosophies and values by which Mr. K lived and worked:

- Treat others as you want to be treated
- Those that produce should share the rewards, and
- Give back to the community

It is from these three philosophies and values that he fashioned a vision of self-sufficient people in healthy communities. It is from this vision that entrepreneurs and youth in the Kansas City community and across the country stand to benefit enormously.

What can be learned from this study of Mr. K's life and philosophy of leadership? The very attributes we searched for in our leaders we should develop in others and demand from ourselves. The essential qualities he demonstrated were integrity, open and honest communication, fairness, consistency, and trust. If we try to practice these ourselves and encourage them in others, I am convinced we will build healthier organizations and stronger communities.

Mr. K was a unique entrepreneur. He devoted his energies to recruiting professional managers who showed the right mix of compassion and intelligence. He was astute enough to hire people *he* considered smarter than himself, and then share with them leadership and responsibility.

Mr. K's philosophies and values not only created a positive and productive environment in which to work, but also a profitable company which created many jobs and great wealth while contributing to the availability of life-saving pharmaceuticals. His philosophies of leadership were directly responsible for generating a legacy far greater than the personal wealth recorded by the financiers.

His legacy means empowering others to achieve greatness for themselves and for the good of others, by reinvesting their strengths in the communities to which they belong. We all believe that he will be best remembered for his uncommon and entrepreneurial approach to philanthropy.

My own experience of being with Mr. K for almost twenty years has been wonderful. I know I have reached a level of my potential I never thought possible before I became associated with him, and I know there is more to come because of the confidence and trust he has placed in me as chairman and CEO of the Kauffman Foundation. I miss him very much and still have difficulty talking about him in the past tense because he continues to inspire me and his other associates at the foundation. We are committed to the pursuit of his goals and dreams for America's youth, his entrepreneurial spirit, and his vision of "self-sufficient people in healthy communities."

Happy reading! I sincerely hope that the following exploration of

Mr. K's experiences, values, and accomplishments lead you to an even more productive and fulfilling life, as it has for so many of his associates.

Robert Rogers
Chairman of the Board and CEO
The Ewing Marion Kauffman Foundation

Acknowledgments

Researching and writing a biography is usually the most solitary of tasks. Grateful for the occasional companionship of helpful librarians, an author normally spends months, even years, traveling to far-flung archives to pore over yellowing letters and documents in an effort to reconstruct the chronology and events of an individual's life. After dusk, when the manuscript collections and libraries are closed, there are the long hours in anonymous hotel rooms. With the mind chock-full of the day's discoveries, the researcher is alternately too stimulated to sleep or too weary to do anything but stare at the flickering television screen.

In the initial stages of a biography, the author feels confused. Names and events flood the mind in a dizzying stream. And as stories and anecdotes pile one on top of the other, it all becomes a bewildering jumble. There is the sense of being overwhelmed and drowning in information. As one tries to make sense out of all the bits and fragments of information, they begin to gather into complex configurations, then shift and change shapes like the shards of glass seen through a kaleidoscope. Then suddenly it all begins to make sense. The subject slowly comes alive in the biographer's mind. Shadowy outlines form into distinctive facial features. Soon there is a palpable figure of bone and sinew, flesh and blood. Then the personality emerges, and the author begins to hear the pitch and resonance of a human voice, to recognize a distinctive gait, to anticipate the precise event that will trigger a certain eccentricity. Only at this point is it possible for the biographer to begin to blend the person and the events into a narrative that chronicles the life and accomplishments of the individual.

This is the process, more or less, whereby most biographical sub-

xiii

jects—who have usually been dead for a number of years—emerge and take on life again in print. The passage of time provides the author with perspective. The individual and the events may be studied and evaluated within the historical context of the era in which the subject lived. The author has the benefit of hindsight and the luxury of reflection. However intriguing and compelling the subject may be, researching and writing a biography is essentially a lonely, solitary endeavor.

Happily for me, this biography has been quite different. Ewing Kauffman was very much alive in the fall of 1991 when I began work on his biography. At our first meeting, he told me that he doubted that he would live to see the book completed. Sadly for everyone involved, he did not. But from the start of the research until a few weeks before his death on August 1, 1993, he was totally involved— cooperative and helpful. He went out of his way to make time for our interviews even when he was feeling unwell and visibly weary. Despite a crowded schedule, he would frequently extend our time to tell me one more story or to let me confirm things I had learned. He searched his mind for elusive details about his naval career; we pored over maps of the period to retrace the voyages; we examined scores of photographs which prompted more long-forgotten memories. Kauffman immediately warmed to the interview process, for he was a masterful storyteller and knew how to build toward a climax with the skill of O. Henry.

As we came to know one another better, he began to discuss subjects which had clearly lain dormant for years. He became more reflective as we talked about my interviews with his old friends and former associates. He confided thoughts and feelings about personal matters with the understanding that I would use my discretion regarding what would appear in print. From the outset, he perceived that I needed to know as much as possible so that I might understand motivations, actions, and consequences, yet he trusted my judgment about what should be included in the book. He had urged all the persons he suggested I interview to be totally candid, and he was committed to do no less. That incredibly trusting nature, on which many of his associates commented in their interviews, challenged and inspired me throughout this process. Just a few weeks before his death, on a day when he was experiencing some relief from the excruciating pain of bone cancer, Kauffman telephoned me. He apologized for not being able to see the project through to completion. However, he had been able to read the draft of the first seven chapters and he said he felt comfortable with the approach and the tone of the manuscript. We talked for another moment or two. Then he said it was time to say good-bye, and I knew that we would not talk again. I have tried to honor and merit his trust in writing the story of his life.

Having the opportunity to know and to work closely with Ewing Kauffman was an experience that I shall always cherish. A man of supreme self-confidence with an ego to match, Kauffman was essentially a modest person. He believed that his successes in life—founding an enormously profitable pharmaceutical company, developing a World Series championship baseball team, and accumulating the wealth to fund a major philanthropic foundation—could largely be attributed to others. He always praised the accomplishments of his associates, saying that his success was because of their efforts and achievements. He did not think of himself as particularly important, or influential, or powerful. And he was genuinely baffled that anyone should consider him of sufficient interest to write his biography. As a boy and young man he had read scores of biographies. He knew he did not measure up to heroic figures like Alexander the Great, Lincoln, or George Armstrong Custer. Why should anyone care about his accomplishments after he was gone, he asked. Authorizing one's biography to be written seemed vain and self-serving to him. He did not want his name emblazoned on buildings, so why would he want to be immortalized in print?

Kauffman resisted the idea until several of his former Marion associates convinced him that it was not merely his life, but the principles by which he lived that should be recorded and preserved. It was not his phenomenal financial success that was to be celebrated but his principled leadership, his skill in motivating others to succeed, and his compassion for young people—all this was what merited a biography.

Ewing Kauffman lived and worked by two simple principles: treat others as you would wish to be treated and share the rewards. He always said that these were the principle keys to success in business as well as to happiness in life. Once he saw the biography as a way of illustrating to people how these simple principles could alter and enhance their own lives—as they had done in his life—he became a willing collaborator on this book.

I shall always be grateful to my dear friend and colleague, Waldemar Nielsen, for suggesting me as a possible biographer. Although I had initial reservations about the project—totally unfounded fears that my work might be censored or that I would not be able to express my own opinions or draw my own conclusions—Nielsen assured me that Kauffman had no interest in a vanity publication. He was correct. At our first meeting, Kauffman assured me he respected my right, as a scholar, to reach my own conclusions. Should we disagree on matters of interpretation, he asked that I cite his views in a footnote. Throughout the entire process of research and writing, Nielsen has been a helpful confidant and a constructive critic.

I appreciate the Kauffman family members' willingness to share their memories. Muriel McBrien Kauffman graciously gave me time from her busy schedule and responded to many follow-up questions. Kauffman's three children, Larry Kauffman, Sue Kauffman, and Julia Irene Kauffman, gave me helpful insights into the private man. And Ruth Kauffman Jianas, Kauffman's older sister, helped me untangle the details of the Kauffman/Winders family history. Her recollections of their childhood proved invaluable to my understanding of Kauffman's relationship with their parents. Mrs. Jianas also graciously shared a number of family photographs which appear in this book.

I owe a special debt of thanks to Robert Barrett, former director of communications at the Ewing Marion Kauffman Foundation. Under his guidance, the foundation's staff conducted a series of videotaped interviews with Kauffman in 1991. These tapes provided me with an excellent introduction to Kauffman and an overview of his life and his ideas. I had the pleasure of working closely with Robert Barrett until his death in December 1993. He shared his talented staff with me—Lynn Spencer, Joy Torchia, Kate Hodel, Barbara Kowalski, Vicki Merriott, and Pam Kearney. They, in turn, always made me feel "at home" in their midst when I was in Kansas City. Marty Krekovich, who worked first with Robert Barrett and later with Robert Rogers, was always ready to respond to any request for assistance.

In every project such as this, there is always one person who quietly assists the author with a myriad of last-minute details. It is a thankless task which requires diplomacy, tact, political acumen, patience, and an appreciation of irony. I wish to thank Steve Roling, who accepted that task and performed it well—with grace and good humor.

There were very few primary documents available for this project. For that reason interviews with Kauffman's associates at Marion Laboratories, the Kansas City Royals, and the Ewing Marion Kauffman Foundation were crucial to this work. These individuals talked fondly of their recollections of this "uncommon man" and his "uncommon company." Lively conversations with intelligent, articulate men and women recalling their experiences with their beloved Mr. K developed into new and valued friendships for me. Although I have not quoted directly from all the interviews, they were all very important in providing useful background and in helping me to understand such a complex and, essentially, private man. Had Kauffman been measured solely by the quality of his friendships, he would have been deemed wealthy indeed. A list of everyone interviewed appears at the end of the book, and I offer each of them my sincere thanks for their cooperation and assistance.

Every historian and biographer builds on the work of others, and I am no exception. Robert Pruitt, an early salesman for Marion Laboratories, wrote an informal history of the company after his retirement. As I stepped through the door of his home for our first interview, Pruitt handed me a copy of that work. He graciously granted me permission to draw upon it as needed. Much of the detail and color about Kauffman and Marion Laboratories during the 1950s and 1960s has been preserved thanks to Bob Pruitt, and I happily acknowledge my debt to him.

Five individuals who were executives at Marion Laboratories and are now directors of the Ewing Marion Kauffman Foundation were more than generous with their time and support. I interviewed each of them several times. They all read the manuscript in draft and made helpful corrections and suggestions. No matter what my needs, they were always supportive and encouraging. I appreciate their trust in me and their efforts to make this book a reality. I value each one as a friend. My warmest thanks to Charles L. Hughes, Robert B. Rogers, James E. McGraw, Michael E. Herman, and Michie P. Slaughter.

Linda Constantine, Kauffman's assistant, smoothed my path in countless ways. I thank her for all her help. Susan Hidalgo, who also assisted Kauffman during much of 1993, was especially understanding of the relationship between biographer and subject. As Kauffman's illness progressed, she would alert me to opportunities to talk with him on "good days" and steer me away when he needed to rest. Her thoughtfulness was helpful to both of us.

For Merle Wood, I feel a special gratitude. When I interviewed him, we agreed at the outset that all his comments would be off the record. For that reason, he is not quoted at any point in the biography, although his interview was one of the most important in helping me understand the nuances of relationships. Merle Wood and Ewing Kauffman had an especially affectionate and trusting friendship. Both men spoke often, usually with tears brimming in their eyes, of their love for one another. It was to Charles Hughes and Merle Wood that Kauffman turned when the time drew near to plan funeral and burial arrangements.

During the last months of Kauffman's life, Wood called me regularly to give me news of "the chief," as he dubbed Kauffman. He knew that Kauffman was in my thoughts each and every day as I pieced together the story of his life. Early on Sunday morning, August 1, 1993, Wood called to tell me that Kauffman had died. I shall always be grateful for his understanding that even though my association with Kauffman had been relatively brief, it was intense, as was my grief.

I had a special cadre of helpers on this book, and I hope never to do another without them. Dory DeAngelo was my research assistant in Kansas City. A historian and author in her own right, Ms. DeAngelo was the ideal colleague. Her knowledge of Kansas City saved me from more than one error, and her ability to ferret out the most elusive and obscure information astonished me at times. She researched and collected more than seven thousand news clippings and articles which I read and kept close at hand for reference in my writing. She reviewed several drafts of the manuscript and always prodded me to greater clarity and simplicity—the hallmarks of good writing. Her friendship has been one of the many delightful benefits of this project.

In Norman, Oklahoma, Andrea Mathis and Michele Moore assisted with the tedious tasks of transcribing audiotapes and proofreading various versions of the manuscript. Through transcribing the interviews, they both succumbed to Kauffman's legendary charm. And as I would prepare for each visit to Kansas City, they always had questions of their own they wanted me to ask. Their constant enthusiasm for the project, as well as their total discretion about the confidential nature of some of the material they encountered, was always helpful to me.

My good friends Dianne and Leonard Bernstein merit special thanks. Early in my discussions with Nielsen, Barrett, and, later, Kauffman, they encouraged me to undertake the project. They saw the biography as the kind of challenge I needed. They sensed it was an opportunity for professional growth. I am very glad I recognized and accepted the wisdom of their counsel.

My closest friend, Rennard J. Strickland, continued to play a supportive role in this endeavor as he does in all the projects I undertake. He was, as always, a patient listener even when I was recounting the same story for the tenth time. He read several drafts of the manuscript and suggested many of the chapter titles when my creativity flagged. I am also appreciative of his willingness to loan me his talented assistant, Jan Young, from time to time to help in transcribing and proofreading.

As always, I owe a profound debt of gratitude to my husband, H. Wayne Morgan. As the author of several biographies, he improved the manuscript in countless ways. As my first reader and chief critic, he always stimulates my thinking about whatever subject I am studying. He challenges me to think more deeply and to write more clearly.

I, of course, accept full responsibility for the imperfections of this work.

Anne Hodges Morgan
Norman, Oklahoma
November 1994

PRESCRIPTION *for* SUCCESS

The Early Years

"Say It Ain't So, Mr. K," pleaded the July 20, 1989, headline of the *Squire*, a Kansas City metropolitan weekly newspaper. But it was so! Ewing Marion Kauffman, the local folk hero who had started a drug company in his basement on a quiet residential street thirty-nine years earlier, was suddenly giving up control of Marion Laboratories, Inc., a *Fortune* 500 company with annual sales topping a billion dollars. Starting with only five thousand dollars, he had acquired a huge personal fortune. And as his wealth grew, so did the wealth of his employees. More than three hundred Marion associates—Kauffman considered the term "employee" demeaning and never used it—become millionaires, too, thanks to the generous profit sharing, bonuses, and stock options available to everyone. And all of this he modestly attributed to two simple principles: "Treat others the way you would like to be treated" and "Those who produce should share the rewards." Now Marion Laboratories was to be merged with Merrell Dow Pharmaceuticals, Inc., in what *Fortune* magazine ranked among the ten biggest deals of 1989.

The *Squire*'s headline, more nostalgic than critical in tone, summed up the sentiments of literally thousands who felt personally acquainted with this Missouri farm boy and his phenomenally successful company. Ewing Kauffman had created jobs that helped fuel Kansas City's postwar growth. His wealth, earned from Marion Laboratories, had saved Kansas City's baseball team and the city's status in the major leagues. In a relatively short time, the Kansas City Royals proved their worth by winning six division championships, two American League pennants, and then the coveted World Series in 1985. One of his philanthropies had meant that on a single weekend thousands of Kansas Citians had learned the lifesaving techniques of cardiopulmonary resuscitation. And for years afterward, Kauffman would receive at least one letter, often two, a week telling him how that training had helped save a neighbor's life or perhaps that of a stranger.

Mr. K, as he was affectionately known, was instantly recognizable. Of average height, balding, with large ears and intensely blue eyes, he dressed nattily in a trademark Royals blue blazer or a bold, plaid jacket. The press and television reported frequently on his foundation's work to help young people get a healthy start in life, resist drugs, and complete school. And his numerous awards for humanitarian service were a part of Kansas City's civic heritage.

There was genuine collective pride in the man and his accomplishments. This was never greater than when the details of the Marion merger became public. In a decision consistent with his business philosophy and career, he had refused the opportunity to sell his controlling interest to the highest bidder. Instead, he instructed Marion executives to secure the best deal possible for all the shareholders. "I could have sold my block of stock for fifty dollars, sixty dollars a share," Kauffman told a financial reporter the day the merger was announced. "But that wouldn't have been fair and I wouldn't have lived as happily afterward." His principles governed the financial arrangements of the seven-billion-dollar merger as they had always governed the daily conduct of business at Marion Laboratories.

When talking about his business philosophy, Kauffman was always quick to disavow the religious connotations. "'Treat others as you want to be treated' . . . is a deliberate misquotation of the Golden Rule," he liked to say. "It is not based on religion. It is the smartest principle I know for making money!" Kauffman's second key principle, the practice of sharing, he declared to be the secret ingredient for personal as well as financial happiness. "At one time I owned 100 percent of the stock of Marion Laboratories," he recalled. "[When] we placed stock on the market, I sold my stock to the point where I owned only 65 percent of [Marion]. Many friends told me that by selling stock and putting our company on a profit-sharing basis I was giving away a lot of money. But which would you rather have?" he asked. "Would you rather have 50 percent of fifty million dollars or 100 percent of two million dollars? We wouldn't be worth fifty million dollars as a company if we hadn't done these things."

Kauffman did not want to be portrayed as especially religious. "I don't feel that I am and I want to be honest." But he did acknowledge a higher power. "I had an ordinary belief in religion and God but not a real concrete one until I was in the navy," he explained. "I was doing navigational work at that time. When you come up on deck just before daybreak and see the stars in the sky and are able to take a mathematical sight of this one and that one and draw lines and say, 'we are right here,' and we are—there has to be some great Being who created such symmetry and order."

The man who would become one of Kansas City's most beloved citizens was born on September 21, 1916, at his parents' farm located in Cass County about a mile southeast of Garden City, Missouri. Kauffman family lore holds that the baby boy was named Ewing after Missouri state senator Ewing Cockrell, and Marion for his maternal grandfather, John Marion Winders. Ewing had a three-year-old sister, Ruth, and the two children completed the family circle.

Young Kauffman's parents, John Samuel Kauffman and Effie Mae Winders, were a handsome couple. John was tall and well built with a nice smile. His son remembered him as being "very friendly, very gregarious, willing to help anybody often to the detriment of himself." Effie Mae was small and slender with expressive eyes. Both husband and wife were descended from immigrants who made their homes in the rural counties of west central Missouri.

His mother's family, the Winders, was of Scotch-Irish lineage and consisted of four girls and two boys. Their father was a renowned stonemason in the region around Warrensburg, Missouri. The family placed a premium on education, and Ewing's mother received the best available. By the time she graduated from Missouri State Teachers College at Warrensburg, she had studied six years of Greek and seven of Latin. Although education in those days consisted primarily of immersion in the classics, it was unusual for a young woman to have such an opportunity to learn.

John Kauffman's parents were first-generation immigrants arriving from Germany after the American Civil War. Both were descended from farmers, and they followed that tradition in their marriage. They had had little education, but saw that their children received the basic schooling available in rural Missouri. John Kauffman was the youngest of their seven children, and the only boy. Ewing recalled in later years, "Only one of Dad's six sisters ever married, and they spoiled my father because he was their baby. All his life he did somewhat depend on them."

Ewing's father attended the first four elementary grades, then left school to help on his father's farm. In spite of having his formal education cut short, John Kauffman possessed exceptional mathematical skills. When Ewing was growing up, his father constantly challenged him with mathematical games. Ewing recalled how he and his father would do calculations to pass the time while working around the farm or driving to town. His father would state the equation, "'Nine times seven, minus three, divided by ten squared— what's the answer?' And I'd say, 'Thirty-six.' And then I'd give him one," Kauffman said. His father taught him by starting out slowly and then getting faster and faster. "This type of thing is just like athletic ability. The more you exercise those muscles, the better you become. As a result, he taught me mathematics and an ability to handle figures which has been very valuable in my business."

Effie Winders met John Kauffman while she was teaching school near Warrensburg. He was selling spices, housewares, and notions door-to-door for the Watkins Company. Ruth Jianas, Ewing's older sister, recalled what it must have been like for this "dainty little person" who knew nothing about farm work. "When they got married, Dad put her in the buggy and took her down to live with his folks. They were Germans. They did speak some English, but they all spoke in German around her." Ruth's mother told her of the isolation and loneliness she felt during those early months with her in-laws. "I knew they were talking about me," she told Ruth.

John Kauffman's sisters were an imposing group. The three oldest were almost six feet tall and they all shared in the heavy work on the family farm. They expected Effie to do the same. The young bride willingly accepted her share of the chores—hoeing the garden, cleaning, cooking, ironing, and canning. As soon as they could afford it, John rented a place nearby where Ruth and, later, Ewing were born. Effie seldom spoke about those first years of marriage, but Ruth remembered, "Mama said Grandpa was awful nice to her and he felt sorry for her." She also recalled that the summer before Ewing was born, her father "took off with my uncle, my mother's brother, and they went to Montana . . . just left Mama there with my grandfather to have the baby."

Shortly after Ewing's birth, his father leased a much better farm near Creighton, Missouri. The new farm was 480 acres of rich bottom land that grew mostly cotton and wheat. Frank Hodgson, a successful grain broker in Kansas City, owned the farm, and John Kauffman provided all the labor in exchange for a comfortable house and a share in the profits. Although Ewing was very young when they moved to the Creighton farm, seven decades later he remembered it as a happy place to grow up. "We did have a very beautiful home for that time, which was made of brick with hot air [central heating], and we had inside water and inside toilets." Ruth never forgot the smooth feel and the freshly scrubbed smell of the kitchen floor where she and Ewing would play while their mother prepared supper.

Located on the rich bottomlands of the Blue River, the farm was an idyllic habitat for childhood adventures. "There were wooded areas with a stream running through the edge of the land right on the boundary," Ewing recalled. "I do remember picking walnuts from down closer to the river where there were lots of trees. I also remember a pond that would be filled when the river overflowed and fish would be washed into it. And I remember my father seining the pond and taking the fish out."

Ewing started school while the family lived on the Creighton farm. He was five years old. Ruth admitted preferring recess over the classroom, but Ewing, like his mother, loved learning. The school was small, so there were three grades in one room when Ewing started first grade. "In those days the teacher graded each student, not on individual subjects, but rather as to the number of students that were in the class," Ewing recalled. "I was number one in the first grade and, of course, if I finished my work early I would listen to what was happening in the second and third grade." One of Ewing's earliest memories of elementary school was of the excitement of spell-downs. "I won the first prize and the teacher gave me a book." More than seventy years later he recalled that the prize was *The Little Lame Prince*, a classic children's tale.

The desire to learn which would make him such a successful entrepreneur later in life was apparent at an early age. "I can remember that there seemed to be a terrific drive within me to get my homework done, to understand it completely. Then I would go to my mother while she was maybe cooking dinner and tell her that I couldn't understand or solve this problem and that I needed help." Whatever she may have been doing, Effie Kauffman always stopped and turned her full attention to her young son.

At the end of the first year, Ewing's teacher decided to promote him to the third grade since he was number one in his class and seemed far ahead of the other students. By the end of the first semester, he had slipped to fourth place. "I went home in tears to my mother, telling her how much I had failed to achieve over what I had done previously." Effie was always there to encourage and guide her bright little son. Soon his confidence was restored and he forged ahead.

Ruth believed those early years on the farm established the pattern of relationships among family members. "I took after my dad's side of the family," she remarked, "and Ewing was more like Mama. I was more tomboyish." After the family moved to Kansas City, "if it came to a choice of who went with Dad to the country down to my grandmother's, it was always me that cried to go and Ewing would say, 'I'll stay home with Mama.'" From the vantage point of her eighth decade, Ruth reflected on her childhood relationship with her mother. "I always thought that she loved him more than she loved me, but after you have children of your own, you know that's not true." While Ewing thrived on the challenges of school, he also joined his father in outdoor activities on the farm. When he was older, sports and Boy Scouts were a key part of his after-school activities. But his mother was to remain the single most important and influential force throughout his life.

Like most young couples who had small children and smaller bank accounts, the Kauffmans enjoyed social activities at home with their neighbors. Ewing remembered many Saturday evenings when his parents had a neighbor couple in to play pinochle. He would stand behind his father intently watching the play. "And, supposedly, according to their stories, I became a very good pinochle player at the age of six or seven just by watching my father play." No player who encountered Ewing Kauffman in a poker or gin game in later years would ever question that he had been a precocious card player.

The first year on the Creighton farm seemed to be the harbinger of good times for the young Kauffman family, but too quickly that changed. John Kauffman had a freak accident that would plague him for the rest of his life. While loading cattle into a railroad car for shipment to Kansas City, one of the steers turned suddenly, and a sharp horn entered John's left eye. He was rushed to Kansas City for medical attention, but eventually lost sight in the eye and the eye as well. He wore an artificial eye so his appearance was unchanged, but the injury, plus his lack of a high school education, kept him from obtaining a number of jobs over the years.

When Ewing was six years old, the weather was especially rainy and the rich river bottomland flooded, ruining most of that year's crop. To a little boy, the high water may have seemed more like fun than disaster since he was too young to understand the implications for his family. "I remember that the flood was up and we went out on the farm and speared fish with a pitchfork." Fishing may have gotten better, but farming did not. After three consecutive years of flooding and ruined crops, the Kauffman family decided to give up farming. Ruth recalled that they all piled into a Model T roadster with the family dog and left for Kansas City. It was raining when they departed, and "it was rainy and muddy when we got up there."

When it became clear that the family would have to leave the farm, John Kauffman's sisters pitched in to help him resettle his brood. Two sisters were already established in Kansas City with good jobs. Elizabeth, known as Aunt Lizzie, was a doctor of osteopathy and doing quite well financially. Another sister, Lydia, was working as a housekeeper for a wealthy Kansas City lumberman and had saved a considerable sum of money. Two other sisters, Minnie and Mary, were still running the family farm. Together they put a down payment on a home for John's family, a large house at 3828 Harrison Street, in a good neighborhood. The plan was for Effie to take in boarders to supplement her husband's earnings, and then the couple would take over the mortgage payments.

The new house was three stories, with ample space to accommodate the family on the top floor. The five bedrooms on the second floor could be rented. The first floor had the usual kitchen, large dining room, and parlor with an adjacent small music room complete with a piano. With these surroundings, and Effie's enterprising approach, the house was soon filled with boarders. From time to time, people who did not live in the house would arrange to take their meals there, as Effie Kauffman enjoyed a reputation as a fine cook. Ruth recalled that when their neighbor, Judge Lukas, died, his widow made arrangements to board with the convivial group of regulars.

Running a boarding house with no help except two young children was difficult and exhausting work. Effie Kauffman was up before dawn to begin preparations for breakfast, which was served from six to eight o'clock. Ewing remembered his mother often awakened him early to run to the grocery store to get something she needed at the last moment for breakfast. After getting her family off to work and school for the day, Mrs. Kauffman then had all the housework to do, plus shopping and preparing the evening meal for boarders and family.

The children helped out after school. Ewing's job was to dust the boarders' rooms, the stairs, and all the woodwork along the stairway and landing. Over the years he recalled the fragrance of cedar oil polish mingled with mouthwatering aromas coming from his mother's kitchen. Ruth helped by cleaning vegetables and washing dishes. "I can remember lots of times that I'd come home from school and the breakfast dishes would still be there because Mother hadn't had time to do them, and she never wasted a minute," she recalled. But the outdoors was always more appealing to Ruth than the kitchen, so often when Mrs. Kauffman set her daughter to a task such as cleaning radishes, "she'd turn around and I'd be outside playing baseball with Ewing and his friends." After a long day's work, Effie Kauffman would often sit up until one or two o'clock sewing a dress for Ruth or cutting down a boarder's discarded but serviceable suit for Ewing.

Instead of being embarrassed that his family was reduced to keeping boarders, young Ewing found the experience stimulating. "As [far as] I was personally concerned, it was no reflection on me having boarders. We had lawyers, schoolteachers, salesmen, and secretaries, really interesting people." His acceptance of the situation reflected the inherent dignity of his mother, who always referred to the boarders as "paying guests." If one of the "guests" were out for the evening, Mrs. Kauffman would have Ewing eat with the other diners and listen to the conversation. He felt at ease and comfortable among adults, and he learned a lot from their discussions. The dinner conversations expanded young Ewing's mind and his palate, too. Mrs. Lukas, the widow who lived in the neighborhood and boarded at Effie Kauffman's, decided she would teach the boy to experiment with new foods. When he announced that he did not like rhubarb and would not eat it, she politely suggested, "You just take a spoonful before you eat anything else." As a result of this culinary prompting, "there isn't anything I don't eat today," Kauffman remembered fondly.

When the Kauffmans first settled in Kansas City, John's sisters, who were still on the family farm, would ship him a case of eggs, thirty-six dozen, to sell. Ewing proved his knack for selling at an early age. "I would take four or five dozen eggs and call on the neighbors, especially the people that lived in apartments, since you could hit six or seven homes with very little walking. Over a period of time I built up faithful customers who looked forward to buying eggs from me. These were fresh and they would sell for a few cents less than the grocery." And they had the advantage of being delivered right to the housewife's door.

Sometimes Ewing and his father used their talents as skilled "noodlers" to catch Grand River catfish, a desired commodity in Kansas City at that time. Noodling was a dangerous way to catch big fish. Ewing would dive into the murky brown waters and make his way along the slippery mud banks, reaching into crevices and holes, feeling for the prey. Kauffman recalled the exhilaration and the terror of swimming blindly "in the velvety mud" and his father pulling him to safety just as he thought his lungs would burst. When they needed larger amounts of fish, they would use the technique of dropping dynamite in certain portions of the Grand River, and the explosion would cause the fish to float to the top. "It would stun them. We would jump in, get them, and clean them. Because we would have maybe a hundred pounds of fish, I would go door to door selling fresh fish to some of my egg customers."

Eggs were easily broken and fish spoiled quickly, so Ewing supplemented those earnings with a magazine route. He delivered the *Saturday Evening Post* and *Colliers* every week. He contributed part of his earnings to the family budget. The rest he saved in a jar on the top of one of the kitchen cupboards. One Saturday when he had accumulated about thirty dollars he went to add to the stash only to find the jar was completely empty. "Mother, with tears in her eyes, said Father had run short and it was necessary for him to borrow it.

Of course, this was quite a heartbreak for a kid," he recalled. "Surprisingly, although we did not have the material assets in life, I never seemed to think that we didn't have money. I didn't miss anything."

Ewing and Ruth enrolled in school while the family was living with their Aunt Lizzie, and the walk from her house, though shorter than the former route to their country school, was their first adventure in discovering city life. Ruth recalled how they had to negotiate several busy streets, make a few turns, and learn to read the traffic signals. Once they were established on Harrison Street, Ewing created his own route to school, which was about a mile away. "I would run through the backyards of the homes on the way to school with my police dog, Larry, chasing me all the time. And after I got to school he would return home. When noon came for lunch hour, he would be there waiting for me and I would run home for lunch and back to school for the afternoon."

Ewing and Larry were inseparable. When the two went sledding in winter, Larry would jump off to block the way of any competitor who tried to pass his master. Ewing taught Larry to stand with his back feet on the car's running board and his front feet on the fender. He would lean his head and upper body against the hood. "That's the way he would go with us driving around town." Although Larry took an occasional spill when John Kauffman turned a corner too sharply, he would jump back on, ready for more thrills. Ewing recalled another time when he and his dad took Larry with them on a fishing trip to Grand River. The dog became a nuisance splashing about in the water and scaring the fish, so John Kauffman locked him in the car. He opened the window enough to give him air, but not enough to permit him to escape. As the afternoon stretched on, Ewing and his dad began to speculate about how Larry might react if they called him. "I said, 'I don't know, let's see. Come here, Larry! Come here!' I called. And he went right through that window," Kauffman remembered laughing. "Broke the hell out of it!"

Larry lived to be thirteen, and when he died Ewing and Ruth both suspected neighbors of poisoning him. "They were a little bit unhappy about the way I'd run over the yard with Larry; he probably trampled their flowers—which was wrong, of course." They buried Larry in the backyard behind the boarding house, and even after Ewing enlisted in the navy he would visit his pet's resting place in the old neighborhood. In his seventies, when asked if he had ever had another dog, Kauffman's eyes shone with tears as he replied, "No, I never wanted another. No, just Larry."

On the surface, everything seemed to be going well for the Kauffman family. Effie had rented all the second-floor bedrooms and taken on extra boarders. Ewing and Ruth were settled in their new school and developing a lively group of friends in the neighborhood. John Kauffman was selling life insurance, so it appeared that they could meet the mortgage payments on the house plus their living expenses. In reality, the Kauffmans were struggling. On arriving in Kansas City, John had looked for work at a number of factories such as the Ford and Chevrolet plants, but because of his eye injury he could not get a job. Finally, he began selling insurance for the Connecticut General Life Insurance Company. John had all the attributes of a good salesman. He was a handsome man with a nice smile and a pleasing personality. But he did not know many people when the family moved to Kansas City and success in selling insurance depended heavily on well-established personal contacts. Ewing reflected that for a man with only a fourth-grade education, selling insurance was very difficult work. "So he actually lived financially off of the income of the boarders at our home. He must have suffered a loss of pride, but he never showed it." Except for his father's difficulties in earning a living, Ewing recalled that the family adapted easily to city living. "There were no problems that I can remember at all."

Faxon Elementary was quite a bit different from the rural classroom in Creighton, but Ewing flourished with the competition of bright classmates and energetic, well-prepared teachers who inspired him. He did well in all the subjects, but he particularly liked mathematics. "We would have mathematics contests where you would add rows of figures to see who could stay at the blackboard the longest, and it was always my pleasure if I could beat the rest of them," he recalled. The mathematical exercises he had enjoyed with his father were beginning to pay off. He also excelled in spelling bees, helped no doubt by his love of reading, which his mother nurtured. But elementary school was much more than homework and academic competitions for the bright Kauffman boy. He joined a Boy Scout troop and became quite interested in athletics, playing baseball on the school team with Les Milgram, who later became a prominent businessman and civic leader.

When Ewing was eleven years old he caught a severe cold which grew steadily worse. The largest bedroom on the second floor happened to be empty, so he was put to bed there. "I can remember him being in bed in that room and the doctor coming and putting sandbags on his feet to pull them down," Ruth said. "The doctor took him to the hospital in an ambulance and he had his tonsils taken out." Ewing remembered that on the trip to the hospital they drove past Westport High School where Ruth was in class. "I asked the driver to turn on the siren so that she might hear it."

The doctor finally concluded that Ewing had endocarditis, or leakage of the heart—a condition in which one of the heart valves fails to close properly and blood leaks through. In those days, there was no medication for this condition. The only treatment known was complete bed rest. The family's physician told Ewing that if he wanted to be healthy enough to play football and baseball again, it would be necessary for him to lie flat on his back, in bed, for a solid year. "The doctor said he didn't even want me to get out of bed to go to the bathroom or to eat or to even sit up in bed—lie flat on my back. Well, he sold me on this and for a solid year I never even sat up in bed."

When Ewing came home from the hospital, he convalesced in what was known as the music room on the first floor. Though small, the room had a large window and opened onto the front porch so the patient could observe the comings and goings in the neighborhood and be closer to his mother as she worked cleaning house and preparing meals for the boarders. "She had to take care of him on top of all this other work," Ruth said, remembering her mother's fatigue at bedtime.

The task of nursing an eleven-year-old boy, plus keeping him flat on his back in bed for a year, was a formidable one. But Effie Kauffman was equal to the challenge. There was little available to entertain the young patient as the family could not afford a radio, so Ewing's mother announced that he was going to read. "And read I did!" he recalled. "As many as forty books a month. And when you read that much, you will read anything. I read the Bible twice, biographies of all the presidents, the frontiersmen, fiction, and particularly liked the novels of Lloyd C. Douglas, who wrote *Magnificent Obsession* and *Dr. Hudson's Secret Journal*." Ruth remembered how she and her father would go the library "sometimes every day, every night. And Ewing just read and read and read."

More than six decades after his illness, Ewing Kauffman remembered a great many of his favorite books such as *Kit Carson and Thirty One Years in the Mountains*. His father had loved this book as a child and found it for him. Reading became for Ewing, as it does for many children, a way to "transfer yourself to various countries and situations. Vicariously I could become a part of it." Between books, Ewing had visitors. His friends would come and talk to him from outside the big window to avoid overexciting him. "You know boys, how they can get rowdy. But Ewing laid there on the flat of his back and [later was strong enough to play] football in high school," Ruth explained.

The year in bed was a long one, but Ewing recovered his health completely and went on to live a normal, active life. And the knowledge and skill he acquired through reading paid important dividends in the years to come. "I think that year of reading was all-important in developing my subsequent vocabulary and also my variety of interests," he recalled. "I know when I became a Boy Scout and during the period after I became an Eagle Scout, they brought out some additional merit badges—they had a readership medal. And I was the first Boy Scout in the country to pass the readership badge." To accomplish this feat, he read thirty-six books and wrote a summary of each one.

When he started his own pharmaceutical business, his ability to read rapidly and retain information proved very useful. In the mid-1950s he enrolled in a class at Kansas City University where he read with a machine. When he started, his reading speed was about 700 words per minute, while most of his classmates started between 180 and 250 words per minute. Within three days he was reading at the speed of the machine—1,200 words per minute—so he dropped the class. In the 1960s, he took the Evelyn Wood Reading Dynamics System course and got up to about 5,400 words a minute when reading fiction. While reading technical material, he would drop back to between 1,200 and 1,500 to ensure good comprehension.

Ewing also gleaned important principles from that early reading which would guide his later endeavors as an entrepreneur, a sportsman, and a philanthropist. The Lloyd Douglas books always held a great appeal for him. He traced the basic philosophy of Marion Laboratories—"treat others as you would like to be treated"—to the fictional physician of *Dr. Hudson's Secret Journal*. This doctor acquired power and energy as he gave away his wealth. From this novel, Kauffman learned "to treat others the way you wanted to be treated and you'll be far ahead. This is the smartest principle to be happy and to have friends. This is also the smartest principle for a company to make money," he would tell those who asked the secret of his phenomenal business success.

With his health restored, Ewing returned to school, but another family crisis was on the horizon. John Kauffman was having a difficult time selling insurance, so he decided to take time off to see about some potential oil leases on land his sisters owned near Beeville, Texas. Ruth had just graduated from high school and, always ready for a jaunt with her dad, decided to go with him. Driving the family's trusty Model T, the two camped along the way, fished, and generally had a jolly time. After a few weeks, Ruth returned home while John Kauffman stayed to pursue the elusive oil leases.

One evening shortly after Ruth's return, Effie Kauffman sat the children down at the kitchen table and told them that she had decided to separate from their father. Both Ewing and Ruth had long been aware of the friction between their parents resulting from their very different backgrounds and personalities. Now their father's difficulty in earning enough to support the family aggravated those differences until they became irreconcilable. In the close quarters of the boarding house, Ewing had become aware of his parents' unhappiness, as his bedroom was next to theirs. "After I would go to bed, they would come to bed an hour or so later, and they would awaken me with their arguing. It was never really bitter. It was mostly about finances," Ewing recalled. Years later as a grown man, he still remembered the child's anguish. "When I heard them arguing, I would cry myself to sleep at night."

Neither Ruth nor Ewing, who were sixteen and twelve at the time, blamed either parent. They told their mother they agreed with the separation "because they couldn't get along." But Ewing did not believe that the financial problems were completely his father's fault. "My father was a physical man, close to the earth, and my mother was quite spiritual and mental. They were both wonderful people, but they were just not the same type. Mother was fastidious and

Dad was careless. Mother liked to stay home and Dad liked to travel. They were just different temperaments."

While Ruth and John were in Texas, Effie Kauffman rented another house at Thirty-sixth and Charlotte. It was about two blocks away and large enough to accommodate the Harrison Street boarders, all of whom agreed to move with her. When John returned, Effie told him of her decision. Ruth remembered her father saying over and over that he could not understand the change. She agreed with Ewing's assessment of the personality differences between the two parents. "I guess you'd call Dad a playboy these days. He wanted to go all the time. He liked to travel."

The parents separated in 1928 and then were divorced. Ruth and Ewing moved to the new house with their mother while John remained at the house on Harrison. His sister, Mary, later joined him and they partitioned the house into rental units—actually rooms with kitchen privileges. Ruth, who shared her father's carefree spirit, often stayed with him and her aunt Mary, moving back and forth between the two parents until she went to work and lived on her own. But Ewing, who was still in school and busy with homework, sports, and odd jobs on the side to help out, remained with his mother.

In spite of his parents' divorce, Ewing had constant contact with his father. As a way to spend more time with his son, John Kauffman became involved in scouting. Ewing was an enthusiastic Boy Scout, returning to school every Thursday evening to attend scout meetings from 7:00 to 9:30 P.M. Scouting appealed to his competitive nature just as math contests and spell-downs did. "I enjoyed the various rankings you could obtain, making the Tenderfoot, the Second Class, and in order to make First Class, it was necessary for me to be able to swim fifty yards in a certain length of time. The nearest pool was at the Young Men's Hebrew Association and, although I wasn't Jewish, they were kind enough to let me learn to swim there." Subsequently, he went on to become Star Scout, Life Scout, and Eagle Scout. One of his most cherished awards in a life filled with honors and awards came through scouting. "I am somewhat proud," he admitted in his seventies, "that I am one of two hundred plus individuals who have been awarded the Distinguished Eagle, which is for Eagle Scouts who later on in their mature life, have accomplished things that scouting seems to think worthwhile."

After his parents' divorce, Ewing began to take on more odd jobs so he could contribute to the family's expenses. Without ready cash to do with as he pleased, Ewing, like generations of young boys before him, devised other ways to accomplish his goals. Throughout his life he never owned a bicycle, "but I was able to travel all around the city by going to the busy streets where the stoplights were. When a truck stopped, I would jump on the back of it and ride to wherever as long as it was going in the direction I wanted. I could travel all over the city, but, of course, my parents were not aware of this."

When Ewing wanted to join his fellow scouts at summer camp, the twenty-four-dollar cost for two weeks was far beyond his mother's budget. So he applied his egg-selling techniques to the problem. The scout troop was offering a scholarship to the boy who sold the most tickets for the Scout-a-rama, an annual exhibition of crafts and activities. Ewing entered to win. He started on the top floor of one of the largest office buildings in downtown Kansas City and went from office to office urging people "to buy a raffle ticket and help send a deserving scout to summer camp." In record time he canvassed several buildings and secured the scholarship. He claimed to have sold almost four thousand tickets. "I'd even have some of my customers so impressed they would say, 'Wait a minute and I'll call Joe down on the fourth floor and you go see him,' and it would pyramid my sales."

As an adult, Ewing Kauffman tempered his youthful pride in winning the scholarship to scout camp, pointing out that his mother's self-sacrifice had enabled him to become a scout in the first place. He wanted to join the year his parents divorced. "My mother had to save diligently for several months in order to accumulate the ten dollars for me to buy the uniform and equipment to become a Boy Scout."

Times were hard, especially for a divorced mother of two, as those were the early years of the Great Depression. But Effie Kauffman managed not only the necessities for her children but a few extras as well. When Ewing was a senior in high school, his mother became concerned when she learned he was refusing invitations to parties because he could not dance. "I can remember that when Mother was very short of money she gave me ten dollars so I could learn to dance. I went up to Professor Wolf's at Thirty-first and Forest. And I was amazed! Here was a man who was about five-feet-seven or -eight, and must have weighed about 175 or 180 pounds. Yet he was so light on his feet that he would be the lady of the dance and eventually taught me a little bit. . . ." Reflecting on his mother's willing sacrifice, Ewing recalled, "This was a big thing for my mother to give me ten dollars for dancing lessons."

As Ewing grew from childhood to young manhood, he seemed to combine the dominant characteristics of both parents. Like his father, he was outgoing, jovial, and happy. He met strangers easily and was very active physically. He shared an acumen for math with his father, which John Kauffman skillfully nurtured while helping to hone Ewing's competitive edge. His self-assurance and love of learning were his mother's legacy. She had high expectations of him, and he responded with extra effort to fulfill these aspirations. From that background he learned a lesson which served him well in business. "I learned from Mother, that the more you expect from people, the more they will give you." Mrs. Kauffman's greatest gift to her son may have been the sense of self-worth which characterized him from an early age. Every morning as he left for school wearing a hand-me-down suit that she had lovingly made over to fit him, she would hug him and say, "Ewing, there may be others going to school that have better clothes or more money in their pockets than you do, but not one of them is better than you are."

Ewing Kauffman was to remain close to both parents throughout their lives. His father lived with him and his family for a time in the late fifties, but his mother was the dominant influence. "I didn't realize at the time how important she was to me, but I'm sure she had some realization of it," he recalled. "But I didn't give her compliments when I should have." Like most children who come to recognize an enormous debt to a parent, Ewing Kauffman believed he did not really understand how important she had been to him until after her death. In his mid-seventies he reflected, "I still awaken and think, 'Well, I'll go by and see Mother today.' And, she must have died ten or eleven years ago, at least. I think you don't really appreciate them until you lose them. You take them for granted."

Effie Kauffman settled her children and boarders in the new house, and soon everyone was back into a familiar routine. Ruth had graduated from high school earlier that year, but she was only sixteen and jobs were scarce so she helped her mother with the work of the boarding house. Before too long, her father introduced her to friends at National Bellas Hess, a Kansas City department store, where she was hired as a typist. She later moved into a better-paying job with more benefits in the Missouri civil service.

Ewing was just entering the eighth grade at Westport Junior High School when his parents divorced. Fortunately, the changed circumstances at home did not affect his schoolwork. He continued to excel in the classroom. His sixth-grade teacher had identified him as the best student in English, and his high school record confirmed her judgment. Ewing liked to diagram sentences, identifying all the parts of speech and placing them in their correct relationships. He also had an exceptionally large vocabulary which he had picked up from his mother and the extensive reading he did while ill. "As a result, when I was in my second year of high school, they gave all high school students in Missouri a vocabulary test and I ranked second in the whole state."

Like most young boys, Ewing loved sports. He had played baseball in elementary school, but in high school he decided to try out for the football team. He was small for a football player, only about five-foot-nine. He weighed 128 pounds and, by his own admission, "I wasn't fast." But he was determined to play and to make the first team, so he began to analyze the positions and quickly developed a strategy. He observed that the position no one seemed to want to play was that of center. That was the position he chose. "I did end up in my senior year making the varsity and playing center at 128 pounds. I played fairly well, but nothing startling."

His academic prowess coupled with a place on the varsity team added to Ewing's self-confidence, but it seldom came through as braggadocio or cockiness. Instead, he appeared self-assured—in command of himself and the situation. He had an inner feeling of being able to do almost any task. He was always the first to volunteer, the speaker at school assemblies, the boy whose hand shot up first. "I don't think I was cocky to the point that it was irritating. Rather, I was willing to take a chance and try to do something because I felt I could."

In addition to schoolwork, sports practice, and Boy Scout activities, Ewing worked for a while as a caddie at a miniature golf course on Troost Avenue. When it became too cold for miniature golf, he went to work on Saturdays at a nearby Milgram's Food Store which his schoolmate Lester Milgram's family owned. He stocked the shelves, sacked groceries, and carried out the packages from seven in the morning until eleven some nights.

During his last two years of high school, Ewing began working for the Long-Hall Laundry on Saturdays and during summer vacation. Years later, Ewing Kauffman recalled that Mr. Long "together with my scoutmaster, R.J. Woods, and my assistant scoutmaster, Cliff Tonsure, was an influence in a small way upon my life." When summer came, Ewing assisted a laundry driver who was overweight and did not like to climb apartment-building stairs in the heat and humidity. Ewing delivered the bundles up and down the stairs, collected the money, and brought it back to the driver. He earned about one dollar per day, and when there was overtime, could make up to two dollars.

Once while Ewing was making deliveries, a customer complained that the laundry was causing her towels to wear out too fast. She pointed to broken and damaged threads in the middle. Since Mr. Long authorized the delivery men to resolve all complaints on the spot, if possible, Ewing apologized and reimbursed the lady the fifty cents she said the towel had cost. When he returned to the laundry, he reported having paid out fifty cents from his collections for the damaged towel. To his surprise, Mr. Long responded, "We didn't do that [to the towel]." Ewing was baffled. If the laundry was not at fault, how had such damage happened? Mr. Long explained that broken threads usually occurred because people folded towels lengthwise and then vigorously dried their backs. Ewing admitted that this explanation had never occurred to him, but it seemed to make sense. He offered to pay for the towel himself, but Mr. Long declined. "No. We'll pay it, but you learned something there." Nearly six decades after the event, Ewing remembered that Mr. Long "had a discerning mind." And he also never forgot that early lesson to look beyond the apparent culprit to the real cause of a problem.

Ewing got his first practical lesson in handling customer complaints at the laundry, but that summer job also taught him other skills that he would use for both profit and pleasure. On Saturday evenings, the drivers would usually have to wait around from thirty minutes to an hour for the last of the laundry to be finished before they could make their final delivery of the week. In order to pass the time, they pitched coins at a line in the dirt—a dime was the upper limit. Then as the winners became fewer, they would raise the stakes to a quarter. One Saturday evening, Ewing got into a game and lost the dollar that he had earned that day. So that following week he went home, drew a line in the dirt, and spent several hours practicing throwing a coin at the line until he became quite skilled. "From then on I was able to win several dollars throwing at the line until it got to the point where they were afraid to play that game with me," he recalled.

Winning the coin toss, like selling the most Scout-a-rama tickets and reading the largest number of books, whetted Ewing's innate love of competition. So when the laundry owner's son challenged him one Saturday late, he took the bait. "Hearing that I had been so good, he asked me if I would like to throw for a dollar. Of course, my pride was involved, so I said, 'Sure.' After I had won five dollars from him, he gave up and quit." It had not taken long for a boy as bright as Ewing Kauffman to learn that overtime was not the only way to supplement his pay.

Ewing was seventeen when he graduated from Westport High School. The country was in the throes of an economic depression. Effie Kauffman's finances had steadily deteriorated after the divorce while the work of keeping boarders had increased and become more tiring. After Ewing's graduation, his mother broke up housekeeping and took a position as a live-in housekeeper for Mr. Hodgson, the owner of the Creighton property where the family had farmed for shares.

The summer after high school graduation, Ewing and another boy decided they wanted to see something of the country before settling into the routine of a job. Their parents agreed that the boys could hitchhike to Colorado and back, picking up odd jobs along the way to pay their expenses. It sounded like a reasonable plan since travel was relatively safe and drivers were inclined to offer rides to young hitchhikers. But in their haste to see the Rocky Mountains, the two boys abandoned hitchhiking and decided to ride the rails.

The year was 1934, the depths of the Depression, with 30 percent of America's workingmen unemployed. Thousands of desperate, haggard husbands, fathers, and sons roamed the country looking for any kind of work, living on food from soup kitchens or what they could scrounge and the kindness of strangers. Some of those on the roads and the rails were merely drifters, some petty thieves, and a few were hardened criminals. The railroads employed burly watchmen, armed with heavy truncheons and sometimes guns, to discourage free riders. And many of those who hopped aboard freight trains at dusk or in a dim dawn missed their footing or lost their grip and were crushed under thousands of tons of moving steel and steam. What seemed like a carefree lark on a summer vacation could have ended in disaster for Ewing and his friend; fortunately, it did not.

When the boys reached Colorado, they picked cherries for money to live on. "These were the Roosevelt days when they were starting the CCC where they would take the youth and the people who didn't have a job and give them work on the highways, building dams, and in forestry," Ewing recalled. Excited at the prospect of a job and the freedom of being away from home and on their own, he and his friend decided to sign up. He called home and told his parents that he was going to join the CCC. But Effie and John conferred and urged Ewing to return home. "My father said if I would come back he would see that I could go to [Kansas City Junior] college."

Ewing thought it all out and decided his father was right. Schooling probably did offer a better future than picking cherries or working on road crews. On the trip home, the boys ran low on money for food. Ewing had heard that cleaning shops would pay so much per hundred coat hangers. He and his friend trudged from house to house only to find that either the people had no coat hangers to return or they were saving them to take back for cash themselves. Ruth recalled that Ewing told the family on his return, "'I just knew if I kept on going that I'd find some.' And he did." That same tenacity and optimism would serve him well in years to come when he began his career as a pharmaceutical salesman.

Upon returning home, Ewing went to live with his father. John Kauffman was still selling insurance, but he made very little money. To reduce expenses, Ewing rejoined him at the old home on Harrison where several of the Kauffman maiden aunts were running a boarding house. He stayed there for two years while attending Kansas City Junior College. Knowing that finances would probably prevent him from going on for a bachelor of arts degree, he took the general curriculum leading to an associate's degree in business. "I was always interested in history, English, and sciences," he remembered.

"But the course I disliked most was psychology and the only one in which I did not get a good grade." Ewing attended classes in the morning and worked at the Long-Hall Laundry in the afternoon. At noon when classes were over, he would buy a couple of ten-cent fried pies and walk two miles to his job at the laundry. His route to work must have made for some interesting banter among his friends at the laundry. "I walked right through the red-light district. Doing it every day, the gals got to know me and in nice weather they'd sit out on the porch and pretty soon they were calling me Ewing." And, as he was already on a first-name basis with the customers, it made sense for him to fill in on this particular route when the regular delivery man went on vacation. "I don't believe I ever told my mother about that," he recalled somewhat sheepishly.

Ewing made A's and B's in his college work while putting in eight hours a day at the laundry. "I did everything from driving the laundry routes to working inside." When he graduated from junior college, Mr. Long hired him to be route supervisor. "Here I was, a twenty-year-old kid, supervising from eighteen to twenty older, more mature adults who were laundry drivers. And because I had worked around the laundry for a couple of years, I knew most of the routes and most of the customers." During that first summer as a full-time route supervisor, Ewing substituted for vacationing drivers. When vacations were over, his supervisory duties also included training drivers to secure new customers. "After a driver would deliver the laundry bundles in his truck, we would park and I would tell the driver to take one side of the street and I would take the other. We would go door-to-door asking for laundry or cleaning, saying that we would like to handle that for them. Since the laundry had a pretty good reputation, we were able to do this. One of the standing bets I had with all of the new drivers I trained is that I would get more customers per block than they would. Of course, this was developing, along with selling eggs [fish, Scout-a-rama tickets, and magazines], my sales ability."

Ewing was not only perfecting his sales skills at the Long-Hall Laundry, he was also observing entrepreneurial talent at work. Mr. Long, the owner, had his desk located in the middle of the laundry so he could keep an eye on everything. One day Ewing noticed him hard at work. "For almost a week, I saw him sitting there with a pair of scissors and cardboard, cutting various shapes." Then about a month later, Mr. Hall called Ewing over and asked him to take a check for $38,000 to the bank for him. When Ewing expressed surprise at the large amount, Mr. Hall asked if he remembered him cutting cardboard? He said he had developed an insert to put into a man's shirt after it was pressed so the collar would stay up. He had patented it and sold it to a national laundry service. The check was the payment for his idea. Suddenly Ewing saw another dimension to making money. "This impressed me how you could make money with your brains instead of your physical activity."

When Ewing finished junior college in June 1936, he accepted a full-time job with the laundry. There was never any question about completing a four-year college degree. He had to work to help support his mother. In later years, when he made it possible for hundreds of Westport High School graduates to earn college degrees, he did not seem to feel that he had been handicapped without one. His love of reading made up for his lack of one. With a full-time job and a salary of $17.50 a week, Ewing felt he could now support himself and his mother. She quit her job as a live-in housekeeper and they moved into a two-bedroom apartment in a fairly low-rent neighborhood of Kansas City. To help pay the bills, they took in one boarder. He stayed only a year, but his brother, Charles Hughes, took his place. "That started our lifelong friendship," Kauffman said.

Charles Hughes and Ewing Kauffman were opposites in most ways. Charlie, as he was known to his friends, was fairly tall, with dark hair and eyes and a quiet manner of speaking. He moved rather slowly, considered his words thoughtfully, and took his time to reach a decision. He was reserved, deferential to others, and somewhat shy. Ewing, by contrast, was shorter, with a slight build, reddish brown hair, intense blue eyes, and a confident, direct manner of speaking. He moved quickly. He spoke well, with authority and conviction. Ewing could analyze a problem and come to a solution with the same speed with which he solved math problems. He was outgoing, ebullient, optimistic, self-assured, and not the least bit shy.

To most young people in their early twenties, adults, and especially parents, have always seemed a bit old-fashioned and strict. And Ewing and Charlie at that age were no different. They shared Ewing's bedroom in the apartment, and since they were both working full-time, Mrs. Kauffman thought everyone should be in bed by

9:30 or 10:00 P.M. at the latest. Often when they were all settled for the night, Charlie would get up, telling Mrs. Kauffman that he had to run an errand. He would walk to the corner bar, buy a six-pack of beer and return to the window where Ewing would be waiting. "I'd lower a little rope and he'd tie the six-pack on it and I'd pull it up. We'd lie there and drink our three bottles of beer each," Kauffman said. "Subsequently, I found out that my mother knew all about it."

Ewing and Charlie both worked full-time, but during their off-hours social life revolved around the Criterion Sunday school class. The class met at a local Congregational church. "But [this] had nothing to do particularly with the church, but rather was just a place where boys and girls of our age, from nineteen to thirty, could attend a Sunday school class. It was our only social activity," Ewing remembered. The Criterion class gathered every Sunday morning to study under O.H. Day, whom they nicknamed "Happy" Day. Along with Ewing's scoutmaster, R.J. Woods, Happy Day had a profound influence on his development. Ewing recalled that Happy Day preached beautiful sermons. "But they were not so religious. However, by taking the principles of the Bible and illustrating how if you followed them in a normal, practical living situation, [he showed that] you were better off. . . ." The homilies of the Sunday school class, coupled with the principles of scouting, reinforced Ewing's reading and thinking about how one ought to live. And they all formed the philosophy of life that would guide him over the years.

After the Sunday school lesson, the class members usually scattered to their homes for lunch and then reassembled back at the classroom at one o'clock. The afternoon might be spent playing baseball at a nearby park or riding rented bicycles. "Then [you would] pair off with a girl, if you wished." A typical date "might be to go to a show, but probably it would be to go to your home and have something to drink and then walk her home or go to her place," Ewing recalled. The Sunday school class was the group's primary social activity, and it was not surprising that romance soon bloomed among its ranks. Charlie Hughes met his future wife, Marjorie, there, as did another close friend who later became an early Marion Laboratories salesman, Paul Danielson. Ewing also met his first wife, Marguerite Blackshire, at the Criterion class.

Ewing's salary at the Long-Hall Laundry inched slowly upward, but there were few prospects for advancement. During this period, John Kauffman was still selling insurance, now for Sun Life Assurance Company of Canada. Like all proud fathers, John found an opportunity to introduce Ewing to the general manager of the Kansas City office. This man knew a salesman when he saw one and quickly offered Ewing a job. The arrangement was that he would draw twenty dollars a week to be repaid out of future commissions. With his ability to sell, this seemed like a golden opportunity for a self-motivated young man. So Ewing quit his job at the laundry and embarked on what he always described as one of the worst periods of his life. "I hated the insurance business. Every time you called friends and said you wanted to drop by and see them, they knew you were going to try to sell them life insurance." Unable to put his heart into the task, Ewing did not set any records for selling insurance policies. In fact, he recalled, "I had the record of having the biggest draw, owing the most money, of any person who ever worked selling insurance for Sun Life of Canada."

Although he knew he was not destined for success in the insurance business, when a friend who worked for Northern Life approached him about selling accident and disability policies, he decided to give that aspect of the business a try. At least with accident policies, he reasoned, the owner could get some money out while he was still alive. There was another reason for Ewing's sudden job switch. The boss had a very attractive daughter, Marjorie Cartwright. They started dating, fell in love, and Ewing asked her to marry him. When she said yes to his proposal of marriage, Ewing sold a local jeweler an insurance policy and took a diamond engagement ring as down payment. Shortly after the engagement, Northern Life offered Marjorie's father the entire state of Kansas as his new territory, with headquarters in Wichita. Since Ewing was soon to be his son-in-law, Mr. Cartwright suggested that he move to Wichita and help develop the territory, which he did. But Ewing was new to Wichita, without friends or contacts, so he had a very difficult time making sales. Then the engagement soured. "I really became a little unhappy because Majorie and I had kind of cooled off," he remembered. "I ran out of money so I sent a collect telegram to Raymond Parshall, this [football] buddy of mine from Westport [High School]." Raymond was working for a soft drink company in Kansas City, and Ewing asked him to wire twenty dollars so he could return home. Raymond sent the money right away, and that was the end of the romance and the insurance business.

It was evident that Ewing would never be an outstanding insurance salesman, but he might have had a successful career in public life. At about this same time, he had an opportunity to test his salesmanship in the toughest arena possible, Kansas City politics. John Kauffman had become active with the reform group attempting to dislodge the Pendergast machine. He was assigned as a ward leader responsible for organizing precincts, identifying registrants, and getting out the vote. He naturally asked his son to help out in one of the precincts. Ewing's job was to get the names of all the householders in the precinct and call on them personally to determine their party affiliation or preference. "If they were for you, then you would see to it that they were registered. Then, on election day, you would see that they got out and voted. If they needed transportation, usually you had somebody you could call or I would drive by and pick them up."

Ewing's assigned precinct was heavily Democratic and an entrenched bastion of the Pendergast machine. He worked tirelessly, but he was very disappointed when the results came out. He lost the precinct by seven votes—207 to 200. When he told his father of his disappointment, John Kauffman responded, "Well, don't you realize what a wonderful job you did? Last time we lost it there were a hundred and some votes difference." In recalling that experience years later, Ewing Kauffman mused, "You know, I thought I always had to win."

The political foray, which he later admitted he had enjoyed, came at a time when Ewing was thinking seriously about his future. "I'd always felt that what I wanted to be when I was old enough to really analyze it, was a trial lawyer, a preacher, or a salesman. If you analyze them, all three are convincing other people to do something. I've always thought I'd enjoy being a trial lawyer." The legal profession's loss was definitely the business world's gain, but Kauffman had one other brief flirtation with politics in the early 1970s. By that time, he was well known in the region as the millionaire founder of a successful pharmaceutical business and as owner of the Kansas City Royals. As a resident of Kansas, and a wealthy Republican, he seemed like an attractive challenger to Kansas's popular Democratic governor, Robert Docking.

The Nixon administration approached Kauffman through his own congressman, Representative John Ellsworth. They talked about the requirements of a political race and the necessity for Kauffman to relinquish leadership of Marion Laboratories and put his assets into a blind trust. Kauffman thought seriously about the contest and the challenges of the governorship, but decided not to run. Later he recalled the thought process which led him to that decision. "I thought to myself, it's almost impossible to be completely honest and be a politician. [For example] you must compromise your principles in order to get votes for your good bill for orphans. Then I have to agree to vote for pork barrel in your area where it really isn't needed to spend that ten million dollars. But if it's the only way I can get your vote, I'll do it. I think it would prey on your mind if you [did] things that are wrong."

That concern for ethical principles became the hallmark of his business career. Just as his parents had taught him honesty and above-board dealings, he would later found his business career and ownership of a major league sports team on those same standards. In his seventh decade, he reported that he had always been able to sleep well at night because, "I know that the IRS can't get me in any way, shape, or form because I've been honest with them. When I traveled overseas, by gosh, when I went through customs I didn't care how much they looked; they were not going to find anything that I didn't declare. I don't worry about it. That freedom of mind is very important."

When Ewing returned to Kansas City after the failed insurance venture in Wichita, he moved back to his mother's apartment. In his absence, his mother had rented his room to two working girls, but upon his return she gave them her room and she moved to the living room sofa. "You can imagine the difficulty of my mother still going through such hard work in order to keep herself and me together."

In the meantime, Charlie Hughes had married Marjorie and they were living nearby. Ewing quickly got a job selling training courses in aircraft, metal work, and engine repair for American Aeronautical Institute. For the next year and a half, life was fairly routine for all the Kauffmans. As the country struggled to break out of the grip of economic depression, they strove to earn an adequate living. News stories of the war in Europe began to dominate the local papers, but the national mood was to let the Europeans settle their own quarrels. Then came the Japanese attack on Pearl Harbor, December 7, 1941, and suddenly every family in America with able-bodied sons and fathers knew they might be called to fight. They also sensed that whatever the outcome of this war or their role in it, their lives would probably be changed forever.

Going to War   2

The Japanese attack on Pearl Harbor and Congress's formal decla-
ration of war the following day changed the lives and plans of all
Americans. Like thousands of other young men who heard Presi
dent Roosevelt condemn the "date which will live in infamy," Kauffman knew that a call from his draft board was inevitable. He was
twenty five and single. But rather than wait for the draft notice, he
decided to enlist.

With his usual thoroughness, Kauffman had investigated the options and decided to join the navy. Sailors, he had learned, could
earn up to sixty dollars a month while draftees in the army were
paid only twenty-one dollars. In addition to the money, for Kauffman there was the age-old lure of the sea. He had topped off his
scouting career with several years as a Sea Scout and loved the sailing exercises and simulated whaling expeditions on Kansas City's
nearby lakes. If one had to go to war, why not enter a branch of the
service that offered some appealing activities and better pay?

Before enlisting, Kauffman went to see Charlie Hughes, who had
been married only a short time and was sure to be drafted. Kauffman
suggested they enlist together in the navy rather than wait for Uncle
Sam's invitation. Hughes agreed. When they reported to the enlist-
ment office, the officer in charge decided that Hughes's experience
as a typist for Folger's Coffee Company qualified him as a petty officer, third class. And the difference in pay was substantial. Had he
entered as an apprentice seaman, his pay would have been twenty-
one dollars a month. However, because he was qualified to do secretarial work for the officers, his pay soared to fifty-four dollars a month.

Kauffman was next. The enlisting officer scrutinized his junior
college record, but without a baccalaureate degree he was ineligible

for officers' training. As an apprentice seaman he would draw only twenty-one dollars a month. Kauffman's salesmanship automatically came to the fore. He described his extensive training as a Sea Scout and persuaded the recruiting officer to let him enlist at the rank of seaman, first class. As a result, his pay would be forty-two dollars a month. "Of course, the navy furnished all your room and board," Kauffman recalled, "so you could live easily on that if you didn't spend too much at the bars."

The two friends said good-bye to their respective families and took the train to the United States Naval Training Station at Great Lakes, Illinois, outside Chicago, arriving on January 18, 1942. Because he was married and wanted to remain as close to his wife as possible, Hughes applied for shore duty. Kauffman requested sea duty. Fate, however, decreed the reverse. Charlie was shipped to California, placed on the cruiser *San Diego,* and was at sea four weeks after enlisting. Kauffman, who longed to go to sea, was selected for additional study after basic training. Almost six months would pass before he was ready for sea duty.

The three months of basic training were essentially uneventful except for a brief scare over a possible scarlet fever epidemic. Because of his heart, Kauffman was considered at high risk and quarantined for two weeks along with twenty other young men. They continued their studies and took all their meals in isolation. As a precautionary measure, each man received daily injections to boost his immunity to diphtheria and scarlet fever. "I really believe that I won't be able to catch any disease when the navy gets through with me," Kauffman wrote to his mother and Ruth. "But all in all, we don't mind the quarantine but time drags heavy." To lighten those hours, Kauffman began playing cards and sent his mother a seventy-dollar check from his winnings. He also asked her to send him a money belt which he anticipated he would need when he went to sea.

After basic training, Kauffman was selected for quartermaster and signal corps school, so he remained in Illinois until June. At some point that spring, he wrote to his mother that he and Marguerite had been secretly married since the previous December. Like his friends Charlie Hughes and Paul Danielson, he had met his bride through the Criterion Sunday school class and they had fallen in love. Kauffman later described Marguerite as "somewhat shy, probably you could call her an introvert. And she had some of the Indian qualities of stoicism. In fact, she could have her teeth pulled with no novocaine. She wasn't book smart, but she was smart from other factors." Marguerite was a small woman with red hair, a descendant of the Cherokee Nation whose family lived in Enid, Oklahoma. She had been widowed a few years earlier when her husband was killed in an automobile accident. Because of litigation involving her former husband's estate, the couple decided to keep their marriage secret, although Kauffman had confided the happy news to Marjorie Hughes at Christmas of 1941.

From a letter that Kauffman wrote his mother while he was still at Great Lakes, Illinois, it appeared that Effie had voiced misgivings about the marriage. She was concerned because Ewing and Marguerite had such different educational backgrounds and temperaments. Kauffman, who had a sunny disposition and a great desire to see others happy, acknowledged that his bride could sometimes be moody and cross. But he wrote, "You also are occasionally [cross] and Ruth has her spells. We all do. You will see faults in Marguerite but I believe you can overlook them because in your eyes she has one great trait—she loves me with a love as great as your own."

In the same letter, Kauffman wrote that they were expecting a child. "It has always been my desire and hope to have children, and I believe that with care all should be all right. Marguerite, due to her physical condition, has to be careful because of a possible miscarriage." The news that Marguerite was pregnant probably lent credence to Effie's worst fears. Ewing was an intelligent, congenial, and clever young man and his mother had envisioned a distinguished career for him in law or medicine, perhaps in teaching. Now with a wartime marriage and the burden of family responsibilities coming so soon, she probably feared that all this would combine to rob him of a promising future. And she may have seen the tableau of her own early life—marriage to an incompatible mate, different intellectual interests combined with young children and the need to earn a living—about to be repeated in her son's future.

Kauffman was correct about his mother wanting his happiness. When she learned of Marguerite's pregnancy, she graciously invited the young bride to stay with her and Ruth while Ewing was away at sea. Marguerite declined, preferring to live on her own and to be free to join her husband on the east coast when he received shore leave. She took a part-time job in a radio assembly plant and began saving for the home that she and Kauffman were planning for their family. Sadly for the young couple, Marguerite had a miscarriage early in her pregnancy, but they continued to plan for the day when they would have children of their own.

When Kauffman completed his additional training, he was sent to Norfolk, Virginia, to board a vessel that would take him to South America to join a naval convoy group. There he boarded a supply ship with a large number of other sailors being transported to various assignments in South America. In addition to the regular crew, a great many extra hands were on deck. The ship's captain was eager to keep everyone busy, and the new seamen were put to work chipping paint off the deck so it could be repainted. The weather was stifling and the work dirty and monotonous, so Kauffman began to look for alternate duty. "You don't want me doing this," he told the boatswain's mate. "I'm a seaman first class." The mate agreed. He had an important assignment for a seaman of Kauffman's obvious ability. Pointing toward the heavens, he told the young sailor, "The coxswain is up there on that mast weaving tackle. You go up and help him."

Years after the event, Kauffman recalled the sheer terror of the assignment. "I had never climbed. I looked up there and it must have been six stories high. I climbed up and was holding on . . . and the coxswain said to hand him the so-and-so, and I would hold on here and try to hand it . . . I just wouldn't go out any further." Subsequently, he was assigned duty below deck making canvas first-aid kits to equip the lifeboats. When the ship reached the U.S. Naval Operating Base at Trinidad in the British West Indies, "they let me off," he remembered with relief.

Kauffman's orders for sea duty had not come through, so he settled into the barracks to wait. He was alone and knew no one. All his buddies from basic training had been scattered. But with a hundred or more sailors in the barracks, it did not take the outgoing Missourian long to get acquainted. Soon he was involved in a spirited card game. With a keen mathematical mind and a love of competition, Kauffman was a natural and gifted card player. He had played with some success on the supply ship during the voyage to the Caribbean, but by his own admission, he was not prepared for what happened at Trinidad. "I was really just starting out in my naval career. I had been in three or four months, so I hadn't built up a stake yet, and I wasn't very smart."

The card game proved disastrous. Each player had a hand of three cards. The player bet that he had a card in his hand that was above the next card to be turned over. At each turn, a player would bet so much money until he ran out of funds. "I had all my money in and the rule there was that I was out. I couldn't play anymore." Kauffman, though usually a winner, had lost all his money and was embarrassed as well. "I didn't have a dime and payday was about six or seven days off." While there was no danger that the penniless seaman would go hungry or have to sleep in the cold, being without any funds at all "was never a comfortable feeling," he recalled. His solution was to fall back on the training of his youth. Except this time, instead of just delivering laundry, Kauffman collected it, scrubbed it with his knuckles in the shower, and then returned it to the owner. "I picked up two or three dollars that way—to see that I had some money. I'll never forget it."

Although his final orders for sea duty were still delayed, Kauffman was eager to escape the scene of his recent humiliation. Every other day he hounded the duty officer with the same plea, "I want to go to sea! I want to go to sea!" Finally one morning at three A.M. the duty officer shook him awake with instructions to "get dressed and pack your gear. You're going to a Norwegian ship that needs an English-speaking signalman."

Because of his extensive vocabulary and his facility with language, Kauffman had been trained as a signalman and was able to read messages flashed at sea with both speed and accuracy. The Norwegian berth was a freighter/passenger ship sailing as part of a convoy traveling from Trinidad to New York. The captain was anxious to have English-speaking assistance as they negotiated the treacherous straits of Cuba and later anchored in New York harbor. Kauffman was the only American on board. Rather than assign him to eat with the crew, the captain invited him to share his table. When he finished signal duty that first day, Kauffman went below to the captain's mess, where he found lunch being served to two civilian passengers, the captain, and himself. "They served cold fish, like sardines, hard—and cold potatoes," he remembered. "I was still hungry after they passed around the food and I asked them for some more. Pretty soon the steward was standing behind me and finally grabbed my plate and they brought on the dinner. I thought that was it. I thought that [cold fish and potatoes] was our entire meal!"

Kauffman not only acquired new culinary knowledge on that voyage, he also had better luck at cards. One of the civilian passengers was an engineer who had helped set up the air base on Ascension Island, where planes refueled on flights from South America to Europe. This man had returned through Rio de Janeiro, where he purchased a number of gifts for his family. On the voyage home, he wanted to relax over a friendly game of cards, so Kauffman obliged. "So I started playing cards with him," Kauffman remembered. "I beat him out of all his money and then he'd bring out a gift and say, 'Well, I paid a hundred dollars for this. You give me credit for a hundred dollars and I'll put it in the pot and we'll play for it.' So we did." By the time they reached New York, Kauffman had won all the engineer's money, an alligator handbag, "the kind with the alligator's face on the flap," and a large, beautifully cut, unset emerald.

Once in port, Kauffman lost no time in contacting Marguerite, asking her to join him as he had seven days shore leave. As soon as she arrived and was settled in a hotel room near Kauffman's barracks, he presented her with the stone and announced, "Let's go to a jewelry store and see about having it set for you." The jeweler to whom they took it commented on the fine cut, but told them it was worthless, "just pure glass." Years later when recalling the incident, Kauffman remarked with his characteristic good humor, "You know, somebody down there had taken advantage of [that engineer]."

After the brief shore leave, Marguerite returned to Kansas City. Kauffman reported for duty, but to his surprise, he found himself in limbo. When he was assigned to the Norwegian ship in Trinidad, the navy failed to transfer any orders with him or to tell him what to do when he arrived stateside. "I could have come on home and they'd never have known it," he recalled. Later in the war, the navy recordkeepers again lost track of Kauffman. But this time, instead of being an anonymous seaman, he was being honored with the Bronze Star for valor in combat. He had been assigned to a merchant vessel ferrying supplies to North Africa, but was transferred to another ship upon reaching the port of Oran, Algeria. The first merchant ship was subsequently involved in combat. "Because I had been on that ship at one time, the naval officer just looked down the register and saw my name there and put my name down for the Bronze Star. Hell, I wasn't even on the ship at that time."

Kauffman continued to agitate for permanent sea duty. Finally the orders arrived. He was assigned to a passenger ship, the *Lauraleen*, which had been converted to a troop transport. Their orders were to take troops in for the buildup following the invasion of Guadalcanal. The *Lauraleen*'s crew did not take part in combat. They simply delivered troops, then returned home through the Panama Canal. Upon returning to New York, Kauffman was assigned to the U.S. Naval Armed Guard Center at Brooklyn. Naval personnel were placed on merchant ships convoying war material to protect them from submarine attacks. "All they had on these merchant ships was a five-inch gun, a fantail, so at least you could fire back at a submarine if they came up on top," Kauffman recalled. "Or you were also capable of dropping depth bombs, but not much." The merchant vessels had to have signal crews capable of taking orders from the navy, so Kauffman's talents were required. He was assigned as a signalman under Captain Edmund A. Crenshaw's command and told to report for duty posthaste. This assignment was to prove fortuitous for both men before the war's end.

Edmund A. Crenshaw, a ruddy-faced, six-foot-three Phildelphian, was an Annapolis cadet of the class of 1911. After graduation, he had remained on active duty until he was retired with the rank of captain in the reduction-of-force efforts following World War I. When the United States entered the war against Japan, Crenshaw returned to active service. Crenshaw's duties were to convoy ships, to protect them from being sunk by German submarines, and to land troops in invasions. Kauffman's first voyage under Crenshaw's command involved taking a group of oil tankers to Aruba, where they would be filled with oil. The tankers then were to be convoyed safely back to the United States, where the oil would be refined to fuel America's war machinery. Convoys of this nature usually traveled at night to avoid German submarines. In order to prevent the enemy from learning of their plans by listening to the convoy's radio frequencies, sailors trained as signal men transmitted messages from ship to ship, either via flashing light or with flags, outlining the various maneuvers for their nocturnal journeys.

Kauffman had all the natural attributes to become a superior signalman. His facility with words, a quick and agile intellect, and the love of almost any competitive enterprise all combined to establish his prowess in this endeavor. Because of his extensive vocabulary, he was often able to identify a word before it was completely spelled out. Kauffman's initial duty was as backup to the man assigned to take the messages on Crenshaw's flagship. Sending messages by flashing light or flag required speed and accuracy. There was intense competition among the various signal crews in the convoy for recognition as the best, and Kauffman's group was no exception. When words were transmitted by flashing lights, the usual practice was for the recipient to turn his light on as an indication that he had received the word. But Kauffman's crew liked to prove how skilled it was, so "we would just leave [the light] on constantly, daring them to send it faster than we could read. Being in charge of the crew, we had one person assigned to take the message, but I was the backup. If he missed it, he would let out a shout and I would give the word that he had missed and we could continue receiving [the message]."

Captain Crenshaw, whom Kauffman remembered as "a very unusual, personable, compassionate, intelligent man," took an interest in the former Sea Scout from landlocked Missouri. Kauffman stood watch from four P.M. to eight P.M. and from four A.M. to eight A.M. He was responsible for waking the captain just before sunrise, the time when German submarines would try to sink enemy ships. Crenshaw wanted to be on the bridge at that time. One morning as Crenshaw stood sipping his predawn coffee, Kauffman recalled that the captain pointed to a bright star in the sky and asked the young seaman if he knew the star's name. When Kauffman said no, Crenshaw replied, "That is Sirius, the brightest star in the sky and so large that if you put the earth in the center of it and the sun ninety-three million miles away from the earth . . . the sun could revolve around the earth and never get outside that star." Kauffman was fascinated. The next morning when the captain came up to the bridge, Kauffman casually pointed to a different star, asking Crenshaw if he knew its name. When Crenshaw said no, Kauffman identified it as Aldebaran. Then he rattled off the names of several other stars. The captain was amused. He grinned and asked if Kauffman had been studying. When the young seaman reported that he had spent the previous day in the ship's library studying some of the stars and reading about astronomy, the captain knew he had an exceptionally keen young man in his crew. He asked if Kauffman would like to learn more about the stars and navigation. When he agreed, Crenshaw had him enroll in a correspondence navigation course so he could study while at sea.

Captain Crenshaw's encouragement did not stop with the suggestion to take a correspondence course. When Kauffman returned to the ship from his next shore leave, Crenshaw presented him with his own sextant, which he had had since he graduated from Annapolis. He also gave Kauffman permission to take sights along with the ship's navigational officer. Now he practiced at every opportunity. "You take sights in the morning before the sun comes up because you can see the stars and see the horizon," he recalled. "You have to be able to see the horizon because you bring the star right down to the horizon and mark the degrees and mark the time. From there you take another sight which could be over in this opposite direction—ninety degrees off. And then you go and draw lines on your chart and see where they cross—a line this way and a line this way—and that's where you are, if you're accurate." Within weeks, Kauffman was so proficient that he was reporting his conclusions as much as fifteen minutes before the navigation officer returned with his own calculations. "Of course, being young and trying to make a name for myself, I probably took advantage of that because my figures were even more accurate than his," he later admitted.

Kauffman's acknowledged ambition and his youthful self-assurance caused him to risk a possible severe punishment. The episode involved a convoy of approximately fifty ships traveling north escorting oil tankers from Aruba back to the United States. "We were passing between the straits by Cuba and, because we were going to be doing it at night, we had to tell the ships that we'd make a turn at one o'clock in the morning. So we passed the message during the daylight before the sun had set, stating that we would make a turn to 095 degrees at one o'clock in the morning. That would enable us to miss the islands because [the] ships were spread out at approximately a five-mile-wide radius across the front."

It had become Kauffman's habit to take sightings along with the navigation officer, a practice the captain encouraged. But that evening, Kauffman's calculations did not coincide with the navigation officer's. "I had us approximately eight miles further ahead than he did, but naturally the captain had to take his sightings because he was the officer and I was still just an enlisted man."

Kauffman got into his bunk that night, but he could not sleep. He was confident that his calculations could not be that far off. Although it was too late to take any more sightings, he thought of another way to check his conclusions. "There was a fathometer on board which measures the depth of the ocean—how many feet it is and you could have a chart that shows you that if it is 1,100 feet here and then it drops to 1,500 there, by doing that over a period of time you can say, 'Well, we're right here.'" While using the fathometer to check his work seemed like a reasonable idea, naval regulations did not permit its use after dark because submarines might pick up the sound and locate the convoy. But to the determined young seaman, the risk seemed worth the prize. "I went up to the cabin. Nobody was there. I turned on the fathometer and after fifteen minutes I was positive that my sights were right. We were eight miles ahead of where the navigation officer had us. If we continued on that course and made the turn at one o'clock in the morning, three of the ships on the right would run aground!"

Without a moment's hesitation, Kauffman went straight to Captain Crenshaw's cabin and awakened him. When the captain asked what he wanted, Kauffman announced, "I think there is a mistake in our navigation and we better make our turn earlier." The captain's response was terse. Calling Kauffman by his nickname, he growled, "Lucky, you'd better be right!" As soon as Captain Crenshaw reviewed Kauffman's fathometer readings, he broke radio silence and ordered the ships to take the turn at 12:30 P.M. instead of 1:00 A.M. "I was right," Kauffman recalled proudly more than a half century later. "As a result, when we got to New York, he had me made an ensign and he named me as his navigation officer."

Kauffman had taken a major risk; in fact, several. He had challenged the work of a senior officer. He had violated naval regulations in using the fathometer to check and confirm his sightings. And most dangerous of all, he had roused a sleeping captain with the news that he would have to risk breaking radio silence to change his orders because unless he did part of his fleet was in deadly peril. All this from a brash enlisted man who had taken a correspondence navigation course and declared the captain's own navigation officer in error. In reflecting on the episode, Kauffman mused, "[This story] illustrates that when you take a risk, sometimes you lose but sometimes it pays off big, and that certainly did."

Kauffman's assignment to Captain Crenshaw's signal crew meant that he was making regular runs between New York and various ports in North Africa and the Mediterranean. And as word of his exceptional navigation skills spread, he was approached about returning to the mainland to be an instructor. Although he had several opportunities to transfer to shore duty and was eager to have more time with his bride, Captain Crenshaw advised against it. He thought Kauffman would be making a mistake in taking shore duty. He knew that in a few months the navy would stop the shore training programs, as they had sufficient men. He warned Kauffman that he would risk being sent to a Pacific island or assigned to a fleet where he would not return to the United States until armistice.

Kauffman was torn between the natural desire to be with his wife and an almost overpowering sense that destiny had intervened in his life. He confided to his mother, "I feel as if my whole navy career has been taken care of by someone above me. That by doing my work well and ably and striving to do right that I [will] come out unscathed and enriched by my experience. That is certainly true up to date. I can't say that this feeling comes through divine consciousness but I do feel it."

Whether surrendering to his destiny or just heeding his superior officer's advice, Kauffman dropped all thought of pursuing shore duty. And with his usual inventiveness, he found a satisfactory way to spend more time with Marguerite. Since he usually had four or five days of shore leave in New York at least every month, he suggested that Marguerite take an apartment there. "I was giving her money from my gambling winnings and she got all my navy salary because I didn't need it while I was at sea. She also had some money of her own from her first husband's insurance," he said. So the young couple's financial situation enabled them to be together as much as military duty would permit. And while her husband was at sea, Marguerite explored museums, began to attend the theater, and even studied violin.

As the United States' participation in the hostilities in the Atlantic theater increased, Captain Crenshaw's command switched from convoying oil tankers to convoying troops. They were involved in

the delivery of fighting men and supplies for the North African campaign throughout 1943. On a voyage to Algeria during this time, the
convoy fleet put into the port of Oran for repairs and refueling.
Kauffman had a few days of unanticipated leave to go ashore and
see the sights. His first afternoon ashore, he wandered into a local
bar for a drink and noticed that in the midst of the French-speak-
ing crowd, the bartender appeared to be speaking in Spanish. Kauffman had taken two years of high school Spanish, so he walked right
in and struck up a conversation. Between the bartender's broken
English and the sailor's broken Spanish, Kauffman learned the man's
daughter was getting married. A happily married man himself, he
said he would bring the girl a present when he returned from the
States. He knew his group had orders to be flown back to New York
shortly and that they would be returning soon with another convoy bringing more soldiers to fight in North Africa. Warming to the
idea of the wedding celebration to come, the grateful father asked
Kauffman if he would be willing to do some additional shopping for
his daughter's trousseau. When Kauffman agreed, the father of the
bride quickly sketched the garments and indicated the appropriate
sizes.

Now, asked this overjoyed bartender, how might he return the
favor? Kauffman had not expected any quid pro quo when he offered to help. His natural friendliness and his Midwestern sense of
hospitality had simply caused him to respond to this man's happiness. After giving the situation some thought, the bartender suggested, "If you can bring some [bed]sheets, I can sell them for you
and you can make some money." The local Arabs were ready customers for sheets, which they fashioned into the loose, flowing garments that were their traditional dress. Who could resist this father's offer to express his gratitude? Kauffman agreed to the scheme.

Marguerite was settled in an apartment and waiting for Kauffman in New York when he returned from Oran, Algeria. Together
they selected the wedding finery for the bartender's daughter and
then bought fifty double bedsheets at two dollars each. Kauffman
packed the bridal gifts and the linens in one suitcase and his uniforms and personal gear in another. Then he and Marguerite
rushed to Kansas City for a few days before he left again for sea duty.
When Kauffman returned from his visit home, he learned that his
ship was to sail from Norfolk, Virginia, not New York harbor. So he

grabbed the two suitcases and caught the train south. "Those fifty sheets weighed damn heavy," he remembered, "and the handle of one suitcase broke. So here I am with this one suitcase with a handle and I have to take the other one—I'm an officer in the U.S. Navy—and put it up on my shoulder and carry it like that. Quite unconventional." But he carried the broken suitcase just the same. And when the bartender sold the sheets for twenty dollars each, Kauffman realized a profit of almost one thousand dollars. This was more than sufficient to assuage the momentary indignity of having to haul the broken suitcase on his shoulder like an ordinary seaman.

The bartender's daughter must have been especially pleased with the purchases, because her father suggested another way for Kauffman to make a little money. He asked Kauffman if he had any cigarettes. "We've got some on board that nobody wants," Kauffman replied. He explained that the Red Cross provided free cigarettes which were the inexpensive, unpopular off-brands that the tobacco companies contributed to the war effort. Even though they were free, the sailors could purchase their favorite brand for six cents a pack or sixty cents a carton. "I couldn't even give them away," Kauffman recalled. He had accumulated a case of Raleigh cigarettes which no one had wanted despite the coupon offers included with each pack. He delivered the cigarettes to the bartender, who in turn sold them for eighteen to twenty dollars a carton and gave Kauffman the money. It looked as if he had stumbled on a very effective way to supplement his seaman's pay. This seemed less risky than playing cards, and cigarettes were not as heavy and bulky as sheets.

But before Kauffman could pursue this potentially lucrative sideline, he noticed an article in the *Stars and Stripes Magazine* that suddenly quenched his entrepreneurial fire. The article reported that there was going to be an investigation to determine why military personnel were sending home more money than was being paid out in salary. When Kauffman received local currency for the bedsheets and the cigarettes, he was obliged to exchange it for U.S. dollars. He would then purchase a money order from the paymaster's office and send the money home to Marguerite. Now he began to worry. An investigation that revealed that he had illegally sold U.S. supplies to Algerians might land him in the brig indefinitely or, worse, result in a dishonorable discharge. He was certain the navy had tumbled to his scheme. He lost his appetite and lay awake to avoid nightmares about his possible dishonor. Fortunately, his ship was scheduled to return to the States right away, so he decided to have a talk with Captain Crenshaw once they were under way.

Their first morning at sea, Kauffman awakened Captain Crenshaw as usual. When the officer was up on the bridge, coffee in hand to watch the dawn, the frightened seaman said that he had a problem and hoped Crenshaw could help. As the captain listened, Kauffman told his story. "I have a friend who made some extra money selling some supplies to civilians over in Oran and they're investigating him . . . because so much money is being sent back home through money orders. What should he do?" Crenshaw reflected for a few minutes, then he counseled the young ensign. "You just tell your friend when he talks to you to see your legal representative." Somewhat baffled, Kauffman asked who that legal representative might be. To which the captain replied, "Have him see me!"

Captain Crenshaw had seen through the ruse immediately, and he knew that one close brush with military justice was all that was needed to keep his navigation officer focused on his official duties. Kauffman was relieved, and he was never investigated. Whether Crenshaw actually intervened on his behalf or the investigation failed to materialize, Kauffman never knew. But he never doubted that Captain Crenshaw would have helped him. "That is just the type of person he was." From then on, a chastened Kauffman confined his income-enhancing activities to card games with his shipmates.

Although Kauffman did not experience combat duty during the war, his ship was frequently involved in dangerous circumstances as they landed troops for invasions. He saw enough bloodshed and carnage never to romanticize his war experiences. Early in the war in the Pacific, he had been with a convoy ferrying troops to support the invasion of Guadalcanal. The usual practice was to anchor about two miles off shore, where the troops would transfer to small boats and landing craft. "As soon as they were gone, we would leave. We might drop anchor ten miles out and wait for wounded to be brought aboard and we did bring back some wounded in the early casualties. I can still remember one of the wounded soldiers jumping overboard in the middle of the sea," he recalled years later. Most of his service took place in the Atlantic theater. "I made South America a half-dozen times and I made North Africa and Iran and the invasion of Sicily. Usually we would get those ships in and out as fast as possible because we didn't want to lose them. And the enemy was more interested in fighting the soldiers than they were worried about the ships. Because we had good air coverage, they couldn't really attack the ships. So, it wasn't really much of a problem as far as we were concerned."

As events in Europe signaled that the war there was near its end, Kauffman began to think about what life would be like when he returned home. This young man who had lavished expensive gifts on his family with the money he won at gambling—a five-hundred-dollar diamond watch and expensive clothes for his wife, gifts of all sorts for his mother and sister—was beginning to ponder the future. "I can't help but feel that ten years or sooner after the war we will have a bad depression and I want to start saving now for it. Thank heavens that [Marguerite] is so thrifty because I need a wife like that," he wrote his mother in November 1944. As the final year of the war began, Kauffman seemed more settled and contented than he had ever been. He knew the end of the conflict in Europe was merely a matter of time now, and he was eagerly thinking about returning to his hometown and beginning normal, civilian life. With more frequent and longer shore leaves and Marguerite in New York in their own apartment waiting for him, he began to relish domestic life. "M. and I are happier than we have ever been," he wrote. "All we need to have our cup overflow is a baby. . . . I do want children so much."

Kauffman was still engaged in convoy duty in the Atlantic when hostilities ceased in Europe. When his ship returned to the United States after V-E Day, May 8, 1945, there was a possibility that he might be discharged. But Captain Crenshaw received orders to go to the Philippines to help prepare for the invasion of Japan, and he wanted his best men with him. He asked Kauffman and two of the signaling crew to go with him. And while they were in the Philippines, Truman dropped the atom bomb. By mid-August 1945, the war in the Pacific was over.

As quickly as the United States had mobilized for combat, the country prepared to discharge hundreds of thousands of military personnel. Release from the navy depended on time served at sea. Kauffman had spent most of his thirty-four-and-a-half months on sea duty, so he was in line for early discharge. But regulations required that he return to the Naval Training Station at Great Lakes, Illinois, to be mustered out. Captain Crenshaw, too, was scheduled for quick demobilization, but he refused the navy's offer to fly him back to the States, preferring instead to remain with his signal crew in the Philippines. They had served throughout the war together, and he wanted to return home with his men. Often during the war, when Crenshaw and his crew were being shifted from one convoy to another, the navy would tell the captain that they would fly him back and his men could follow on the next ship. But Crenshaw always declined special treatment. "He'd say no," Kauffman recalled. "He'd say, my crew goes together." The captain's style of leadership was an example that Kauffman emulated years later in his business. "I think [those experiences] taught me something—that loyalty goes down as well as up," he told an interviewer in the 1960s. "And we do try to carry that forward here at Marion Laboratories."

Within a few days, the captain secured an airplane ride for himself and his signal crew to Pearl Harbor, but not before they had what may have been their most harrowing experience of the war. On the flight from the Philippines to Hawaii, the plane had engine trouble and landed on the sea. With only one engine intact, they coasted into a small island. And there they sat waiting for spare aircraft to take them on the next leg of their journey back to the States. Within a week or so, Captain Crenshaw managed to get the only seat on a small plane heading for Hawaii. He left his crew behind only because he had pressing orders to report in Honolulu. Ever resourceful, Kauffman finally managed to ferret out a pilot who was making a run to Hawaii the next day. Even though he was forced to ride cramped and freezing in the fuselage, he arrived at Pearl Harbor only a day or so after his commanding officer. When he told Crenshaw about the hard time he had getting off the island and the cold flight in the fuselage, the generous captain promised they would go home together.

With nothing to do but wait for transportation, Kauffman settled into the officers' quarters at Pearl Harbor and passed the time playing cards. He got into a high-stakes poker game; five thousand dollars was required for entry. The noted bridge champion Oswald Jacoby was among the players. Kauffman started the game flush with cash, happy about going home, and eager to test himself against the great Jacoby. "[He] was a very interesting poker player because maybe the final bet he would bet $572," Kauffman recalled. "Well, I'd sit there and think why did he bet $572? Why didn't he just bet $500 or $600? And I'd worry so much about the seventy-two dollars that it bothered my decisions whether to call him or not. It was strategy on his part." Jacoby's idiosyncratic method of betting so distracted the other players that he would almost always win. Kauffman, who never forgot the excitement of the encounter, had no wish to tangle with the bridge champion again.

Fortunately for Kauffman's bankroll and his confidence, transportation back to the United States materialized quickly. Captain Crenshaw was offered a flight, but he declined, saying he wanted to make the last voyage of the war with his men. The captain and the ensign sailed to San Francisco on the aircraft carrier *Lexington* with several hundred other naval personnel all about to be released from active duty. "I told Captain Crenshaw good-bye because he was going one place and I was going another," Kauffman said. Two or three days later, he was ordered to Great Lakes Naval Training Center in Illinois and released from active duty November 16, 1945.

The wartime adventure had ended. The young enlisted man who had dreamed of the ocean as a Sea Scout had experienced the exotic ports of the Far East, South America, and the Mediterranean. He had been an integral part of the incredible war machine that moved men and matériel all over the globe. And although he had not been in combat, he had helped transport enough wounded and dying men to hold no illusions about the glories of battle. In his thirty-four months of active duty, Kauffman had matured. He had risen to an officer's rank because of his intelligence, his diligence, and his willingness to take a risk. And he had served under an officer who was first a mentor and later a trusted friend and confidant. The relationship with Captain Crenshaw had a profound effect on Kauffman because it was based on mutual respect. Crenshaw was the first person beyond Kauffman's immediate family and circle of friends in Kansas City to affirm the young man's intelligence and to recognize and nurture his potential. The two men carried on a regular correspondence throughout the fifties and sixties as Kauffman was building Marion Laboratories. When Kauffman received the Horatio Alger Award in 1967, together with Dr. Michael Debakey and Lawrence Welk, he remarked that what honored him most was that his former commanding officer had shown his respect in attending those ceremonies in New York. Crenshaw died shortly thereafter, but his memory remained a powerful influence with his young ensign, Lucky. Within hours of his release from active duty, Kauffman was on his way back to Kansas City, to his wife and family and to a life that he could never have imagined.

Civilian life was a major change from the routine of the past two and a half years at sea, and Kauffman decided to take his time before entering the job market. He was able to do this because he had accumulated a substantial nest egg from his winnings at cards while in the navy. After the one bad experience early in his naval career when he lost all his money and was reduced literally to "taking in washing," Kauffman planned his gambling the way he would later plan the financial aspects of Marion Laboratories.

"Here's the reason I won money," he recalled. "I never went to sea but what I carried two money belts with two thousand dollars to three thousand dollars each." Kauffman learned to play poker as a Boy Scout and had an advantage over the young boys from the small country areas who had never played. Since there was little to do on board ship, they would play poker. If they had a bad streak, they were finished. But if Kauffman had a bad patch of luck, he could stay in the game until his luck changed. "So just having more money was one of the reasons I won. It got to the point where I won so much that they changed my name to 'Lucky.'"

Indeed, Kauffman was lucky. But mathematical skill, intellectual curiosity, and competitive spirit also contributed to his success at cards and dice. Two decades after his naval service, he told an interviewer that he continued to follow his early strategies when gambling. "I play percentages in cards. Depending on the size of the pot and how much the bet is, I would draw to a flush. What I never do is stick in a five-card stud game when somebody has me beat." Always determined to excel in any activity that appealed to him, he learned as much as possible about the games he played. "I studied dice and I knew how to shoot. I read books on it. I read many books on dice and gambling and I studied gin until I became one of the better gin players in Kansas City."

Kauffman won about ninety thousand dollars at cards during his naval tour of duty, an enormous sum when translated into 1990s dollars. However, since Marguerite disapproved of gambling, they reached a compromise about how to handle the winnings. He gave her half the money to put in the bank and they agreed to spend and enjoy the other half. These extra funds meant that Marguerite and Ewing had a different experience during wartime than did most young couples. With no money worries, the young couple was able to travel back and forth to Kansas City to see their families whenever time permitted and transportation could be arranged.

Most young couples dream of a home of their own, and children. The Kauffmans were no different. But with Kauffman at sea and Marguerite wanting to be free to travel to meet him when he had stateside leave, purchasing a residence seemed premature. However, the steady flow of Kauffman's winnings prompted Marguerite to start making plans for their life after the war. As victory in Europe emerged, people began to focus on what their lives might be like in a postwar economy. To even the most casual observer, sufficient housing seemed a likely problem. The country's housing supply had remained static since the Depression. Once the war was over there would be large pent-up demand.

With the prospect of other returning servicemen wanting to buy houses and the likelihood of rapidly escalating prices, Marguerite decided to invest some of the gambling winnings in a home. She wrote Kauffman that while driving around on a Sunday, she had seen a house she thought they should buy. He responded that this was a foolish idea because they would not need a house until the war was over. Four months later while he was in Kansas City on a seven-day pass, Marguerite suggested that they go for a drive one afternoon. They passed a small bungalow on 78th Terrace and Marguerite asked Kauffman what he thought of the house. When he commented that it was very attractive, she proudly announced, "Well, we've bought it." Surprised, Kauffman asked, "What are you going to do with it?" She replied, "I've already rented it for ninety dollars a month and the mortgage is only sixty dollars a month, so we'll have a little extra coming in."

When Kauffman returned from the navy, the couple moved into the house. "We paid off the mortgage on the home, bought two cars, one for me and one for her, and lived pretty high," Kauffman recalled. "And we were gradually spending [the savings]." Years later, when asked if he had given any thought to using part of his gambling stash to finish his college education, Kauffman replied,

"It never occurred to me. I was married and we wanted a child. It just never occurred to me." Several years later, they sold their house for $12,500 and moved to a larger, more expensive home at 6705 Locust. Marguerite's investment had been a wise one. It had provided supplemental income for a time and the equity to improve their living arrangements without the struggle typical of most veterans and their families.

As soon as they were settled, Kauffman decided to use a portion of his wartime savings to pay off a debt that had been gnawing at him. He went to the Sun Life Insurance Agency and said that he thought he owed two thousand dollars or three thousand dollars which he was ready to pay back. In response to the agency manager's baffled look, Kauffman attempted to explain his offer. "I tried to sell insurance for you and you let me draw so much. How much do I owe? I'll pay it." The agency manager was astonished. This was the first time anything like that had ever happened in the history of the company. He told Kauffman the company did not expect him to pay it back. In fact, they did not want him to repay it since that would confuse their bookkeeping. "At least it made me feel better that I offered to pay back the money they had advanced me during my failure as a life insurance salesman," Kauffman said.

His offer to repay the debt was a genuine gesture stemming from his personal sense of accountability. Sun Life had advanced him salary with the expectation that his sales would cover the outlay. When those anticipated sales did not materialize, the company had accepted the loss. But Kauffman believed it was his obligation to repay the losses because of his inability to sell insurance. Fortunately, his winnings at cards now made that possible. To repay what he owed seemed only fair to him, and he expected others to view debts to him in the same light. This commitment to fairness in relationships with others and to giving people value for their money would be the hallmarks of his business career.

For the first few months after his return to civilian life, Kauffman kept busy with all the usual tasks of a new homeowner. His savings were such, thanks to Marguerite, that he did not need to find work right away. Although he was not actively looking for a job, he scanned the want ads regularly. "I answered an ad for an insulation salesman which was door-to-door and I didn't care for that particularly. But then I saw an ad one Sunday for pharmaceutical salesmen. I knew nothing about [the pharmaceutical business] but what intrigued me is they gave an aptitude test. I always did enjoy taking tests," he recalled. Once again, he responded to the allure of a challenge just as when he sold the tickets to win the scholarship to Boy Scout camp, or competed with new drivers to secure accounts for the Long-Hall Laundry. "So I went and talked to the man and took the aptitude test. It turned out that out of around fifty people that answered the ad that I was maybe at the top or close to it." The impressive score landed him an offer of a job with Lincoln Laboratories of Decatur, Illinois, and he accepted without any hesitation.

The financial terms of Kauffman's first job in the pharmaceutical business did not presage the great wealth that he would one day earn as an entrepreneur in this field. The job paid no salary. He worked for a guaranteed 20 percent commission on all sales. There was no expense account, no car, and no additional benefits of any kind. To be successful under those conditions required that a salesman be aggressive, self-motivated, and extremely confident of his sales ability. All of these qualities characterized Ewing Kauffman, especially self-confidence.

By his own admission, Kauffman "simply fell in love with the business." In 1947 when he started with Lincoln Laboratories, the pharmaceutical business had changed little since the turn of the century. "In those days," he explained, "you didn't have prescription drugs the way you do now. Instead, the doctor gave shots in his office—liver shots, vitamin shots, everything. Country doctors, in particular, did not write prescriptions but would have their own drugstore or pharmacy and have their nurse fill a bottle of pills. The doctor would then sell them to the patient and make money on them." Kauffman thrilled to the challenge of making sales directly to physicians. He had grown up in an era when the local doctor was a revered and admired member of the community. His youthful reading of Lloyd Douglas's novels where the healer was hero had nurtured his view of the physician as a well-educated, caring humanitarian.

His daily routine was to see doctors in their offices—sandwiched in between patients' appointments, surgery, or house calls—and to sell them medications that they would then administer to their patients as injections or dispense as pills. Making a direct sale in the pharmaceutical business after World War II was basically an "all or nothing" proposition. "It was more a *selling* job than what our people do today," Kauffman recalled in the early 1990s. "If we didn't get an order [from the doctor] when we were there, it wasn't likely that we were going to get anything." He was a natural salesman, but he did not rely solely on his innate ability to fuel his career at Lincoln Laboratories. Just as when he wanted to be the best poker or gin player, he began to read widely in the pharmaceutical literature and to study the scientific properties of the various products. And as he became more familiar with chemistry and more knowledgeable about the interactions of various drugs, he was able to talk with physicians with even greater persuasive skill.

When Kauffman joined Lincoln Laboratories, they were just branching out into new territory. He became their first salesman west of the Mississippi. Whatever he may have lacked in formal training, he made up with enthusiasm, energy, and self-education. Within nine months, his volume of sales was such that he was promoted to manager of the entire Midwestern region, an area stretching from Chicago to Dallas. In this new position, he continued to earn a 20 percent commission on all his own sales plus a 3 percent commission on everything the salesmen under his direction sold.

With this extra incentive, Kauffman began hiring salesmen. During the first few weeks as Midwest regional manager, he hired a new man every week. At first, hiring did not seem too time-consuming or difficult, but training proved quite a challenge. Even as a regional manager, Kauffman still worked on straight commission. He received no base salary, no expenses for transportation, meals, or lodging, to say nothing of other benefits. So it was imperative that he devise a way to train new people while still selling and earning a living. The strategy was simple, but shrewd. "The first week I went down to Wichita and hired a salesman and brought him back to Kansas City to train him. That meant that I could be selling and making a living while I was training him. Then I would send him back to Wichita, and I did that every week for six straight weeks." A week spent accompanying Kauffman as he made his calls let the new recruit observe firsthand how to obtain an appointment with the physician, how to open a presentation, what aspects of a given product to emphasize, how to respond to questions, and, most important, how to secure the actual sale. After five long days of what must have seemed like trailing a comet, the new man would be dispatched to his own territory while Kauffman repeated the weekend search for another salesman to work yet another part of the territory.

The extent to which Kauffman's training regimen was effective is doubtful, but it was definitely exhausting. At the end of six weeks, he had lost the first three salesmen. And eventually he lost all six of them. As one recruit after another fell by the wayside, Kauffman pondered what to do. The prospect of having to repeat the Sisyphean process of recruiting, hiring, and training was daunting. This, plus the loss of the anticipated 3 percent commission on sales, spurred Kauffman to learn more about hiring.

As was his custom, he began to read everything he could find on hiring. Because of his competitive nature, he was attracted to the work of a Stanford University professor on aptitude tests. He was excited by what he read, so Kauffman called the professor and said he would like to spend a day with him in California. The professor was skeptical that Kauffman could absorb a semester course in a few hours. However, when he pleaded, "How about giving me a weekend? Will you tell me everything you can in a weekend?" the Stanford professor graciously agreed. After a flying trip to the west coast and a weekend's tutoring, Kauffman returned to Kansas City. He started hiring again using an aptitude test that measured aggressiveness, intelligence, emotional stability, and various other factors. "I really thought I had something," he recalled. "So I didn't care if a person had three eyes. If he made a good grade on that aptitude test I would still hire him!"

The aptitude test helped weed out a great many unsuitable candidates and Kauffman devoted a bit more time training new recruits, but he still had not "found the secret." With improved hiring and training techniques and Kauffman's incomparable powers of motivation, sales in his region soared. "By the end of the second year, my commissions alone amounted to more than the [company] president's salary. That wasn't right in his judgment, so he cut my commission." The injustice of having his commission reduced stung him, and the shortsightedness of this strategy completely baffled him. Yet Kauffman continued to outperform others while salesmen under his supervision began to capture significant numbers of new customers.

In his third year with Lincoln Laboratories, Kauffman again astonished, and apparently annoyed, his superiors. "That year I again exceeded the president's thoughts of what a sales manager should earn. So he took away some of my territory which was the same as taking away some of my income. So, I quit and I started Marion Laboratories in the basement of my home."

Kauffman's decision to start his own pharmaceutical company was not as precipitous as it may appear. He had chafed at the initial inequity of having his commission reduced because he earned more than the company's president, but he accepted the challenge as if company officials were merely testing his mettle. But when he rebuilt his income through his own sales and the success of his recruits working in a new territory, he was genuinely angered to be rewarded with a reduced territory. He silently vowed that he would never treat anyone who worked for him in such an unfair manner. He would treat them with the same courtesy and fairness that he wanted for himself. He also determined that he would never be so shortsighted as to penalize an employee for doing a good job. He would share the rewards and the successes because he knew from his experience at Lincoln Labs that sharing success was the easiest and surest way to multiply success.

In severing his relationship with Lincoln Laboratories, Kauffman moved cautiously. He had learned the lesson of preparedness well in his Boy Scout training and his naval career. He began carefully to lay the groundwork for his next move. First, he went to his former scoutmaster, R.J. Woods, for counsel. Woods was a successful pharmaceutical representative for Parke-Davis Company, but he was skeptical about Kauffman's chances for long-term success. "I asked [Woods] his opinion and he recommended against it since I had no pharmacy background and not very much scientific education," Kauffman remembered. This was not advice that he wanted to hear, because he already loved the pharmaceutical business. He enjoyed the challenge of convincing a physician to try his products. He studied long hours to increase his knowledge so he could persuade a client of the efficacy of one scientific product versus another. And dealing with products that had the potential to relieve pain and better people's lives appealed to his idealistic nature. He had total confidence in his ability to succeed and, of course, Ewing Kauffman simply loved selling. So, in spite of Woods's skepticism, he began to make plans for the day when the unfair situation at Lincoln Laboratories would no longer be tolerable.

In the three years that Kauffman had been with Lincoln Laboratories, there had been substantial changes in his personal life. Unable to have children of their own, the Kauffmans had adopted two infants, Larry in 1947 and Sue in 1948. A larger family needed a larger house, so they sold their home and moved to 6705 Locust. Like most young families starting out, Kauffman admitted, "We were probably spending about everything we made—then we moved to the next home and that took all our money." With the exception of about five thousand dollars in savings left from his wartime winnings at cards, Kauffman's capital for the new enterprise was all personal and intangible—supreme self-confidence, incredible energy, enthusiasm for his work, and the desire to earn a good living for his family.

To start a business of his own, Kauffman had to have a dependable supply of products. At that time it was common practice for one company to manufacture a single product, such as vitamins, that might be sold under the labels of several different pharmaceutical houses. He found a company that made excellent injectables and had them manufactured for him. But a little capital and a small inventory were not enough to launch a new business. There had to be customers to buy the drugs. So Kauffman began to scout for potential customers. "It was easier [to start Marion Laboratories] than it sounds because I had doctors whom I had been selling to for several years. Before I made the break, I went to three of them and said, 'I'm thinking of starting my own company. May I count on you to give me your orders if I can give you the same quality and service that you had with my previous company, Lincoln Laboratories?'" All three physicians responded that they liked doing business with Kauffman, and agreed they would be regular customers "as long as you have the quality." With those assurances and three accounts as a base, Kauffman took the greatest gamble of his life. He drew out the five thousand dollars left from his war winnings, created a makeshift office in the basement of his home, printed up a business card and plunged into the fray as the one and only salesman of Marion Laboratories.

Launching Marion Laboratories

As Kauffman started Marion Laboratories in June 1950, the modern pharmaceutical industry was beginning to emerge. World War II had produced an array of wonder compounds such as sulfa drugs, penicillin, and the first generation of antibiotics. But many physicians, particularly those in rural areas and small towns, still relied on tablets of various kinds, vitamins, and the traditional injectables. These medications, in combination with large doses of listening and counseling, were the typical medical regimen of the time. The practice of giving the patient a prescription to be filled at a pharmacy was not widespread except in large cities. Most physicians purchased drugs in bulk and dispensed them directly from their offices, with the cost usually included in the office-call fee.

In addition to dispensing tablets, doctors in the 1950s also made extensive use of injectable medications. In many instances, the efficacy of injections, when compared to that of tablets taken orally, was unquestionable. By injecting a drug directly into the patient's bloodstream, the physician was assured of a more rapid response than could be obtained by use of an oral dosage. The doctor also knew that the patient had received the correct therapeutic dosage and was relieved of relying on the patient's memory of how and when to take the medication. Since the patient would have to return for further injections, the doctor could monitor the medication's effectiveness. And, of course, there was the issue of cost. The price of an injection was not usually included in the physician's office fee, so the doctor could charge an extra one to three dollars for an injection that may have cost him between ten and fifteen cents.

When Kauffman started Marion Laboratories, he wisely decided to continue doing what he knew best. He concentrated on selling injectables to family practitioners located in suburban Kansas City and nearby rural areas. "It was easier to sell to country physicians than it was to the city physicians," he recalled years later. "[The city physicians] were more sophisticated. And also they were in a position to call up a drugstore and say, 'I need the following injectables. Send me one vial of each.' Well, I wasn't interested in selling just one vial. I wanted to sell one dozen or four dozen—big orders. So that was one reason that I developed a country business first."

Dr. Gordon Stauffacatr of Sedalia, Missouri, was one of the three accounts that followed Kauffman when he established his company. A country doctor, Stauffacatr had a mammoth practice built on exceptional skills and a willingness to stay in his office until nine or ten o'clock at night to accommodate hardworking farmers and their families. Kauffman's strategy in rural areas was to try to end the day in a town where he knew doctors worked late so he could call on them at night. After a long day of selling elsewhere, Kauffman would arrive in Sedalia at about six o'clock in the evening. He would check into a motel, shower and change, then call on doctors who were still in their offices. Several physicians in that area kept evening office hours, but he always called on Dr. Stauffacatr last because he worked later than anyone else. "He wouldn't see me until he had taken care of all his patients. Then we'd talk business. Later we'd go out and the doctor would have his dinner. I would go with him, although I probably would have already eaten earlier."

Kauffman enjoyed Dr. Stauffacatr's company and, as the Sedalia physician was one of his largest customers, took special care to adjust to his schedule. In late-night conversations over after-dinner coffee, Dr. Stauffacatr might compare the therapeutic value of one treatment to another, argue the merits of a long-acting single dosage versus smaller, more frequent doses, and suggest special properties that he hoped to find in this analgesic or that prophylactic. From these visits and conversations, Kauffman learned to communicate skillfully with physicians. He also took mental note of ideas for possible new products while nurturing the relationship between a satisfied customer and good salesman.

Although Kauffman concentrated on building his business with rural physicians in those early days, he also had two large accounts in Kansas City, Missouri. Drs. John A. Growdon and Ralph R. Coffey, internist and surgeon, respectively, with offices in the Professional Building at Eleventh and Grand, had been his clients at Lincoln Laboratories. They continued to give him substantial orders when he established Marion Laboratories. His other major customer in Kansas City was Dr. Milton B. Casebolt, a family practitioner who had offices at 4000 Baltimore. Mrs. Casebolt ran the office, and the doctor made house calls for three dollars. He had a very large practice and purchased a lot of injectables; Kauffman accorded him the kind of attention he gave to Dr. Stauffacatr. Dr. Casebolt was so busy that Kauffman would often drop by to see him on Sunday morning. The doctor frequently saw patients on the Sabbath who could not keep an appointment during the workweek. If Casebolt had house calls to make, Kauffman would ride along. Dr. Casebolt was a very intelligent man, and Kauffman learned much from him during those drives. The physician had worked in a drugstore while in medical school, first as a floor polisher and later as a salesman, so he and Kauffman shared a mutual interest in the retail drug business. The two men developed a respectful and friendly business relationship, but never saw one another socially. "He probably didn't have time," Kauffman mused later. Neither did the ambitious, hard-driving young salesman. The energetic Kauffman steadily added new customers to this base of physicians. Fortunately, the volume of business from his original clients was large enough that first year to provide a reasonable income for him and his family. "Everything else, which probably was equal to what those doctors gave me, was extra," he recalled.

From the start of Marion Laboratories, physicians responded to Kauffman's professionalism and salesmanship, and most customers never suspected that the entire effort was literally a "one man show." In naming the company, he wanted to create the impression of a substantial pharmaceutical enterprise. "Laboratories" in the title was purely aspirational, as it would be many years before Marion would have any kind of internal research capacity. And, as it turned out, virtually all the company's successes were to be licensed products, not those created by their own scientists in their own laboratories. Kauffman also made a deliberate decision to use his middle name, Marion, rather than his surname. "I would have liked to have called it Kauffman Laboratories. But for Ewing Kauffman to walk into the doctor's office and say, 'I'm Ewing Kauffman of Kauffman Laboratories,' immediately you'd get the idea it's a pretty small operation.

So I took my middle name, Marion, and called it Marion Laboratories. Therefore, no one knew whether we were large or small as I called on new accounts."

To save on rent, Kauffman operated out of his home's basement. He purchased large quantities of injectables and a range of tablets from a pharmaceutical house he knew from his days at Lincoln Laboratories. He had labels printed with the company name and address, and the statement "Manufactured for Marion Laboratories." Weekends were usually devoted to counting tablets and labeling injectables. "I would label these vials with my own label and put them in a box. I would count the tablets out and put them in bottles of one hundred, five hundred, or a thousand."

During the week, he had a different routine. If he worked outside of Kansas City, he started early and stopped only when the last weary physician had locked up for the night. "If I were in the city, and I did spend about half of my time in the city, I would come home at night and type up the orders—hunt and peck—go to the basement, package the orders, and ship them through the mail. They were small enough in volume and weight that I could use the postal service. And maybe it would be eleven or twelve o'clock at night when I would run down to the post office, leave those packages, come home, and finally go to bed." Somewhere in the midst of traveling, selling, sorting, bottling, labeling, packaging, and mailing, he found time to post checks in the ledger book, record orders for inventory control, and write up notes on sales calls. Although Kauffman may not have been slaving away in his basement every evening he was in town, thoughts of business were never far from his mind. He recalled years later that when he took Marguerite to a movie, on the way home he would always try to stop by any physician's office where he saw a light on and squeeze in one more call.

Kauffman worked feverishly to expand his territory. Soon his former employers realized that he was taking some of their business away. Their first response was to add another sales representative to the Kansas City area. When that strategy failed, they dispatched their attorney to call on Kauffman's customers. The attorney told several physicians that, "I was competing with them which I was not supposed to do—which was not true." When the attorney called on Dr. Casebolt, he quickly perceived he had met his match.

Dr. Casebolt made it clear that Lincoln Laboratories' attempts to crush the fledgling Marion Laboratories could be met in kind. He said, "Now I'm just an old country practitioner, but I do belong to the American Academy of General Practice which is an association of all the general practitioners in the United States which happens to have its headquarters in Kansas City. And, I just happen to be one of the founders. I would hate to go tell that academy and all the doctors that belong to it that you're doing this to this young man, Ewing Kauffman." The attorney fled, and Lincoln Laboratories made no further attempts to counter superior salesmanship with implied threats.

Within the first six months as an entrepreneur, Kauffman could see "that financially it was going to go." He waited a few more months, then when one of the neighbors asked why so many trucks were coming and going on their street, he knew it was time to move the operations out of the basement and into a larger space. He leased a small building at 4215 Troost, previously a store-room. "It was twelve feet wide and forty feet deep with a hardware store on one side and a used car lot on the other . . . not very prepossessing." But the name, Marion Laboratories, emblazoned in large letters on the tiny building, was a harbinger of the growth to come.

At the end of the first year, Kauffman had sold $36,000 worth of drugs, realizing a net income of about $18,000 after expenses. In reflecting on that initial year, he recalled, "I wouldn't have the courage to do it again, but it was enjoyable. Of course, I worked eighteen hours a day, and it was fun. What I was trying to do was just to make a living for my wife and two children. I had no dream of building a fabulous company such as we ended up with thirty or forty years in the future." In one year, Kauffman had proved that he could establish and manage a business and make a respectable profit. But if the business was to grow, he knew he would have to have help. His first decision was to find a way to increase his time for selling. He hired a helper to handle the routine office chores, plus his after-hours and weekend tasks of preparing orders for mailing. Then he decided to begin recruiting additional salesmen so he could expand sales to cover a larger geographic area.

Kauffman hired the first salesman in St. Joseph, Missouri, and the second in Des Moines, Iowa, but neither of them succeeded. A salesman's biggest hurdle, regardless of his experience and talents, was gaining acceptance among physicians for a new drug company. "The doctors are used to dealing with this one [company] they've dealt with all along. They know the products are good and they know and like the representatives," Kauffman said, analyzing those early years. But even then he knew instinctively that the acceptance would come if the right people were on the job. "It takes superior salesmanship and hard work, in that order."

After two failures, Kauffman began giving the aptitude test that he had used at Lincoln Laboratories. The test helped eliminate a great many unsuitable candidates, and Kauffman used the interview to identify characteristics he believed would make a successful salesman. Instead of academic credentials such as a college degree in science, Kauffman was interested in the applicant's life experience and personal qualities. He looked for people who had work experience; who were willing to persist and defer gratification in anticipation of future rewards. He wanted builders, team players, men who believed in themselves and in the future. Formal credentials were not important; personal character was.

Together with the improved hiring strategy, Kauffman devoted a bit more time to training new recruits. The aptitude test helped him identify better qualified people, but it was still not the complete answer. Over time, he learned that hiring effective, productive sales people was more complex and more time consuming than he had ever dreamed. He also grew to understand that sales training had to be thorough in the initial stages, and continuing, for consistent and long-term success. While the company was still small, Kauffman trained all the salesmen personally. He would accompany them on their calls with the understanding that they would detail the product and attempt to close the sale. "We would go in and I could see that they were butchering the sale, yet I knew the doctor could use what we had. So I would elbow them out of the way and take over the sale, close the order, and walk out with a commission that I made." In spite of his eagerness to capture every sale possible, Kauffman knew he was not providing effective training. But it would be a long time before he was able to turn the training over to someone else.

While Kauffman was struggling with ways to identify and hire superior sales talent, he remembered an earlier conversation he had

had with his close friend Hughes. After the war, Hughes and his brother had opened a trade school offering courses in auto mechanics and repair to veterans who needed training for jobs in the growing automobile industry. Kauffman had worked at a variety of jobs before he began selling pharmaceuticals, and the two friends would occasionally meet for lunch to catch up on the news. Hughes was aware of his friend's growing dissatisfaction with the unfair treatment at Lincoln Laboratories, and he was not surprised when Kauffman had announced at lunch one day, "Charlie, I'm going to start my own company." Hughes confided that he, too, was dissatisfied with his work and was thinking of making a change. Half-kidding, he added, "I've never tried selling, so who knows, I may sell for you someday." Kauffman was in no position to act on Hughes's suggestion at that point, so the conversation turned to the name of the company. With his usual thoroughness, Kauffman had reviewed the major drug companies and concluded, "It's the history of the industry that the pharmaceutical companies are named after founders." Wanting to be helpful, Hughes recalled that he offered the suggestion, "'Your middle name's a girl's name. I sure wouldn't use it.' So he did!"

Even though he had ignored Hughes's advice about the company's name, Kauffman did remember his friend's comment about becoming a salesman. One evening he called Hughes to say that he really needed help with the business and suggest that he come on board as a salesman. Hughes talked it over with his wife, Marjorie, but she was not enthusiastic about his joining Marion Laboratories because she thought the company was too young and its future seemed so uncertain. "It's a joke now among us," Hughes recalled more than forty years later. "Even Marjorie loves to tell it. But she says, 'Whenever Ewing and Charlie asked my advice and I said, 'No!' they said, 'Go!'" Hughes was anxious to quit the trade-school business, but hesitated to start a new job because he had some surgery scheduled within a few weeks. "Can you pay me during that period when I'm off?" he asked. Kauffman replied, "You bring your typewriter that you're using right now and I will."

Hughes joined the sales team of Marion Laboratories in March 1952, at a monthly salary of $303.00 plus twenty-five dollars per week to cover expenses. For two and a half years he worked the area north of Kansas City almost to the Iowa state line. He was a popular and successful sales representative, but no one could have been more different from Ewing Kauffman. "You could consider us complete opposites," Hughes recalled. "He was the aggressive type, which was the reason he was successful at selling." Hughes's approach to selling was understated. Kauffman recalled that he had a high record of sales despite his unwillingness to put pressure on a doctor or keep asking for an order. "He was so well liked, especially by the nurses—now he was not a ladies' man—that they would send in mail orders. We'd leave a card with them and they'd say, 'Please send such and such a product,'" Kauffman recalled. But in spite of his high sales record, Hughes never liked selling. So when the business prospered to the point that Kauffman could afford an office manager, Hughes moved into that position. "That meant that he did everything from labeling to boxing to typing orders, and more," Kauffman remembered. "And as we got bigger and bigger, why, his job got bigger and bigger."

As Marion Laboratories grew, Kauffman hired Paul K. Danielson, another chum from the Criterion Sunday school class. He was a good salesman who also had the ability to train others, so Kauffman asked him to become a division manager. In that position, he trained and supervised eight sales representatives in a given geographic area. The job required a lot of travel, which Danielson did not like. But Kauffman was so determined that he was right for the job that he "gave him more money than I wanted to." Danielson turned in a good performance, and when Kauffman needed more help in the Kansas City office, he turned again to his old friend. He eventually promoted Danielson into the office, not as a sales manager—Kauffman thought no one could do that job as well as he—but to handle other responsibilities, especially the development of new products. Paul Danielson became Marion Laboratories' first vice president in charge of new products and research.

In those early days of Marion Laboratories' history, the word *research* was somewhat misleading. The company was not directly engaged in scientific research and discovery. Danielson's job was to work with Midwest Research Institute of Kansas City and others to engage their help with new product development. With only a high school education, Danielson was soon out of his depth. "I realized it," Kauffman recalled decades later, the pain of that episode still near the surface. "I should have either offered him the opportunity to go back to sales or have fired him, but I vacillated. I was wrong. I vacillated for two years. When he was forty-three years old I told him that he just couldn't make it in the research job and offered to let him go back to sales, which his pride wouldn't let him do. But my mistake was that I should have made the decision when I knew he couldn't do it, when he was forty-one. Instead, I kept hoping and hoping and kept him on an additional two years, which hurt him."

Fortunately, Danielson immediately got another selling job, and within six months his new employer wanted to promote him to sales manager. His wife objected, reminding him of the Marion experience. "You're a better salesman," she said. "You just stay there." That was wise counsel. He followed her advice and had a very successful second selling career. Kauffman always regretted having promoted Danielson beyond his capabilities. He also regretted his own inability to deal with the problem as soon as he saw the mistake. But that experience taught him the value of quick corrective action for the sake of the employee, as well as the company. While he was pleased that his friend went on to another successful sales position, Kauffman felt a lingering sadness. "Paul left before we went public and so he missed the opportunity to make a lot of money on his stock."

Building a strong and effective sales team was Kauffman's major priority during Marion's formative years. Even with the aptitude test to help identify potential sales talent, turnover continued. Now with Charlie Hughes's assistance, Kauffman increased recruitment efforts. Hughes described the process. "We would run an ad in the paper and then we'd hire a room in a hotel. We used the hotel over on Linwood Boulevard quite a bit. The candidates would show up, we'd pass out the forms, actually a test, and then we would interview them. And that's the way we hired Sperry; that's the way we hired Pruitt."

Jean Sperry and Bob Pruitt, two salesmen hired in 1953 and 1955, respectively, played prominent roles in building the young company. Sperry's decision to join Marion Laboratories was fortuitous because he knew nothing about the pharmaceutical industry. In 1953, Sperry was a recent graduate of the University of Denver with a degree in economics and communications. He had served on an aircraft carrier briefly before the war ended and was still active in the Naval Reserve. When the Korean War started, he was in danger of being called to active duty. Because of his military status, he was having a difficult time finding employment. Out of near desperation, he took a temporary job working for the Canteen Company of America. The vending machine business was hectic yet routine, not the place where Sperry wanted to build a career. So when a close friend and college classmate working in pharmaceutical sales urged him to try for a similar position, he listened.

When he saw an advertisement for a pharmaceutical salesman which promised a good salary plus a substantial commission, he probably thought, "nothing ventured, nothing gained" and answered it. He called the number listed and Kauffman answered the telephone. At Kauffman's invitation, Sperry took the aptitude test, with good results. Then Kauffman invited him for a personal interview, as he would do with every potential salesman he seriously considered hiring in those early years. Typically Kauffman started off those interviews by asking the sales candidate if he had ever done any selling. He also asked about other work experience—odd jobs and part-time stints of any kind interested him as much as full-time selling experience. He was looking for people who had a need to work and who had worked.

Once Kauffman had established the candidate's work ethic, he would probe for intuitive sales ability. He usually began by asking the applicant to sell something in the room, perhaps a picture on the wall or a lamp. He was curious to hear what the individual would say about the item. Then he would respond, "No, I don't think I want that," while listening carefully to see what new tack the potential salesman might take. He not only used this technique himself, but as the company grew, he trained all the managers to have a potential candidate sell them something.

In Sperry, Kauffman found the characteristics he was looking for: a history of working since boyhood, intelligence, ambition, persistence, and the desire to succeed. After another brief interview, Kauffman offered the job, and Jean Sperry's thirty-year career with Marion Laboratories was launched.

With Sperry's arrival, the Marion Laboratories' sales force grew to four: Charlie Hughes, Paul Danielson, Sperry, and Kauffman. From March through July 1953, Sperry spent most of his time in Wichita, Kansas, which proved to be a very lucrative market for Marion Laboratories. Very few other pharmaceutical companies bothered to call on physicians in towns the size of Wichita in those days, so an ambitious and articulate salesman could do well quickly. Kauffman quickly recognized Sperry's talents and believed he had the ability to train others as well as to rack up high sales numbers on his own. But the Wichita market was too small for a man of his potential, and Danielson dominated Kansas City. So Kauffman offered him the choice of Dallas or Denver to open new territory for Marion. Sperry studied the potential of both locations and quickly perceived the implications of geography. In August 1953, he moved his young family to Dallas—the place he had chosen to make his reputation in the company. Six years later when Kauffman asked Sperry to return to Kansas City as sales manager, his district extended from Phoenix, Arizona, in the west to Columbus, Ohio, in the northeast. Sperry's district set sales records, then broke them and set new ones. Reminiscing about those heady days, Kauffman chuckled, "Sperry was the most obnoxious district manager I ever had. I got more letters from him complaining about literature, about the products not holding up, not being stable. He was writing me all the time, but because of the smallness of our company we just had to put up with some of those obstacles." Yet when Marion Laboratories grew so large that Kauffman had to relinquish his responsibilities as sales manager to attend to other aspects of the business, Jean Sperry was his first choice for the position.

Kauffman and Sperry were both aggressive, competitive men, and it was inevitable that they would clash from time to time. Kauffman felt that Sperry kept too much control in his own hands. "We lost his assistant sales manager because Jean didn't give him enough authority. Also he was very stubborn, dogmatic—bullheaded. If he were not sold on an idea, why, it would not succeed. I can remember that I would force him to introduce a certain product. But if he didn't like it, it just wouldn't go. But if he liked it, then he carried that attitude and he did a beautiful job."

Bob Pruitt, who joined the Marion team in 1955, had an experience similar to Sperry's. Pruitt's family was in the restaurant business in Sedalia, Missouri, and he started washing dishes at age nine. From that job, he progressed to selling shoes for fifteen cents an hour. He then worked his way through Central Missouri State College playing with a band and working in a music store. When band jobs were scarce he filled in as a fry cook. After leaving college, he operated two drive-in restaurants—often working sixteen to seventeen hours per day. By the time he applied for a position with Marion Laboratories, Pruitt had sold everything from pianos and real estate to fast food. Like Sperry, Pruitt was encouraged by a friend to look for a job in the pharmaceutical industry. He arrived at the hotel in Kansas City to take the aptitude test on a snowy January day. The sight of more than one hundred other applicants seeking the position nearly caused him to turn around and drive back home to Sedalia, but he stayed. After the test, the field narrowed to thirty-seven, and Pruitt interviewed with Kauffman. Their talk went well, and Kauffman asked Pruitt to return the next day with his wife. There would be four more interviews before Kauffman made an offer.

In those early years as the company was getting started and Kauffman was still doing all the hiring personally, he made it a practice to interview a prospective salesman's spouse. "I learned in hiring sales people a lot of factors came in, and one that I couldn't overlook was the wife," Kauffman said. "Here is the husband who is traveling on the road every other week and his wife isn't used to this. So a minor problem comes up at home and she has to call him long-distance and say, 'Well, the baby broke his arm', or 'The dog got run over.' This detracted from his ability to stay on the job and keep his mind on selling." In a nonthreatening manner, Kauffman would probe to determine how the wife might handle an emergency situation when she was dependent on public transportation or the kindness of friends and relatives. He looked for signs that she was ambitious to help her husband succeed and that she had the pluck to cope with temporary difficulties in exchange for the promise of future security and stability.

Helen Pruitt recalled her shock when she and her husband arrived for their interview. "I remember the storefront on Troost was crude, tacky looking. It just didn't look like anything at all. And we stood across the street and we thought, 'I wonder what kind of company this is that we're going to interview with?'" More than three decades after that initial interview, Helen Pruitt could not recall the specific questions Kauffman had asked. "It seems to me that most of the questions he had for me were things like: What I wanted out of life? What I wanted to get to? Of course, I was pretty unsophisticated and I really didn't have big dreams at that time. I thought with a few thousand dollars in the bank, we'd be sitting pretty. And a little savings, you know. But I think he wanted to find out what would keep me satisfied at that point. I think he just wanted to kind of get a feel for the kind of people we were."

Whatever Helen's fears or misgivings may have been when she saw Marion Laboratories' modest facilities, Kauffman soon allayed them. "Once you talked to him, you'd think you'd be the luckiest person in the world if you could go to work for him," she said. And her original impression never changed. It only grew stronger and more vivid over the years. She recalled that as the company struggled in those early years, Kauffman remained steadfast in his promises and kept everyone's spirits up as well. "When you'd get down all you'd have to do was just talk to him a little bit or hear him at a national sales meeting and you'd be back up on top of the world. You knew everything was going to work out. If you were worried about how am I ever going to educate these children, he'd say, 'Trust me. You're not going to have to worry about that, it's going to be there.'"

Helen Pruitt also recalled those years when the family barely scraped along financially. Bob would be out of town selling two weeks out of three, and she was at home with three children and no car. When he was in town, Bob Pruitt often worked nights and weekends to earn a bonus. "We'd look at that money and we'd think, 'Well, we can do one of two things: replace this sofa that's worn out or we can put [the bonus] back in stock,'" she said. "The company would always offer you the chance to buy just about the same amount of stock that the bonus was. Luckily, we were smart enough to put it back into the stock."

Kauffman's inclusion of the salesman's wife in the interview was not mere window dressing. He knew that giving the wife an immediate and tangible stake in her husband's success would motivate him. He liked to offer prizes such as jewelry or all-expense-paid vacations as incentives. Kauffman recalled, "I would say the top five salesmen would be able to give their wives a fur jacket. Then I would send the message to the wife that 'if your husband really loves you, he'll go out and earn a jacket for you.' You can imagine the pressure that was put on [the husbands]."

Another idea he tried that stimulated sales was the establishment of the "Bank of Marion Trust." He told the wife that if she would make sure her husband was out of the house on the way to work by 7:30 in the morning and did not come home until 6:30 at night, still trying to call on doctors or pharmacists, then she could write a check. He sent her a little checkbook with which she could write herself a check for two dollars that day and every day her husband kept that schedule. When she accumulated five of them, she could mail them to Kauffman and he sent her a check for ten dollars. Kauffman said this tactic did stimulate sales, and he used it on several occasions. "It was amazing the influence those wives had on seeing to it that their husbands worked because this was extra money to them."

Even as the sales force grew larger, Kauffman continued to acknowledge the importance of the wife to the husband's success. When Marion Laboratories began to hold national sales meetings in the mid-fifties, wives were included, all expenses paid. While the men were in business meetings and training sessions, the wives would enjoy various planned sightseeing tours, and of course, shopping. Pruitt remembered, "Mr. K would give them a little bit of cash so they could go shopping. He really romanced the wives. He realized how important that wife was to the success of her husband."

The young Pruitts were exactly the kind of people Kauffman was seeking to join him in building Marion Laboratories. And salesmanship flowed both ways in that interview. Bob Pruitt remembers that, "Helen was trying to sell him as hard as he was trying to sell her, because she knew I wanted the job." The final interview was on Saturday, and rather than wait until Monday, Kauffman offered Pruitt the job at 10:30 Saturday night. Helen spent a frantic Sabbath washing and ironing, and Bob Pruitt left for his new sales territory in St. Joseph, Missouri, at six o'clock Monday morning.

Pruitt started with Marion Laboratories in 1955 at a salary of $303.00 per month plus the opportunity to earn a bonus. Kauffman had stopped paying commissions when he opened the Dallas office. After that, all sales contracts were salary plus a bonus. Pruitt remembered that, "You had a quota and if you went over your quota you got a bonus. The higher you went over the quota, obviously, the more bonus you got." The Marion salesman furnished his own car and received twenty-five dollars a week, every week, for expenses. "When I say twenty-five dollars for all expenses, that was postage, meals, car expenses, and lodging," Pruitt said. "I stayed in a lot of dollar-fifty hotels that were pretty scroungy. Some of them didn't even have heat. You had to go downstairs to the old potbellied stove in order to get warm."

When asked what it was that kept him selling week after week, away from his family and often living in less than desirable conditions, Pruitt quickly responded. "It was Mr. K that kept people with him by continually telling them how big, how good things were going to be. We just had to watch our p's and q's right now." Then looking around his beautiful home in the rolling countryside east of Kansas City where he and Helen had retired, he mused, "Some stayed and some didn't. Those that didn't, I am certain, rue the day."

Marion Laboratories' first year's sales produced a reasonable living for the Kauffman family and a modest profit. Within a short time, Kauffman's original plan of just earning enough to support his young family began to change. "As I saw the business was successful, I realized that if I could do it, I could train other people to do it," he recalled. The only obstacle was capital. In order to add salesmen, Kauffman borrowed five thousand dollars from the Commerce Trust Company in Kansas City. The federal government guaranteed the loan because he was a veteran. He hired a second salesman in Des Moines, Iowa, and a third in Joplin, Missouri. These first three salesmen did not last long, but they produced enough sales, with Kauffman's own increased earnings, to permit him to repay the loan quickly. Caution was the hallmark of his business planning in those early days. He hired salesmen one at a time as he could afford them. "I would always operate on the basis that my budget for next year would be based upon what our sales were for this year," he said. "I knew we could sell as much next year as we did this year, and probably quite a bit more. So if I budgeted on what we did this year, then we'd make a greater profit the next year!"

Within two years, Kauffman knew his strategy was correct. "I could see that if I hired more salesmen, then we could make even more money. But I needed outside capital to do it." Kauffman estimated that each new salesman required an investment of about eight thousand dollars before his work began to pay off. Instead of going back to the Commerce Trust, he devised a different plan. He decided to offer investors the opportunity to buy common stock in the company. Since he was reluctant to sell too much of the company, he decided on a purchase/loan strategy. "They could buy one thousand dollars' worth of common stock, but they also had to lend the company one thousand dollars for a bond that would pay 5 percent. The bond wouldn't pay anything for five years, at which time they would get back $1,250."

The first individuals he approached about investing in Marion Laboratories were the four physicians who had shifted their business to him when he started in 1950. All four promptly agreed. "Dr. Growdon said he had a friend, Marvin Marsh, president of Marsh Steel, who would like to put one thousand dollars in, so I let him," Kauffman remembered. "That was five." Kauffman next invited his insurance agent, Wylie Craig, to participate. A few months earlier, Kauffman had purchased a hundred-thousand-dollar life insurance policy to insure that the company would have some money if something happened to him. Craig was a very personable and capable individual whom Kauffman liked and respected, and he was happy to have him as a shareholder. The seventh and last of the initial group of investors was Raymond Parshall, Kauffman's former Westport High School classmate and football buddy. He had never forgotten Parshall's kindness in wiring him twenty dollars when he was stuck and without funds in Wichita, Kansas—and on the rebound from a broken engagement. He believed that giving Parshall the opportunity to get in on the ground floor of Marion Laboratories' growth was an appropriate way to show his continuing gratitude.

The original seven investors decided to put in two thousand dollars each. Then two decided to risk another two thousand dollars each, bringing the total to eighteen thousand dollars. With these funds Kauffman began to add the men who would become the core of Marion Laboratories' sales team—Hughes, Danielson, Sperry, and, later, Pruitt. "I built on these people and we became profitable." All of the original investors except Marsh, who sold half his interest when the steel business experienced a downturn, were still with Kauffman in 1965 when Marion Laboratories went public. The one thousand dollars in common stock was worth about $900,000, and each investor had earned about $25,000 in dividends since 1952. In 1991, while recalling those early investors, Kauffman said, "Wylie Craig, who is now in Denver and must be eighty-something, has never sold a share." Although Kauffman counseled his old friend to diversify his investment portfolio regardless of the capital gains penalty, Craig always replied, "I made my money in Marion stock. I'm going to leave it there."

Kauffman's notion that the best way to thank Raymond Parshall was to invite him to become an original Marion investor proved correct. "Raymond retired right after we went public in 1967 because he had so much money," Kauffman said. The kindness had been repaid many times over. If all of the original investors had retained their original one thousand dollars' worth of common stock, Kauffman noted in 1991, it would have been worth more than $21 million. "The six [other than Craig] did diversify," he said, "and all of them are millionaires. It couldn't happen to better people because they helped me out when I needed the help."

With funds now available to hire additional salesmen to cover a larger geographic area, Kauffman turned his attention to Marion Laboratories' products. After a year or two, he realized that the most lucrative part of the business lay in prescriptions. If the doctor ran out of injectables, he usually bought from the next salesman that called on him. To get the order, the salesman had to be on the scene. "But with prescription drugs, the doctor would write a prescription for a certain medication and tell the patient to take it to the drugstore and have it filled," he said. "This meant that you could be fishing and still doing business because the doctor was writing the prescriptions on your products. So seeing the value and the finances involved in prescriptions, I started going more toward that side of the business."

In the early 1950s, the Food and Drug Administration exercised modest regulatory control over pharmaceutical companies. "It was probably ten or twelve years before they knew I was in the business," Kauffman recalled with a smile. "So I would sit down at my desk and devise a formula, have it manufactured for me, write the research on it, and come up with the literature that the salesman would hand the doctor as he gave his sales presentation." These formulas were usually not single-entity chemicals, but combinations of chemicals. The first significant prescription product Kauffman devised was a high-potency vitamin B complex with vitamin C and three amino acids added. VICAM, available in both tablet and injectable form, was designed to help the physician respond to the universal complaint, "Doctor, I'm tired all the time." Kauffman reasoned that since a physical examination usually showed nothing organically wrong with such patients, the doctor was at a loss as to what to prescribe. Here was the very product that would interest him.

Kauffman got the idea for VICAM from a story in the medical literature. The article said chronic fatigue was brought on by too much Coca-Cola, too much coffee, and too many cigarettes. This combination produced a toxic condition in the upper digestive tract. So he decided on a product to cleanse the upper tract and give the patient a sense of renewed energy. "VICAM had all the vitamins and minerals which detoxify the upper tract. So it was a good, logical story that I made up out of my own mind," Kauffman said years later. In addition to treating chronic fatigue, VICAM filled another market niche. Pruitt recalled that the product's detoxifiers were widely used at the time to treat alcoholics. "In fact, many physicians who treated alcoholics swore that they could get these patients back on solid food within days after starting VICAM therapy."

VICAM was virtually an all-purpose medication. "I put everything in it so it was as big as my thumbnail. And the doctors would say, 'That's an awful large tablet.' I said, 'No doctor, it's shaped like a football and it goes down easy.'" Leaving nothing to chance in a sales presentation, Kauffman admitted he practiced swallowing the tablets rapidly with no water. But there was one drawback to this demonstration: VICAM had a slight laxative effect. "So by evening," Kauffman remembered with a chuckle, "I was not only making the call at the doctor's office, I was also running down the hall to the restroom."

As with VICAM, most of Kauffman's ideas for new products grew out of his extensive reading. At the end of a long day, he would settle down at home and browse through the stacks of literature he kept near his favorite chair. "[I read] everything from sales, marketing, research journals, medical journals, to scientific proceedings." Kauffman sometimes got ideas for new products from conversations with physicians or manufacturers. "But at Marion we usually did it on our own," he recalled. "You could take an item for arthritis which was sodium salicylate, a pain reliever. And with that we added . . . a [muscle] relaxant. It was logical when you suggested that. You could write a good sales story on it, and the doctors tried everything for arthritis and nothing worked. So, they'd try this.

That was, of course, before we got into the real scientific products that we later developed."

One day while Kauffman was scanning the mail, a letter from a physician in Hiawatha, Kansas, piqued his interest. The doctor wrote that he sent patients with compound fractures to a Dr. Francisco at the University of Kansas Medical Center. The simple fractures he took care of himself. Over time the Hiawatha physician observed that Dr. Francisco's patients, in spite of their more serious injuries, healed faster than his own did. There seemed to be only one discernible difference in the treatment. Each of Dr. Francisco's patients came home with a brown paper sack of ground oyster shell with instructions to take six teaspoonfuls per day. Could the oyster shell make the difference, he wondered?

Kauffman was intrigued. He wrote Dr. Francisco, but learned that he had died and that his patient records were not available. He then consulted his old friend, Dr. Milton Casebolt, who said he thought this "oyster shell therapy" sounded like a reasonable idea and encouraged Kauffman to pursue it. Then he wrote the University of Wisconsin and asked them to analyze the chemical composition of oyster shells from the east coast and the Gulf coast. "I think that analysis cost about three hundred dollars, a lot of money in those days," Kauffman said. "It turned out that the Gulf oysters had more ingredients of the various elements that man has discovered. In fact, you will find in oysters all the elements except the inert gases, nitrogen, oxygen, and so forth." The analysis also revealed that Gulf oyster shells contained high concentrations of calcium carbonate. Kauffman knew that the calcium tablets then on the market contained only low levels of elemental calcium. Why not develop a tablet that would provide more beneficial elemental calcium? he asked himself.

Producing a superior calcium tablet was easy; persuading physicians to prescribe it was more difficult. In order to introduce the new product, Kauffman decided on a gimmick to attract physicians' attention. "I would have the oyster shells shipped to me after the oyster had been removed. Of course, you would still have a little residue of that oyster, so I would take them to my basement and try to scrub them with a wire brush to get all that out because I didn't want the odor. That took so much time that I thought, 'Why can't I put them in the washing machine?' So I put them in my wife's washing machine and almost ruined it." Once it was cleaned, he would drill a little hole through the shell, put a tag on it, and address it with a note telling the doctor that he would be by to see him at a certain time and date. "This would titillate his interest so that he would let me talk to him." Once through the door, the master salesman was usually successful in persuading the physician to prescribe oyster shell calcium for his patients.

OS-CAL, the name of the Marion Laboratories calcium tablet, was developed because of its apparent therapeutic properties in healing broken bones. However, a search of the medical literature failed to produce much supporting evidence for this use. So Kauffman urged his salesmen to listen carefully when they called on physicians for reorders to see if their experience with the tablet might provide some leads for a stronger sales story. Pruitt recalled that as the salesmen made the rounds to generate reorders for OS-CAL, doctors began volunteering, "I've used your OS-CAL and a strange thing has happened. My OB patients are telling me their leg cramps are going away after three or four days."

With that lead, Kauffman went back to the specialists in the laboratory. Further analysis revealed that oyster shell calcium contained 97 percent calcium carbonate, which was easily absorbed into the system. By contrast, 95 percent of all the other calcium tablets in use contained high concentrations of phosphorus, which was thought to inhibit calcium absorption. Since it was general medical practice to put all pregnant women on calcium, Marion Laboratories began concentrating on the obstetricians and general practitioners doing obstetrics. Pruitt recalled, "At one time, by actual birth records, Marion sold enough OS-CAL and OS-VIM in Dallas, Texas, through Sperry's leadership, to have supplied 87 percent of all the pregnant women in that area."

OS-VIM, oyster shell calcium tablets fortified with vitamins and iron, quickly followed OS-CAL and was marketed as a complete prenatal tablet. With the introduction of these two prescription products, Kauffman and his salesmen began to experiment with new approaches to marketing and sales. And what the company lacked in financial resources to promote its products, it more than made up in the imagination, ingenuity, and sheer enthusiasm of the founder and his sales team.

To help the physician remember Marion Laboratories' products,

Kauffman had the salesmen prepare samples to leave at the end of the sales call. These were not sample doses as later used throughout the industry, but merely examples to show the physician the product's size and appearance. Since the company had no funds for promotion, Marion salesmen and their wives prepared samples in their homes. Helen Pruitt recalled that when Bob returned from a week or two out of town on a sales trip, they spent Sunday afternoons at the kitchen table preparing samples for the next trip. The company supplied little cellophane bags similar to cigar wrappers, lengths of coiled cotton, small plastic vials, labels with the product name and Marion Laboratories' name and address, and, of course, the tablets in bulk containers. Whatever the product, the process was virtually the same. Kauffman wrote all the promotional literature, which was sent to the salesmen in large sheets. "We couldn't afford to pay to have it cut," Pruitt recalled. "So we would take a pair of scissors and hand cut every little piece of green literature." The next step was to package the samples. "We would take a cigar wrapper and put one tablet in the wrapper, fold it over and staple it to the literature."

OS-CAL was easily packaged, but OS-VIM, a sugarcoated, pinkish tablet, required special handling. In order to preserve the tablet's luster, salesmen and their wives used teaspoons to fill the small cellophane sample packets. These lovingly prepared samples reinforced the wives' importance and involvement in the sales process and gave them a way to participate in building their own and the company's future.

The oyster shell promotion had worked so well with local physicians that Kauffman decided to introduce it at a national medical meeting. Pruitt remembered that Marion's participation at medical meetings astounded the pharmaceutical industry. "In the midst of large, elaborate exhibits sat a small Kansas City company with literally a 'homemade exhibit,'"Pruitt said. Kauffman, Pruitt, and other salesmen "would leave the home office with one twenty-five-foot roll of dark blue and light blue corrugated paper, a staple gun, razor blades, fish-net, and oyster shells with small holes drilled in them." Upon arriving at the exhibition hall, they rented an eight-foot table and literally constructed a display on site. Even with a crude, homemade exhibit, they always had one of the busiest booths at a meeting. "One of the 'tricks' we used was to tip the bellman and have him walk through the hotel lobby and cocktail lounge from 4:30 until 5:30 paging Mr. O.S. CAL," Pruitt wrote in his history of the company.

To attract those physicians who missed the booth or failed to respond to the page in the cocktail lounge, Kauffman and his sales force had yet another ploy. Armed with oyster shells to which a small stop sign was attached imprinted with OS-CAL STOPS LEG CRAMPS, Marion salesmen roamed the corridors of the headquarters hotel hanging a shell on the doorknob of every physician registered. "You can imagine the intrigue this caused as those physicians, returning from a night on the town, reached for their doorknob and grasped an oyster shell," Pruitt said. Rival drug companies were astonished at Marion Laboratories' rather unconventional and aggressive approach. In retaliation, they began stuffing the physician's hotel mailboxes with so much literature that the American Academy of General Practice finally asked that Marion discontinue the oyster shell calling cards.

Even without the "calling cards," the oyster shell repertoire seemed inexhaustible. The exhibit booth had a supply of "oyster flowers" to attract attention. These were small shells with crepe paper flowers inside. When the shells were dropped in water, the crepe paper would absorb the liquid, swell, and force the shell to open. The flower would then float to the top. Pruitt estimated that hundreds of thousands of these oyster flowers were given away over the years. "Occasionally a physician would stop by our exhibit and say, 'I don't have time for a visit, but I need some of those oyster flowers for my kids.' Usually, we would get to visit with each physician for five or ten minutes." Marion salesmen usually wrote an order as well.

Kauffman had a special flair for attracting attention to his small company and its limited product line. In 1957 at the annual meeting of the American Academy of General Practice, he produced a hospitality event that became legendary in pharmaceutical-convention lore. Pruitt believed that the party they hosted "was probably the single most influencing factor in Marion's gaining national recognition, particularly with the general practitioners, but also with the pharmaceutical industry as a whole."

Lavish hospitality suites with champagne fountains, elaborate, if tasteless, hors d'oeuvres, and even dance bands were the order of the day at medical conventions in the 1950s. The fall prior to the annual meeting of the American Academy of General Practice, which was to be in St. Louis, Kauffman decided Marion Laboratories would host a cocktail party, its very first, at the meeting. When he asked the board of directors to allocate funds for the event, most were skeptical. Little Marion could not afford to compete with the elaborate affairs the industry giants hosted, they argued. Such an expenditure would waste precious capital. But Kauffman shocked them further when he announced he was not planning to compete with champagne and caviar. Marion would serve only beer and raw oysters on the half shell. And he planned to hire an accordion player to provide the entertainment! Although several board members thought Kauffman's plan would result in a social fiasco and the company would be the brunt of industry jokes for years to come, they finally relented. Who could argue with this man who believed that he and his company's products were exceptional? That is what his mother had told him each day as she saw him off to school, and he had acted on that belief all his life.

Kauffman reserved the Gold Room on the fourth floor of the Sheraton Jefferson in St. Louis, the headquarters hotel. He ordered four thousand oysters trucked in directly from New Orleans. Anheuser-Busch set up four Michelob beer stations in the room. The invitation list included all the general practitioners plus the top executives in the home office of every pharmaceutical company exhibiting at the meeting. Pruitt recalled, "This was absolutely unheard of—no one except physicians, and they had to wear the convention name badges, was ever allowed in a hospitality suite. And here was Marion Laboratories, whoever they were, inviting even the competition to a beer and oyster party! All we asked was that the competition not wear their name badges."

The Marion sales team was as nervous about their social debut as a new bride hosting her first dinner party. They decided if at least 350 physicians attended the party, they could go back to Kansas City and tell the board it had been a success. The party was scheduled to begin at 5:30 P.M. At 4:45 two salesmen slipped away from the Marion booth to check on arrangements in the Gold Room. "As the elevator doors opened on the fourth floor level," Pruitt remembered, "we were greeted by a mass of humanity. There was no room even to get off the elevator! Riding to the fifth floor, we worked our way down to the fourth and finally got into the room. Everything was ready except putting out the trays of raw oysters. Even the accordion player was unpacked and ready to go."

Pruitt managed to get word to other Marion salesmen and the party got under way shortly after five o'clock with the accordion player swinging into a spirited rendition of "St. Louie Woman." By 5:40 P.M. the catering manager reported that they were running out of oysters and getting low on beer. Getting more beer was no problem, but by 5:50 P.M. every oyster was gone. "That didn't seem to dampen the spirits," Pruitt said. "Physicians and their wives and our competitors—most of whom had closed their suites early due to lack of attendance—continued singing with the accordion player. It was 10:30 P.M. before the last physicians gave up and headed for their rooms."

The next morning physicians began stopping at the Marion booth even before the official opening time. One general practitioner confessed that he had eaten more than a dozen oysters and had stayed drinking beer and singing long past his usual bedtime. But his reason for stopping at the Marion booth was not to order OS-CAL or OS-VIM. He wanted the name of the advertising agency that had written the poem printed on the Marion cocktail napkins. It read:

> ENJOY YOUR OYSTERS
> WE BID THEE WELL
> YOU NEED THE PROTEIN
> WE NEED THE SHELL
> OS-CAL

It was doubtful that any advertising agency would have admitted penning that doggerel. Marion Laboratories could not afford an advertising agency at that time in its corporate history, but the authorship was irrelevant. The rhyme was not the reason for the successful evening. Kauffman's instinctive ability to step into the spotlight, to get the customer's attention, to be different, and to take pride in the distinction did the trick. For the rest of the meeting, Marion Laboratories' booth enjoyed a brisk business with physicians. "It almost seemed as if they were looking for something to buy because we had to keep pulling out new order books all week long," Pruitt said. "Even our competition began speaking to our salesmen as they walked down the aisle. Marion had finally arrived!"

The Company Grows   4

Promotional gimmicks and zany convention antics could have become counterproductive had Kauffman not insisted on quality products. Because of the founder's often unconventional and flamboyant style, Marion Laboratories steadily gained recognition in the
medical community. In the fall of 1956, an article appeared in *Obstetrics and Gynecology* comparing the clinical and laboratory effects
of OS-VIM with two other calcium tablets, all designed for the prenatal market. The study concluded that OS-VIM tablets provided
pregnant women the best protection from leg cramps during the
last trimester. Strangely, as calcium blood levels rose, phosphorus
levels decreased. Subsequent research in medical texts established
that calcium and phophorus levels occur in inverse proportions in
the human body. This medical recognition was far better than nods
and glances from competing salesmen. Confirmation of OS-VIM's
effectiveness translated directly into increased sales. And Marion
Laboratories began to earn respect for the quality and efficacy of its
products.

The sudden surge in sales created a dilemma for Kauffman. The
entrepreneur in him wanted to expand into the national market,
hire more salesmen, and tote up increasing profits. But the card
player in him counseled caution—evaluate the risks and calculate
the costs of each move. Kauffman recalled the mental tug-of-war he
experienced as OS-CAL and OS-VIM sales mounted. "My thinking all
the way through was to grow safely," Kauffman recalled. "And
growing slowly would help me do that. I added salesmen only as we
could afford it. After we introduced the oyster shell calcium, we
could have gone national. I could have gone and borrowed, pledged
the company and gone national trying to sell [calcium tablets] and

made it. But I preferred to go slowly and in the long run it proved better. I took very little salary, just enough to live on, kept investing all the money in the company."

Kauffman may have been willing to risk his personal resources at Las Vegas casinos or in poker games at the Kansas City Club, but Marion Laboratories was not a part of his private stash. Kauffman the entrepreneur may have been unrelenting and aggressive in pushing his people to break sales records, but Kauffman the patriarch felt a genuine responsibility of stewardship to his associates and their families. "I couldn't take that big a risk [with OS-CAL earlier] because I had about fifteen families depending on the company. I would have been taking a risk with their future."

Kauffman's preference for slow, orderly growth financed out of earnings was as much a product of the frugality he had learned from his mother as it was a fear of the unknown. "The odds were strongly against me when I started," he remembered four decades later. "There were two or three thousand pharmaceutical businesses started after World War II, and only three ever really succeeded." He was in a business that was rooted in science and fueled by research, and he had only a smattering of the former and could not afford the latter. Every decision, every step in a new direction, must be measured and weighed carefully.

During those early years, he was literally learning all aspects of the business. All he knew was selling. Never shy and always eager to learn, Kauffman sought counsel from those he had met while working for Lincoln Laboratories. He went first to an injectable manufacturer at Taylor Pharmacal in Decatur, Illinois, to ask him to manufacture certain medicines for Marion Laboratories. Much to Kauffman's surprise, the man tried to discourage him from entering the business. "Here he was turning down an order for a thousand—two thousand dollars." But Kauffman persisted. He knew how to sell drugs, and he was confident he could learn the rest. "I knew nothing really of budgeting and purchasing." Fortunately for him there was another pharmaceutical company in Kansas City, B.F. Asher & Co. Kauffman often called on Mr. Asher for advice. In recounting that experience, Kauffman said that he frequently advised other entrepreneurs to follow the same strategy. "When I call somebody up on the phone and say, 'I need to learn something. Could I come by and see you for a few minutes and have you teach me?' it makes the recipient of that phone call feel good. It shows your impression of him, that he is intelligent and capable, and therefore, he is all the more willing to help you."

As Kauffman applied what he learned, the young company grew steadily and sales climbed. Income from sales was $39,000 in 1950 and up to $176,000 in 1954. With net earnings of six thousand dollars, Marion Laboratories was now a profitable concern. As sales grew, so did the staff required to support the Marion representatives in the field. Soon the tiny facility on Troost was overflowing with people and pills. As an interim measure, Kauffman acquired the adjacent building, broke through the wall, and created a packaging facility to streamline distribution.

Pruitt declared that practices in the expanded facility were an improvement over the old way, although the tablet counting and labeling were still manual operations. Each product had a special "board" with one hundred holes that conformed to the shape of that particular tablet. The product was spread on the board, the holes would fill and the board would be slowly drawn over a funnel where the tablets would drop into the bottle. If the order called for a bottle of a thousand tablets, the process had to be repeated nine more times. The staff put a label with heat-sensitive glue on a common hot plate and then attached it to the bottle. "Some of the labels were not quite straight because once the glue touched the bottle, the label was there to stay," Pruitt recalled. Burned fingers seemed to be the most consistent result from this "improved" process.

As the company grew, Kauffman decided he needed someone to manage the burgeoning office chores. It was at this point that he decided to take his best friend, Charlie Hughes, off the road and make him office manager. Hughes, who was a successful and productive salesman, had never liked the life. He preferred not to travel and happily accepted the office assignment. Now with a trusted confidant overseeing daily operations, Kauffman could concentrate totally on what he did best: selling, and directing and managing sales activity.

The expansion on Troost was merely a holding operation until a new facility could be built. In 1956, with sixty-five associates, Marion Laboratories relocated to eight thousand square feet of floor space on a ten-acre site at Twenty-ninth and Grand. "This was the first building we had built for us," Hughes recalled, "and we rented it from the man who built it. We leased out half of that building to start with to a wholesale grocer. Then we decided to venture into manufacturing ourselves. So when his lease ran out, we opened our first manufacturing plant." Pruitt remembered that the new facilities were palatial compared to the cramped office on Troost where he and Sperry had started. There were four private offices and "even enough space that we set up a conference table so we began holding sales meetings at the home office."

Marion Laboratories' steady growth continued throughout the last half of the decade. As earnings climbed, Kauffman added more salesmen and began to do more manufacturing. By 1959, the company had achieved sales of one million dollars and was planning yet another move to a new and larger headquarters in the southwestern section of Kansas City. All of the growth was financed from earnings. Kauffman kept a close watch on the balance sheet and a firm grip on the company purse. "The financial area was not a problem with me because I had a mathematical mind," he said. "I was good with figures. [Finances] were never a problem as long as I had the money to pay the bills. Here I think my father's German trait of never spending more than you have paid off because I would always try and see to it that we didn't overspend."

With the two exceptions of the five-thousand dollars from the Commerce Trust Company to finance hiring the first salesmen and the seven-thousand dollar, five-year loan from the original Marion investors, Kauffman borrowed no money. However, in 1960 he became concerned about the company's future and decided it would be prudent to have some cash in reserve. Sensational congressional hearings that year had raised the specter of potential legislation aimed at the pharmaceutical industry and greater regulatory powers for the Food and Drug Administration. Estes Kefauver, the crusading Democratic senator from Tennessee who had captured national attention in the early 1950s with his investigative hearings on organized crime, had turned his attention to the pharmaceutical industry. It was probably not accidental that the drug industry hearings were timed to coincide with his tough reelection campaign in 1960. Strapped for campaign funds and facing a unified opposition backing a single candidate, Kefauver was in a race for his political life. He decided to campaign from Washington rather than in Tennessee. He reasoned this strategy would be less costly, less tiring, and more effective in attracting attention from the media. And the Senate hearing room was the perfect forum to revive his image as a crusader against corruption and privilege.

As chairman of the Antitrust and Monopoly Subcommittee, Kefauver initiated a series of investigations in 1959 about alleged excessive costs of drugs and questioned the efficacy and safety of pharmaceutical products. As the 1960 Tennessee senatorial election campaign heated up, so did the drug industry hearings. Kauffman had good reason to be concerned about Marion Laboratories' future as the talk on Capitol Hill and in the national press ranged from amending drug patent rights to regulating drug prices. "I could see there might be trouble ahead," he recalled. As a precautionary measure, he wanted to have a cash reserve to help the company weather whatever might come. He asked his Kansas City bank, the Commerce Trust Company, for a fifty-thousand-dollar loan, but the response was negative. The official who examined the Marion Laboratories' balance sheet could not see that Kauffman needed to borrow. Kauffman responded, "I know I don't, but I want to because I don't know what will happen a year down the road." Unmoved, the loan officer insisted primly, "Well, until you need it, we won't lend it to you."

Kauffman protested that this was unfair. Marion Laboratories was a good customer and a good risk. He felt the Commerce Trust Company should be willing to honor that relationship with a good-faith loan. The bank officer suggested that if such a loan were made, the decision would have to come from a senior official, and referred Kauffman to another department. The senior official agreed to the loan, but only in return for an option to buy 25 percent of the company any time within the next ten years. Kauffman flatly refused the banker's terms. "I looked at him and said, 'No thank you' because that was the same as selling part of the family."

He decided to pursue another course. Since he was planning a trip to New York, he called the Chase Manhattan Bank loan division and asked for an appointment. They agreed on a time, and Kauffman showed up promptly for the meeting. After studying the Marion balance sheets, the loan officer asked how he planned to use the money. "I'm just kind of worried about the next year or two in the pharmaceutical business because of the Kefauver investigation," Kauffman replied candidly. "I just want the safety of having that money. I know I don't really need it, but I want the safety of it." Kauffman's rationale was more than satisfactory. "Do you want the funds put in this bank or shall we wire them to your bank in Kansas City?" the loan officer responded. A bit surprised at the quick answer, Kauffman said it would probably be more convenient if the funds were available to him in Kansas City.

Before they completed the arrangements, the loan officer said there was someone else in the bank who wanted to meet Kauffman while he was in town. And with that, he ushered Kauffman in to see the bank's chairman, David Rockefeller. Years later Kauffman still remembered the sea motif of Rockefeller's office, the captain's chest around which they sat, and the atmosphere of subdued elegance. After an exchange of pleasantries, Rockefeller commented that the Rockefeller Foundation had no investment in pharmaceutical stocks. If the day ever came that Marion Laboratories went public, Rockefeller said he would like to have the opportunity to purchase stock. Justifiably flattered, Kauffman assured the Chase Manhattan chairman that he would personally guarantee that opportunity. As Kauffman was preparing to leave the office, Rockefeller said, "Now I want you to go back to Commerce Trust because they are an affiliate of ours in Kansas City. Tell them that if they don't want to lend you fifty thousand dollars, we will." Continuing in a quiet manner which hinted at the irony of the situation, he concluded, "I imagine they'll lend it to you." The line of credit was established, just as Kauffman wanted, but he never needed to draw on it.

Kauffman's cautious approach to company finances was a contrast to the way he handled personal resources. Over time he became freer with his personal funds, but there were still occasional lapses into the frugality of his childhood. He enjoyed the excitement of casino gambling in Las Vegas. He always bet at cards and when playing golf. For a time in the late 1960s, he owned a stable of winning racehorses started with an initial purchase from Desi Arnez, the television entertainer and producer. Hughes recalled that Kauffman once roused him from a sound sleep telephoning to report that one of his horses had won seventy thousand dollars in a race in New York. "I'm having a ball," Kauffman shouted into the telephone. "I've been passing out hundred-dollar tips to everybody I come across." It was not until the following morning that it occurred to Hughes that Kauffman had reversed the charges on the long-distance call. "That character had won seventy thousand at the track and then called me collect!"

In his public role as founder of Marion Laboratories, Kauffman was circumspect and cautious. He believed strongly that a company that did not owe money could withstand the rigors of the free market. While he was willing to take a personal risk when starting the company, success in the pharmaceutical business brought his thrifty German nature to the surface. "Once you become successful or halfway successful, [and you are] making a living and making a profit, you better not gamble [with the company]. You might lose everything," he said. "After you accumulate so much or achieve so much success, you don't want to take the risk of losing it."

The combination of conservative financial management, new or enhanced products, and aggressive salesmanship fueled Marion Laboratories' growth throughout the 1950s and into the next decade. There were further variations of the basic calcium supplement. OS-CAL led to OS-VIM. Then vitamin C was added to OS-CAL to make TEX-MAR, a product designed for patients having their teeth extracted in preparation for dentures. Vitamin D was later added to OS-CAL. Throughout the 1950s, oyster shell calcium products were the foundation for Marion Laboratories' steady growth. The company had neither the funds nor the personnel to conduct basic research, so Kauffman added to the standard offerings with new products which he licensed from other pharmaceutical houses or drug manufacturers. By the mid-sixties, purchasing marketing rights of a specific product for a specified term and territory would become standard practice for Marion. Recognizing that the company lacked the resources to develop and sustain an in-house scientific research program, Marion Laboratories became dependent on locating, licensing, and bringing to market the discoveries of others.

In late 1955, Marion introduced GLYCAMINE A.M., an antacid, licensed from a custom pharmaceutical manufacturer in St. Louis. Early the following year, Kauffman acquired marketing rights to DUOTRATE, a long-acting capsule used in the treatment of angina. With DUOTRATE, Marion began to challenge the larger drug firms in an attempt to acquire a portion of the lucrative market for heart medicine. This marked the beginning of Marion Laboratories' long-term attachment to the internist and the cardiologist. And those relationships would prove invaluable when in the 1980s, the company introduced the blockbuster drug licensed from Japan, CARDIZEM.

During those early growth years, Marion's products were "probably no better than 50 percent of our competitors' products," Pruitt admitted. But Kauffman trained the sales force to emphasize and promote the quality of their products. Marion's success in selling vitamin B_{12} illustrated this strategy. The pharmaceutical giant Merck & Company had successfully isolated vitamin B_{12} from liver extract in 1948 and Marion purchased it from them in injectable form. Even though Merck sold a 30cc vial for $4.80 and Marion's price was $6, Marion salesmen frequently outsold their competitors. Kauffman instructed the salesmen, "If you go out and sell quality, you can get a quality price." Often when a Merck salesman attempted to persuade a physician that he could purchase the same vitamin B_{12} at a lesser price, the doctor would counter, "Little old Marion Laboratories forced you into making a better product, huh?" Pruitt conceded that Merck and Marion had the identical product all along but "Merck just forgot to sell quality."

As a superior salesman, Kauffman was a shrewd observer of human psychology. He learned quickly to appeal to the physician's pride and sense of self-worth. In an effort to expand direct sales of injectables and calcium products, he hit on the idea that physicians might prefer to buy tablets with their personal label on the bottles. After selling the physician OS-VIM or OS-CAL, the salesman would determine how many babies the physician delivered each month. Then doing a quick mental computation to figure what a six-month supply would be, he would explain Marion's latest service. "Doctor, we will print personalized labels for you and then attach them to bottles of one hundred OS-VIM. You'd be surprised at how much time this will save your staff. They no longer will have to count out those one hundred tablets." Then the salesman would begin asking questions to help design the label: Did the physician want his name printed as Joe A. Jones or J.A. Jones? Should both the office and the home telephone numbers be included? What type of printing did the doctor prefer, script or block letters? Then the questions switched to the merits of a six-month supply versus the substantial savings available if the physician ordered a full year's supply.

Bob Pruitt remembered the success of this approach with delight. "It was not unheard-of for a salesman to walk out of an office with a 288-bottle order—*on the first call!* The beauty of this "subordinate close" was that the physician had not made a decision about whether to buy 28,800 tablets. His decision was about the information to be placed on the bottle." Pruitt also noted that ego played a part in the physician's willingness to place a large order. "He didn't want to admit that [288 bottles] were too many for his practice."

Sales continued to grow as the company expanded into new territories. Physicians located outside of Iowa, Nebraska, Kansas, Missouri, Oklahoma, and Texas who dispensed medications from their offices had little chance of using Marion products. Drug wholesalers beyond Marion's home base did not stock them, so neither physicians nor pharmacies had access. In 1956, Kauffman decided to make a foray into "foreign territory" following the American Academy of General Practice's annual meeting scheduled to be held in Washington, D.C. In preparation for what became known as the "Marion blitz," Kauffman contacted the major drug wholesalers in the Washington, D.C., area and secured their agreement to stock OS-CAL, OS-VIM, and TEXMAR. With ample supplies of Marion products readily available, the challenge was to create the demand among physicians. Kauffman selected four of his top salesmen to remain in Washington following the academy meeting. They spent the weekend dividing the city into four quadrants and preparing physician record sheets on every general practitioner and obstetrician in each quadrant. They also made a backup list of dentists to call on when no physicians were available. The goal was to launch OS-CAL and OS-VIM, the company's moneymakers in the prenatal market. But if a salesman had time on his hands, he was ready to call on dentists to introduce TEXMAR. "Armed with the local Yellow Pages, a map of the area, and red 'velvet' calling cards . . . on Monday morning . . . [we] set out to blitz Washington, D.C." Pruitt remembered.

Kauffman instructed the salesmen to vary their usual approach to the doctor's receptionist because time was of the essence. In established Marion markets, Pruitt described the approach as a "soft sell" designed to ensure access to the doctor. Knowing that they would be back in the area every six to eight weeks, the salesmen were careful to cultivate good relationships with doctors' receptionists. If they did not, "she just might not let us in to see her physician on subsequent calls," Pruitt said.

The goal of the "blitz" was to see as many physicians as possible in a limited time. So the approach was direct and hard hitting. The salesman would introduce himself, saying he was from Marion Laboratories in Kansas City with a new product that would be of great interest to the physician. Explaining that he was only in the city a short time, he asked for an appointment in the next twenty minutes, then sat down to wait. Whether the approach so totally disarmed the receptionist, or she was so impressed with the red velvet calling card, no one ever knew. But in a surprising number of cases, he and his colleagues would get to see the physician within twenty minutes. More often than not, the receptionist would apologize for the doctor's being unable to see the Marion representative at the moment, but she would usually set a time for the salesman to return. No one knows how much sales volume the first blitz produced because a flood destroyed company records in 1961, but it was successful enough to be repeated again and again. Throughout the late 1950s, experienced Marion salesmen fanned out from Kansas City as if following the four points of the compass, opening up markets using the "blitz" techniques in Indiana, Ohio, Florida, Arizona, and Wisconsin.

As Kauffman staffed new territories, he also continued the search for new products. In 1959, he obtained nonexclusive marketing rights to a product for anemia which he called ANASORB. He understood that name recognition was as important in the drug industry as in any other kind of sales. He believed his sales force more than capable of selling the physician on the advantages of this new treatment for anemia, but he puzzled over a way to get the physician in the habit of writing the product's name—preferably on a prescription form. The solution was simple, yet imaginative and very successful. To acquaint physicians with ANASORB, Kauffman announced he was offering women employed in physicians' offices in the company's fourteen-state territory the opportunity to win an all-expense-paid, round-trip, week-long vacation in the Bahamas. Press releases explained the rules for nominating potential winners by postcard. "Each doctor may submit one vote each day for any member of his staff simply by writing ANASORB, the contestant's name, and his own signature on a postcard or prescription blank which he then forwards to a designated firm of certified public accountants."

ANASORB was a rosy pink tablet. So Kauffman had a large supply of pink, self-addressed, postage-paid cards printed and distributed to each salesman. Pruitt said that most salesmen would end their visit with the nurse or receptionist by confiding, "Now, you're only supposed to send in one card a day, but I don't think they'll ever catch two or three cards with the same postmark. Here's a supply with my calling card. Call me if you need more." Sales of ANASORB soared as pink postcards deluged the accounting firm. The grand prize winner was Mrs. Evelyn Ransom, a registered nurse who worked for three physicians in an Enid, Oklahoma, clinic. Kauffman's strategy had worked. ANASORB had become an oft-repeated product name and a frequently prescribed medication in hundreds of doctors' offices. The contest had created so much interest in the product that one physician complained to Pruitt, "You and your . . . ANASORB contest! I wake up in the middle of the night and start writing ANASORB."

By June 1959, Marion had achieved annual sales of one million dollars. Clearly Marion products and salesmen were successful, but Kauffman recognized the need to make some major changes if growth were to continue. As the company expanded, he found the demands on his time overwhelming. He was managing an increasingly complex organization while still trying to recruit, train, and lead the entire sales force. He had started as a salesman. He thrived on the competitive aspects of selling and genuinely liked talking directly with physicians, pharmacists, and drug wholesalers. But he understood he would have to relinquish some control in the sales area if he were to have the time and energy to focus attention on other areas crucial to Marion's continued development. These included public relations, the development of manufacturing facilities and quality control, and the nagging issue of research needed to secure FDA approval to bring new products to the market.

Relinquishing day-to-day responsibility for the Marion sales force was a wrenching decision for Kauffman, but one he knew he had to make. He selected Sperry to succeed him. Sperry had gone to Dallas in 1953 with the charge to develop the southwest region for Marion Laboratories. By 1959 when Kauffman tapped him to return to Kansas City, he had eleven salesmen spread throughout Oklahoma, Kansas, and Texas. Kauffman complained that Sperry could be difficult at times, but knew that he was highly motivated to succeed and unfailingly loyal. Sperry had a nose for sales talent; he recruited selectively and trained the men well. He was the epitome of what would later be called the "hands-on manager." He buoyed the sales team up in down times and prodded them to achieve even more in good years.

When Kauffman approached him about returning to Kansas City to become general sales manager, Sperry naturally wanted to know what his responsibilities would be. "Everything you feel capable of handling," was Kauffman's response. Armed with this all-inclusive mandate, Sperry returned to the company's headquarters at Twenty-ninth and Grand. "Headquarters" consisted of two private offices, one for Kauffman and the other for Hughes. The rest of the building was an open area that housed the computer, all the secretaries, and the new general sales manager. As soon as he was settled in the Kansas City office, Sperry tried again to pin Kauffman down. But as usual, Kauffman was so busy with a multitude of responsibilities and commitments that he neglected to outline Sperry's specific duties. He simply expected Sperry to "sit down and manage." The goal was clear: to build a small sales organization into a national pharmaceutical company. And he trusted Sperry's intelligence to decide how best to do it. As would often be the case during Marion's formative years, Kauffman chose the individual he believed could do the job best and then he let the person do it. His choice of Sperry was to be a good decision for both men and for Marion Laboratories.

Placing the new general sales manager at a desk in the middle of the secretarial pool dramatized the need for larger quarters. Fortunately, plans were under way for a new building. In May 1959, Marion Laboratories had acquired a 6.9-acre tract in the newly announced Swope Park industrial district. The three-hundred-thousand-square-foot site seemed ideally suited for the company's needs. The plan was to construct a fifteen-thousand-square-foot, one-story building to house the general and executive offices, distribution facilities, a sales unit, and a quality control lab. Within a short time, Kauffman planned to add two additional buildings, a laboratory, and a manufacturing unit. Rail access was located nearby, while Swope Park was to the north and east and the Blue River ran near the site.

Kauffman's announcement that he had retained a professional architectural firm to design "a contemporary facility for Marion Laboratories, Inc.," glossed over the more prosaic reality of the situation. The land was located in a river bottom just as the leased farm had been where he spent his early childhood. Kauffman and his father, who was helping him find a suitable spot for expansion, understood from personal experience the possibility of flooding in that type of location. Building there was a calculated risk that he decided to take. The deal had seemed too good to turn down. Kauffman recalled, "The only reason we even moved there [was that] we needed to have bigger quarters and a land developer had bought that acreage wanting to develop it. But he was having trouble getting the first tenant. We didn't quite have the money to make the move so I persuaded him to give us the land in exchange for an IOU. We would build our building and repay him from the profits earned on increased sales." The arrangement benefited both parties. The developer acquired an initial tenant who would help attract others to the site. And Marion got the land needed for expansion, but delayed the payment.

Just prior to moving to the new site, Kauffman wrote to the senior management staff acknowledging the strain that the company's cramped facilities and rapid growth had caused. He cautioned them that with expanded physical space and additional growth in sales, communications among various departments could become more difficult. Because of the pressures of overwork, Kauffman admonished his executives to guard "the congenial relationship between each department that has been the history of Marion Laboratories. We do not ever want bickering or conflict between departments. We do not ever want one individual to be derogatory in his comments concerning others." Being thoughtful of others was not an empty homily. For Kauffman it was the principle on which Marion Laboratories had been founded, and he was determined to translate it into daily action. Anyone who doubted the sincerity of his commitment to a caring, congenial, and profitable workplace had only to read the concluding sentence of his memo. "Together we rise; divided, changes will be made." And anyone who mistook his friendly demeanor as weakness soon learned that he did not hesitate to fire an individual who did not carry his part of the load.

The move to the new headquarters in April 1960 seemed a fitting way to mark the company's remarkable first decade of growth. Kauffman had established and nurtured a successful enterprise against seemingly incredible odds. Money was often scarce in those early years, so product refinements, more attractive packaging, and other improvements had to wait until the cash flow improved. Sperry was impatient with the pace of improvements, nagging Kauffman to pay attention to details such as the color variations on the coatings of certain pills. Although Sperry's perfectionism could be exasperating, Kauffman admitted it was "extraordinarily helpful prodding. Irritating though it was, it kept us moving toward more quality control."

As with all fledgling businesses, there were times when there were more bills to pay than money in the bank account. And given Kauffman's aversion to borrowing, the solution was to work harder, work longer hours, and sell more. There were times during those early years when Kauffman literally did not know if he was going to be able to pay monthly salaries. Yet while he may have had to forgo his own salary from time to time, he never missed making a Marion payroll, even in the leanest of times.

The move to the new facility was a giant step in the growth of Marion Laboratories. Earnings from sales continued to climb; all the associates seemed reinvigorated in the new surroundings; and the company's future seemed secure. But Kauffman's home life had become increasingly insecure. Marguerite was frequently ill and often away from home for extended periods in the 1950s undergoing treatment for depression. She also suffered from severe back pain as a result of an automobile accident prior to her marriage to Kauffman. Having experienced two miscarriages before she and Kauffman decided to adopt, Marguerite became a strict parent who seemed overly protective of the children. "I never remember having a lot of friends. I do not recall ever having people spend the night," her daughter, Sue Kauffman, said.

Kauffman, like most men of his time, left child rearing primarily to his wife. He was trying to build a business and had limited free time for family outings. But he was eager for Larry to become a Boy Scout since scouting had been such a happy experience for him. He had grown closer to his own father when John became a Scout leader, and doubtless he believed the same could be true for him and his son. However, according to Larry, reality did not quite match Kauffman's romanticized memories of father-and-son camping trips. "We had an overnighter somewhere and it was cold," Larry recalled. "[Dad] decided he had time; he was going to go. We'd been out there all weekend when he showed up that evening. We had a tent pitched, and when he showed up it became rainy and cold. I spent one night in that tent with him, and he snored constantly. He grinds his teeth, too. Oh, terrible! The worst sound you ever heard in your life. It would scare you. I think we had one blanket and, of course, he had to have it around him. I was up all night long. The next morning, being wet, cold, and tired, Dad said I told him not to come to any more over-nighters! I'll never forget that as long as I live. As miserable as it seemed at the time, later in life it came to mean a lot to me that he was there that night."

Sue's childhood memories of activities with her father were less specific than Larry's. "He didn't ignore us, but I don't recall him going out and playing ball with us. I don't recall him going to the zoo . . . or to the art gallery. You know, things that were available to all of us at that time. He wasn't an active father."

When Marguerite was away for medical treatment, Kauffman had the burden of caring for two young children added to a heavy travel schedule and the usual worries associated with running a business. "About the only thing Dad could cook was oatmeal," Sue said. "So we ate a lot of oatmeal in those days, morning, noon, and night." When the children were very small, Kauffman's mother would frequently take them for a Sunday. "We'd have fried chicken," Sue recalled. "[Grandmother Kauffman] had a very active role in my early upbringing. The only place Dad had to turn was her." Later Ben Blackshire, Marguerite's nephew, lived with the young family while attending college. "As I look back, I think part of the reason was to take care of us in case something happened to Marguerite while Ewing was traveling," Sue said. Kauffman confided the private anguish of those troubled years to his daughter after she was married and had children of her own. "He told me one time he was walking down the street and tears were rolling down his cheeks. He was thinking to himself, 'How am I going to take care of two children and now a woman who is in a mental institution, or a woman who's very ill with no money?'"

As Marion's first lady, Marguerite tried valiantly to keep up with her ebullient, outgoing husband, but she felt inadequate and intimidated. Marion Laboratories had grown rapidly throughout the 1950s, and Marguerite's social responsibilities grew as well. "Part of her problem was that as Dad began to progress with Marion, she started to regress. She was not as well educated . . . she only finished the sixth grade. He needed someone who could entertain. His needs were grander and greater than she had ever imagined or could foresee in her life," her daughter said with the benefit of hindsight. Marguerite's physical problems, her insecurity about her role as a hostess, and the lingering despair over two miscarriages all added to the stress of raising two lively youngsters. These mounting pressures began to take a toll. She would become withdrawn and despondent for days, then overwhelmed with sadness. Then as fall gave way to winter, personal tragedy struck the Kauffman family.

Kauffman awoke on December 15, 1960, to find his wife's lifeless body, clothed in her nightgown, lying on the front seat of the family car. The motor was running and the garage door was closed. Sue recalled that on the evening before her mother's death, Marguerite was in exceptionally good spirits. "She was talking on the telephone and laughing with one of her friends as I was getting ready for bed. I kissed her goodnight and started to my room, then I remember, for some reason I can't explain, I went back and kissed her again. She seemed so happy." Sue, who was only twelve when her mother died, was especially sensitive to her moods, as were the other family members. Stunned and shaken, Kauffman told the authorities that she had left no note and that she had not been despondent. The coroner's finding was accidental death.

For more than nine months after his wife's death, Kauffman struggled to find a way to juggle his huge responsibilities. After experimenting unsuccessfully with several full-time housekeepers, he reluctantly decided the only alternative was to place the children in boarding schools. Larry was enrolled at Wentworth Military Academy in nearby Lexington, Missouri, and earned his high school diploma there, but he never adjusted to the military environment. His father recalled, "He hated it. He went in as a private and came out as a private." Sue's experience was more chaotic, but in the long term, more satisfactory. After a year at Kemper Hall, a girls' school in Kenosha, Wisconsin, she enrolled at Judson, a private coeducational school located in Phoenix, Arizona. "Judson was the sort of school that took everybody," she recalled. "It was a small school and that was my saving grace, without a doubt. . . . I started making friends and started making my niche in life. School became my ground; it became my family."

Marguerite's unexpected death remained a painful memory for Kauffman throughout his life. He tried to wall up those years. He seldom mentioned Marguerite's name, and he never discussed the circumstances surrounding her death. His work, which had always been important to him, became all-consuming. "Dad was devastated. Then he put all of his efforts into Marion. I think he had a choice at the time," Sue said, reflecting on the aftermath of her mother's death with no trace of bitterness or self-pity. "I think his choice was family or Marion Laboratories. And I think he chose Marion Laboratories. There's no doubt in my mind."

After settling the children in their respective schools that fall, Kauffman returned to Kansas City and plunged back into his work. On September 11, the skies darkened and it began to rain. The downpour continued for three days in the wake of Hurricane Carla. After plundering the Texas Gulf coast, the powerful storm moved inland and straight up the center of the country. Torrential rains caused inland streams and rivers to leave their banks while people in their paths scrambled to higher ground. As the rain drummed down on Kansas City, Kauffman began to worry. "We were real small and didn't have too much money," he said, recalling his fears that Marion's new headquarters and a decade of effort might be washed away. When he finally went to bed on September 13, he did not sleep well. The sound of the rain and his concern for the company kept him awake. At four in the morning, Kauffman got up and went out to the plant site. "I sat down by the river." he said. "I drove a stake into the edge of the river to see how fast it was rising. And by 5:30 I could see it was really coming up fast."

Although the Blue River was a quarter of a mile from Marion headquarters, Kauffman knew there would be flooding. He immediately alerted the top executives. Hughes was instructed to call all the truck lines that serviced Marion and ask for their help in moving raw materials and packaged goods to higher ground. If they could not provide sufficient help, he was to rent moving vans. The priority was to save the marketable products. Kauffman also told him to locate several loads of sand and bags to be filled. These would be used to block the doors and help to stem the rising river.

His next call was to Danielson. He told him to organize a team of executives to find warehouse space for Marion products and any equipment that could be moved. The warehouse would be a temporary shipping station until the regular distribution facility dried out. Then Kauffman summoned the rest of the Marion associates. By 7:30 A.M., local salesmen and janitors were working alongside executives and secretaries boxing up products, filling sandbags, and transferring desk drawers and desktop items to the tops of filing cabinets.

Although Marion Laboratories was not extensively involved in manufacturing drugs at that time, they did make some of their products. As a consequence, the company owned heavy machinery which Kauffman hoped to save from the corroding effects of flood waters. But without sturdy equipment for moving the cumbersome machines, it looked for a time as if this major capital investment would be lost. Then Kauffman remembered a cough medicine in the inventory which had never been a big seller. "We poured it on the floor which made it slippery," he said. "Then we pushed the machines . . . underneath the girders and jacked them up with a pulley as high as we could so if it did flood, the machines wouldn't be destroyed."

By ten o'clock water started coming into the building. At noon it was waist high, and Kauffman ordered everyone to evacuate. "I really waited a little too long," he recalled, "because three of our automobiles in the company parking lot flooded. But by that time, we had moved almost all of our drugs out." Floodwaters from the Blue River rose three and a half feet in the Marion buildings. But the morning following the deluge Marion was filling and shipping orders from the facility Danielson had found. It took two days for the water to recede, and then the task of cleaning up lay ahead. "Mud just covered everything," Kauffman remembered. "You'd open drawers and you'd even find snakes in there." In a memo illustrated with staff cartoons and photos, Hughes reported to sales representatives in the field on the damage at company headquarters. Referring to a sketch showing where the water line came on the file cabinets, he wrote, "Some of our most cherished and obsolete records were lost. But reposing on the top, high and dry and quite safe are some extremely valuable items we did save: A potted plant, crayons, fly swatter, electric fan, and jump rope." Another drawing showed capsules overflowing from a toilet bowl. Hughes identified the product as DUOTRATE and concluded, "We feel that this represents the most unorthodox moisture test ever performed on that product."

With the help of staff from a neighboring firm, Marion associates had the building cleaned and operational within six days. But during that time, they were able to fill and ship orders because of Kauffman's quick decision to move the shipping operations to a leased facility. In recalling the relative ease with which they survived what could have been a genuine disaster, Kauffman said, "You know how you try to turn adversity into an asset? Well, we sent wires to all the doctors in the seven or eight states that we covered at that time. We told them that Marion Laboratories had whipped the flood, our products were moving again, and their druggist would be able to fill their prescriptions." After a slight pause and with just the hint of a smile, he admitted, "Which, of course, we always were able to do anyway!"

Changing with the Times 5

During the decade of the 1950s, Ewing Kauffman and Marion Laboratories had earned the respect and trust of the medical community. As Kauffman began to move toward becoming a contender on the national level, he was determined to guard and preserve the company's reputation for integrity. He noted that the greatest compliment a physician ever paid him was when he introduced a new product and the doctor said, "I will use it because you have never lied to me." Although he might employ rather flamboyant marketing ploys to call attention to a product, he was scrupulous never to exaggerate a medication's probable effects. He cautioned the salesmen to explain the specific application of every product, to promote the quality of Marion's drugs, but never to inflate their potential efficacy. And success seemed to breed success as the company prospered in the 1950s. "It just illustrates that when you do what's right," Kauffman concluded, "good things happen."

But even in the midst of dynamic growth and mounting success, there had been problems and lean times. Turnover remained fairly high among the sales staff, and Kauffman experimented with trying to find the right combination of recruitment, training, benefits, and motivation to keep Marion's growth curve moving upward. In 1957, he had substantially increased the expense allowance for salesmen. And, for the first time, each salesman drove a company-owned car. Pruitt remembered that his first Marion car was a 1957 Chevrolet. "It had a straight stick shift with a radio and heater, but no air conditioning. By 1961, all the salesmen had cars with automatic transmission and air conditioning as standard equipment. And by 1963, all the managers started driving Cadillacs." The salesmen enjoyed the status and prestige which a company vehicle implied.

Their wives were overjoyed to have use of the family car. Instead of being dependent on family, friends, or public transportation when their husbands were away, wives of Marion salesmen were among the first women in Kansas City to experience the luxurious freedom of the "two-car family."

In spite of increased compensation packages, bonuses, and special perks, turnover in the sales force continued to be a worrisome problem. Usually it was because a man was unwilling or unable to work the extra hours Kauffman expected of Marion salesmen. And if one salesman did not produce, Kauffman was quick to find another who would. But his handling of the sales team was not based solely on sales numbers. If a man was having a problem in his territory, Kauffman tried to give him an opportunity to improve his performance before deciding to replace him. For example, in 1957 Pruitt was transferred to Columbus, Ohio, to begin an eastward expansion developing markets for Marion products. He was picked for the job because he already had an exceptional sales record after only two years with the company. His forte was selling to physicians who dispensed medications directly from their offices. He was constantly studying the medical literature to increase his knowledge so he could converse easily and knowledgeably with physicians.

Pruitt was excited about the challenge of opening the eastern United States for Marion, but "when I got out to Columbus, I tell you I was just falling on my face," he recalled. The Buckeye State was an intensely competitive market. Seventy-five pharmaceutical companies were located there, and all sold directly to physicians. "There were pink aspirin, blue aspirin, green aspirin, purple aspirin," Pruitt said as he tried to re-create the sense of the flood of products. And the name, Marion Laboratories, initially proved a handicap. Most physicians thought this was yet another little drug company that had sprung up in Marion, Ohio. In addition to the ruthless competition and the lack of name recognition, Pruitt was having difficulty selling to doctors who bought only by price, with no regard for quality. There were also tensions in Pruitt's relationship with the regional manager. The supervisor might go along on a sales call where Pruitt had already convinced the physician that Marion had the superior product. But the sticking point would be that the doctor was unwilling to pay the price to get the better product. "And [my manager] would come out—and offer him the million-tablet price if he would buy twenty-five thousand packets. I couldn't do that!" Pruitt said. He struggled for two years to make inroads into the Ohio market, but lacking the authority to match competitors' lower prices, he became increasingly frustrated. Several drug companies were eager to recruit him, and finally he agreed to an interview with Geigy. Pruitt was earning $450 a month, plus bonuses, so he told Geigy's district manager that he would not move except for a guarantee of $650 a month in salary, plus commissions and bonuses. These were not exactly the terms expected from a man eager to sever relations with his employer.

While the Geigy recruiter was negotiating Pruitt's compensation with executives in Cleveland, Pruitt had to attend a Marion regional sales meeting in Indianapolis. He told his wife that if Geigy agreed to his terms, she should call the hotel and leave the message, "Everything in Cleveland is okay." Shortly after the sales meeting began, Pruitt received the message. Geigy had agreed to his terms. And there he was, trapped in a meeting with Ewing Kauffman outlining a new compensation plan and graciously asking all the associates for their comments. When Kauffman reached him, Pruitt hesitated, then said he preferred to discuss the matter in private. "Bob, you can discuss anything you want right here," Kauffman responded. Then, as if on cue, the refreshment cart appeared and everyone broke for coffee. Kauffman, betraying annoyance, pulled Pruitt aside and asked what was so important that they needed to talk in private. Pruitt blurted out that he was resigning to take a job with Geigy. Clearly shocked, Kauffman growled, "You meet me and Jean Sperry in my suite immediately!"

When Pruitt arrived at the suite, Sperry, who was back in the Kansas City office with the responsibility of developing a national sales team, and Kauffman were already there. Kauffman seemed genuinely hurt that Pruitt was even thinking of leaving Marion Laboratories. "You know, Bob, you've been with us for all of these lean years and we're just beginning to see the light of day. You'd be making a big mistake," he argued. Pruitt finally admitted that a great part of his frustration was his inability to work with his district manager, who he felt was of no help to him. "Well, that's certainly no problem," Kauffman replied with relief in his voice. "You're now working for Jean Sperry."

Kauffman's response to Pruitt's attempted resignation was typical of his management style. Flow charts and diagrams of hierarchical relationships were an anathema to him. He knew Pruitt was a committed, ambitious, and persuasive salesman who was experiencing a temporary difficulty. That Pruitt was unable to work effectively under a certain regional manager was a minor problem. Both men were highly effective sales representatives, and Kauffman intended to keep both working at their maximum potential. In confirming Pruitt's story years later, Kauffman reluctantly admitted that if there ever had been a salesman whose ability surpassed his own, it was Don Ludwig, the regional manager in question. So the solution was self-evident. As a result of Kauffman's quick decision, Pruitt became the only salesman in the field who reported directly to the national sales manager.

This unorthodox arrangement worked flawlessly. But, of course, Pruitt was not just any salesman. Shortly after the Indianapolis meeting, Sperry flew from Kansas City to Columbus to work with Pruitt for a few days. He saw immediately that Pruitt had difficulty making sales to dispensing physicians who wanted to haggle about price. Together they went through Bob's record book. Sperry tore out all the pages of physicians who bought strictly on price, and told him to concentrate on prescriptions. Pruitt followed those instructions and was soon setting sales records again.

The decision to have Pruitt focus on prescription sales was a natural response to the evolutionary process that was taking place within Marion Laboratories and throughout the pharmaceutical industry. Kauffman had recognized that the physician who dispensed tablets and gave injections at his office was disappearing from the medical scene. Scientific advances in medicine after World War II, the development of specialties among medical practitioners, and the growth of suburbs and cities all required pharmaceutical companies to respond with more specialized and sophisticated drugs, targeting specific diseases. Not only were pharmaceutical products changing, but the system of delivery to the medical professional was changing also. Kauffman grasped the importance of developing new business arrangements with drug wholesalers who supplied pharmacies with specialized prescription products. Marion was selling a limited number of prescription items by the end of the 1950s and the company was beginning to work with wholesalers for distribution. But the majority of their sales still came from direct contact between the salesman and the physician who dispensed remedies directly from his office. All of that was about to change.

Once the salesmen began focusing on prescription products, it became imperative that the company strengthen its prescription product line. Sperry had been pushing to "get rid of the injectables" for some time. As the medical profession became more specialized and demanded ever more sophisticated drugs, Marion Laboratories began the intensive search for drugs or new applications of existing compounds to complement its strongest markets—internal medicine, obstetrics, and cardiology. Kauffman's selection of Sperry as sales manager was tacit confirmation of a new strategy and direction for Marion Laboratories.

Just as Marion Laboratories changed during the decade of the 1950s, Kauffman's goals also changed. He had started with the idea of creating a fair and equitable working environment that would produce a good standard of living for his family and the men and women who were associated with him. Now the goal was to become a major competitor in the pharmaceutical industry, but without sacrificing the principles on which Marion Laboratories had been established. Regardless of how large the company might grow, Kauffman was committed to treating his business associates as he would wish to be treated, and to sharing the rewards with those who helped produce them. Once he decided to become a major competitor in the pharmaceutical world, the next step followed logically: Marion began looking for new products.

Even though he had been in the pharmaceutical business for more than a decade, Kauffman had not developed an internal scientific research capacity within Marion Laboratories. He had neither the funds nor the personnel necessary for doing hard science in pharmacy. Instead, the firm often purchased applied research from organizations such as Midwest Research Institute in Kansas City or provided grants to universities to assist in their research programs. They had also begun to license a few products from other pharmaceutical houses. But as late as 1962, Marion Laboratories was still introducing products developed from a staff member's after-hours study of the scientific literature, a manufacturer's suggestion, or from Kauffman's discussions with a friendly physician who was seeking a certain treatment for a specific complaint.

In an attempt to bring some kind of order to this informal and unorthodox process of discovery and development, Kauffman created a "new products committee" in the early 1960s. The members were Kauffman; Sperry, sales manager; Danielson, vice president for research; Dr. A.R. Haskell, Marion's technical director in charge of clinical trials; and George Grinham, whose duties ranged from marketing and public relations to personnel relations and export. Kauffman designated Danielson as head, but it was never a formal process. They all gathered from time to time in the company cafeteria and shared ideas about what they needed to introduce. As the search for a major prescription product got under way, the committee members read about all the different things that would be available without research. The group agreed on the need for a drug that was already being prescribed, one to which they could add some significant improvement. Then with their formidable sales force, they were sure to succeed.

There seemed to be two likely candidates: salphenisen and papavarine. Kauffman and Grinham thought salphenisen could be marketed as a drug for arthritis because it contained properties to relax muscles and had aspirin for pain. Sperry lobbied for papaverine because it had a good sales story behind it. He was so convinced that papaverine was the right product for Marion Laboratories that he laid his job on the line. Pruitt recalled that Sperry pledged to Kauffman, "Let me introduce it. If it's not successful, I'll resign."

Papaverine was a proven vasodilator. By relaxing the smooth muscle surrounding arteries and arterioles, it enabled the arteries to carry more blood to a given part of the body. The only problem was the drug had a short half-life. Within ninety minutes of taking a tablet, its effectiveness began to diminish rapidly. But Marion had perfected a sustained-release method with another product, DUO-TRATE, used in the treatment of angina. Sperry argued that if the sustained-release technology could be married to the drug papaverine, it could be used for certain heart conditions and possibly for stroke victims. Furthermore, the competition was negligible. The only company marketing the drug was Eli Lilly, and it sold only about $50,000 worth per year. Kauffman listened carefully to all the arguments, as the final decision was his. Sperry pushed hard for papavarine and Danielson went along with him. Dr. Haskell, the only pharmacist working for Marion said, "Well, both of them are just concoctions. I don't think it makes too much difference. But I think

I might vote for papavarine." Kauffman, who had initially favored a treatment for arthritis, changed his mind. "Sperry had pushed so hard, was so dogmatic, his mind was closed. So, I said, 'Okay. We'll introduce papavarine.'"

But there was still another hurdle. The people who were to manufacture the drug maintained that ETHAVERIN, an analogue of papaverine, was much easier to make. So they argued, why not use ETHAVERIN. Sperry countered that no one was prescribing ETHAVERIN, but many physicians were already prescribing papaverine. He argued that it was pointless to try to create a market for ETHAVERIN when papaverine was already well established. Convinced of the logic of Sperry's argument, the manufacturer agreed to produce papaverine, which became an immediate sales success. Regardless of how flawed the selection process may have seemed, Kauffman's decision to back Sperry's choice proved fortunate. He knew if Sperry were not enthusiastic about a product, it would not sell well. But PAVABID, as the product was named, was Sperry's pick, and he poured all of his talents and energies into promoting it.

Although Kauffman backed PAVABID because he knew Sperry's total commitment was crucial, he also had another reason. He believed in giving his associates the responsibility and authority to do their jobs, even if it meant making a mistake. When Sperry first returned to Kansas City as sales manager, he approached Kauffman with a new program he wanted to start which would have cost about fifteen thousand dollars. "Boy, it didn't look good to me at all," Kauffman remembered. "It was a lot of money, but we could afford it. But I didn't think it would work." Kauffman took his time before giving Sperry the green light. He asked for a second presentation, reexamined the budget and rethought his concerns about the program's potential for success. Reluctantly, he concluded that he had to authorize Sperry to proceed. "I thought to myself, 'I can say no and he won't do it, but he will always believe it would have worked.' So I said, 'All right, Jean, you go ahead and do it.'" As Kauffman feared, the program failed. But he resisted the natural impulse to blame Sperry for the outcome. When he called Sperry in to analyze why the idea had not worked, he deliberately couched the discussion in terms of shared responsibility. "I said, 'Jean, that program that you and I put in . . . didn't succeed. We didn't figure that one right did we?'" In recounting the story more than three decades later, Kauffman emphasized that an entrepreneur must be willing to give away some of his own authority if the enterprise is to grow. "If you give people responsibility, you must be willing to give them authority. You have to permit them to make a mistake sometimes in order for them to develop themselves for the future." But, he pointed out, it was equally important to know when and under what circumstances to say no. "Now if Sperry's program had cost $100,000, I wouldn't have done it. We couldn't have afforded it."

In the case of PAVABID, the history of Marion Laboratories might have been very different if Kauffman had not backed his general sales manager. In spite of the gloomy prediction of an outside market research firm that PAVABID had the potential to sell only about $100,000 per year, sales mounted quickly, then soared. Kauffman recalled that PAVABID was introduced in December 1962, halfway through the fiscal year, yet sales that year exceeded $200,000. "PAVABID was the big, big . . . first big product for us," he said, remembering the euphoria of those days. "That was the product we were selling when we went public."

Kauffman was correct about Sperry's unflinching commitment to PAVABID. With his usual thoroughness, the sales manager selected five salesmen from various territories to test-market the PAVABID sales literature a week before the product was introduced at the company level. Pruitt and Charles Feld were among the five who were "to call on doctors and find out what their hot button was." They were then to report back to their respective regional sales meetings concerning which points in the literature captured the physicians' interest. The plan was for the literature to arrive at each salesman's home by Friday. The men would have the weekend to study it, a week to test it, and then they would report the results the following Saturday at the regional sales meetings. But, thanks to the U.S. mails, the plan went awry. The material failed to arrive on the designated Friday. Early Thursday morning of the following week, it finally showed up in the seven A.M. mail delivery. There were only two days before the regional sales meetings. Since Thursday was the day that most physicians were out of the office, the chances were fairly slim that many doctors would be around. Pruitt remembered he read the literature quickly and took off for downtown "looking for offices with lights on." Ironically, he and Feld both found only neurologists in their offices at eight A.M. All the cardiologists seemed to be away playing golf or making hospital rounds. In their quick scan of the sales material, both salesmen had noticed the statement on the back page that papaverine was often used for "cerebral ischemia"—lack of quality or quantity of blood to the brain. So they figured they had a sales story that might interest neurologists.

Pruitt's first call was on Dr. Christopher B. Theodoto, a neurologist. He introduced himself to the receptionist and asked her to tell the doctor that he had papaverine hydrochloride in a sustained-release mechanism. Within minutes he was ushered into the physician's office. "I got in there and he nearly took the product away from me." The neurologist told Pruitt he had had experience with papaverine. "I saw my old professor at Kansas University open up a brain, expose a blood vessel, and all he would do is put papavarine topically on that vessel. You could see it relax. I've been looking for something like this for years. Your PAVABID, with its sustained release, just may be the answer to my prayers," the neurologist declared.

That evening, Pruitt called Feld and learned that he, too, had had a similar experience on his first call. Feld, who was located in Detroit, then spent the rest of the day at Wayne State University in the Neurology Department trying his PAVABID presentation on as many interns, residents, and staff as he could find. Even though that first piece of literature had very little scientific data supporting PAVABID's use in cerebral problems, both salesmen encountered almost general acceptance of the sustained-release application among teaching neurologists. They, too, had had experience with papaverine in an intravenous form but found oral tablets ineffective. Pruitt and Feld agreed that when they got to their respective sales meetings on Saturday they would advise the other salesmen to "forget the cardiologists." Their message was simple. Concentrate on neurologists, general practitioners, and internists because they see stroke patients and patients with senility. "Because of the neurologists' [endorsement and] use of PAVABID, it was almost like the heavens opening up and a booming voice saying: 'Attention all GPs and internists . . . prescribe PAVABID!'" Pruitt recalled. Jean Sperry's job was saved, Ewing Kauffman's judgment was confirmed, and Marion Laboratories was on its way to becoming a serious contender in the pharmaceutical world.

As the first half of the decade of the 1960s brought major changes in Kauffman's business career, there were changes in his personal life as well. In March 1961, he was attending a meeting of family physicians in Miami, Florida, when he met the woman who would become his second wife, Muriel Irene McBrien of Toronto, Canada. When Kauffman saw the petite blonde and her mother sunning alongside the Deauville Hotel's pool, he probably never guessed that his life was about to change dramatically.

Muriel was the daughter of Frederick George McBrien and Irene Zella Jarrott. Her father had left home at age thirteen, and by sixteen he had opened Fred G. McBrien's Hardware Store. Seven years later he had branches all over Toronto and began to invest the profits in real estate. At an age when other men were finishing college and beginning their careers, Fred McBrien entered the University of Toronto to study law. He became a barrister and solicitor-at-law and served as a Tory member in the Canadian parliament. Muriel's mother was equally accomplished. Irene McBrien earned a teaching and music degree from the Royal Conservatory of Music in Toronto and was a member of the Toronto Board of Education for more than thirty years, the first woman to serve in that capacity. She was also the first woman director of the Canadian National Exhibition and a leader in a variety of cultural and civic organizations throughout her long life. Her daughter noted that Irene McBrien was a very independent woman "who did not need women's lib."

Both the McBriens imbued their daughter with a spirit of achievement, but she credited her father with challenging her to develop business skills and giving her the experiences that would permit her to feel at ease in a male-dominated business world. "I spent all my time trying to prove to my father I could do everything as well as my [older] brother," she recalled. Muriel's father taught her to write checks at a very early age. When she was sixteen, he financed her first business venture. He bought her a small house to fix up as rental property. When she was eighteen, the father she had idolized died suddenly. With her older brother away at war, Muriel began to manage the family businesses—the law office, an insurance company, and the real estate holdings. After graduation from Ontario Ladies College, she earned degrees in economics and finance from McMaster University.

Muriel McBrien had been widowed two times, and had a teenage daughter from her second marriage. She was also just recovering from a near-fatal automobile accident when she met Kauffman. Her mother, who had become acquainted with him earlier in their stay, introduced them. Muriel's first impression was not favorable. "I didn't care for him at all. I thought he was very forward and asked personal questions that weren't any of his business. He asked how old I was and how much I weighed and all those kinds of things which I wasn't accustomed to from a gentleman." At first Kauffman thought this five-foot-two Canadian beauty was "stuck-up," so he playfully tried to annoy her. But his annoyance soon gave way to admiration. "In the first place, she was a beautiful lady. Second, she was high-spirited. She had a smile, a glint in her eye, and she was intelligent. That intrigued me."

After a rather prickly beginning, they dated a few times in Florida before returning to their respective homes. But Kauffman remained interested. A few weeks later, he flew to Toronto and showed up on Muriel's doorstep. Muriel was giving a dinner party when the houseman announced that there was a man at the door saying he was a friend from Kansas City. "Since the only man I knew from Kansas City was Ewing Kauffman, I said, 'Invite him in and set an extra place at the dining room table,'" she recalled.

Kauffman checked into the Park Plaza Hotel, the closest accommodations to Muriel's home. For the next two weeks he went with her on dates, being introduced as "my friend from Kansas City." As he got to know Muriel better, he became even more impressed with her educational background and her self-assurance. At the end of his stay, he paid her what he considered the supreme compliment: He asked her to become a director of Marion Laboratories. "Your little company?" she sniffed. "I don't have the time." However, she finally relented and agreed to fly to Kansas City to "look it over" before dismissing the offer completely.

Although Muriel seemed uninterested in the directorship, Kauffman had yet another offer in mind. "I'm not very good looking," he told her. "These other men may be younger and have more hair, but I'm smart and I have a whale of a personality. These guys with hair will love you while you're young and pretty, but I'll love you when you're old and crummy." Muriel was smitten with this rather unorthodox proposal. "Put it in writing and I'll consider it," she replied. Kauffman wanted to marry right away, but Muriel reminded him, "The young lady you fell in love with takes care of her responsibilities." There was the green card to arrange so she could work in the United States. There were homes to sell and regulations to be checked with the immigration authorities. Muriel also hoped to find partners for her business interests with her brother, and she was still undergoing physical therapy for injuries sustained in the automobile accident. It was not until later that year that they announced their engagement at an elegant party at the Waldorf Astoria in New York. The prospective groom marked the occasion by giving the bride-to-be a dazzling, eight-carat diamond engagement ring, the first of many lavish pieces of jewelry he would give her in future years.

Ewing Kauffman and Muriel McBrien were married on February 28, 1962, in the chapel of the Village Presbyterian Church in Prairie Village, a suburb on the Kansas side of Kansas City, Missouri. The couple bought a home at 10111 Wenonga and began the process of melding their two families. There were, of course, the usual adjustments for the children, as well as for the adults. Kauffman had two adopted children from his first marriage, and he wanted to adopt Julia Irene as soon as he and Muriel were married. But Irene McBrien objected. "You're taking our daughter. You can't have our granddaughter, too!"

After the wedding, Julia Irene returned to complete her piano and theory studies and examinations at the Royal Conservatory of Music at the University of Toronto. Then she joined the Kauffmans in Kansas City. She had been an only child, so the prospect of having a brother and sister seemed appealing. "I was just elated by it all," she recalled. "I was the oldest and I followed the younger two around because that was such a novelty. [Having] other kids in the house brought a great deal of freedom because there were three to be watched. There were two other messy rooms; two other people to get in on time; two other people to leave dishes out; two other people got phone calls. There were all kinds of good, great things about it to me."

Kauffman and Julia Irene enjoyed a good relationship from the beginning. "I liked him immediately," she recalled. When Julia Irene came to live in Kansas City, Kauffman gave her a car. "And I treated her differently than I did my own," he admitted. "Mine were [younger] and I treated her like an adult. But it was the right way to treat her. She learned so much more. And I was tougher on her. And because I thought she was somewhat like an adult, I made her do things that I probably didn't make [the other] kids do when they got to be sixteen." Kauffman often talked to Julia Irene about various problems at Marion—posing real situations involving inventory control, or personnel, or new construction—to stimulate her thinking and to teach her problem-solving skills. She recalled one such session when Marion Laboratories was constructing a new building. There would be parking lots both in front and behind the building. The question was: which associates should park where? "His answer was, 'Let anybody park where they wanted.' He was constantly driving me with questions that way and I had the wrong answers a lot in those days," she recalled. In addition to trying to develop and hone her ability to solve problems, Kauffman was trying to imbue her with the notion that "treating others as you wanted to be treated" extended to every aspect of the workplace.

Julia Irene seemed to thrive under Kauffman's tutelage. Although her father had left her a comfortable inheritance at his death, Kauffman insisted on providing all her support. He encouraged her to save the monthly allowance she received from a trust in Canada. "Of course, I always bought all the Marion stock [I could afford]," she said. She worked at various jobs throughout the company from doing bulk mailings and packaging tablets on the assembly to taking over the work of executive secretaries when they went on vacation. "He expected a lot, he demanded a lot," she recalled. "And I've always been more than delighted he gave me the experiences."

Blending families has always been a formidable task, and Muriel and Ewing neglected to anticipate the potential problems, especially where their respective children were concerned. "We should have discussed it," Muriel said years later, "but we didn't." Kauffman's children, Larry and Sue, were still grieving for their mother who had died only fifteen months earlier. The decision to send them away to boarding school the fall following her death was understandable given the circumstances. But it was another painful separation not only from their father but from the grandparents whom they loved dearly. Kauffman's remarriage compounded their sense of abandonment. Holidays were the only times they saw their father, and now they had to share his attentions with a stepmother and a new, older sister. Muriel recalled that Julia Irene had an equally difficult adjustment to make. "All of a sudden she had a new daddy, a new brother, a new sister, a new country, a new school, and no friends." Tensions were bound to arise. "Being a stepmother, I think, is the toughest job I've ever done in my life," Muriel said, reflecting on those early years. "If I didn't correct [Ewing's children], my own daughter would say, 'Mother, you're not correcting them. You're not being fair.' It was horrible! You're always wrong. You can't win!" The Kauffmans experienced the usual differences of opinion that arise when strong-willed individuals marry. And blending two families that included three teenage children challenged them both. "I think the biggest argument we ever had was about kids," Kauffman told a reporter in the mid-1970s. "But they're all grown and away from home now, so we don't have that anymore."

After settling the family in its new home, Muriel Kauffman assumed additional duties as treasurer of Marion Laboratories. "It was very exciting," she said, remembering those early days. "I'd never been in the health care industry, and when you could help people with products that made their lives better, it makes you happy." It was not happenstance that Mrs. Kauffman viewed the pharmaceutical industry as a compassionate partner with the medical profession in the healing arts. The near-fatal accident she had survived prior to meeting Kauffman had changed her. While lying in the hospital for two months with a broken back, three broken ribs, a crushed foot, and a concussion, she had become a more sympathetic person. Another three and a half months in a wheelchair had given her time to reflect. "I feel God used the accident to change my life," she said. "Because until then, I had no real sympathy for people who hurt or had medical or health problems. I had never been particularly compassionate. But [the accident] made me feel more sympathetic to others."

Muriel quickly established a warm relationship with Effie Kauffman Smythe, Kauffman's mother, who had remarried after the divorce. Muriel knew that his mother had been an inspiration to him as a young boy, and she knew her influence on his values. Muriel admired the special bond between mother and son, and she was always thoughtful and considerate to his mother, her husband recalled. But there was a longer period of time before Muriel felt really comfortable socially in Kansas City. "I found the people very friendly, but a little insular in their outlook," she remembered. "They thought a woman's place was in the home. But I was a business and professional woman and most of the people in Kansas City were not accustomed to a lady like me. I'd spent all my life in a man's world and I had a lot of lady friends in Canada, who I'd gone to school with, but in my courses, I was the only woman."

Muriel and Ewing Kauffman were both outgoing individuals, but their ideas about how to spend recreational time clashed from the beginning. Mrs. Kauffman recalled, "When we first got married, Ewing would go to parties. Not that he liked them, but he'd go." Later on as his health declined and his energy level diminished, Kauffman rarely accompanied his wife in the social whirl she loved. "I'm used to being by myself, having been a widow so many times. It really doesn't bother me," she would reply when people asked why she went to social functions without him. "I'm always the un-claimed treasure wherever I go!"

When the couple entertained, it was usually a relatively small dinner party at home. Kauffman, who relished any kind of com-petitive activity, liked to break the ice with parlor games. One night the guests might have to find their dinner partners by matching fa-mous quotations and their authors. Another evening they might have to identify a historical event being described in a well-known quote. Or they might be given only a date and asked to identify the event that had occurred on that day. As the years passed, Kauffman preferred evenings reserved for reading or playing computer chess more and more. Often if Mrs. Kauffman hosted a party at home, he would greet the guests at the door, then discreetly slip upstairs. Mrs. Kauffman also learned early in their marriage that her husband "wasn't much interested in the arts or music or the [cultural] things that I was very interested in. Where music is concerned he knows 'The Star Spangled Banner,' 'Onward, Christian Soldiers,' and 'Take Me Out to the Ball Game'!" But Kauffman always encouraged his wife's participation on boards supporting arts and cultural activities in Kansas City, and Mrs. Kauffman became a generous patron and fund-raiser for a wide range of cultural and educational endeavors. At every opportunity she reminded her husband, as well as other Kansas City business and civic leaders, "To attract top executives, you need other things besides baseball and football. You need the arts."

Over the years, the Kauffmans built a stable and enduring relationship. "They seemed to blend an ideal combination of together-ness and separateness," a local observer wrote in the early 1970s. Muriel had a flair for fashion and Kauffman gladly bowed to her expertise and taste in dress and in decorating. "I do not buy one sin-gle article of clothing I wear," he said. "Nothing! She picks it out and if she buys 'em, I wear 'em." He also gave her free rein to select the furniture, paintings, and interior decoration for Marion Laborato-ries when he built a new headquarters in 1973, and for the entire Royals baseball stadium and complex of offices. "She's decorated all of that. And I never have questioned anything because I have such confidence in her ability," he said with pride.

Muriel Kauffman's first priority was creating a comfortable, re-laxing home environment for her husband. After Marion Labora-tories became a publicly traded company, Mrs. Kauffman decided the family needed a larger home, nearer to downtown. They also had the cash from the public sales of Marion stock which would permit them to live and entertain in a grander style. "I didn't like it away out there [in the suburbs]. I felt like I was in the country, and I was a big-city girl." The house she selected was one befitting a suc-cessful entrepreneur. Located on the crest of a hill in the exclusive Mission Hills area, it was a massive stone and brick mansion de-signed in the Lombardi Italian style. There were seven bedrooms, eight bathrooms, five fireplaces, three kitchens, a ballroom in the basement, and an organ room with a full-size church organ. Kauff-man's first reaction was not enthusiastic. "Oh, it looks like a mau-soleum," he groaned. But she assured him, "When I get finished with it, you'll love it." And love it he did. Years later, when all the children were gone, Mrs. Kauffman occasionally suggested moving to a smaller, more manageable place. But Kauffman staunchly re-sisted, "No, I'm not moving!"

After their marriage, the Kauffmans quickly settled into a domes-tic routine, and their partnership extended to the corporate world as well. To avoid the stiff formality of addressing one another as Mr. Kauffman and Mrs. Kauffman in business settings, yet wishing to maintain a professional attitude and environment, the couple began using the first initial of their surname. They quickly became known affectionately at Marion Laboratories and in the press as Mr. K and Mrs. K. Muriel had declined a seat on the Marion board, but after her marriage she accepted the position of treasurer at Marion Laboratories. The couple consciously managed their activities to avoid the conflicts that often occur when spouses work together. "Mrs. K and I work together effectively because we recognize each other's authority," Kauffman told an interviewer in the early 1970s. "There are phases of business where I am especially proficient and she recognizes those. On the other hand, her talents are in economics, law, interior decorating, and other areas—and I respect her for that." He also noted as the scope of Marion Laboratories' activities had grown, "Mrs. K and I don't have close interplay on the job as we would in a smaller firm." Kauffman also cited another important reason for his wife being closely involved in his business affairs: in the event of his death, she would become the major stockholder in Marion Laboratories.

At the time of Kauffman's marriage to Muriel, the company was poised for major changes. In the early 1960s Kauffman had realized that he needed people with more specialized skills and experience in the pharmaceutical industry if the company was to become a national concern. The only staff member with a degree in pharmacy was A.R. Haskell, the technical director and a member of the new-products team. "And I had not had too much pharmaceutical experience either," Kauffman said. "Mine was mostly selling and now we were manufacturing a little bit and we had started a little research." Many entrepreneurs are initially successful, but fail to respond to changes, however subtle, in the market or are unwilling or unable to associate themselves with other strong, talented individuals. But Kauffman was constantly alert to opportunities, ideas, and especially people who could help to spur growth. Supremely confident of his own abilities, he was not blind to his own inadequacies. He knew that he was the best salesman in the pharmaceutical industry. But he never for a moment pretended to scientific knowledge or boasted of a sixth sense in plotting market strategy. Persons who had specialized knowledge or skills he needed never threatened or intimidated him. Instead he sought them out, wooed them to his enterprise, and then stood aside and let them perform.

Kauffman seemed to have a nose for talent, but was even more successful at motivating people to perform. Cocky executives and respectful clerical assistants all succumbed to his personal warmth. They recognized that Kauffman instinctively cared about them as individuals. "My greatest ability is people-orientation," he said. "I think that is the secret of my success. I care for people. I may not like them, and you can't like everybody, but I do care for them." To illustrate what he meant, Kauffman recalled a purchasing manager whom he had not liked. "As I look back, I think the reason [I did not like him was] because he looked like a kid that beat me up when I was eleven years old. But he did a beautiful job." Kauffman acknowledged that the man worked for Marion Laboratories long enough to become a millionaire through profit sharing and the company's generous stock option program. Later, he ran across this former associate who had become a successful vintner in retirement. "I cared for him and I think the greatest thing that an executive— a leader, or so-called manager—must have is a caring relationship with people. If they know you care for them, they know you expect a lot from them. They will try to live up to those expectations, and if you don't expect much, they will live down to those expectations."

When the company was small and there were few associates, it was easy for Kauffman to know and to establish a personal relationship with everyone. Yet even as Marion Laboratories grew into a large and complex organization, he never lost that personal touch which assured associates that they, as individuals and as a team, were important to him. Often this involved a spontaneous gesture. One secretary recalled a Kauffman Foundation board meeting when Kauffman, well over seventy "and moving slower than he used to," was the first person out of his chair to hold the door for a repairman struggling to remove some defective audio-visual equipment. He might call an associate, asking if he knew why that particular day was important. When the associate said he had no idea, Kauffman would respond jovially, "Why, this is your eighth anniversary with Marion Laboratories!" He would continue the conversation thanking him for his hard work and talking about his particular contributions to the company's success. Sometimes Kauffman made a discreet inquiry about a spouse who was ill and then sent a reassuring word. Or he might send a handwritten thank-you note to the secretary who had cross-stitched a Royals logo for him or autograph a baseball for an associate's elderly mother who lived for the Royals' season. "It all came so naturally to him," remembered Rosemary Godbout, a secretary who joined Marion in 1983. "These were not isolated incidents. There were hundreds of them."

While Kauffman was accessible to Marion associates and desired to create a caring environment, he was scrupulous about separating business relationships from social ones. He and Charlie Hughes were closer than most brothers, but during the years that Hughes was Kauffman's most trusted associate in the company, they deliberately did not see one another outside of business hours or at business-related functions. "Yet we always knew in our hearts we were still each other's best friend."

Beginning in the mid-seventies, the company began holding quarterly "Marion on the Move" meetings for all associates. Originally conceived to prepare associates for relocating to Building C, the format was so successful that Kauffman began using it to share the results of the previous quarter's performance and to focus on goals for the coming months. These meetings were crucial to reinforce the sense of caring about one another and for everyone to recommit to the team effort. Godbout attended her first "Marion on the Move" meeting after being on the job only two weeks. She admitted being skeptical of all the talk among fellow associates about the "Marion Spirit." The meeting was in the auditorium of the Baptiste Junior High School, a building that had been renovated to accommodate Marion's growing research-and-development staff. "Here were all these people talking about all this spirit, and I just thought, Hmmmmm," she remembered. "Then Mr. K got on stage and people stood up and clapped loudly. I'm looking around and I'm thinking, 'Wow! This is kind of like a cult. I'm not sure I like this.'" Three months later when Godbout attended her second "Marion on the Move," she was at ease. "I didn't feel in any way, shape, or form that it was a cult or a commune. I felt very comfortable clapping." By the third meeting, "I noticed I was leading the clapping!" she said.

Godbout recalled that at first it was hard to define the "Marion Spirit" that all the associates talked about. But she soon began to understand that it was an accumulation of day-to-day happenings. "It made for a teamwork situation because everybody felt it. Everyone was uplifted. You'd walk down the hall and people you didn't even know would smile at you and say hello. They knew you were new because they hadn't seen you around. They would chat with you. I had never worked anywhere like that before." Godbout remembered later telling her fellow workers that whenever she answered the telephone, "I answer with the idea that Mr. K could be on the other end. And we should answer every phone call like that." But what impressed her most was Kauffman's pride in the associates and their accomplishments. "He would never take the credit himself. He always said, 'I didn't do it. You did it.' He set his expectations high and we wanted to meet his expectations," she recalled.

While there were extra perks for senior executives and top-producing salespeople, Kauffman instituted a profit-sharing program for all associates very early in Marion's history. Charlie Hughes had been working for Marion Laboratories only a short time when Kauffman announced that he was calling his attorney to discuss establishing a profit-sharing plan. "I'd never heard of such a plan, very few people had," Hughes remembered. Kauffman made an appointment with his attorney, Gene McGannon of Hoskins, King, and McGannon, to work out the details. The general idea was to put a certain percentage of each year's profits into a fund that would later be distributed according to a salary formula. When McGannon asked Kauffman what the plan's vesting period would be, it was clear that he had not settled on the exact time frame. "He said, 'Charlie, you came with me what, in 1952? So let's make it twenty years. That'll be about long enough for Charlie,'" Hughes recalled.

Kauffman believed that the profit-sharing plan was one of the most effective incentive programs the company had. In the early days, the company would put an amount equal to 15 percent of associates' annual salary into their accounts. If associates left of their own volition or were terminated, then the amount they had that was not vested would be split among the associates still in the plan. Turnover among the sales force was very high in those early days, and in later years Kauffman often boasted that those loyal associates who had stayed with Marion had received credit to their personal accounts for as much as 30 to 40 percent of their annual compensation, not just the 15 percent that the IRS permitted.

The profit-sharing fund's value grew, but not quite in the way the founder remembered. The reality was that if people left the company before being vested, their forfeitures were used to reduce Marion's contributions. This resulted in the company not having to make a contribution during most of the late 1960s and early 1970s because the forfeitures at the higher stock value covered the maximum 15 percent contributions the IRS allowed.

It was easy to espouse the virtues of profit sharing in those early years of steady growth. But the test of Kauffman's commitment to the principle of sharing the rewards did not come until the mid-1970s when the share price began to decline and sales slumped. "I remember that . . . I had to tell the associates that we couldn't put 15 percent into the profit-sharing program. We could only put 11 percent in because we didn't make enough money." But Kauffman promised that when market conditions improved, he would make it up. For the two succeeding years, profits were such that he added only 11 percent one year and 12 percent the next. By the time profits improved to the point that the company could pay in 15 percent as well as make up the shortfall of the previous three years, there had been so much turnover that legal restrictions prohibited retroactive contributions for persons who had not actually earned the profits. Yet Kauffman was determined to keep his word to those who had stayed through the bad times and had worked so hard to help Marion return to profitability. He had founded Marion on promises, and he was committed to keeping faith with his associates. "So just to take care of the people that we owed it to in my judgment, why, we wrote out checks to them. I presented them checks for the difference between eleven and fifteen."

The profit sharing, the generous sick leave, educational and vacation benefits, and the stock-options plan—the latter of which came after the company went public in 1965—were all powerful incentives for accelerated performance. But the intangible ways in which Kauffman motivated people were equally valuable. As employees and facilities multiplied, Kauffman was concerned about retaining the convivial, family-like atmosphere that had always characterized Marion Laboratories. As the company grew, he continued to work as hard to motivate Marion associates as when he was the single sales representative, president, and chief executive officer of fledgling Marion Laboratories. For the first fifteen years or so, he met for a half hour or longer with each new associate as a part of their orientation. As Marion grew, time pressures and complex schedules forced him to begin meeting informally with small groups in which two or three of the participants might be newly hired personnel. These sessions gave him an opportunity to communicate his philosophy of teamwork. He might ask one participant when and why he first thought about coming to work for Marion Laboratories; another to name the employee benefit she valued most. He often shared anecdotes from the company's early history so the new associates could develop a sense of continuity with what had gone before. It was also a time to learn about people's families, their ambitions, and aspirations for the future.

He understood that it was important to morale that employees see the company founder, shake his hand, have the opportunity to ask him a question or share the good news of a family milestone. Warm embraces between old friends and misty eyes marked some of the visits, for Kauffman was a sentimental and affectionate man, not embarrassed to show emotion. Throughout his entire active tenure as chief executive officer, Kauffman did "walk-throughs" on a regular basis. With old-timers, he might stop briefly to chat about their families or some special hobby he knew they enjoyed. With newer employees, he might ask them to explain some aspect of their job. The result was to reinvigorate and remotivate people who were already doing a terrific job. People thought "this guy is really interested in us." And he genuinely was. This was one additional way that Kauffman could demonstrate how much he cared for his associates.

Marion Goes Public 6

In the 1960s, PAVABID was for Marion Laboratories what OS-CAL had been in the previous decade. When PAVABID was introduced in December 1962, the company's net sales were almost three million dollars. Four years later, they had grown to eight million dollars. By the end of fiscal year 1970, net sales passed the thirty-million-dollar mark. Market analysts had gloomily predicted that PAVABID would do well to sell $100,000 a year, but by 1970 it was Marion's leading product, accounting for 45 percent of sales. The associates of Marion Laboratories were giving life to their founder's message in the first annual report when he had written, "One of the basic purposes of Marion Laboratories is to cause common men to do uncommon things."

How was it possible for a pharmaceutical company that was essentially a marketing enterprise—a company that invested no resources in research to produce new drugs, but reformulated existing compounds and licensed drugs that others had developed—to become so successful? Kauffman attempted to explain this conundrum to Marion shareholders in 1966 by posing several questions: "What is the difference between a mediocre company and a good one? And even more important, what is the difference between a good company and an excellent one?" The best companies, he maintained, were not necessarily the ones with the biggest research efforts, the most sophisticated training programs, the largest marketing departments, or the most complex and voluminous charts and graphs. "The best company," he wrote, "is one in which a favorable environment reflects management philosophies which one trusts and respects, an absence of restraints limiting individual development, and assurance to the individual of recognition, opportunity, and fair treatment." In Marion's first year as a publicly traded company, Kauffman wrote of leading the industry, of setting the pace in profits and products, and of associates with a "glowing enthusiasm for work and life." He closed that first report to new stockholders with the ringing tones of an Old Testament prophet. "Lift your eyes and look far beyond. . . . There is only one way to pursue our future and that is to move forward, looking to see where we are going—not where we have been."

If those words had not come from Ewing Kauffman's mind and pen, they could have easily been dismissed as the scribbling of an overwrought publicist. But they were vintage Kauffman, grounded in his life experience, authentic and inspiring. Kauffman was determined that Marion Laboratories was going to the top, or as near to the top of the pharmaceutical industry as it could climb. As the profits from PAVABID began to roll in, he began planning for expansion. The first priority was to find suitable property for future facilities. It was imperative that the company relocate because of the ever-present threat of flooding from the Blue River, and it was crowded at the Swope Industrial Park facility after only two years. Portions of the enterprise were already being conducted in leased space elsewhere. Kauffman planned to combine all Marion activities in one location. But as usual money was tight. Losses sustained in the 1961 flood, plus the costs of getting PAVABID to market, had strained finances. Then expanding both the sales force and the manufacturing process to respond to an ever-growing demand for PAVABID stretched resources even more. Kauffman turned to his father, who was retired and living in Kansas City, to help him find a suitable location for expansion. He hoped to acquire the needed land for a reasonable price, but above all it must not be susceptible to flooding.

John Kauffman combed the area and finally decided to show his son a parcel of fifty acres located at 103rd Street and U.S. Highway 71 South. The land his father was recommending for Marion Laboratories' future corporate headquarters was made up of several lots zoned for residential construction, some vacant ground, and a sewer lagoon. On the drive out to look at the property, the younger Kauffman became concerned. "It smelled terrible," Kauffman recalled. "I told Dad we just couldn't move there." The senior Kauffman reminded his son that it would be several years before they could afford to build and make a move. When that time arrived, the city would probably have sewers in place and the lagoon could be drained. "So we bought the land for two thousand dollars an acre, which was very, very cheap then. And the sewers did come out there. We drained the lagoon, put in fish, and there's a beautiful lake there today," Kauffman said. A short time after the purchase of the initial acreage of what became known as Marion Park, Kauffman bought an adjacent seventy-five acres. "So we had plenty of acres very inexpensively," he said. In purchasing land for future expansion, Kauffman was doing what he challenged the associates to do: "Look to see where we are going—not where we have been."

With increased earnings from PAVABID, Kauffman decided to augment the already-generous benefits package Marion associates enjoyed. Hughes recalled, "He wasn't greedy. One thing he did not do—to his credit —he did not bleed the company which so many men have done. He was always trying to further the employee situation. Continuously, as profits would warrant, [he] would increase benefits." The profit sharing plan had been in place since 1956. In 1964, Marion's board of directors agreed to his request for a disability compensation–salary continuation plan to supplement the existing health care benefits. "I had hired on promises," Kauffman recalled. "I told people that if they would come to work for me, someday they would have an automobile, hospitalization, profit sharing, disability compensation, and stock ownership. They lived on faith." The mounting PAVABID profits on top of the stable base the calcium products provided meant that another promise could be redeemed.

While Kauffman was acquiring land and developing new benefits programs, he also began pondering the idea of "taking the company public." He held about 60 percent of the stock, but over the years he had permitted Marion associates to buy in. By the early 1960s, a substantial majority of Marion associates had become stockholders. For many, it was their only significant asset. The problem, as with all private companies, was that the stock had no value on the open market.

How would he feel in the associates' position, he wondered? "The associates who owned stock couldn't sell it to anybody. They couldn't borrow money on it. If we fired them, they had to sell it back, and if they quit they had to sell it back," he said. Viewed from that perspective, it was not a deal that he would want for himself. Many of his friends who had joined him at Marion and had worked so hard to make the company grow had their life savings in the company's stock. "Charlie Hughes, especially, had nothing outside of the stock he had accumulated over the years," Kauffman recalled. Hughes remembered that in the early years he received a salary, and if sales goals were attained, a modest bonus. It was his habit to use part of the money for the annual family vacation. With what remained, he purchased stock. "I was paying fifty dollars a share in those days, and they weren't worth five cents!" Hughes admitted that he invested all his extra cash in Marion stock without his wife's knowledge. "I went so far as to cash in an insurance policy one year and bought stock," he said. "I would buy whatever number shares I could because I was convinced of three things. One, that we were good friends. Secondly, that I was investing in a man. And third, of course, I was on the scene. I could see the growth and see what was happening and how the business was run." The more Kauffman thought about Hughes's situation and the other associates whose assets were all in Marion stock, the easier the decision became. "So, I decided, 'We'll have to go public.'"

In recounting the story more than three decades later, Kauffman seemed to be reliving each detail of the initial encounter with officers of Smith, Barney and Company, the brokerage house selected to handle the sale. First they instructed him to bring Marion's financial records for their review. "They looked at them and said, 'You can't go public now; you're not making enough.'" Kauffman responded that he did not intend to offer Marion stock for sale at the moment. "I want to go public in about three years, say 1965. Tell me what I need to do."

Smith, Barney's concern was Kauffman's auditor, a small Kansas City firm. Its work was accurate and its fees reasonable, but the New York brokers said Kauffman needed the experience, as well as the cachet, of a national firm, preferably one of the "big eight" accounting organizations. "So we changed auditors to Peat, Marwick and Mitchell," Kauffman said. The next obstacle was the crucial one and would take longer to resolve. Marion was not yet earning sufficient profits to be attractive in the publicly traded stock market. Even so, PAVABID sales were exceeding all predictions, and the prospects for continuing growth looked very promising. "You will need to make at least $300,000 in profits," the advisers announced. Then, they began to probe. They asked Kauffman to project how much he would earn the following year. "So I gave them a little lower figure than I knew I was going to earn," Kauffman confessed.

The following year Smith, Barney's counselors expressed surprise at the increase in profits. "Why, that's more than you said you were going to earn!" they exclaimed. "Yeah, we're pretty good," Kauffman responded with just the right blend of farm boy modesty and Midwestern pride in his voice. When asked to project profits for the second year, Kauffman again stated a figure that he knew the sales force could exceed. "I said our profits would be so much, then every year I would earn more than I told them," he recalled.

When Kauffman returned to Smith, Barney at the end of the second year, having come very close to the $300,000 goal, he was in for a shock. The executive who was reviewing Marion's records that year was an Englishman, "kind of stiff-laced and sour-pussed," he recalled. He told Marion's founder that the Securities and Exchange Commission had raised the threshold for companies wishing to sell stock to the public. Marion would have to produce $500,000 in profits to qualify. Kauffman was visibly irritated. Whether this broker was condescending to a farm boy from Missouri or the criteria had changed that much was irrelevant. Kauffman was confident his sales force could produce the profit level needed and more. But he had no intention of dealing with the haughty Englishman again. Before leaving New York, he announced coolly, "I'll have my interview with somebody else next year."

When Kauffman returned the third year, Fred Frank was assigned to handle Marion Laboratories. It was the beginning of a trusting and cordial business relationship. Frank reviewed the financial statements and assured Kauffman that the company was now earning enough to go "over the counter." What Frank saw must have been astonishing to everyone except Kauffman. When Smith, Barney first reviewed Marion's sales and profits for the fiscal year ending June 30, 1963, volume had reached $2 million with profits of approximately $53,000. In fiscal 1964, sales rose even higher and profits surpassed $130,000. Although growing steadily, net profits were still far short of the new goal of $500,000. Then the big spurt came. Largely because of the success of PAVABID, volume reached almost $4,800,000 in the twelve-month period ending June 30, 1965. Net profits soared to well beyond the $500,000 threshold. Marion Laboratories was ready to take its rightful place among

America's publicly owned companies. The first stock offering would be "over the counter" and then, within four years, Marion would be listed on the big board, the New York Stock Exchange.

Frank had warned Kauffman that preparing a public stock offering was a tremendous and costly job, and it was. But by late July 1965, most of the details had been completed. The underwriting team, headed by Smith, Barney and Company, planned to offer 187,470 shares to the public by mid-August. The *Wall Street Journal* reported that the combined offering consisted of 87,050 shares from Ewing and Muriel Kauffman. If they all sold—and everyone anticipated that the sale would be oversubscribed—the Kauffmans' ownership position would still be secure, though reduced to about 50 percent. The remaining stock was to come from a percentage of the holdings of seventy-eight Marion employee-shareholders and from the employees' profit-sharing plan.

Excitement mounted at Marion Laboratories and elsewhere in Kansas City as the day for the public stock offering approached. Nerves were frayed and tempers occasionally flared. "But finally we had everything settled; all the legal work was done," Kauffman said. "We were ready to go public." The night before the sale the Kauffmans met with Smith, Barney officials in New York to make the crucial decision—the sale price of the stock. The consensus was to offer the stock at twenty-one dollars a share. Kauffman, ever the salesman, countered, "If you want to cut it to twenty and a half, it's all right with me.' I wanted to give the stockholders a ride for their money," he recalled. Fred Frank dismissed the suggestion. "That's a hatcheck figure," he commented. "We don't want that. We'll just sell it at twenty-one." When the stock market opened on August 19, 1965, the first bid for Marion stock was twenty-eight dollars. "It never dropped below that price," Kauffman said, recalling the euphoria of that day. "We had sold it for less [to the underwriters] but the main thing was that everybody was happy that bought it."

In recalling that heady time, Kauffman remembered that some who had wanted to invest in Marion while it was still a private company might not have been so joyful. Shortly before the public offering, he confided to Frank, "I have some friends who want to buy Marion stock." Frank counseled him to deflect those entreaties. "It's the wrong thing to do to sell to your friends, because if the price goes down, they'll hold it against you," he cautioned. "Instead, it went up!" Kauffman recalled with a sigh. "Even my father didn't buy any at twenty-one!"

Kauffman was understandably disappointed because he was eager to share the good fortune with everyone, especially his family and friends. But his father, for whom Kauffman had set aside a handsome allotment of Marion stock when the price was at three dollars a share, did reap the benefits of Marion Laboratories becoming a publicly traded company. He just missed that adrenaline rush of actually buying on that special day. "It was thrilling, nonetheless," Kauffman recalled, his eyes alight with good memories. "And then that night I remember Fred Frank took us to the French Buffet where we had a big celebration dinner."

The celebration in New York may have been elegant, but the festivities in Kansas City were beyond comparison. Pruitt recalled that each shareholder in Marion had to sell 25 percent of his holdings. "What a celebration we had that night! Associates who had previously lived on a shoestring now had thirty or forty, yes, some had $100,000. And just think what [going public] did to our profit-sharing plan!" he exulted. All the anxiety that Helen and Bob Pruitt had felt that day in 1955 when they stood across from the tiny building on Troost and decided to cast their lot with Ewing Kauffman faded from memory. The years of buying Marion stock instead of a new sofa or a late-model car had been worth it. The men and women of Marion had worked with messianic zeal. Salesmen kept calling on doctors long after the competition had retired to the local motel for dinner and bed. Whole families had devoted their weekends to helping package samples for Dad's Monday morning sales calls Marion associates and their families had been tempered in the fire of intense competition and had survived an actual flood which bound them even more closely as a team. And Kauffman had kept them motivated with their eyes set on the distant prize of security. He had also kept his word and his promises. Now, with the wealth and the renewed energy that the public sale of stock had generated, all those dreams pinned to Marion Laboratories might actually come true.

The public sale of stock produced the infusion of cash Kauffman needed to accelerate the program of long-term growth he had begun to formulate in the late 1950s. The plan was straightforward: expand the sales organization, augment the salesmen's training, and keep them motivated; plan and build the facilities necessary for growth; enlarge the research effort; and, most important of all, find the products to keep the profits flowing. Kauffman had taken the first crucial step toward becoming a national contender in the pharmaceutical business in 1959. For him it may have been the most difficult one. That was the year he brought Sperry back to Kansas City as general sales manager in his place. He recognized that if Marion Laboratories was to grow, he must be willing to share authority as well as responsibility. He also understood the imperative to find and attract other executive talent, preferably persons with experience in the pharmaceutical industry. They could help him learn, as well as grow.

Sales were Marion Laboratories' lifeblood, so it was natural that Kauffman would want to augment his own strength there first. In 1962 he had recruited Warren Perryman, an executive with Meade-Johnson, to serve as vice president for sales and marketing. Upon his arrival, Perryman immediately recognized Sperry's capabilities and the salesmen's loyalty to him. He gave Sperry carte blanche to continue recruiting new personnel and opening new territories for Marion's products. Perryman focused his own energies on developing a long-term, cohesive marketing strategy for Marion's product line. In reviewing the history of the sales force with Kauffman and Sperry, Perryman concluded that the major reason for the relatively high turnover was the haphazard and sporadic training the salesmen received. Kauffman had always acknowledged that this was one of his own shortcomings. During the mid-fifties, many of the salesmen were making outrageous claims for their products. Fortunately, a friendly doctor or another colleague might take the novice under his wing and teach him how to communicate effectively with physicians.

In Pruitt's case, he had been his own teacher. Although he had only minimal science education during his three years at Missouri State Teachers College, he was curious about pharmacological questions. He was never satisfied with the information in the company brochures. There always seemed to be questions the sales material did not answer. In 1955 when he started with Marion, he traveled a great deal in the St. Joseph, Missouri, area. In the evenings, instead of retreating to a depressing motel room, Pruitt went to the local hospital library. There he read up on calcium therapy, treatment for angina, or any other medical subject relevant to Marion's product line. Later, when he was transferred to Columbus, Ohio, he took advantage of the resources in the Ohio State University medical school library and of the faculty as well. He became so conversant with the scientific literature that he began holding technical sessions for fellow salesmen at their regular regional meetings.

Sales training improved somewhat when Sperry took over as sales manager in 1959. Pruitt recalled that Sperry might gather a group of six new salesmen and talk to them in his office for an hour. Then he would go to another executive's office and, if he was not busy, he would ask that individual to talk with the recruits about his span of responsibility. "The disadvantage [of this approach] was that you didn't have any idea what Jean had said and he had no idea what you were going to tell them," Pruitt recalled. One of Perryman's first decisions was to assign Pruitt to develop a formal, structured sales training program. Perryman recognized the value of having a sales veteran training new recruits. Bob Pruitt was an excellent choice, with the right mix of sales savvy and scientific curiosity needed for the job. At the same time, Pruitt also assumed full responsibility for exhibits, contracts, and other details involving Marion's participation in any professional meeting.

Shortly after the company became public in 1965, Perryman decided to retire and enjoy the freedom his new wealth afforded. Kauffman, for whom every aspect of Marion Laboratories was intensely personal, felt betrayed. He had given Perryman the opportunity to join Marion as the company was preparing to go public. And he had counted on him to help sustain the momentum. When Perryman announced he was taking the money he had made in the public sale, retiring to California, and taking up avocado ranching, Kauffman was stunned. At the very moment when he needed an experienced executive trained at a highly successful pharmaceutical house, Perryman faded into bucolic retirement. So Kauffman turned again to a trusted colleague and promoted Sperry to vice president for sales. However, he split off the marketing and planning functions that had been a part of Perryman's former position. The challenge then was to find just the right person for those responsibilities.

With the introduction of PAVABID and the ongoing search for additional new products designed for medical specialists, Kauffman recognized the need to expand the company's communication with these potential clients. The sales force was excellent in personal visits with physicians, but he decided that there needed to be additional follow-through. He began toying with the idea of investing in some advertising to reinforce the message about Marion's quality and to build name recognition. "At that time I had never spent a dollar advertising in medical journals or advertising any of my products. I thought it was a waste of time [and money]. The way to get doctors to use our products was through salesmen," he recalled. Perhaps, upon reflection, it was time to make some changes.

While Kauffman was mulling over all these thoughts, he met Malcolm M. Dalbey, an executive with Neisler Laboratories, Inc., a pharmaceutical company located in Decatur, Illinois. Kauffman was impressed with Dalbey and some of the things he had done from a marketing standpoint. At Kauffman's request, Sperry flew with him to Chicago and participated in the interview. In spite of Sperry's reservations, Kauffman hired Dalbey. He believed Dalbey's strength in marketing and advertising, as well as his pharmaceutical experience, complemented his own and Sperry's expertise in sales. In getting to know Dalbey, Kauffman had observed that he seemed to have a special talent for analyzing doctors' requirements. He had a knack for determining the reason physicians would use a particular product. This kind of knowledge was crucial in deciding on new products and planning how to introduce them to the medical profession. "Mac" Dalbey joined Marion Laboratories in March 1966, with the impressive title of executive vice president. His primary responsibilities were planning and marketing. "I was not preparing him for the eventual role of CEO," Kauffman said. "I was still in my early fifties and had no idea of leaving the CEO position. His title was solely to cover any type of duties that I might want to give him."

Dalbey was a large man with a tendency to be bombastic. Some of his fellow associates remembered him as having to be "top dog all the time." Kauffman recalled that he was "a little bit uncouth in his language" as well. Whatever his personal shortcomings, Dalbey successfully launched Marion's first advertising program. He also recruited Al Mannino and Stu Gold, both of whom played key roles in Marion's growth in the subsequent decades. Kauffman credited Dalbey with "the idea that there were new products overseas in pharmaceutical companies that were not being sold in the United States, and that we should scour the world to license them." And scour the world they did. All of Marion's major moneymakers— GAVISCON, SILVADENE, CARAFATE, and CARDIZEM—were to come through licensing, rather than research.

When Sperry became vice president for sales in 1966, he and Kauffman agreed that he should focus his attention on finding the salespeople they would need to become a national company. He inaugurated Marion's college recruiting program, which required all of the field managers to spend several days a year on college campuses in recruitment. While Kauffman and Sperry were interested in people with some science courses among their college credits, they were not looking for pharmacists or those with a lot of biology. Kauffman always urged Sperry to look for people who not only had good sales personalities, but who had done something during their college years in selling. They also concentrated their search on people who were doing some part time work related to sales. Sperry's initial approach to recruitment differed little from Kauffman's except that he began interviewing and hiring more college graduates.

For a time in the mid-sixties, Sperry instructed Marion recruiters to concentrate on hiring teachers. This was a period when colleges and universities were turning out an excess of students with degrees in education, and many were unable to find teaching jobs. It seemed reasonable to assume that teachers would make strong pharmaceutical sales representatives because they could learn quickly and were already accustomed to teaching. Then he toyed with the notion of trying to hire M.Ds. He was particularly intrigued with the idea of hiring British physicians after reading about a small town in southern Missouri that had lured an entire clinic of English doctors, assuring them much better pay than they were then earning under socialized medicine. Sperry proposed to offer British physicians a guaranteed salary of twenty-thousand dollars a year plus a car if they would give Marion Laboratories two years service as sales representatives. Kauffman, somewhat reluctantly, agreed to the plan. He understood the importance of permitting an executive to experiment with new approaches as long as the costs were within reason. Fortunately, Sperry abandoned the plan when he got word of opposition within the British Medical Association.

Even without the addition of the illusory British physicians with their upper-class accents, Marion Laboratories grew at an astonishing pace throughout the 1960s. By the end of the decade, the goal of national market coverage was almost within sight. Starting with 117 salesmen in 1966, Sperry had 241 representatives in the field at the close of fiscal 1970. They were aggressive, competitive, productive, and young—the average age was under thirty. Those who survived the grinding pace—and many did not—always seemed hungry for more. Kauffman often boasted that "the typical Marion representative completed almost twice as many doctor interviews as his average competitive counterpart."

There were concrete reasons why Marion sales representatives were more productive than was typical of the industry. Kauffman gave special attention to every aspect of sales motivation. He talked frequently with Sperry and the regional managers about specific problems they might be experiencing with the salesmen, and they brainstormed probable solutions. The Marion M Club was developed from that scenario. As the company began to grow rapidly in the mid-sixties, there were more demands on the sales force. As those demands grew, there were the usual problems of keeping the salesmen happy and keeping their families content, as the men were away for most of the week. Kauffman had always believed that a happy and supportive home life was necessary to free a salesman to concentrate fully on his job. For that reason, he balked at hiring bachelors, believing that marriage made a man more stable. In the early years when he was personally doing all the hiring, he always interviewed the wives of serious contenders. Even as late as the mid-seventies, he often requested that a man being considered for an executive position bring his wife so that he might interview them as a couple.

The Marion M Club was a way to recognize the exceptional salesman who did not aspire to a management position. Because the company had so many reward programs for managers, salesmen's wives sometimes became unhappy when their husbands did not seek or were not recruited for management positions. Managers drove Cadillacs while salesmen drove Chevrolets, and ambitious spouses often chafed at other differences in perks. Kauffman and Sperry began to look at how they could develop a professional sales organization within the sales force that carried sufficient prestige to be acceptable as an alternate route to success. They recognized that any such organization would have to be highly selective and membership would have to carry many of the same benefits previously available only to managers.

Membership in the exclusive Marion M Club was limited to no more than 8 percent of the sales force. The criteria for admission included a combination of various existing measures of success plus years of service and the number of Marion rings a salesman earned. Then M Club candidates had to be nominated by the vice president of sales for having met the additional criteria of being a favorable influence on fellow salesmen and being positive people toward Marion Laboratories. Those few who satisfied the nomination process then had to pass muster with the existing M Club membership. Because both Kauffman and Sperry had started their careers as salesmen, they believed that field salesmen often knew things about their colleagues that managers did not. Right up to the end of the process a candidate could be blackballed. Nomination was in no way tantamount to selection.

M Club members and their wives enjoyed many tangible and visible rewards that affirmed their importance to the company. They drove luxury cars, received extra vacation days, and were invited to a special resort club meeting every year with all expenses paid for their wives. They received extra training sessions to keep them fresh and up-to-date on the latest developments in the pharmaceutical industry. During the Kansas City training sessions, the Kauffmans would host social events personally. It might be a reception and dinner in their Mission Hills mansion plus special shopping tours and cultural activities for the wives. Mrs. Kauffman often worked late into the night before such events, personally cooking the dinner, assembling the appetizers, and supervising all the other details from table settings to flower arrangements. This was one of the gracious ways she demonstrated her own respect for the Herculean efforts of the salesmen and the sacrifices of their wives. After the Kauffmans became the owners of the Kansas City Royals, they often entertained M Club members at the stadium with festivities surrounding a game. Marion folklore was replete with anecdotes about the Kauffmans' lavish hospitality extended to their associates.

There were also other little privileges or perks that Kauffman and Sperry designed to show the respect within the company for M Club members' extraordinary contributions to Marion's success. M

Club members enjoyed "open menu" privileges at sales meetings. This meant they could order steak or lobster for lunch even though their colleagues were being served creamed chicken and peas. They also had "bumping privileges" that permitted them to move to the head of any line or take any seat, even if already occupied, at a company function. In order to emphasize and reinforce their prominence in the company, Sperry decided to demonstrate how bumping worked. Kauffman recalled the incident many years later with good humor. It seems that Sperry told one of the more aggressive M Club members that it was his responsibility to bump Ewing Kauffman at the next sales banquet. Seeing Marion's founder ensconced at the head table surrounded by senior executives and invited dignitaries, the salesman boldly stepped forward and announced that he would like to exercise his prerogative of bumping Mr. K. "And he did!" Kauffman recalled with a chuckle.

Kauffman was always sensitive to the need to recognize and celebrate performance. He understood early in Marion's history that cash bonuses were only one part of a reward system. Prior to the M Club's creation, Kauffman had developed the Marion ring as a visible symbol of a salesman's success. Working with Sperry, he set individual sales quotas every year. They tried to set the quotas high enough so that there would never be more than 60 percent of the salesmen who made the goal in any one year. They preferred that only about 40 percent make the target. Each year that a salesman "made quota," he earned a ring or added a precious stone to an existing ring. When the program started, rings were designed to reflect four years of achievement. Before long a new ring was needed to last six years. Finally two rings were created that would last twenty years. During the first year, a salesman earned the ring, then nine diamonds could be added for each year of exemplary service. In the eleventh year, the salesman received a new ring with a one-carat diamond as a center stone signifying the previous decade's accomplishments. Then nine more diamonds could be added. As of 1992, Kauffman noted that no one had yet reached that accomplishment.

Kauffman recalled that very emotional things often transpired involving Marion rings. The ring was a privilege so restricted that even Marion's founder and greatest salesman was not entitled to wear it. Kauffman always made a point of showing them that neither he nor Sperry had a Marion ring. One salesman who was being promoted to a district manager had earned thirteen rings. As a manager, he would never be entitled to earn another. He took the diamonds and gave one, mounted in a new setting, to each of his nine children. With each gift, he included a written account of his career with Marion Laboratories and what that experience meant in the life of each family member. For Kauffman that one story, out of scores of similar stories, was proof of the special joys of sharing the rewards.

The Marion sales force may have looked like an elite corps, and it was. But Kauffman also recognized and acknowledged that every Marion associate was a vital contributor to teamwork and success. He developed generous incentives to keep all Marion associates, not just the salesmen, working at top capacity. Profit sharing had been in place since the mid-1950s, and with the annual gain in profits averaging more than 50 percent from 1966 through 1970, each associate's share grew steadily. In March 1966, the board of directors accepted Kauffman's recommendation to adopt a stock option plan available to all associates. This was a major departure from earlier practice and from industry practice in general. While the company was still privately held, Kauffman would offer stock primarily to executives and high-producing salesmen—usually in lieu of a bonus. "The option available was dependent on the importance of the job the person did for the company," Kauffman recalled. One hundred shares was the minimum option offered, and executives often qualified for up to two thousand shares in those early days of the program. But every associate was included, from the janitor to the chief operating officer.

Kauffman recalled that stock options typically took a period of time to motivate people because the stock price had to increase above the option price. But at Marion Laboratories in the late 1960s, "we had stock splits where the share would double and that would mean that those associates who held options would have their options doubled," he said. Stock splits, coupled with escalating share prices and growth in earnings, compounded the benefits. "Without exception, our associates would purchase their stock options prior to the time they expired," Kauffman remembered with visible pride.

As sales and profits grew in the mid-sixties, new associates were hired and production and packaging facilities were strained to the limits. In the fall of 1965, the new manufacturing plant and administrative offices had been completed at 10234 Bunker Ridge Road, the site which became known as Marion Park. Pruitt remembered the luxury of space after being crammed two to an office at the old location. There were twenty-two private offices, a board room, large quality-control laboratories, a large packaging and manufacturing area, a huge warehouse, a small maintenance shop, and a coffee shop seating fifty people. "What a showplace!" he recalled. Once in the new facility, Marion began manufacturing some of its own products, which were then packaged with state-of-the-art equipment. "No more hot plates for labels," Pruitt rejoiced. "But we still filled liquid bottles by hand . . . but six at a time now!"

The new facility was designed for easy expansion, and within nineteen months bulldozers and construction cranes appeared again. By 1968, administrative offices and plant operations occupied ninety-three thousand square feet of floor space. By the end of the decade, Marion Laboratories was "virtually self-sufficient in the ability to manufacture everything we market," Kauffman proudly announced to the shareholders.

Quality products and the most aggressive sales force in the pharmaceutical business fueled Marion Laboratories' phenomenal growth. The company sold approximately twenty pharmaceutical products in a variety of dosage forms when its stock began to be offered "over the counter" in 1965. The products were clustered in three primary areas. The OS-CAL group, a line of nine calcium products, provided a stable foundation of steady and predictable sales. Marion Laboratories first marketed a calcium tablet for prenatal care in 1951. Over the years other therapeutic agents, and later, hormones, were added for the relief of osteoarthritis and osteoporosis. These calcium products for the expectant mother and the senior citizen built valued customers for the long-term. They provided the foundation for the company's earliest growth. In later years, while less significant as a part of total volume, they sold consistently and well.

The DUOTRATE group of products was to treat cardiac conditions such as angina pectoris and coronary insufficiency. Introduced in 1956, DUOTRATE was soon available in various combinations and dosage forms. The company perfected its plateau cap, or time-release dosage, with DUOTRATE. This refinement meant that instead of taking five or six tablets a day, a patient might be able to take only two or three while the dosage level remained more constant in the system. Relief was more continuous. With fewer pills to take, a patient was more likely to stick with a treatment regimen. This technological breakthrough was to be even more important with PAVABID.

The third major product group was composed of the PAVABID products. With the time-release feature applied to an old drug, papaverine, PAVABID was introduced in 1962 for the relaxation of vascular spasm associated with coronary, cerebral, and peripheral disorders. With PAVABID in their detail kits, Marion salesmen pushed net earnings beyond the million-dollar threshold for the first time in 1966. Once past that hurdle, profits soared.

In the first annual report to the public shareholders, Kauffman outlined Marion Laboratories' strategy "for the months and year ahead." The plan was to build primarily on the strengths of the PAVABID and DUOTRATE groups. There would also be more emphasis on searching out products to be licensed for the U. S. market. And finally, management planned to "make acquisitions in fields related to the talents of Marion's people."

There were sound reasons for building on the strength of PAVABID and DUOTRATE that had roots in the company's first fifteen years of existence. First, PAVABID was the leading money earner. The drug had rapidly surpassed all market projections, even the most optimistic ones of its chief advocate, Jean Sperry. Second, Kauffman wanted to avoid the cyclical business of seasonal remedies, such as cold and allergy medicines. "Since we did not have a patented product at that time, we would have had to spend the salesman's time detailing doctors every year to get them to remember that a year ago they used this product and now was the time to use it again," Kauffman said. And finally, Marion salesmen were well acquainted with the general practitioners and were getting to know cardiac specialists, as well. "These doctors were our best customers and our real customers," Kauffman said. "Coronary and cerebral diseases were quite often handled by the G.P., with whom we had a very good rapport." This was still the era when the general practitioner dominated medicine. The specialists were mostly attached to hospitals, clinics, and medical schools, and their numbers were still relatively small. The average person still went to see the family doctor so familiar to Kauffman from the pages of Lloyd Douglas. Although that would all change over the next twenty years, and the change would pose major challenges for Marion Laboratories, in the mid-sixties the general practitioner reigned supreme.

The strategy that produced PAVABID—identify a well-known drug and enhance its efficacy through technology—had worked so well that Kauffman decided to try to harness the true potential of another well-known standby, nitroglycerin. For almost a hundred years, physicians had been prescribing a nitroglycerin tablet placed under the tongue for the relief of angina. The problem was that relief was transitory. Patients often had to take several tablets a day.

NITROBID, nitroglycerin in a time-release dosage, could be taken just twice a day, with the medication entering the patient's system uniformly over a ten- to twelve-hour period. NITROBID was introduced in January 1966, with a marketing ploy reminiscent of the days of blooming oyster flowers. Each salesman carried a supply of hot pink, cylindrical-shaped boxes about three inches tall with a bit of pipe cleaner sprouting from the top. The object was supposed to look like a small stick of dynamite. When opened, it contained fifteen tiny wooden matches with a strike plate on the bottom of the cylinder. A salesman would walk into a physician's office, open his detail bag, and toss the "stick of dynamite" onto the desk to attract the physician's attention. Since nitroglycerin is the explosive ingredient in dynamite, the analogy was supposed to be apparent. A serious discussion of NITROBID's therapeutic benefits was supposed to follow this unorthodox opening.

The dynamite stick sales gimmick—another promotional piece whose authorship was lost or, at least, denied—disappeared in a few months as the sales force worked to appear more professional and sophisticated. But it was a reminder of the freewheeling early days when Marion Laboratories was an upstart company determined to attract attention and business any way possible in an intensely competitive and somewhat snobbish industry. In spite of the theatrics, NITROBID was quickly and widely accepted among cardiologists. PAVABID with Phenobarbital was also introduced late in the same year and helped to extend that product's use even more.

The combined sales of all Marion Laboratories products was large enough by 1969 to permit the company to list its stock for sale on the prestigious New York Stock Exchange. As Kauffman described that day almost a quarter of a century later, the awesome quality of the occasion could still be seen in his face and heard in his voice.

"That was quite an honor. To think that this farmer boy had started in the basement of his home and was now on the New York Stock Exchange!" The Kauffmans were invited onto the floor of the exchange and permitted to purchase the first one hundred shares that went across the ticker tape. "That moment was somewhat a fulfillment of our growth, although never in my wildest dreams did I ever think that event would occur."

In addition to the excitement of being present on the floor of the exchange that brisk February day, the Kauffmans also had the pleasure of picking the initials for the Marion Laboratories listing. "I wanted MAR for Marion, but that was already being used by Marathon Oil, I think. So we went to MKC, which was Kansas City, Missouri, backwards," Kauffman said. But for those who profited from the stock over the years, the designation would always stand for Marion, Kansas City.

Changing the Corporate Culture 7

Being traded on "the big board" was more than a thrilling experience. It also meant that Marion Laboratories had proven that its business practices were sound enough to attract large investors such as institutional, pension, and trust funds. The nagging question for investors in pharmaceutical stocks has always been "Where are the new products going to come from?" In Marion Laboratories' case, the question was especially bothersome because the company spent a relatively small portion of its resources on research. But Kauffman never ducked the issue. Instead, he usually brought up the subject because he knew the research question was always in the potential investor's mind. In speaking before the Kansas City Society of Financial Analysts in November 1967, he quoted from the *FDC Reports*, the pharmaceutical industry bible, heralding Marion Laboratories as the foremost marketing company in the pharmaceutical industry. Then he asked, "But where is Marion Laboratories going to get new products in the future? What is the research program?"

Having erected the straw man of research, Kauffman delighted in battering it to the ground. Marion Laboratories had a multifaceted research program, he explained. The company's research activities at the Kansas City plant were devoted primarily to insuring the quality of its own products and developing improved dosage forms and combinations of existing drugs. Five universities and scores of private physicians assisted Marion Laboratories in clinical trials. This research had produced the OS-CAL, PAVABID, and DUOTRATE groups, and the most recent big moneymaker, NITROBID. Then he would point to Marion's five-year-old research association with the Department of Pharmacy at the University of Tennessee and recent grants to the University of Missouri for work on drugs affecting the central nervous system. Reining in his natural tendency to "sell" Marion Laboratories at every opportunity, Kauffman did not make unrealistic or insupportable claims about these research ventures. "Is this research worthwhile?" he asked rhetorically. "I don't know yet."

Although Kauffman acknowledged the company's expenditures for research were relatively small compared to the enormous outlays of a Merck, a Lilly, or a Hoffman-LaRoche, he explained that Marion was intensely involved in a worldwide search for new products to license and market in the United States. With Marion's aggressive and productive sales force and their penetration of key prescription markets, the boast was justified. "Our door is knocked on monthly by foreign companies bringing us products because we are recognized as the foremost marketer in the pharmaceutical industry. When we introduce a product, we're going to get more than our fair share."

The summer of 1967, prior to Kauffman's speech to the financial analysts in the fall, Marion Laboratories and the Syntex Corporation of Panama announced an agreement in principle for the Kansas City firm to market various Syntex products in the United States. News of the Syntex deal spurred investors' interest in Marion stock, which gained eleven points in two days to close at sixty-three dollars a share. One Wall Street observer was quoted in the *New York Times* as noting that "the Syntex magic still works." Smith, Barney's analysts concluded in their monthly report to investors that the agreement with Syntex, "in effect, catapults Marion into the equivalent position of a highly regarded research organization." Kauffman was the most bullish of all in predicting success with the Syntex relationship. "I predict Syntex will make $100 million from their stock option and I hope they do, because the rest of us stockholders will make $400 million."

With the exception of FLUONID, a topical steroid introduced in 1969, everyone's predictions about the riches the Syntex licensing agreement would produce were never realized. But FLUONID was a landmark product for Marion because it was the first product to achieve sales of over one million dollars in its introductory year.

Fortunately, other efforts to obtain marketing rights to foreign products did succeed. William T. Doyle, Marion's vice president of corporate affairs, initially headed the global search for products to license. In 1971, James W. Church succeeded Doyle. His charge was to develop new business within the health field, through acquisitions and the licensing of new products, both foreign and domestic. Church joined Marion after serving as vice president for new business development for Meade-Johnson, a division of the Bristol-Myers Company. Like many other executives recruited to Marion in the 1970s, Church had a degree in pharmacy. Kauffman, too, spent a considerable portion of his time and energy in the mid-sixties traveling throughout Europe to persuade foreign pharmaceutical houses to entrust their products to his company's marketing genius.

The antacid GAVISCON, Marion's first licensed foreign product to become a significant moneymaker, was acquired through licensing from the Swedish firm Ferring AB. It was introduced in 1970 at the national meeting of gastroenterologists in New York City. Pruitt, who was now in charge of exhibits for all medical meetings, mused that New Orleans, with its hot and spicy Cajun food, might have been a better place to introduce a new therapy for heartburn. But New York City, with its diversity of ethnic eateries, proved more than adequate. "We were also fortunate to be next to a Coca-Cola exhibit," Pruitt remembered. "GAVISCON required that you chew the tablet, which would create a foam in the mouth. To wash this foam down you needed to take liquid of some form, and Coca-Cola was handy!"

Securing the rights to GAVISCON and bringing the product to the market was a classic instance of how the licensing relationship worked. Church wrote to a number of pharmaceutical firms to determine their interest in licensing products to Marion Laboratories. Ferring AB in Malmö, Sweden, replied affirmatively and forwarded copies of patents, samples, and extensive clinical data on various products. The second step was for all the appropriate departments at Marion to analyze the information. From that study, the drug which was to become known in the United States as GAVISCON was identified as the most likely candidate. All the departments involved in the analysis reported favorably. The technical department saw no major problems. The medical department agreed that the product had unique patient benefits, and market research predicted a promising sales potential.

Next, the new-product-screening committee evaluated position-

ing the product for the U.S. market given the number of potential
sufferers from heartburn caused by hiatal hernia, gastroesophageal
reflux, and esophagitis. Once again the signals were positive. But
there was concern about the product's grayish appearance and less-
than-agreeable taste. So Marion's research-and-development team
concocted a more attractive looking, palatable, chewable tablet. Finally, four medical centers conducted studies to document patient
preferences—tablet versus powder, the product's foaming action, its
effectiveness, and potential side effects, if any. All of this activity,
analysis, testing, and evaluation took only two years following the
initial contact, and less than a year after the appropriate product
prototypes had been developed. Licensing clearly had significant
advantages both in terms of time and money over the industry's
traditional approach. Marion Laboratories had found a way to combine its marketing talents with the scientific work of others for the
benefit of both. This basic approach of licensing and marketing fueled Marion's growth through the next two decades.

GAVISCON's rapid acceptance in the medical community and its
substantial contribution to Marion's growth in sales and profits
proved the merit of this "search and develop" strategy. Pruitt also
noted that the arrangement with Ferring AB was a vivid example
of how Kauffman applied his basic business philosophy to every
corporate activity. Marion continued paying royalties to Ferring for
a number of years beyond the terms of the original agreement.

The licensing strategy was an effective and efficient way for Marion Laboratories to wire around the costly research-and-development process that most pharmaceutical houses employed to obtain
new products. But there were still significant costs involved in acquiring the product rights. By then lengthy and expensive clinical
trials were necessary to obtain FDA approval. Often, by the time a
licensed product reached the marketplace, more than half its patent
protection would have expired. So there would then be a limited
time to recoup the investment before the product was subject to
generic competition. In the competitive pharmaceutical world, an
approach to product acquisition which reduced the up-front investment seemed worthy of careful consideration.

In the 1966 annual report Kauffman had announced the company's intention "to make acquisitions in fields related to the talents of Marion's people." The idea was to marry the company's

marketing and motivational expertise to other health-related enterprises whose products had high profit potential. Acquiring other
companies had not been Kauffman's idea, but he understood the
logic. "Wall Street felt that having 80 percent of our earnings come
from one product, PAVABID, was dangerous," he recalled. "They said
that we should diversify and bring in earnings from other businesses."

Kauffman moved quickly to establish a diversification program.
In 1967, he chaired an acquisition committee of key Marion executives whose job was to locate and screen companies and products
for potential acquisition. He reported to the shareholders a set of
standards against which potential candidates for acquisition would
be matched. "The essential element is to acquire successful, non-
competing companies in health, nutrition, and allied fields, managed by competent people," he wrote in the 1968 annual report.
Marion intended to acquire successful companies with strength
in their specialty markets. That strength might have been gained
through patent positions, proprietary trademarks and products,
strong distributions systems, or from some other aspect of the enterprise which assured profit potential for above average growth.
Kauffman wanted companies headed by aggressive and dedicated
executives with entrepreneurial ability, selling quality products in
a market that was not yet saturated. In turn, Marion Laboratories
would provide a range of services, including financial expertise,
market research, access to capital for "growth by design," plus data
processing, major employee benefit programs, and support in key
management selection and development. And Kauffman would be
available with his innovative business philosophy to shape and articulate the vision, to lead and to motivate as he had done so skillfully with Marion Laboratories.

The acquisition's strategy was state-of-the-art thinking in the late
sixties and seventies about how businesses could grow to become
more profitable. Although Kauffman pursued the strategy vigorously, his first love was the pharmaceutical industry. Understandably, the passion he felt was not easily transferred to other enterprises. But his commitment to the Marion associates and to the
company's future well-being meant he would pursue vigorously
any strategy for the long-term good of "Mother Marion." In recounting the story of the company's diversification he noted, "These

decisions were made solely on the basis that we needed to get extra earnings from other sources."

Over the next decade, Kauffman and his senior executives acquired a dozen companies across the United States selling everything from legume inoculants for the farmer to home stairway elevators for persons unable to manage steps. In response to growing consumer demand for proprietary drugs, they also started efforts to develop in-house products that could be purchased without a prescription. And they stepped up their worldwide search for proven products to market in the United States.

By the fifth year after Marion Laboratories had become a publicly owned company, Kauffman could proudly report uncommon growth. The company had experienced five consecutive years of record sales and earnings. Over that time the consistent annual sales gain averaged 41.4 percent, while the annual gain in earnings averaged 50.3 percent. Shareholder equity for the same period had averaged almost 40 percent. The company had grown from a single pharmaceutical house to a diversified company of associated enterprises serving various markets in health care, agricultural science, and industrial safety. The reputation of Marion's sales force as the most productive in the industry facilitated licensing agreements with major research-oriented corporations. And Marion's enviable cash position meant she could fund additional growth wherever needed without borrowing at high interest rates.

Marion's prosperity also meant that Kauffman was a wealthy man with the resources to acquire a stable of winning racehorses, a mansion, and a baseball team. With his wife's encouragement, this man who loved business was learning to enjoy the fruits of his labors as well. As he recruited able executives to help him run Marion and the associated enterprises, he began to relinquish control in more areas. And with the luxury of some leisure time, he played golf more frequently and enjoyed his vacation home in the desert near Palm Springs. The Missouri farm boy who always regretted that he never owned a bicycle bought a Falcon jet to fly to football games or to see his horses run in New York or California. "You know, I never really felt rich until I bought that jet," he admitted to a *Time* magazine interviewer.

"Mrs. K taught me how to enjoy money," he liked to say. But even more than his personal wealth, Kauffman gloried in what he was able to share because of the combined efforts of Marion employees. In 1968, the Associated Press reported that a score of people working for the eighteen-year-old pharmaceutical company had become millionaires. And the big news was that among those mentioned was a thirty-year-old assistant office manager, a widow who worked in the accounting department, and a fifty-six-year-old plant maintenance worker. That fall at the shareholders' meeting Kauffman announced that three long-time associates had already accrued the maximum, a million dollars, in their retirement accounts. "For the three who have over a million dollars each in the fund, Marion Laboratories actually contributed only $28,000," he said. "And next year, Marion will have six more employees who will pass the million-dollar mark." Sharing Marion's wealth with the people who helped produce it "hasn't hurt me personally," Kauffman said. "I still own 43 percent of the company. Which would you rather have—100 percent of $2 million or 43 percent of $175 million? I am more proud that twenty of our people are millionaires than I am of anything I've got."

With these impressive results, word spread that Marion Laboratories was the pharmaceutical house to watch. Potential investors liked Marion's aggressive sales force, the company's successful penetration of several significant markets, and its purchase of health-related businesses to beef up its product line. Potential employees, especially those already experienced in the pharmaceutical industry, saw Marion's profit-sharing and stock-option plans as avenues to personal wealth. These benefits were simply not available elsewhere in the industry, or else were restricted to the highest echelons of management.

Marion Laboratories and its flamboyant founder also captured public attention when Kauffman emerged as the successful bidder to purchase a major league baseball franchise for Kansas City. Suddenly it seemed as if everybody in Kansas City and sports enthusiasts across the country were asking, "Who is this Ewing Kauffman? Where did he make his money? What is Marion Laboratories?" Kauffman, who loved the limelight, still chafed a bit at the sudden notoriety attracted by being a ball club owner. He expressed that frustration in a speech to the Kansas City Junior Chamber of Commerce. "I worked twenty years of my life to build the finest pharmaceutical company in America. During that period I was asked to make six speeches. I've owned a baseball team for two years and seven months. This is the two-hundredth speech I've been asked to make. It seems to be what you own, not what you've done, that counts."

Although he would exult in the league pennants and the World Series championship that the ball club would earn, throughout his life he remained most proud of the company he and his associates had built. For it was Marion Laboratories, "Mother Marion" as he so affectionately called the business, that produced the wealth that made all his other accomplishments possible. The stewardship of that wealth as a businessman, sports owner, and philanthropist governed his actions over the ensuing years.

When Kauffman purchased the baseball franchise in 1968, there was considerable speculation that he might relinquish the reins at Marion. Developing an expansion club into a World Series contender was going to require considerable expertise as well as financing, and Kauffman intended to be a winner. But he knew that his primary contribution to the ball club would be his financial strength and acumen plus his personal skills in motivating both management and players to excel. He was determined to recruit strong management talent with a proven record in baseball and to let them do their job. His primary responsibility was still as president and CEO of Marion Laboratories, and he was beginning to formulate a plan to build a $100 million company.

One of Kauffman's greatest strengths as an entrepreneur was his accurate assessment of his own abilities. His experience and instincts had been appropriate for a fledging company struggling to find a toehold in an increasingly sophisticated and complex industry. But the marketplace was changing. Medical specialists, not general practitioners, were the physicians eager for the latest products. If they could be persuaded to prescribe PAVABID, NITROBID, or GAVISCON, the family physicians would follow their lead. And physicians and pharmacists were no longer the primary dispensers of drugs. Institutions such as nursing homes and hospitals were becoming major customers, and salesmen with special abilities to communicate with these various audiences began to supplant the old "detail man of the fifties." Third-party payers, whether insurance companies or entities of government, altered the landscape. Generic formulations began to compete more aggressively with established brand-name medications, and the market for over-the-counter drugs boomed. It seemed that every aspect of doing business was becoming more competitive and more expensive.

The explosion of scientific knowledge following World War II caused drug companies to invest hundreds of millions of dollars in the search for new compounds. And the Food and Drug Administration's tedious and lengthy regulatory process added further to the rising costs. It took seven or eight years, sometimes a decade, to bring a new product to market. And changes in the distribution system accompanied changes in the customer base, as regional and national drug wholesale operations became the conduit between the pharmaceutical company and a more complicated marketplace.

As Kauffman reviewed the complexities of his business commitments, he sought the counsel of financial analysts who specialized in the pharmaceutical industry. They were unanimous in their advice, and he concurred. He needed to build a strong executive management team. If the goal was to become a $100 million company, he must recruit experienced managers from pharmaceutical companies substantially larger than Marion Laboratories. That was, of course, exactly the strategy he had followed when he recruited Perryman and Dalbey earlier. But Perryman had left shortly after Marion became a public company, and Dalbey was approaching retirement. Kauffman was conscious of the need to replace him with a more sophisticated team-oriented individual with good interpersonal skills. While he appreciated Dalbey's many contributions and innovations over the years, he realized that those methods and ideas were becoming outdated. Although Dalbey was unpopular throughout the company because of his abusive language and his bear-pit style of management, Kauffman was unwilling to force him into retirement before he was ready to go of his own initiative. "Mr. K was a very loyal person," recalled Al Mannino, who took over many of Dalbey's responsibilities when he joined Marion in 1968 as vice president of marketing. "Kauffman had a lot of strengths. But . . . he took a lot on face value. And when he had somebody who was totally loyal to him, then he was totally loyal to them. And Mac Dalbey came in when Mr. K needed him." While Kauffman tolerated the situation because of the personal debt he felt to Dalbey, he knew he would have to work around him. So he instructed other senior executives to be on the lookout for talent.

Mannino was the first of the new executives who would help re-shape Marion Laboratories in the 1970s and prepare the company to maximize the potential of its two major products, CARAFATE and CARDIZEM, in the 1980s. He was a trained pharmacist who had had a distinguished career in marketing before joining Marion Labora-tories. At McKesson & Robbins, the world's largest drug wholesaler, he had developed the hospital division, which became a significant part of their business. He had also been responsible for sales to gov-ernment agencies. These experiences would prove to be crucial in Kauffman's plans for growth. Mannino had been aware of Marion Laboratories long before he considered the possibility of joining the firm. "They had a reputation because of Mr. Kauffman's flamboy-ance. He was going to make this the best company in the world, and the district managers drove Cadillacs. No other company in the industry—no matter how high you went—drove Cadillacs in the field." Mannino wanted to know more about this small company where a district manager in charge of ten field representatives drove a luxury car. He had heard that Kauffman wanted those managers to feel better than any other managers in the industry. "It was that kind of thing that intrigued me," he admitted.

In 1967, Mannino attended a Marine Corps reunion in Kansas City. While there he looked up an old friend, Bill Doyle, Marion's vice president for corporate affairs. Doyle insisted on introducing Mannino to Kauffman. They ended up visiting for more than half an hour about Kauffman's philosophies of sharing rewards and treat-ing others as one would like to be treated. Mannino, who by his own admission had grown up on the wrong side of the tracks in a New Jersey town, shared Kauffman's history of having worked hard as a young boy. As one of seven children in an Italian working-class family, Mannino started working alongside his father when he was only ten. He had worked hard all his life to accomplish the things he wanted. And he thought, "I'm going to work hard anyway, no matter who I work for. I ought to work for a company that appre-ciates it . . . somebody who will reward me for it!"

The following year when Kauffman began to search for a vice president for marketing, Mannino decided to campaign for the job. The applicant pool was a rich one, which meant that others in the industry had learned what was going on at Marion Laboratories and wanted to be a part of it. Among the fifteen finalists was the president of Massengill, a company which was much larger than Marion at that time. But Mannino landed the job. When he reported for work, Kauffman invited him into his office for a "get acquainted" session. Leaning back in his chair and taking a deep draw on his pipe, Kauffman asked if Mannino knew why he had landed the job. Mannino replied that he did not know, but he was pleased to be a part of the Marion team. Kauffman said there were two reasons. "I realize that if we're ever going to grow, we're going to have to have the support of the wholesalers. And you were the only one [of the candidates] with ten years' experience with wholesale methods. And someday the institutional market is going to be a big part of our business. You're the only one who has experience in that area." In that brief conversation, Mannino found out why he got the job, learned Kauffman's plans for the future, and received his marching orders. He also gained considerable insight into his new boss's thinking.

Mannino decided to tackle first the challenge of placing Marion Laboratories' products with major wholesalers. "Mr. Kauffman recognized that there were fifty thousand drugstores and that as you grow, you can't be servicing fifty thousand separate customers," he recalled. But because Marion Laboratories was a small company, only one of many hundreds of pharmaceutical houses trying to place products with the wholesalers, it had encountered apathy, if not outright resistance. The wholesalers, who had to pay large storage costs to keep drugs on hand and large transportation costs to deliver them, necessarily limited their inventories. "Kauffman had tried to get in with the wholesalers," Mannino learned. "But because the company was so small and unknown, the wholesalers would generally say, 'When we get a call for your products we'll put them in.' And that kind of made the people at Marion angry; they were sort of antiwholesaler."

By the time Mannino joined Marion, the firm's drugs had been placed with a small number of wholesalers. A wholesaler typically carried the products of a hundred or more companies, so Marion still had to compete for the wholesaler's attention and shelf space along with such household names as Gillette, Parke-Davis, Bristol-Myers, and Procter & Gamble. "Now the wholesaler can't promote everybody's products all the time. Everybody wants them to promote their product [exclusively] and they can't," Mannino said.

Marion Laboratories was paying the wholesalers 20 percent to distribute its products, and Mannino found a growing resentment among the sales force. Sperry, in particular, who was now vice president for sales, was critical. He complained that Marion was paying them to do a job and they were not doing it. Mannino's response was one he used time and time again to chip away at the parochial attitudes that characterized many of those in management who were resisting Kauffman's willingness to change the company in order to help it grow. For Mannino, the strategy was obvious: "We've got to sit down with [the wholesalers], talk to them, get to know them, and come up with a program with some mutual benefit. Then together it'll work to help both of us." He cautioned his Marion colleagues that they could no longer ship products to the wholesalers with the ultimatum: "I expect you to do all these things because I am paying you a commission!" Mannino was shocked at the depth of animosity among the Marion sales associates toward the wholesalers. After more than a decade in that business, he knew that continued ultimatums and animosity were a strategy for disaster. He also understood, as did Kauffman, this was not the way to treat other people.

Mannino began calling on the wholesale companies, one by one. Over the years he had worked with or met a great many of the individuals who were now running the major wholesale houses, so he could go right to the top. He would call the chief executive and say, "'I need to come out and visit with you.' Then I'd go out and we'd sit down and they'd agree, 'Well, let's work out a program.'" Mannino always took one of the field sales managers on these calls to open up communications and to establish personal relationships and goodwill. "I was showing these men that they could work with these people. I'd say, '[The wholesalers] are good people. They are our friends. But they've got twenty thousand items to promote. They can't sit around just waiting for you to tell them something.'"

As Marion sales managers began to think of the pharmaceutical wholesalers as partners and to treat them as colleagues, attitudes changed and sales climbed. When GAVISCON was ready to be introduced in 1970, Mannino had his first opportunity to test the working relationship he had been building with the wholesalers. GAVISCON was also Mannino's first product as vice president of marketing, so its rapid acceptance was doubly important to him. However, he encountered interference from Dalbey with the marketing plan from the beginning. "No matter what I did, he felt it was wrong," Mannino remembered. Frustrated and angry as the time neared to introduce GAVISCON, Mannino announced to Dalbey that he was going to introduce the product his own way. "If it fails, there'll be a resignation on your desk. You won't even have to fire me. I'll quit," he said. But Mannino was in no danger of losing his job. His careful nurturing of the wholesalers on behalf of Marion's product line was about to pay off. "What Dalbey didn't know was that I had four hundred wholesalers who were going to do it. They would get distribution for me. They would move it. No way it was going to fail!" Mannino recalled with the echo of triumph still in his voice.

In spite of Dalbey's resistance, Kauffman backed Mannino from the beginning. He trusted him to do whatever was necessary to get the wholesalers working in tandem with the Marion team. He was holding Mannino responsible for GAVISCON's successful distribution, so he had to entrust him with the authority to act. Kauffman told him, "I recognize we've got to work with them and I'm going to turn it all over to you. You're in charge of the wholesalers," Mannino recalled. By the early 1980s, these relationships had been tuned to near perfect pitch. "We had distribution . . . with CARDIZEM and CARAFATE that placed those drugs in 75 to 80 percent of the drug stores within ten days," Mannino recalled. "This speed was unheard-of in the industry before that time."

Kauffman always told the associates that caring about the people you did business with was an important part of the job. And Mannino found a great many ways to translate that principle into action. He began with meetings, first among the pharmacists and then with wholesalers, to determine what Marion Laboratories needed to consider when preparing a new product for market. George Grinham, an executive in Marion's advertising department, had suggested asking the pharmacists questions about dosage sizes, packaging, shelf cartons, and promotion. Grinham's idea spawned what came to be called the Service to Pharmacy programs. It started with a one-day meeting of ten pharmacists in the Kansas City area. That worked so well that Mannino decided to bring in pharmacists from all over the country. His strategy for identifying who should attend was simple but shrewd. "In order to find the best pharmacists, I'd call my wholesaler friends and say, 'Who are the best pharmacists in Arizona? Give me the names of two or three. Who are the best ones in all these different states?'"

Over the years, Marion Laboratories held seminars with persons from all the different enterprises employing pharmacists—hospitals, retail, wholesalers, chain stores, deans of pharmacy schools—to learn about the specific needs and the problems of each specialty market. Kauffman always made it a practice to be present for a substantial portion of each meeting. He was keen to learn what Marion's customers were thinking, and he loved the repartee and camaraderie of his chosen industry. In the 1970s, senior executives such as Fred Lyons and Jim McGraw followed their CEO's example, participating in each seminar in its entirety. But it was Kauffman's presence that was so special. Here was the founder of an important pharmaceutical house listening to an individual pharmacist's concerns, asking questions, trying to think from another person's point of view. And of course, there was the added attraction of Kauffman as the owner of a major league baseball team. As Mannino summed it up, the message was clear. "It was not just lip service, we all really cared about them."

With Kauffman's wholehearted support and participation, Mannino developed similar focus groups with the wholesalers building on what had been learned from the pharmacists. If Marion was planning to introduce a new product in dosages of one hundred tablets to the bottle, Mannino would query the wholesalers. How many bottles should be packaged together to be shipped to the wholesaler? Should there be twelve bottles to a carton, or twenty-four, or thirty-six? How many cartons could be shrink-wrapped for easier handling? "These were the things we would come up with," he recalled. "What makes it easier for you, the wholesaler? What makes it easier for us, the manufacturer? When you got their input, they were going to work twice as hard for you when the product finally came out."

The small group meetings with pharmacists and wholesalers were so productive that Marion Laboratories began hosting the presidents of state pharmaceutical associations and the leadership of the various states represented in the Association of Independent Wholesalers. These individuals were active in state matters relating to the selection of drugs for public institutions, and they became an important part of Marion Laboratories' legislative network. In order to get Marion's products on each of the fifty states' approved drug lists for Medicaid reimbursement, Mannino recommended hiring Merle E. Wood as director of government services. Several senior executives interviewed Wood, and they all praised him highly. When Wood arrived at his office for the final interview, Kauffman was surprised. "He was five feet, eight inches tall, weighed 240 pounds, and dressed like a hick. He really was a kind of a farmer-type of guy and a horseman. I asked myself, 'How can this man be effective at the Washington, D.C., level?'" In spite of his initial reservations, Kauffman decided to follow his executives' advice and hired Merle Wood. Within a short time, Marion Laboratories' business with entities of federal and state government began to grow rapidly. It seemed as if Wood always knew the right person in the right place to get a task accomplished. He had an extensive network of contacts that had been building from his days as a chief pharmacist mate in the navy. During the Kennedy administration, he had been the president's personal pharmacist. "Every place that *Air Force One* would go, Merle would go," Kauffman said. "He had the back six seats [on the presidential plane] so he would say, 'Senator So-and-So, or Representative This-and-That, would you like to fly back to Washington with us?' So he built up some clout." But Wood's contacts were not limited to the legislative branch. Many of the employees at FDA during the 1970s were former naval personnel, so he often called an old friend to help break a logjam there.

As always, the Kauffmans helped when and where they were needed. If Mannino was holding an industry-related association meeting on the west coast, it would be near the Kauffman's home at Palm Springs. They would invite the wholesalers or pharmacists to their home for cocktails around the pool and then take them to the nearby country club for dinner. If the gathering was in Kansas City, the scenario might be a bit different, especially during baseball season. "I would open the meeting," Mannino recalled. "Then I would introduce Mr. K. He'd talk about the background, how he started Marion Laboratories. They would ask him questions, usually about the Royals. One night he'd have the group come to the Royals Stadium as his guests. We'd have them in the box and sometimes he'd bring them into a suite, and we'd take them to dinner. He and Mrs. K always participated. He was always making them feel special and always was a part of making our life easier."

Kauffman's external role as host to colleagues in the industry was an extension of his most important role within his own company. Mannino remarked that by the time he joined Marion Laboratories in 1968, Kauffman had realized that the company was growing, and as such, he was going to play a different role. He could find others who could train salesmen better than he. He could recruit advertising gurus, market analysts, and manufacturing authorities, but there were no other specialists who excelled in his field. His greatest skill was as the motivator, the dreamer, the visionary. Mannino recalled that when he started, Marion Laboratories was doing about fourteen million dollars in business a year. One day Mr. Kauffman said, "Al, someday we're going to do a hundred million dollars [a year]." Mannino was justifiably skeptical, given the limited product line and the lack of basic research. But when that goal was achieved in the 1980s, he stopped by Kauffman's office to remind him that his prophecy had come true. "Mr. K, did you really believe that when you told me?" Mannino remembered asking. "No," Kauffman replied with a big grin. "But it sounded good, didn't it?" No matter how he might downplay his role as the dreamer and the motivator, Kauffman had a vision for the company and consummate skill in getting everyone to work together. He generated an esprit de corps that galvanized everyone from external suppliers of raw materials to wholesalers to senior executives within the firm. He articulated the goals, held out the incentives, and, with genuine pride and pleasure, shared the rewards.

Developing an effective working relationship with drug wholesalers was a relatively easy task for Mannino, but that was not his major responsibility. "My [primary] charge," he recalled, "was to make the company professional, but not lose enthusiasm." Kauffman had recognized that the industry was much more sophisticated than when he started in the 1950s, and he had hired Mannino primarily to develop a sales force that could produce a hundred million dollars in sales. That task was neither easy nor painless. As he began to evaluate the sales force, he found that salesmen were still being hired using an aptitude test that measured two attributes: aggressiveness and ability to sell. "It wasn't measuring their professionalism, their ability to interact with people. . . ." he said. Within a short time, he saw a telling example of the kind of salesman this strategy often produced. Mannino had two brothers who were pharmacists in

New Jersey. After about three weeks at Marion, he received a call from his brother Russ, who thought he should know about an incident that had occurred in his drugstore. "Your salesman walked in, took off his raincoat, and walked right into the back of my drugstore," Russ, reported. "So I looked up and said, 'Hey, where are you going?' and he said, 'I'm going to check your inventory.'" When asked what company he worked for, the impulsive salesman announced that he was the new Marion representative. "Now if he had not said Marion, I'd have thrown him out," Russ reported. Making allowances for the man's inexperience, Russ tried to tell him about the etiquette and protocol of making a sales call. It did not involve barging into a pharmacist's private work area and rummaging through his inventory. Concerned that he might be overdoing the lecture on what to do and what not to do, Russ asked the salesman if he knew Mannino, who was the new vice president of marketing and sales. To this friendly overture, the salesman replied, "Oh, there're a bunch of Jews and Italians back in Kansas City and I don't know them all."

Mannino was shocked. His first inclination was to confront Sperry, but his better judgment prevailed. He knew that if Sperry recognized the problem himself, it would be much easier to change the hiring strategy. Mannino did not have to wait long. Within a month, the salesman was fired. Thinking that he might be able to avoid a confrontation with Sperry, Mannino decided to talk first with Pruitt, the head of sales training. But when he recounted the story, Pruitt seemed nonplussed. "What's wrong with that? We've got to get into those drugstores and we've got to get into the back room to check the inventory," Pruitt responded. Now Mannino realized that the situation was going to be more difficult to change than he had anticipated. Not only did the hiring strategy give priority to aggressiveness, but the training encouraged rather unconventional behavior, all in the name of "making the sale." The hiring system was also costly in terms of turnover. "Marion had a philosophy of hiring people and then throwing everything at them. If they worked out, fine. If they didn't work out, that was okay. But turnover was between 35 and 50 percent," Mannino recalled. Kauffman never acknowledged the obvious dichotomy between his rhetoric about caring for the associates and the trial-by-fire sales apprenticeship.

After several conversations with Sperry and Pruitt, Mannino recognized that there was little incentive for them to change their programs. He believed, "They didn't like my ideas and they didn't like me." As a trained pharmacist and successful executive in the industry before joining Marion, Mannino felt handicapped by being from New Jersey and of Italian ancestry. The men who had built Marion Laboratories through the fifties and sixties were primarily Midwesterners with little or no formal science education but with exceptional sales skills and powerful ambitions to succeed. "But none of them were pharmaceutical people," Mannino observed. His only recourse was to persuade Kauffman that major changes were needed. To his dismay, "Mr. Kauffman was not totally sold on changing that a lot, either. He realized that [the turnover] was expensive. But he said, 'We only get the best. And if we hire somebody and he's not the best, then we want to get rid of him.'" Mannino's response was that this was a very costly way to get good people. He showed Kauffman that the company was wasting $300,000 to $400,000 a year in the process. Then he suggested developing specifications for the type of person they would need if Marion was to grow substantially. With a plan in hand and the prospect of substantial annual savings, Kauffman relented. "Well, change it."

Mannino's profile for salesmen was substantially different from Sperry's, although there were some similarities. At one time Sperry had recruited teachers because of their perceived ability to learn about pharmaceutical products. The new recruit was to have a science or business degree with the demonstrated aptitude to learn about Marion's inventory. "I knew that someday we would have scientific products. We had to have people who could learn to sell scientific products if they didn't have a science background," Mannino said. But instead of recruiting inexperienced college graduates, Mannino preferred to hire someone who had been with another pharmaceutical company for about two years. "They have trained him. He's been with the company long enough to know that they may not fulfill his goals and needs and desires, and most of it was money." From his own experience, Mannino knew that large pharmaceutical houses were slow to promote and reward young people. The potential rewards through Marion's profit sharing, stock options, and bonuses for salesmen were to be powerful recruiting tools.

As Mannino began to search for new salesmen, he called his colleagues among the wholesalers and the pharmacists. He asked them to identify good salesmen with one to two years experience. He shied away from persons with more experience on the grounds that they were "pretty well set in their ways." He also believed that after five or ten years in the business they were probably at a salary level where an offer from Marion would not be especially attractive. His network produced a stream of likely candidates. "We began to hire a lot of young people who were aggressive, yet professional; already trained by somebody else. And we could give them the finishing touches and training, but they already had that professional background," Mannino said. Just as Marion Laboratories leapfrogged the expensive basic research stage by licensing drugs which other companies had developed, they now applied a similar strategy to upgrading and professionalizing the sales force.

Changing the way Marion Laboratories hired and trained new sales personnel was a constant struggle. Mannino, as the outsider from the east coast, had new-fangled ideas that threatened the established way of doing things. Both Sperry and Pruitt were as baffled as they were defensive. "They didn't understand what I was trying to accomplish," Mannino said. "They had already been successful. They were already making money personally [through stock options, profit sharing, and bonuses]. Their question was, 'Well, who needs you?' They were taking it all personally." Mannino tried to be patient. He began building alliances among several regional sales managers who welcomed his ideas about recruiting people with science training and experience elsewhere in the industry. Slowly Sperry and Pruitt began to see some merit in the changes, and reluctantly they went along. But Mannino credited Fred Lyons, who was then the chief operating officer, as being the driving force behind the changes. "Fred recognized that we had to change and Mr. K recognized that we had to change. The two of them said to me, 'We'll back you up, we'll make this thing work,'" Mannino recalled.

Along with the changes Mannino was brought in to effect, Dalbey convinced Kauffman of the need for more sophisticated market research and analysis. In studying larger, profitable pharmaceutical companies, Kauffman was learning that they all invested substantial resources in formal, systematic market research. Now that Marion Laboratories was acquiring other companies serving a variety of markets, Dalbey helped Kauffman see the value of a separate department to study market conditions as predictors for developing sales strategies. Prior to 1968, Kauffman had subscribed to a syndicated market research service from Lea Associates, Inc. of Philadelphia. From time to time, Marion Laboratories would also contract with the Philadelphia firm for individual market studies. Through this work, George Grinham developed a good relationship with a young pharmacist-M.B.A. there named Stuart Gold. So when Kauffman agreed that it was time to establish a marketing research function within Marion, Grinham asked Gold to suggest potential candidates to head the new division. Gold had been monitoring Marion's growth as a part of his job and was intrigued with the company's policy of providing stock options to all employees. "As far as my own career was going at that time, I was progressing very nicely but Lea Associates was basically a closed corporation," Gold recalled. The company's five principals were only a few years older than Gold, who was in his late twenties. "All the stock was with them and it didn't appear that they were going to open it up," he said. There seemed to be no good reason not to pursue the opening with Grinham, so he replied, "George, I'd like to throw my hat in the ring."

Grinham encouraged his young colleague to submit a résumé, and within a short time Gold flew to Kansas City for interviews with Dalbey and Kauffman. As late as 1968, Kauffman was still requesting that spouses be included in the interview process, so Mindy Gold reluctantly left her five-month-old baby with her sister and flew with her husband to the Midwest—a part of the country where she had never dreamed of living.

Being a research professional, Stu Gold did his homework. Prior to the interview, he read all the "client call reports" on Kauffman which colleagues at Lea Associates had prepared after their visits with the entrepreneur in Kansas City. "I remember one trip report [in which] one of our fellows said he had met with Mr. Kauffman. Dalbey had given this fellow some background information on the company, yet when he talked with Mr. Kauffman, Kauffman kept talking about sales that were three times higher [than the material indicated]. The impression I got from that, and the impression my colleague got, was that Mr. K was . . . eccentric." An article in the December 1, 1967, issue of *Time* had colored Gold's view of Kauffman. The writers described him as "a frenetic businessman who smokes five packs of cigarettes and averages seventeen cups of coffee a day . . . spends [his] money on a twenty-eight-room mansion . . . equipped with his and her poodles, an Olympic-sized swimming pool, pistol range and organ." It concluded that he was "waving four million dollars in earnest money . . . to bring a major league baseball team back to Kansas City to replace the recently departed Athletics." Gold's impression of Kauffman as merely eccentric seemed mild, given the recent press.

Gold's interview with Dalbey was routine. Then he and his wife were ushered in to see Kauffman. In recalling the interview a quarter of a century later, Gold said that initially he found Kauffman intimidating. "Now I would probably use a more encompassing term because I got to know him and it was more than just intimidating. It was just a tremendous persuasive ability that he had." The passage of time also changed Gold's view of Kauffman as an eccentric. "Only years later when I was with Marion did I realize that Mr. K had really been talking about a vision and that's why the sales were three times higher than what Dalbey said."

With Gold's résumé before him, Kauffman asked a few perfunctory questions, then raised the question of salary. Gold was disappointed with Kauffman's offer. Although it was a bit of a raise from what he was earning in Philadelphia, he had expected a greater increase if he was to move his family from Philadelphia to Kansas City. "At the time, having never had equity in the company that I was working for, I didn't realize what the value of that could be," Gold said. "So I was more interested in the salary." When Kauffman offered several hundred shares of stock, but a lesser salary than he had hoped, Gold balked. He told Kauffman he was expecting more in salary. Kauffman then asked him to name a figure, and he did. Then Kauffman immediately agreed to the salary, but said he would halve the number of shares of stock. Surprised at Kauffman's response, Gold backed off, deciding to stick with the original offer. "I wasn't real savvy at thirty-one, but I was savvy enough to know that I'd be a fool to mess this thing up for a couple of thousand dollars a year at my stage."

Reflecting on the process, Gold said that Kauffman's strategy in hiring management talent was to offer stock instead of salary and to handle the negotiations personally. He recalled as they were walking to Kauffman's office, Dalbey had remarked in a rather offhand way, "Maybe Kauffman can get you here for less than I can." The strategy worked. It was one thing for a prospective employee to bargain with a senior vice president. It was markedly different to haggle with the company founder.

Mindy Gold was present at the interview. As they talked, Kauffman seemed sensitive to what a move away from family and friends would mean to her. "It was like he was reading her mind, because in those days I think a spouse depended pretty heavily on her husband's business contacts for part of their social life," Gold recalled. Kauffman sketched out what life would be like for the wife of a Marion executive. He said that Marion was not a social company; business would come first. But he promised there would be some social interaction as he and Mrs. Kauffman entertained Marion executives and their wives at their Mission Hills mansion several times a year. Just as with the sales force, spouses of executives were expected to facilitate and support their husband's work, and social life was secondary.

Gold remembered that Kauffman used the terms "uncommon company" and "uncommon people" in talking about the productivity of Marion associates. As a way of telling Gold how special Marion people were, Kauffman cautioned him not to overestimate his own abilities. "You may be smart, Mr. Gold, but here you'll be only average. Everybody here is smart!" A less secure individual might have taken offense at Kauffman's remark, but Stu Gold's appetite was only whetted more. He was skeptical that Marion Laboratories was really so different from other companies despite Kauffman's claims, but he recognized that the company was going to grow. "I thought, 'I'm getting in on the ground floor and I can go somewhere with it.' I wasn't sure I believed everything he was saying, but I wanted to be there."

Both parties knew that they had struck a deal, but toward the end of the interview Kauffman asked if the Golds had any questions for him. "Mr. Kauffman, you may or may not know I'm Jewish," Gold stated. "I'd like to know if you think that would be any kind of problem for the company or for you. If it is, I'd like to know it right now." Kauffman pondered the question for a moment and then summoned Dalbey to ask if there were Jewish associates at Marion. Assured that there were indeed several on the team, Kauffman replied, "That should be no problem at all." Then he asked, "By the way, Mr. Gold, are you prejudiced? Some Jews are, you know." Gold assured him that he accepted people without concern about their race or religion. As the Golds were preparing to leave, Kauffman walked around his desk and said with evident pride, "I want you to know that the Kansas City Club was closed to Jews. And I got one of the first Jews admitted there. I hope that answers your question."

As the outsiders, Gold and Mannino quickly allied to introduce change at Marion Laboratories. Even though they combined efforts, the struggle to professionalize all parts of the company lasted well beyond Dalbey's retirement. Mannino remembered that shortly after Gold arrived, the two men decided to collaborate on a very small market research project. When Dalbey saw the bill, five thousand dollars, he seemed to snap. "He came in my office screaming and yelling, 'What you're doing is a sophomoric approach!'—his exact words," Mannino recalled. Dalbey maintained that the most useful market research was talking to people in little towns such as Stanley, Kansas, a small farming community near Kansas City. "You go there on Saturday morning at the gas station and when the farmers come in they sit around that potbellied stove and they talk about issues. You ask them what they feel about the product. You'll get the grass roots," Dalbey announced, dismissing their approach. "That's what we were up against from a professional point of view in marketing and [market research]," Mannino recalled with a sigh.

In spite of these newcomers' frustrations in trying to work around Dalbey and frequent clashes with Sperry and other old hands, Kauffman seemed oblivious to the mounting tensions. Earnings continued to grow, and net sales for the year showed an increase of more than 55 percent over the previous twelve months. Sales and earnings were also rising among the various subsidiaries. And Kauffman continued to espouse the practical wisdom of buying companies with high profit potential which needed marketing and motivation expertise. In his personal message to the shareholders in the 1969 annual report, he noted, "It would be improper if I did not comment on the performance of our executive vice president, Mr. M. M. Dalbey, who took over the management of Marion Laboratories a year ago." Kauffman praised Dalbey for initiating many changes and programs which were proving beneficial, and he predicted, "Under his leadership you can expect Marion to maintain its past performance record." Until he could find a way to ease Dalbey into retirement, Kauffman continued to treat him with respect and to attribute positive change to his administration. Whether the euphoria that surrounded Marion's stock being traded on the New York Stock Exchange clouded Kauffman's judgment or he was distracted with the demands for time and money from the newly acquired baseball franchise, his optimistic prediction soon proved to be a hollow one.

Surviving the Seventies 8

The decade of the 1970s opened in an unfavorable economic atmosphere, but Kauffman announced to the shareholders that Marion's growth continued on schedule. In the five years since the company had become publicly owned, the consistent annual sales gain had averaged 41 percent. The annual gain in earnings for the same five-year period averaged just above 50 percent. Return on stockholder equity averaged a little better than 39 percent. As the company grew, Kauffman acquired six subsidiaries as a part of a broad plan to develop a flow of new products that could be marketed in various related health care fields. Efforts to license new products had also intensified with 266 possibilities screened in 1970. Twenty-one had been identified for further investigation and possible development. The sales force had grown to 214, the cash position was strong, and plans were being drawn for a new laboratory to accommodate the company's expanding research-and-development activities.

Within this milieu, Kauffman was steadily building an executive management team to lead a $100 million company. After much thought and investigation, he decided to seek help from Bill Gaberini, an executive recruiter in New York. With Gaberini's network of contacts and Marion's own reputation in the business, by 1975 he had assembled the team that would lead the company through some rather grim years in the second half of the seventies and then on to the blockbuster decade of the 1980s.

The major challenge facing Kauffman as the decade began was to groom a successor. Although Dalbey was handling day-to-day operations, Kauffman never saw him as a successor. Four years Kauffman's senior, Dalbey was already in his fifties when he joined Marion Laboratories. At that point in Marion's history, Kauffman was the only person with previous experience in the pharmaceutical business. Dalbey had extensive management experience in the industry and he was skilled in marketing and advertising, neither of which were Kauffman's forte. By 1970, Dalbey was approaching sixty and beginning to plan for retirement. Although reluctant to acknowledge it openly, Kauffman was fully aware of Dalbey's difficulties in working with other executives, as well as the growing antipathy toward him. So the first step was to recruit an understudy for Dalbey's role in the hope that the person would be suitable to move into Kauffman's position when he, too, was ready to retire. The ideal candidate would also have solid operational experience and previous sales experience with another pharmaceutical company—preferably one significantly larger than Marion Laboratories.

After an extensive search, Kauffman selected Fred W. Lyons Jr., a thirty-five-year old pharmacist trained at the University of Michigan and a graduate of the Harvard Business School. Prior to joining Marion Laboratories in 1970, Lyons had been vice president and general manager of Conal Pharmaceuticals, Inc., a Chicago subsidiary of Alcon Laboratories, in Fort Worth. Lyons was attracted to Marion, as were Mannino and Gold, because of the opportunity and potential to accumulate wealth through the generous stock-options and profit-sharing plan. Kauffman recalled that during the search which resulted in hiring Lyons, he had also talked extensively with a vice president for sales at Parke-Davis. As the field of prospective candidates narrowed, the Parke-Davis executive spelled out his terms. "I work for a company with hundreds of millions of dollars in sales each year and you're doing thirty-three million," he said. "I've got to at least have the presidency." Kauffman replied that if the man proved himself within a year on the job, the title could be his. They reached an impasse and Kauffman hired Fred Lyons instead. "Thank God, I did!" he exclaimed more than two decades after the event.

Lyons and Kauffman were as different as any two men could be. Where Kauffman was the ebullient salesman, Lyons was the reserved manager. At ease whether making small talk with a potential customer or negotiating the details of a complicated business deal, Kauffman fairly radiated warmth and confidence. Lyons by contrast was more urbane, smoother, and more reserved. Some associates described him as being rather cool and detached. Kauffman tended the vision of Marion's great future with an evangelical zeal. Lyons was to focus on translating that vision into reality, employing all the techniques and methodologies learned as an Ivy League business school graduate. Each saw complementary strengths in the other. Kauffman became the mentor and Lyons the attentive understudy. Whatever the precise chemistry, it worked.

Lyons, as vice president and general manager, reported to Dalbey, the executive vice president. And the two clashed from the start. Mannino remembered the initial confrontation, which occurred the first day Lyons was on the job. "Mac, this company is not big enough for both of us to run it," Lyons said. "Either you run it or I run it. If you're going to run it, then I'll leave. If you want me to run it, then let me run it." Lyons quickly established the reputation for being an adroit executive and an effective manager. And Kauffman began to see that this bright young colleague might have the potential to guide Marion along the course to become a $100 million company.

In 1973, Kauffman began to struggle with the problem of how to ease Dalbey into retirement. That same year, he redesigned Marion's corporate structure to reflect the company's multidivisional character. He presided over the "mother company"—Marion Laboratories, Inc. The associated companies were grouped into six divisions under this umbrella. The sixth and largest division was Marion Pharmaceutical, with Fred Lyons at the helm. Each division had its own staff, as did the parent company. "Mother Marion" set the policy, determined the direction of the divisions, and provided services—legal, financial, market research—that were well suited to centralized control.

Kauffman was moving steadily to broaden and deepen the base of executive talent, so he was caught off guard, and a bit annoyed, when a concerned investor at the 1973 annual meeting publicly expressed misgivings about the depth of management. "Is Marion basically a one-man company?" he asked. "Definitely not!" Kauffman shot back. "It is to my own personal interest and that of my family to see that there is excellent future management for Marion Laboratories in the event of my death." He lauded the executive ability of the two senior vice presidents, Church and Lyons, as well as Dalbey, whom he characterized as "chief adviser to me and the executive staff generally." In spite of Kauffman's assurances about the depth of talent, the questioner had touched a sensitive nerve. Dalbey was not well liked within the company and unaware of new developments in the industry. He was nearing retirement age, although he had not announced his intention to go. Church and Lyons were still relatively new to Marion. There was substantial strength in Mannino and Gold, who had been in their respective positions in marketing and market research since the late 1960s. But more talent was needed on the operations side and in the financial area. Kauffman later admitted, "I personally wanted to take it easier and not work as hard." It was clear that he would have to accelerate efforts to build the executive team which he knew was crucial to the company's future growth.

While reviewing the recruiting efforts with Gaberini, Kauffman concluded that he needed to create a personnel department within Marion Laboratories of professionals specifically trained in that field. The right talent there was needed to identify and recruit top-quality executives. And with the many subsidiaries, the number of Marion associates was growing rapidly. "We needed greater direction for all of them," he concluded.

Using Gaberini's network, Kauffman recruited an exceptionally skilled human resources specialist, Gerald Holder. Trained as an industrial psychologist, Holder had started his career at Union Carbide in New York City. He then moved into the pharmaceutical industry, holding various positions at Abbott Laboratories in Chicago and later at American Home Products in New York. Holder's challenge at Marion was to build his own staff while simultaneously recruiting an executive management team. In addition, there were myriad personnel issues relating to staff turnover, training, compensation, and benefits that had grown like Topsy over the years. They all needed to be addressed in a systematic, professional manner. Clearly, the job was bigger than one man. So with Kauffman's blessing, Holder set out to recruit the staff talent he needed.

Holder's first call was to Michie Slaughter, an executive he had recruited to American Home Products after previously working with him at Abbott Laboratories. As a favor to his friend, Slaughter agreed to an interview at Marion, but he had no intention of working for a small company in Kansas City. Holder knew that Slaughter had developed serious professional reservations about the move to American Home. To compound the problem, he and his family intensely disliked commuting from the Connecticut suburbs into Manhattan. Slaughter respected Holder and had enjoyed working with him, but he approached the interview at Marion cautiously and with some misgivings. He had already experienced a situation in which "They said all the right things in the interview process, but when I got there they didn't really want somebody to do what I can do." Slaughter was determined, if at all possible, to avoid a similar mistake. He was on his way to Atlanta to interview with several consulting firms when he had the fateful conversation with Holder. Vowing to himself that he would "be real suspicious about the whole process," he agreed to fly to Kansas City to investigate.

In spite of his initial caution, Slaughter's suspicions quickly melted. When he asked cab drivers, people in bars, and the personnel at his hotel about Marion Laboratories' reputation in the community, he got positive responses. When he met Fred Lyons and Jim Church, he liked them. When he met Kauffman, Slaughter admitted to being charmed. Although he recalled that Kauffman asked tough questions in the interview, he probed primarily to find out what kind of things were important to Slaughter. "He asked more about personal stuff than job stuff. So I really felt he was trying to get to know me as an individual." The interview was brief, no more than fifteen minutes. Shortly afterward, Marion made a job offer. There was a bit of dickering, then Slaughter accepted. That evening he called his wife to report the situation looked promising and he was inclined to accept. "You know I'll go anywhere to get out of Connecticut," she replied, "but where is Kansas City?"

Slaughter moved his family to Kansas City in early 1974 to take up his duties as director of personnel and organizational development. He and Holder had decided on that title "because nobody knew what it was. And we were able to decide what it ought to be as the need arose," Slaughter remembered. Since the most pressing need was to put together an executive team, when people asked Slaughter what his primary responsibilities were he would reply, "executive recruiting."

In January 1974, the Marion executive team consisted of Kauffman and Dalbey with Lyons and Church reporting directly to Dalbey. "Fred had the pharmaceutical marketing division. Jim had everything else—research and development, licensing and acquisitions, and all of the various subsidiary companies Marion had acquired," Slaughter recalled. When he arrived, Holder was about to bring off his most significant early accomplishment, which would pave the way for new management to help Kauffman realize his dream of a $100 million enterprise. Kauffman had become convinced that after several years of drift, it was time for Dalbey to retire. Since 1968, Kauffman had focused a lot of attention on the ball club. During that period, he had given Dalbey almost free rein in running the company. With his attention diverted to the Royals, Kauffman was somewhat out of touch with the company. His trusting nature also compounded the problems. "Mr. K was the most complex person I've ever known," Slaughter recalled. "At times, he was much, much too trusting. He had a unique ability sometimes to overdelegate and abdicate. And then at times, he was not nearly trusting enough."

Holder pressed his concerns about the general malaise within the company until Kauffman agreed to ask his trusted friend, Hughes, to appraise the situation for him. Hughes had retired as corporate secretary in 1972, but he visited Marion headquarters from time to time to meet friends for lunch and to keep up old ties. If people saw him chatting with various Marion associates, Kauffman knew there would be no sinister connotation attributed to his gentle questioning. "Charlie would come in and just sort of wander around the organization and say, 'How're you doing?'" Slaughter recalled. Within a short time, Hughes confirmed that there were, indeed, serious problems.

Kauffman concluded that Dalbey would have to go if the company was to prosper and if he wanted to retain the new management talent he had recruited. But implementing that decision was quite another matter. Kauffman had never been comfortable in the role of "executive disciplinarian." He had anguished and vacillated for two years before relieving Paul Danielson of executive duties early in Marion's history. And the intervening years had not made firing a long-term associate any easier. Dalbey's case was especially difficult.

Slaughter recalled that Kauffman hesitated so long in resolving the turmoil that Dalbey created because "he simply did not know how to do it. One of the most difficult things for a chairman or a president to do is to take out the single individual between him and

John Kauffman and Effie Mae Winders Kauffman,
Ewing's parents, on their wedding day. John, the son of
a farmer, was easygoing and loved to travel. Because of
an eye injury sustained while farming, he had a difficult
time finding steady work when the family moved to
Kansas City. Effie, a college graduate, was more practical-
minded, and kept the family afloat by taking in boarders.
Their differences led to a parting of ways when Ewing
was twelve years old.

Ewing and his older sister, Ruth. "I took after my dad's side of the family," Ruth said of their childhood, "and Ewing was more like Mama."

Ewing at age eleven with his faithful police dog, Larry. The two were an inseparable pair throughout Ewing's youth.

Seaman First Class Ewing Kauffman, at Great Lakes Naval Training Station in 1942. Kauffman's substantial poker winnings during the war earned him the nickname "Lucky" and provided the seed money used to start Marion Laboratories.

Marguerite Blackshire and Ewing Kauffman were secretly married in 1941, just before he left Kansas City to begin naval training in Great Lakes, Illinois. Kauffman described Marguerite as "somewhat shy . . . She wasn't book smart, but she was smart from other factors."

Kauffman (bottom left) and fellow shipmates with Admiral Edmund A. Crenshaw (bottom center). Crenshaw was the first person outside of Kauffman's family and friends to affirm his intelligence and nurture his potential. The two would carry on correspondence throughout the 1950s and '60s.

Kauffman at the time he went to work for Lincoln Laboratories in 1947, following his naval duty in World War II.

Kaufmann started Marion Laboratories in 1950 in the basement of the family residence on Locust Street.

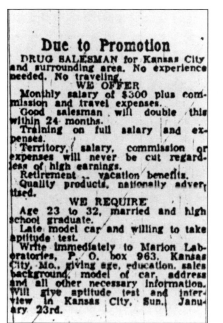

Due to Promotion

DRUG SALESMAN for Kansas City and surrounding area. No experience needed. No traveling.

WE OFFER

Monthly salary of $300 plus commission and travel expenses.

Good salesman will double this within 24 months.

Training on full salary and expenses.

Territory, salary, commission or expenses will never be cut regardless of high earnings.

Retirement .. vacation benefits.

Quality products, nationally advertised.

WE REQUIRE

Age 23 to 32, married and high school graduate.

Late model car and willing to take aptitude test.

Write immediately to Marion Laboratories, P. O. box 963, Kansas City, Mo., giving age, education, sales background, model of car, address and all other necessary information. Will give aptitude test and interview in Kansas City, Sun. January 23rd.

A typical Marion solicitation for salesmen, from the January 5, 1955, *Kansas City Star*. Kauffman emphasized success on an aptitude test and the stability of married life over academic credentials. He also made clear that none of his sales staff would ever experience what he had at Lincoln Laboratories, where his territory was cut because of his high earnings.

Zany promotional materials such as this miniature stick of dynamite pitching NITRO-BID helped attract attention to Marion's early products.

Within a year Marion Labs had moved out of the basement and into a former storeroom at 4215 Troost Avenue. "It was twelve feet wide and forty feet deep with a hardware store on one side and a used car lot on the other," Kauffman recalled. "Not very prepossessing."

Larry and Sue Kauffman compare scrapes garnered at summer camp, as Larry tries to teach his sister to play the ukelele.

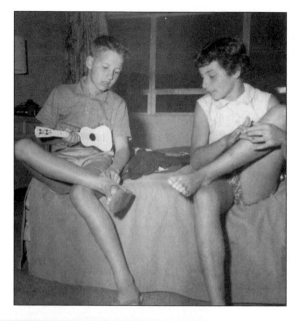

Muriel and Ewing Kauffman on their wedding day, February 28, 1962. Larry served as his father's best man, and Julia Irene attended her mother.

Muriel McBrien Kauffman was raised in Toronto, and at an early age began managing her family's extensive business interests. Upon marrying Kauffman, she put her business skills to work for Marion as the company's treasurer.

"Like father, like son . . ." Kauffman and his father, John, shared a gregarious nature and a ready smile for all they met.

Effie Mae Winders Kauffman Smythe, Kauffman's mother (pictured here in the 1960s), was a college graduate, an unusual accomplishment for a woman of her generation. Her greatest gift to her son was the sense of self-worth which characterized him at an early age.

Marion's early leadership included Charles L. Hughes (above), Kauffman's closest friend throughout his life and the second full-time Marion associate; Jean R. Sperry (top right), Marion's first national sales manager; and Malcolm M. Dalbey (bottom right), recruited as executive vice president to handle marketing. The three are shown here in pictures from Marion's 1966 annual report.

Bob Pruitt, one of Marion's early and most successful salesmen. He wrote an informal history of Marion following his retirement.

One of Kauffman's trademarks was his pipe, which he would smoke while contemplating Marion's future or resolving difficult issues.

Kauffman in 1968 with his first grandchild, Julia Irene Power, the daughter of Julia Irene Kauffman.

Kauffman with OS-CAL, the oyster-shell calcium tablet that was Marion's first nationally successful product.

Marion's stock began trading on the New York Stock Exchange on February 25, 1969, under the ticket symbol MKC. Lee D. Arming (left), the exchange vice president, and John A. Barry (right) of Silver, Barry & Van Raalte welcome Kauffman to the trading floor.

Marion executives Jim Church, Lowell Miller, and Stuart Gold confer in a photo from the 1977 annual report.

Marion's senior management team of the early 1980s. Standing, from left: Gerald W. Holder, senior vice president; James E. McGraw, executive vice president; and Michael E. Herman, senior vice president and chief financial officer. Seated: Fred Lyons Jr., president and chief operating officer, and Kauffman, chairman and chief executive officer.

Al Mannino, known as "Mr. Wholesaler," pictured here in 1985, served as Marion's vice president for corporate affairs.

Fred Lyons Jr. with Kauffman in 1983. Lyons was named chief operating officer and president of Marion in 1977. Kauffman handed over the position of chief executive officer to him in 1984.

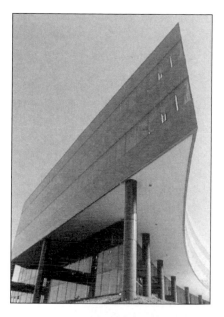

Marion's corporate head-
quarters in 1985 made a
dramatic contrast to the
company's humble begin-
nings in Kauffman's base-
ment on Locust Street.

Kauffman, Jim McGraw, and Muriel Kauffman at a
quarterly "Marion on the Move" meeting in the 1980s.
The meetings were held to celebrate company performance and outline goals, and were attended by all associates. Kauffman's infectious enthusiasm marked the
events, which typified the "Marion Spirit."

Kauffman on his birthday in 1991 with Merle Wood, Marion's vice president for government affairs, and Wood's wife, Ellen. Kauffman's first impression of Wood was of "a kind of a farmer-type guy and a horseman," but Wood's Washington experience and connections proved a valuable asset for Marion.

The so-called Six-Pack of operational executives, pictured in 1990: Standing, from left: Harley Tennison, Jim McGraw, and Lloyd Hanahan; seated, from left: Michie Slaughter, Brant Cotterman, and Lowell Miller. Under McGraw's leadership, the group was a key element in Marion's phenomenal growth in the 1980s.

Kauffman shakes hands with a Marion associate at one of the annual
Marion Appreciation Nights at Royals Stadium.

Kauffman with Joe Temple, the Merrell
Dow executive who became chairman of
the board and CEO of Marion Merrell
Dow upon the completion of the merger.

Jim McGraw and Kauffman reminisce at the Marion visitors' center
after the merger.

A *Kansas City Star* cartoon lampoons some of the more unlikely suggestions made for the name of Kansas City's 1969 expansion baseball club.

Missouri Democratic senator Stuart Symington, who had been instrumental in Kauffman's securing the Royals franchise, throws out the first pitch in the team's inaugural season, 1969.

Kauffman made it a point to leave day-to-day operations of the Royals in the hands of "baseball people." Key figures in the team's development have included: Cedric Tallis (left), the Royals' first general manager; Joe Burke (center), team president from 1981 until his death in 1992; John Schuerholz (top right), general manager from 1981 to 1990; and Herk Robinson (bottom right), Schuerholz's successor.

Kauffman addresses the pupils of the Baseball Academy, his brainchild for player development. The academy taught baseball fundamentals to outstanding athletes from other sports who were inexperienced in the game.

Muriel and Ewing Kauffman relax in the stands of new
Royals Stadium in 1973.

Frank White was a fixture at second base for the Royals from 1976 to 1990, during which time he earned eight Gold Gloves for his spectacular fielding. A Kansas City native, White was the most successful product of the Baseball Academy.

Royals players (including young star George Brett, center) give Kauffman a champagne shower in 1976 after winning their first division championship. The team would win its division again in 1977 and 1978, only to lose in the playoffs each year to the New York Yankees. In 1980 the Royals met the Yankees again in the league championship series—and this time the Royals swept their rivals in three games.

Avron B. Fogelman, a Memphis real estate developer, purchased a 49 percent share of the Royals from Kauffman in 1983, with an option to buy the rest of the team between 1988 and 1991. Fogelman experienced financial difficulties in the late 1980s, and as a result the succession plan never came to pass.

In the locker room after the final game of the 1985 World Series, key participants in the Royals' victory are interviewed for television. Pictured, from left, are interviewer Reggie Jackson, manager Dick Howser, Series MVP Bret Saberhagen, Fogelman, Brett, and Kauffman.

Kauffman and Fogelman (opposite page) were riding high as they flew to Washington, D.C., to receive congratulations from the president following the 1985 Series.

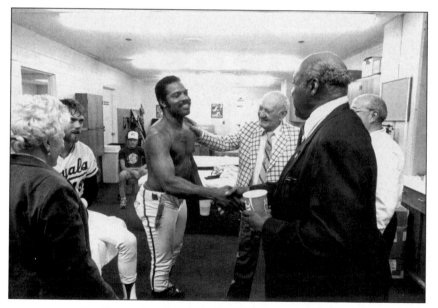

Kauffman's chauffeur, Blanchie Blevins, congratulates longtime Royals star (and future manager) Hal McRae following the 1985 World Series victory, as Kauffman looks on.

From left, Steve Balboni, Muriel Kauffman, Mark Gubicza,
Fogelman, Kauffman, and Burke meet President Reagan
in the White House rose garden.

From 1987 to 1991, Bo Jackson was a center of attention and controversy on the Royals. The erratic but often spectacular two-sport star put fans in the seats and attracted media attention unprecedented for a Royals player.

Brett and Kauffman embrace during an October 3, 1992,
celebration at Royals Stadium recognizing Brett's 3,000th
career hit. Brett solidified his place among baseball's all-
time greats when he became only the eighteenth player in
major league history to reach the 3,000-hit plateau.

Kauffman talks with Mark Seals, a PROJECT CHOICE participant, in 1991 about his plans to attend college.

Kauffman on the field at Royals Stadium with participants in the CPR NOW! program. As part of their effort to give back to the community, the Kauffmans set a goal of teaching one hundred thousand Kansas Citians CPR. During a single weekend in the spring of 1981, volunteers taught ten thousand people at the stadium.

On the field at Royals stadium in 1988, Kauffman and
Mike Herman explain the workings of PROJECT CHOICE,
a program through which Kauffman offered to pay college tuition for a group of eighth graders if they stayed in
school, kept out of trouble, and earned their high school
diplomas.

Robert Rogers, chairman of the board and CEO of the
Ewing Marion Kauffman Foundation.

Calvin Cormack, director of
PROJECT STAR.

A meeting of Kauffman Foundation associates. From left,
Ray Smilor, vice president and director of the Entrepreneur Institute; Michie Slaughter, president, the Center
for Entrepreneurial Leadership, Inc.; and Marilyn Kouril-
sky, vice president and director of the Institute for
Entrepreneurship Education.

Associates who helped Kauffman with the Youth Devel-
opment programs at the Kauffman Foundation, from left:
Jerry Kitzi, director of PROJECT EARLY; Tom Rhone, di-
rector of PROJECT CHOICE; Leslie Reed, director of PROJ-
ECT ESSENTIAL; and Carl Mitchell, president of the
Youth Development Division.

Kauffman acknowledges the cheers from the fans as he is inducted into the Royals Hall of Fame on May 23, 1993, a few months before his death.

Kauffman waves to fans from his limousine at the conclusion of his induction to the Royals Hall of Fame. The event
would be his last public appearance.

The championship pennants at the rechristened Kauffman
Stadium fly at half staff to mark the passing of Mr. K.

the organization. It's hard to admit that you've made a mistake," he commented. But in Kauffman's case, Slaughter also acknowledged that there were even greater obstacles. "If you are, down deep inside as I believe Mr. K was, a very warm and caring, generous person, it is doubly hard to fire somebody."

With Holder's guidance, Kauffman structured a scenario that permitted Dalbey to depart with dignity. Dalbey was six months shy of being fully vested in Marion's retirement system when Kauffman finally decided to dissolve the relationship. He called Dalbey in and told him simply, "It's not working. I'm not sure whose fault it is that it's not working, but I'm going to have to ask you to resign." After some discussion, they agreed that Dalbey would announce his retirement to take effect in six months. In that interim he would assume new responsibilities for planning. "As a matter of fact," Slaughter recalled, "he announced his resignation [to occur at a date] six months in the future, and then went on an extended trip to the Far East to make contacts with potential licensers for new technology. He did not return to Kansas City until after his resignation became effective. Everybody felt that was the best thing that could happen."

With that very prickly personnel problem resolved, there was only one more critical decision to make. The selection of a new chief operating officer was the most crucial decision of Kauffman's professional life. Marion's founder had already decided he did not want to devote all his time to the daily pressures of building a company. He was enjoying his new life as a member of that elite group of wealthy individuals who owned major league baseball teams. Talk of pennant races, league championships, and even the World Series was exhilarating. At fifty-four years of age, Kauffman was ready to take life a little easier. He wanted more time on the links with Bud Dahner, Don Stein, and George Bernard. And he delighted in the camaraderie and the good-humored competition among the regulars of the Kansas City Club's exclusive inner circle where he usually passed every afternoon playing gin rummy with his cronies. Yet, even though Kauffman was settled into the comfortable routine of the "good life," he was always mindful of the source of the wealth that made it all possible.

Although Kauffman was thoughtful, he was neither reflective nor introspective, certainly not at that point in his life. As a card player and businessman, he carefully calculated risk. At cards, he studied the odds and analyzed the possible outcomes. He always went into a game with a sizable reserve to tide him over a patch of bad luck. He never bet recklessly. He had none of the traits of the gambler. He assessed the risk involved and wagered accordingly. His style was similar in business. He made conservative financial projections. He always set the target for the coming year below what he believed he could earn, then worked hard to surpass that number by a substantial margin. Kauffman the entrepreneur might adopt the rhetoric of the visionary, talking expansively about annual earnings of $100 million, but in daily business he was an earthbound pragmatist. He eschewed bank loans, preferring to finance Marion's growth from reserve capital. He kept a sharp eye on expenses, remembering those early days when he often shared a drab motel room with one of the salesmen to keep travel costs down. He bartered stock in lieu of salary to ambitious young executives. And he aggressively pushed programs that rewarded associates for money-saving suggestions.

Yet when it came to people, Kauffman trusted his instincts. He wanted certain characteristics in the sales force—men who had worked from a young age, who had any kind of retail experience, and with wives who were supportive and ambitious for their husbands' success. In Marion's early years he relied on former school chums for the executive staff. And he turned to old friends or early benefactors as initial investors, confident that he was giving them the chance to be a part of something that would be very successful. He believed in himself and was supremely confident in his abilities as a salesman. He was determined to succeed and was eager to share that material success with friends, colleagues, and supporters.

All of these seemingly contradictory characteristics in Kauffman's nature and personality came into play as he considered who among the young executives was the right person to inherit his mantle at Marion. Most Marion associates concluded somewhat prematurely that Lyons was the heir apparent when he was promoted to executive vice president of Marion Laboratories in 1974 after Dalbey's retirement. But Kauffman reserved judgment. Lyons was only thirty-eight years old, the youngest of a relatively youthful cadre in which the average age of the Marion executive suite was forty-seven, and forty-five among the heads of the subsidiaries. Kauffman was only fifty-seven and in excellent health. He decided to observe Lyons and

Church closely to see which man seemed best suited to the task. If neither turned out to be the right fit, he could always look beyond Marion. But the more pressing challenge was to complete the executive management team.

Kauffman's first priority was to augment his own strength regarding financial matters. Initially he thought of hiring a senior comptroller or chief financial officer since money matters were his strong suit, along with sales. Instead, he hired Michael E. Herman, an exceptionally versatile financial strategist from Wall Street, as vice president of finance. Herman was a thirty-three-year-old founding partner of Dryden Company, a private investment-banking firm, when he decided to change his life by joining Marion Laboratories in 1974.

Herman's first Wall Street job was with Laird & Company, an investment-banking firm that was an innovator in management buy-out of companies. That was 1966. Within a few years Herman was head of Laird's mergers and acquisitions department. In the early seventies, he and four other partners left Laird to found Dryden Company, where they were primarily involved with venture capital projects.

The heady Wall Street life quickly paled. Herman became very unhappy with the ethics of Wall Street. "I just didn't like the orientation being fee-driven, very financially driven, not people-driven at all," he said. When Herman broached selling his share of the firm, he was stunned to learn that the partnership agreement he had signed "said basically you could be taken out at cost." In spite of his significant contribution to the firm's healthy balance sheet, the other partners demurred at buying his interest at market value. Herman's outcry, "That's not fair!" met unyielding resistance. He parted company, poorer but wiser. He left Dryden vowing, "I would not have treated people that way."

Rather than join another investment banking house, Herman decided to make a fundamental change in his life. "I liked entrepreneurs who started their businesses—first-generation entrepreneurs, not the old establishment. So I went out . . . looking for someone who might need me with my financial background and my desire . . . to help with an entrepreneurial business." As he was planning the strategy for approaching entrepreneurs, an executive recruiter suggested he add Ewing Kauffman to the list. As an avid sports fan, he knew of Kauffman through his ownership of the Kansas City Royals. He also knew of Marion Laboratories because Laird had been one of the underwriters of the initial offering of Marion stock. When he vetted Kauffman and Marion among his Wall Street contacts, they all scoffed at his even thinking about Marion Laboratories. "They didn't think it was a real [pharmaceutical] company. It didn't do research, it didn't have its own chemistry—just marketing and sales. This company really should never exist," Herman recalled.

An instinctive contrarian, Herman was curious and decided to investigate for himself. His initial interview with Kauffman was scheduled for thirty minutes, but it lasted four hours. Holder told Herman that Kauffman rarely spent that long with anyone, and inquired what they had talked about all that time. "We talked about everything!" Herman remembered. By the end of the interview, Kauffman offered Herman the vice presidency of finance. Reading hesitation in the younger man's face, the master salesman trolled more bait past him. "I know you think that Marion might not be big enough, but I can keep you interested. I have the Kansas City Royals. We have our family investments and—just a whole bunch of things."

The combination of possibilities was appealing. "Working with this small company called Marion Labs, being with this man and the things he was in—I liked that whole entrepreneurial spirit. That sounded like fun," Herman declared. But salary became a sticking point. "He wanted me to take a 50 percent cut in pay because I was to learn a lot here and the move would be good for me and my family and, therefore, the right thing to do," Herman said, recounting the negotiations. Kauffman refused to meet Herman's salary expectations because it would mean paying the new vice president for finance more than either he or Fred Lyons was making. And the usually impulsive Herman stifled the desire to suggest that Kauffman give himself and Lyons a raise. The salary was only one obstacle. Herman also learned that Marion Laboratories did not reimburse moving expenses and had no contracts. "Mr. Kauffman didn't believe in them. I was trying to explain to him that I was going to move my family from New York to Kansas. And Mr. Kauffman explained to me how they couldn't afford me," Herman said.

That fall following Herman's initial interview in August, he and his wife, Karen, visited Kansas City. They decided that this Midwestern town would be a delightful place to raise a young family and that they could change their standard of living. Karen Herman caught her husband's enthusiasm for what was a major career gamble. "This seemed to be the right thing for me. And, besides, it seemed like fun!" Years later as he thought back to that fateful decision, Herman again and again praised Karen's willingness to risk their future.

Kauffman decided to promote Fred Lyons to executive vice president in 1974, but not until the right executive was in place to direct the daily operations of the Pharmaceutical Group, Marion's oldest and most profitable division. The man recruited for that job was Jim McGraw, a Midwesterner who was president of General Diagnostics, a division of the pharmaceutical giant Warner-Lambert. His educational background was in preveterinary medicine, but an interest in business coupled with science led him to pharmaceutical sales after college. He started as a salesman with Dorsey Laboratories in Lincoln, Nebraska. When he left sixteen years later, he was acting general manager. During his years in Lincoln, McGraw recalled being aware of Marion Laboratories when it was extremely small. "In fact, we tried to buy them at one time and that was not successful." Later on when Marion began to grow rapidly, a representative contacted McGraw to see if he had any interest in working for them. "My answer was no because my track at Dorsey was too fast, and so I admired Marion from afar." But in 1974 when Holder and Lyons contacted McGraw at Warner-Lambert, he was more inclined to listen. Like Slaughter, McGraw had become involved in a situation with a lot of unkept promises. He bridled at the inequity and was ripe for persuasion to join another firm.

McGraw's interview with Kauffman was fast-paced, but lasted longer than the usual half hour. On his second trip back to Marion, he met with Kauffman again. "Mr. K was very forthright. He said I had made a very favorable impression and he wanted to bring it to a positive conclusion." He made an offer, but it was not up to McGraw's expectations. He told Kauffman he would think it over seriously and then left to return to the east coast. "Fred Lyons called up at the airport and increased the offer before I got on the plane to go back to New Jersey." McGraw joined the company in September 1974, and his wife and family followed six months later.

After five years of planning, thinking, and searching for the right people, Kauffman's executive management team was in place. Not even he could have imagined how complementary the mix of talents and the balance of skills would be. But before the legendary successes of the 1980s, the team would prove their mettle navigating the company through the troubled and treacherous waters of the late 1970s.

June 1975 marked Marion Laboratories' twenty-fifth anniversary. As Kauffman reflected on the preceding quarter century, he wrote confidently to the shareholders. "Marion, it seems to me, has never been in more capable hands, or its future more energetically committed to excellence." An experienced yet youthful executive team was in place. With net sales in excess of $84 million in fiscal 1975, the company was experiencing the momentum created earlier in the decade with the successful launch of GAVISCON and SIL-VADENE, a topical antimicrobial cream for serious burn-wound infections. Kauffman justifiably boasted that Marion Laboratories was the most productive company in the pharmaceutical industry. "We've had the most sales per employee in our industry," he told a local writer. "We've had the most profits per employee. Way above anybody else!" He credited the sales representatives' willingness to call on twice as many doctors as others in the industry as a major contributor to the growing profits. Marion pharmaceutical salesmen led the industry in sales per employee, with the number two company lagging behind by 38 percent. What made this performance so extraordinary was that up to this point, Marion Laboratories did not have a single patented product. As Lyons noted, "There is no so-called 'protection of the pricing structure' by patents. Anyone else could compete with these products."

But beneath this healthy facade and the silver anniversary rhetoric, signs of deterioration were apparent by summer 1974. Slaughter recalled that when he joined the company in February 1974, the stock was selling at fifty-two dollars a share. "Over the next four or five months, FDA difficulties with PAVABID, which was the leading product at the time, hit the street. There was a real risk of [the Food and Drug Administration] taking PAVABID off the market. And the stock began to drop like a rock. By August 1974 it was at eleven dollars a share."

Questions about PAVABID symbolized Marion Laboratories' vulnerability. Without the resources to support scientific research, Kauffman had relied on repackaging and enhancing existing compounds and on licensing drugs. Both of Marion's major products, PAVABID and NITROBID, were vasodilators marketed initially as "old drugs" enhanced with a sustained-release mechanism. Together, they accounted for more than 45 percent of the company's total volume in 1974. Neither product had ever cleared the Food and Drug Administration's new drug application licensing procedure because the main ingredients in both, papaverine and nitroglycerin respectively, had long been thought safe in medical application. But in the early 1970s, Congress empowered the Food and Drug Administration to demand evidence of efficacy as well as safety. The resulting situation was one of great uncertainty for Marion Laboratories. *F.D.C. Reports* cautioned investors that there was no guarantee that the Food and Drug Administration would determine that the sustained-release data Marion had already submitted on both drugs was adequate to permit the two products to remain on the market, pending completion of the efficacy studies. And these studies could take up to five years. In their filing with the Securities and Exchange Commission that year, Marion officials conceded that, "the removal of either PAVABID or NITROBID from the market would have a material adverse effect on earnings." This bearish language was probably more a reflection of Marion's lawyers' caution in dealing with the Securities and Exchange Commission than an accurate assessment of the FDA regulatory situation. However, it was evident that the company needed a strategy to weather what everyone hoped was only a temporary slump.

Kauffman's program to offset the effects of potential regulatory vulnerability to PAVABID and NITROBID and to ensure continuation of the company's sales and profit record was hardly new. It was, in fact, a continuation of the strategy for growth which he and Dalbey had devised in the years immediately following the public offering of Marion stock. Kauffman announced that Marion Laboratories would continue to diversify by acquiring companies in health-related fields with products ranging from safety devices to cosmetics. And the parent company would intensify efforts to search out and develop new drugs as an alternative to the large amounts of money and time required to create an in-house research capability. He characterized the approach as a "low-risk road to growth." He continually reminded shareholders and potential investors that this strategy gave Marion two advantages. It broadened the company's scientific and technical base far beyond what it could possibly afford through an in-house program. And it concentrated the search on relatively risk-free products that had already been proven efficacious and safe through testing in other countries and, in some cases, through marketing as well.

Kauffman's continuing efforts to acquire related companies were questionable. Marion's nondrug businesses had never performed too well on the profit side, and fiscal 1974 was no exception. Total sales and earnings continued to move upward despite general nationwide economic distress. And while all the associated enterprises contributed to the improved showing, the gains were exceptionally strong in the pharmaceutical area. Kauffman attributed the lassitude of the nondrug businesses to inflation in raw materials costs and price controls in the early 1970s. However, their historical performance overall did not merit the optimism and faith he seemed to place in them. While Marion's nondrug businesses accounted for 32 percent of sales, they contributed a mere 8 percent of pretax profits. Yet, Kauffman remained optimistic. He believed that Marion's prowess in pharmaceutical marketing and sales could be transferred to the other businesses. With an aggressive sales force, any one, or perhaps several, of the related businesses could take off in a big way at any time.

Although he continued to cling to this outmoded business strategy, Kauffman had completely transformed Marion's senior management team. With guidance from Jerry Holder, he hired executives with educational backgrounds in science and business and solid experience in larger pharmaceutical houses. They were relatively young, energetic, intelligent, and ambitious. He was deliberately positioning Marion Laboratories' pharmaceutical division to become a more sophisticated and aggressive competitor in a rapidly changing industry. Because of his faith in his own judgment, his willingness to share both responsibility and rewards, and his trusting nature, he would permit these new executives to undertake radical measures to restructure the company. And with his eyes fixed firmly on the goals of the future, he would sanction major changes, however wrenching they might be for him personally. As these new executives learned to work as a team during the last half of the decade, they would jettison the ancillary companies and concentrate on the pharmaceutical side of the business. Experience would temper their relative youth, but it would not blunt their willingness to wager that two compounds out of the scores they licensed in the 1970s had the potential to become major products. Yet never in their most expansive moments did they imagine that CARDIZEM and CARAFATE would be the blockbusters of the 1980s.

The young executives would remake and retrain the sales force, easing some men into new positions and some into retirement. When the federal government began pressing corporations to hire more women and minorities, they would move quickly to recruit both for positions throughout the company. They would discard the hucksterism of the earlier years without sacrificing the drive and commitment that had always distinguished Marion sales representatives. They would persuade Kauffman of the need to revise and extend what he believed was already a generous compensation schedule and benefits program. The result would be powerful incentive packages for the entire company, from the manufacturing plant's assembly lines to the inner sanctum of the executive suite. These incentives, combined with Kauffman's unparalleled ability to motivate the associates to sustain peak performance, fueled the explosion in sales and profits when CARDIZEM and CARAFATE finally reached the marketplace in the 1980s.

But before the phenomenal successes of the eighties came the doldrums of the late seventies. Stu Gold recalled, "The bottom started to fall out in the mid-seventies. I don't know how others felt but from my vantage point, we didn't have much to look forward to." When Jim McGraw arrived to head the pharmaceutical division, Marion stock was at an all-time low. "The business had frankly just topped off and the products were very mature," he recalled. "But what intrigued me was the program to license products from overseas. I was given some reasonable assurances that there were some big things . . . that were going to materialize. What I didn't realize was that the next two years were to be two very, very difficult years for the company."

McGraw's first task was to reach some accommodation with the FDA over PAVABID, which accounted for more than 50 percent of the pharmaceutical division's annual sales. When Marion Laboratories first began marketing PAVABID in 1962, the FDA had ruled that a new drug application was not required. They subsequently changed the decision, and a tug-of-war ensued with FDA threatening punitive action by 1974. McGraw, who believed in swift and direct response to a problem, went to Washington to visit personally with FDA officials. He proposed a compromise. Since both Marion and the FDA were conducting a series of studies on PAVABID's efficacy, he agreed that Marion Laboratories would not promote the product until the studies were finished. This was acceptable from a regulatory standpoint since the company would cease all efforts to advertise or otherwise promote the product. "But it was very, very hard from the marketing standpoint." Almost overnight, PAVABID sales began to decline. The earnings per share dropped dramatically as a result.

As earnings fell, the stock price continued downward and PAVABID sales lagged further. It seemed as if there was no stopping short of the basement. As a result, the associates' profit-sharing plan also suffered. "Mr. K was very defensive, or sensitive over that, because he felt he had let the associates down," McGraw recalled. Kauffman admitted that he realized he had probably been pushing the associates too hard for earnings. "We have just overstretched ourselves," he reflected. "The key is to put everything in order and make sure it doesn't happen again." That was McGraw's first opportunity to work with Kauffman in a very difficult situation. "He handled it very, very well," McGraw remembered. There would be many more difficult situations to resolve, many more tough decision to make, but McGraw knew that he could rely on Kauffman to be thoughtful, evenhanded, and remarkably resilient.

Slaughter recalled that Kauffman's response to the decline in the stock's price convinced him that Marion Laboratories was the right place to be. When Slaughter joined the company, the dichotomy between Kauffman's rhetoric about working at Marion and the reality of functioning in an environment where Dalbey held sway struck him forcefully. Dalbey's actions were the antithesis of Kauffman's rhetoric. Slaughter quickly learned there were other gaps between rhetoric and reality. Pay levels as well as benefits were low in comparison to the rest of the pharmaceutical industry. The only part of the benefits package that was really good was the profit-sharing plan. "But when the stock went from fifty-two to eleven, the profit-sharing plan really became a strong demotivator," he concluded.

The week that the stock suffered the biggest drop, Slaughter's original faith in Kauffman's promises was reaffirmed. Late on a Friday afternoon in the summer of 1974, Kauffman called Holder and Slaughter to his office. "Marion stock is down as low as it has ever been," he said calmly. "This is a real good opportunity for our folks to make some money with stock options. The only problem is you've got to put together a program to grant those options quickly. Can you do this over the weekend?" Kauffman asked. Holder and Slaughter worked around the clock for two days to develop a plan to help Marion employees take advantage of the low stock price. Throughout the weekend Slaughter could not help thinking of the enormous financial loss Kauffman had sustained. The Kauffman family owned 35 percent of Marion stock, and their personal fortune was now greatly diminished. Yet, instead of bemoaning his own losses, Kauffman was saying, "Now is a good time for our folks to make money on stock options because I think we can get this stock turned around." For Slaughter, Kauffman's rhetoric about sharing the rewards was becoming reality.

When Kauffman told McGraw that the key to avoiding a repeat of the adverse business conditions that plagued the company in the mid-1970s was "to put everything in order," he may not have been fully cognizant of the implications of those instructions. Marion Laboratories had fundamental problems that went far beyond the regulatory flap over PAVABID and NITROBID. Even if the FDA had never challenged those two products, the company's underlying weakness was the lack of a growing product line. Although rights to the compound which became known as CARAFATE had been acquired in 1974, and CARDIZEM would be licensed in 1976, they were part of a much larger group of drugs whose potential marketability was yet to be determined. Beyond that decision lay the long road through the FDA to secure regulatory approval. Strengthening and broadening the product line was clearly a priority, but there were other problems—high turnover among the sales force, low salary levels, an uneven benefits package, and lackluster performance from the associated businesses. All these issues would need to be addressed if Marion Laboratories was to survive, much less fulfill Kauffman's dream of becoming a $100 million enterprise.

When Kauffman named Fred Lyons as executive vice president, he acknowledged the need for change. One of the most vexing

problems was how to increase the profitability of the numerous associated businesses. Lyons's first move to bolster performance among
the associated companies was to hire Thomas W. Olofson as corporate vice president in charge of the health products group's operations. Then he began an analysis of market opportunities, resource
requirements, and resources available within each business. He structured a new planning process and developed strategies for the re-
allocation of resources and a measurement-and-controls system to
support implementation. Lyons attempted to assure the stockholders in 1975 of "meaningful opportunities for market penetration and
profit growth in these health care areas. We now feel that we have
in place the organization, concepts, and people capable of leading us
to that growth."

The subsidiary companies' lagging performance was only one of
the problems the new management team faced. The more ominous
cloud on the horizon was the continuing instability of the sales force,
which was the envy of the industry and the company's most valuable asset. But it had always had high turnover. Sperry first, then
Mannino had worked to upgrade and stabilize the group, but the
problems continued. Slaughter recalled that when McGraw took
the reins of the Pharmaceutical Division, turnover among the sales
staff was "killing us. . . . The doctors were saying, 'I see a new guy
every six weeks.'" But changing anything about the Marion pharmaceutical sales force would take finesse, tact, and not a little courage.

Kauffman took special pride in the Marion sales force. These were
the people who consistently out-performed all industry sales indi-
cators and produced the ever-growing revenue stream. He was one
of them. He had experienced the special terror of making a cold call
on a harried physician to tout the virtues of a new product. He
knew all about the tedium of the doctor's waiting room and the relentless push to make a few more calls at the tag end of a long day.
He had eaten indifferent food in late-night diners, slept in lumpy
motel beds, and experienced that hollow, lonely feeling of being too
far away to go home for the weekend. Kauffman also knew their
joys. He had felt the exhilaration of surpassing a quota and landing
a bonus. He knew the satisfaction of developing a collegial relationship with a respected physician. There was that intoxicating
feeling of being part of an elite corps, complete with the trappings
of sleek, air-conditioned, luxury automobiles, specially designed

gold rings, and expense accounts. Some of the salesmen who began their careers at Marion when Kauffman was still selling were in managerial positions or involved in sales training. Some were still on the road. But whatever an individual's history or length of tenure, the sales force, as a body, enjoyed the mantle of Kauffman's gratitude, loyalty, and his benevolent protection.

McGraw knew he must move cautiously. Kauffman had to be an ally in any changes. To test his subjective conclusions about the extent of the problem, McGraw asked Holder's group to analyze the turnover. Slaughter, who had completed a similar study for American Home Products just before he was recruited to Marion, compared the two situations. Both were financially successful drug companies, but both were "taking it out of the hides of their people. Can you make money that way? Yes. Is that the way you want to live?" he asked. The answer at Marion Laboratories was no.

Slaughter's team studied the problem from every angle. They asked who was leaving. When they were leaving? Why did they say they were leaving when they left? To test the results of the exit interviews, they did postexit interviews. They telephoned people all around the country three or six months after their departure to ask, "Now that you're gone, why did you really leave?" The study results were clear and troubling. Slaughter concluded that the primary problem with the sales force was twofold. "We learned that it was largely a matter of management style, the tone of which was set by Jean Sperry and complicated by the low compensation for the sales force." Kauffman, unwittingly, compounded the problems. In his speeches to the sales force, he always boasted that the company's pay and benefits were the best in the industry. "That's what he wanted, but at this point, it just wasn't true," Slaughter said. "Both Sperry and Mr. K were very frugal, as entrepreneurs must be, but when applied to salaries for the sales force, this was destructive. Mr. K, in spite of being the most generous person I have ever known, was also very tight! And whether or not it was a matter of Mr. K setting the tone or of Jean Sperry overdoing it, we will never know. . . . But it was clearly an operating style in the sales force." The study also revealed a lack of scientific education among the sales staff, compounded by outdated training and insufficient initial training of new sales representatives and a general style of management by intimidation.

The proposed strategy required to remake the sales force was straightforward: hire people with a strong science background as well as an ability to sell, give them the best training possible, compensate them competitively, and devise an incentive system to keep them challenged. But the reality of implementing the strategy ran smack up against the human problem of how to change the temperament, management style, and lifelong habits of a single individual. Mannino had attempted to upgrade the sales force and its training in the late sixties and early seventies. But many of the young professionals he had recruited from other companies felt stifled. They considered management practices to be out-of-date. Others felt alienated from a group that had a lengthy internal history and was inherently suspicious of outsiders. Clearly, the only way to remake the sales force was to change it from the top down.

Sperry continued to manage the sales force, a position he had held since the late fifties. He was one of the original pioneers of Marion Laboratories. He was the third person Kauffman had recruited to help in the dingy storefront on Troost. Sperry had opened the Dallas market and quickly achieved record sales for OS-CAL and OS-VIM. As general manager, he opened territory after territory across the country for the young company. His arguments had persuaded Kauffman to bring PAVABID to market over serious objections from his colleagues. And his concept of the M Club and the Marion ring had become known industry-wide for motivating and rewarding a sales force. He was as aggressive, tenacious, and ambitious as Marion's founder himself, but Sperry lacked Kauffman's insight into his own shortcomings and was stubbornly resistant to change. McGraw recognized the significance of Sperry's role in building the sales force which had helped the young company to survive and then succeed. But the two men had very different work styles, and they clashed from the beginning. This tug of wills continued for almost two years. "We worked at it and worked at it, and finally I said, 'It's just not going to work out,'" McGraw recalled. He recommended to Lyons that Sperry be made president of the new international division which was about to be started.

For Kauffman the decision to replace Sperry was as difficult personally as any decision he would make as Marion's chief executive officer. He was aware that Sperry's relationship with both Lyons and McGraw had been uneasy from the beginning. He conceded that "Sperry was quite dogmatic" and resistant to ideas not his own.

But Kauffman understood that the industry which he and Sperry had entered in the 1950s was profoundly different by the mid-1970s. Where tenacious salesmanship alone had once carried the day, a strong science education and sophisticated marketing skills were now necessary. "The only experience in pharmaceuticals Jean had was what he learned from me, and I didn't know very much myself," Kauffman said. "There were gaps in our knowledge, and this is what hurt him in his relationship with Lyons and McGraw. I agreed with the change because we just outgrew Jean."

While Kauffman accepted the need for different leadership in the sales force, he was sensitive to the human dimensions of this decision. He felt deep loyalty toward Sperry as a trusted colleague. And he was concerned about the possible financial ramifications for him and his family. Sperry was still a young man, only in his late forties, but Kauffman thought it unlikely that he could afford to retire because of the recent steep decline in Marion's stock price. Furthermore, he recognized that Sperry had extensive experience and skills that could still be of great value to the company. He agreed that launching Marion products abroad was just the kind of challenge to call forth Sperry's best performance. They had been pioneers together once. Now Sperry would have the opportunity to pioneer again.

True to his nature, Sperry resisted the plan. Kauffman recalled that he dismissed the idea as preposterous, saying that anyone familiar with Marion's product line would know the ideas could not be successful. Sperry spent an entire evening at Kauffman's home trying to convince him to rescind the decision. He argued that he had no qualifications for such an assignment. He spoke no foreign languages and he did not particularly like traveling outside the United States. But Kauffman would not budge. He was confident that Sperry's in-depth knowledge of Marion and its products, plus his innate abilities as a salesman, insured the success of the new international division.

Kauffman felt that Sperry left that evening with the impression that he was supporting decisions that had been made by his upper management. That impression was accurate. When Kauffman transferred day-to-day management control to Fred Lyons and the executive team, he did so with the full recognition that some of their specific decisions might be personally painful, as the one regarding

Jean Sperry certainly was. In recalling the incident years later, Kauff-man said quietly, with no hint of self-justification, "I protected Jean as far as I could."

In spite of Sperry's gloomy predictions, the International Division was successful from the beginning. While learning the ins and outs of the foreign pharmaceutical markets, Sperry paid his way with licensing agreements to sell products from the subsidiaries, primarily Kalo, Stair-Glide, and Marion Scientific. Within a few years he had successfully negotiated arrangements with foreign companies in the Pacific Rim and in Europe to sell a number of different products from Marion's basic pharmaceutical line. By the time he retired in 1987, the International Division employed twenty-four people and was producing in excess of fifteen million dollars in sales each year. Kauffman's view—that if senior management felt the environment had outgrown the person, they should put the person in an environment where he could succeed—was vindicated. "Here was Sperry's genius," Slaughter explained. "He could go over there by himself, solely by himself, start up an International Division, go eke out, scratch and claw his way into several marketplaces around the world, so within three or four years, he's selling fifteen million dollars worth of product! . . ." It was an even more impressive accomplishment because it was done without the major products, CARDIZEM and CARAFATE, that were so successful in the United States and Canada in the 1980s.

Attacking the problems in the sales force involved a great deal more than new leadership, better educated recruits, and more competitive compensation and benefit packages, although all those were important. McGraw sensed a genuine need for the sales representatives to become better listeners, to know more about how a given product helped a patient—in short, to be more empathetic. "I'd been with the company not too long when I asked at a meeting, 'How many of you have ever been to a burn ward?'" he recalled. When very few hands went up, he decided it was time to change that. He told Bob Henderson, the Marion medical director, to set up a tour of a burn ward for the next meeting of regional sales managers.

McGraw's decision to have Marion's sales managers, and later all hospital sales representatives, visit a burn ward as a part of their sales training to introduce a new product was a strategic one. In the late sixties, Marion had obtained the rights to SILVADENE through a combination of risk taking and blind luck. Bill Doyle, whose job was to find new products, told Kauffman about a burn cream therapy that scientists at Columbia University had developed. They were getting ready to put the licensing rights up for bid, and Doyle thought Marion should make a bid. "I sent him up there with a blank check and said that he could go to fifty thousand dollars," Kauffman recalled. "And that's how we ended up with it. I spent fifty thousand dollars not knowing too much about it, but if we lost, I could afford it." SILVADENE was exceptionally important because it was Marion's first patented product, which meant that no other pharmaceutical house could manufacture or market it until the patent protection expired. "[The patent on SILVADENE] helped both our morale and our ability to interest doctors in our products," Kauffman recalled.

Never one to ask his associates to do something he had not done, McGraw flew to San Antonio to visit the world's largest burn ward at Brooke Army Hospital. There they interviewed the physicians and nurses who attended severely burned soldiers. They talked with the patients and with their families as well. "I remember this one father and son, who said, 'You know, SILVADENE is such a wonderful product. We can barely wait for the nurse to come around and put it on. It soothes and fights the infection and just makes us feel so much better,'" McGraw remembered. McGraw was convinced every Marion hospital representative needed a personal visit to a burn ward, plus thorough instruction in burn management and pharmacology, to help them present SILVADENE more effectively to health care professionals.

With assistance from Dudley Hudgins, Marion's chief sales trainer, McGraw developed a preceptorship which required the hospital representatives to spend five days in a burn unit. An abbreviated, but equally effective program was also devised for the so-called "Six-Pack," the executives who reported directly to McGraw. "Once a year I'd take the Six-Pack and their wives on an off-site meeting," McGraw recalled. "One year we took them to a burn ward up in Boston where we were working on artificial skin. We took them to MIT in the morning, then we went over to Boston General. The burn surgeon brought us right into the intensive care unit where a patient had third-degree burns over 80 percent of his body. Everybody but [one man] made that one. These aren't pleasant things to see." However difficult aspects of the experience may have been, the overall effect was positive. And it was quickly reflected in rising sales for SILVADENE.

McGraw was pleased with the effect on sales, but he was primarily concerned with teaching the salesmen to listen to the physician, as well as to engage their compassion for the patient. Jim McGraw was an emotional Irishman with a quick intelligence, wit, and temper. He believed passionately that if the sales staff understood how the products affected individual human lives, their work could be transformed. And he also believed the same could be true for senior management. Kauffman, who loved nothing better than interacting with customers, eagerly offered to participate in a trip to Indianapolis to set an example for the sales force. He had always loved being on the road for Marion Laboratories. Now he sometimes longed to be in the thick of things, especially when a new product was being introduced. Yet, as was his policy and habit now, he deferred to McGraw's judgment. McGraw knew that Kauffman's near-celebrity status as the founder of Marion Laboratories, and more importantly, as the owner of the Kansas City Royals, would distract everyone involved from the task at hand. The founder was grounded, but he took it with good grace.

That week in the field was revealing and disturbing. The same group did two more "sales trips." Again they came home unsettled. "Those trips were very traumatic for the organization," McGraw recalled. "They found that the sales literature didn't work, and things like that. Harley Tennison, who was the vice president of sales and marketing at that time, was incensed. He said [company records showed that] the doctors he was to call on had been 'visited regularly' but the building had been torn down two years earlier!" During the high-growth years, Marion employees had become careless. They were more eager to garner the profits of the moment than to ensure the good relationships and the accurate records that would help the company continue to prosper over the long term.

McGraw and his executive team responded quickly to what they had learned. They revised sales literature and the training programs. They implemented new recruiting standards and practices. "I'm a nut on getting out and listening to the customer," McGraw admitted. "You come back to the office and implement ideas, but first get out there where the action is. You can't do that all the time, but I'm saying you have to get involved with the customer."

The marketing strategy used with SILVADENE came to be known in the company as "the empathetic focus concept." And it proved to be highly effective when applied to other products as well. Many elements of this strategy—preceptorships at hospitals that specialized in cardiology and gastroenterology, intensive seminars with specialists, field testing the sales literature—were refined and utilized with even greater success when CARAFATE and then CARDIZEM were launched in the 1980s.

Listening and responding to physician and patient needs was important to Marion Laboratories' success in the 1980s. But Marion executives also listened carefully to the wholesalers who were their crucial link to pharmacists throughout the country. McGraw, who admitted he loved "to get out there where the action is," took several members of his executive team to Los Angeles to visit Emil Martini, the head of Bergen Brunswick, "one of the most innovative wholesalers, bar none." Martini was the first large wholesaler to automate a warehouse, and McGraw was eager to pick his brain for ideas about how their respective firms might work together more effectively. Martini visited with McGraw's team in the corporate offices, then suddenly announced that he wanted to talk somewhere other than his office, some place very private. McGraw chartered a boat and they had lunch in Los Angeles harbor. "Obviously, we were a captive audience," he remembered.

Martini got right to the point. He told the Marion people that their shipping and payment schedules were unacceptable. "It takes you people sixteen days to get a shipment from Kansas City to California," he complained. The financial arrangements permitted a 1 percent discount if the wholesaler paid within thirty days. But given lost days in shipping, the wholesaler was actually having to pay within fourteen days to get the discount. McGraw's first response when he returned to Kansas City was to request an audit to verify Martini's complaint. When he received the results, he immediately called Martini to announce, "'Emil, I want to tell you that you are wrong! You said it took sixteen days to get a shipment. It takes us nineteen! We're working on it and we need your total commitment to work with us on this.' Martini said, 'No problem,'" McGraw recalled.

The standard practice among pharmaceutical manufacturers was to establish a shipping date and require that the wholesaler must order on that date. Gary Sears and Bob Slater of the Pharmaceutical Division's program management staff developed the "preferred order date program." "We said, 'Mr. Wholesaler, you are in southern California and if you will order on every other Monday, we'll guarantee that shipment to be there in six days or less. In addition, we will give you an additional cash discount if you will order on that day and in case lots. Now if you want to order on other days, that's your business.'" All parties agreed that this sounded like a win-win solution. So the "preferred order date program" was introduced at the annual meeting which Marion hosted for the wholesalers' chief executive officers. Kauffman was in attendance, as always, and he personally made the announcement. He praised Emil Martini for stimulating the idea and gave him a plaque to commemorate the occasion. McGraw recalled that Martini was "very touched by Kauffman's praise. And he got a lot of publicity out of it and every wholesaler benefited."

In practice, the turn-around time was astonishing. Marion products were on pharmacists' shelves in record time, and the revenue stream flowed more swiftly and more evenly. Later, the order process was enhanced again and again as Marion people listened more attentively to the wholesalers and the pharmacists. The particular innovation of shrink-wrapping orders, which quickly became standard practice throughout the industry, came from a wholesaler in New Jersey. This man noted that he regularly ordered a certain number of cartons of CARDIZEM which cost $750 each. Since the cartons were shipped in a large container, it was often difficult and time-consuming for him to verify that he had received the exact number ordered. In a large warehouse operation, a single carton might become separated from the rest of the shipment and then be placed on the wrong shelf. Whether missing from the original shipment or placed with the wrong inventory, it was lost. And that meant lost profit to the wholesaler. Shrink-wrapping was the answer, as well as securing an agreement among the wholesalers about the standard number of cartons in each order.

McGraw described these innovations as the result of "another example of listening to the customer." Kauffman agreed. But he always reminded the managers that being attentive to the customer, seeking his advice, implementing his suggestions, and giving him the credit for good ideas was at the heart of his basic philosophy of "treating people the way you want to be treated." And it was. These practices, which forged mutually profitable relationships among Marion and its various distributors were also consistent with Kauffman's second principle: "Those who produce should share in the rewards." In the case of the wholesalers and the pharmacists, having their needs considered and seeing their suggestions implemented meant additional discounts for them, better inventory control over product, and enhanced sales and profits.

By as early as 1975, problems within the company and with the FDA over PAVABID and NITROBID were beginning to take their toll. The distribution channels were stuffed to overflowing and, for the first time in Marion Laboratories' history, more product was returned in July than was sold in June. "We found out that the sales force had been working the distribution game," Slaughter recalled. "In fact, we have very high levels of returns in the month of July." Since bonuses were calculated on product shipped instead of product sold, some overzealous salesmen had been persuading wholesalers to take delivery of product they had no intention of selling. Marion had a 100 percent returns policy, so the accommodating wholesalers would ship the product back the next month. However, the sales would have already been credited toward the bonus of each person along the line, from the man in the field to the sales executives in Kansas City.

McGraw discovered other questionable practices. He found that it was standard practice to bring in a lot of sales at the end of a quarter to try to meet projected goals. Even if the product was not shipped until after the end of the quarter, it was still being recorded in the books as having transpired the prior quarter. From a financial standpoint, "it was," according to McGraw, "like trying to shoot pool with a rope." Then he uncovered a half-million dollars of promotional literature stored in a warehouse. The explanation was that if the Sales Division found its expenses too high in one quarter, it would put the material in escrow and not book it against that quarter's earnings. McGraw demanded an immediate end to such practices. "We're going to write that stuff off, get rid of it, and clean up the books," he announced. "We were becoming a big-time company here, and I'm a nut on having clean books." What had happened was that the company's expansion had gotten ahead of the sales revenue. McGraw noted that this was not an uncommon situation, especially in a company with maturing products. Marion Laboratories continued to behave as if in a growth mode. They were attempting to squeeze additional earnings out of the health products' growth; instead, losses occurred. "It was growing pains," McGraw said. "It has happened to a number of firms. But the key is, you don't want it to happen again."

But problems within the sales force and questionable accounting practices were only part of the decline that became acutely apparent in 1976. The biggest stumbling block was Marion's pharmaceutical product line. It was ordinary—a "me-too" group of products that were collectively and inherently weak. Slaughter described it as "a 'salesman-intensive line' as opposed to a 'technology-intensive line.'" Lyons and McGraw knew that to survive in the pharmaceutical industry, much less grow, they had to improve the product line substantially and then upgrade the sales force to move it. And they had to move quickly. The pool of licensed but as-yet-undeveloped drugs the company had acquired would have to provide the genie as well as the lamp if the old magic of Marion was to be revived.

Lowell Miller, a biochemist who joined Marion Laboratories in 1973, was acting head of research and development. In that capacity, he led the team that studied and recommended which compound or compounds from among the batch under consideration had the greatest potential to be a significant product in the marketplace. A variety of factors had attracted Miller to Marion Laboratories. "I certainly had a lot of respect for Mr. Kauffman as a person, based mainly on rumor [rather] than fact," he recalled. Like so many others in the pharmaceutical industry in the central United States, Miller was familiar with the stories about Kauffman's generous treatment of his associates. He had watched Marion's astonishing growth from a close range. In spite of Kauffman's success and how well the company had done without a research program, Miller believed there would be great opportunities there for scientists like himself. He was confident that the company would either be forced into more scientific research and development or be forced out of business. He was betting on the former and wanted to get on board while the company was still relatively small and growing.

After months of intensive analysis, Miller became convinced that CARDIZEM, licensed as an antianginal agent without a clearly defined mechanism of action, was "something different . . . something of real significant potential," Slaughter recalled Miller telling his colleagues. Early in the review/licensing process there had been initial speculation that CARDIZEM might have some beta-blocker activity. However, based on some very early preclinical data generated by outstanding scientists, Miller was convinced CARDIZEM belonged to a new and exciting class of drugs. German scientists investigating the drug verapamil described this new class of drugs as calcium channel blockers. Based on their mechanism of action, this class of drugs was thought to have fewer side effects—less drowsiness, less disorientation—than the existing beta-blockers. Miller had a similar hunch about CARAFATE, which had been licensed as an antacid.

Acting out of respect for Miller's scientific judgment and visceral intuition, McGraw secluded himself with Miller and his four-man scientific team at the Crown Center Hotel for three days to ponder the choices. "We've got to think through which of these projects we can drive a white stake through and which of them we can put our money behind," McGraw announced. "It's clear that we are not going to be able to turn PAVABID around, and we're just holding on by the skin of our teeth to keep it on the market. We've got to get some new products!"

The planning team reviewed each of the two dozen products in the process. After listening carefully to his scientific executives and blending their ideas with what the marketing executives were saying, McGraw framed the recommendation: "If we'll take the money and put it behind CARDIZEM and CARAFATE . . . we can accelerate their development by as much as two to three years." His associates in the planning meeting gasped, "It's the biggest gamble we've ever taken." In the end, they all agreed. Lyons then persuaded Kauffman and the board that their best hope for Marion Laboratories' future was to adopt McGraw's strategy: They would "bet the company."

In order to free up the resources—both people and dollars— needed to accelerate the development process on CARDIZEM and CARAFATE, Kauffman finally acknowledged that the subsidiary companies were not making enough money to justify the executive time that they required. Lyons made the case repeatedly and with great conviction: The pharmaceutical business was Marion Laboratories' rootstock. The subsidiaries had been grafted on rather haphazardly and, as a group, had sapped the parent company's strength. Pruning them away would give the company an opportunity to flourish again.

In retrospect, selling the associated businesses seemed like a series of swift, clean cuts. In reality, it was slower and messier than Kauffman remembered. He did not proceed with the sale of the subsidiaries in a cavalier manner. In fact, the divestiture process had actually been going on for some time when the final decision was made to concentrate on pharmaceuticals exclusively. What finally became a policy to divest started as an effort to make all the subsidiaries more profitable.

Signet Laboratories, located in Burbank, California, was the first candidate. Signet produced and sold health food supplements, vitamins, minerals, and cosmetics. The rationale for purchasing Signet a few years earlier had seemed very persuasive at the time. Signet had more than a hundred different products in its inventory, plus laboratory facilities and staff for developing more. Kauffman reasoned that since Marion Laboratories had been so successful with a simple product like OS-CAL, they could surely do the same with a much larger inventory of similar products. But Signet Laboratories had performed far below expectations from the beginning. By 1975, it was clearly foundering. Tom Olofson, the executive responsible for the subsidiaries, decided to replace Signet's president. He hired a young entrepreneur, Brant Cotterman, who had owned one of Signet's competitors. Cotterman, an engineer and marketing graduate of Michigan State, was already living in California when he accepted the position. "Within three months, I realized what needed to be done," Cotterman recalled. "Actually, within thirty days. Actually within thirty minutes I realized what needed to be done with Signet!"

Fortified with facts and figures, Cotterman flew to Kansas City prepared to recommend a solution. But it was the opposite of what he had been hired to do—namely, to restore the company to profitability. He talked first with Olofson, then with Lyons. They, in turn, decided he must talk directly with Kauffman. "That was about the hardest meeting I've ever had in my life," he remembered. "I was the first person that went in and said, 'This is a failure. It's a bad decision.'" Cotterman tried to deliver the bad news in positive terms.

He recommended selling Signet Laboratories as quickly as possible. "'If you wait six months, you are going to have six more months of losses; wait a year, you are going to have a year of losses. And plus, the company today is still worth something and I don't think it'll be worth very much a year from now.' This was very, very hard for Kauffman [to hear]," Cotterman recalled.

At first Kauffman seemed to think this was to be a routine report on Signet. However, he quickly sensed the direction. "And as I got about two-thirds of the way through the presentation, he took out . . . three matches. He was stuffing this tobacco down this great big [pipe] bowl and lit up and started puffing the smoke. I looked up and this smoke is increasing and increasing. I thought it was going to be like one of the Houdini acts. I thought I was annoying him so much that when . . . that cloud [of smoke] disappears, he's not going to be there!" Instead of disappearing, Kauffman sat, silent amid the smoke. Cotterman rose to his feet, but no one spoke. He was sure this was the end of his association with Marion Laboratories and Ewing Kauffman. Finally Lyons broke the awkward stillness, telling him they would be in touch. Cotterman was at the Houston airport later that day, halfway home to California, when Olofson tracked him down. He was to return to Kansas City at once. At Lyons's urging, Kauffman had agreed with the recommendation and now wanted to know how quickly Cotterman could sell the company. "That was the end of it. It took me thirty days. In thirty days, I had a signed contract."

The decision to sell Signet Laboratories had been difficult for Kauffman. It forced him to acknowledge that he had ignored the advice he had always given any person launching a business: "An entrepreneur who starts in business should stick to what he knows." At the time he purchased Signet Laboratories, the health food business was very profitable. Signet's founder was making over a million dollars a year in profits and was ready to retire and enjoy the good life. As Kauffman considered the purchase, it looked as if he could acquire the company without a significant cash outlay. "Here we were selling [our stock] at fifty times earnings and we could trade stock. We could buy the company for six million dollars, which is six times earnings, but Wall Street was giving us fifty times earnings ratio. [It] sounded like a deal to me, and when you get greedy, you lose." Kauffman later admitted that he had been somewhat suspicious because he thought the man was selling out too cheaply. He was also concerned because the financial records were not as good as they should have been. "So being very smart, I insisted that [the] Peat, Marwick & Mitchell accounting firm go in there and spend three whole months, very expensive, about sixty thousand dollars, to see that he was telling the truth—that he was making that type of profit." After careful and costly study, the outside accountants agreed that the company was indeed making that large a profit. Kauffman bought the company, but Marion executives were never able to realize anything close to the previous owner's profits.

Signet Laboratories was the first of the associated companies to be sold. Rose Manufacturing Company of Denver, which made fall protection devices for the construction industry and therefore attracted costly lawsuits when plaintiffs became aware of Marion's deep pockets, was the next to go in 1978. By 1980, all of the associated companies had been sold. But in selling each of the subsidiaries, Kauffman followed his own dictums about how the owners and employees should be treated. Regardless of how great Marion's revenue needs might be for growth in pharmaceuticals, the associated businesses were not to be plundered.

The specific task of building an incentive system that would cause the president of each of the subsidiaries to support the sale as being in his own best interest fell to Herman and Slaughter. "We worked out a way in which the president of the subsidiary got a specific bonus that was a function of how much money we got out of the sale." Under such a system, the president was highly motivated to facilitate the transaction. The human resources staff devised either separation packages or transition packages. "And we negotiated hard with the potential buyers to protect our people," Slaughter recalled. As a result of these incentives and protective measures, the management teams in a number of the subsidiaries actually helped significantly in the buyouts.

Michael Mahoney, the president of American Stair-Glide—the most profitable of the associated businesses—recalled his experiences working with Kauffman and Marion Laboratories. Newly married in 1968 to a TWA airline attendant from Kansas City, Mahoney had left Los Angeles "with no place to go; about a buck and a half in my pocket, a suit of clothes . . . and a 1964 Mustang." He liked his wife's hometown and decided to pursue leads in the banking industry, in which he had worked in California. After the chief executive officer of a Kansas City bank told him, "We can't hire you because your personality test showed that you're too aggressive to be a banker," he decided to try sales. Mahoney's father-in-law knew Kauffman and asked him to counsel with Mahoney in his job search. Although Kauffman generally preferred to hire men with previous sales experience, he liked Mahoney's personality. And he was impressed enough with the test results to offer him a position as sales promotion manager for American Stair-Glide.

Kauffman's nose for talent served him well. Within a few years Mahoney was promoted to general manager and then to president in 1974. Under his leadership, American Stair-Glide became the most profitable of the Marion subsidiaries, but it, too, would have to go on the block. In December 1979, McGraw met personally with Mahoney over lunch. He told Mahoney that the Marion board had decided to divest everything that was not directly related to the pharmaceutical business. Although American Stair-Glide was the star among the associated companies, Mahoney knew that as a group, they diverted resources from the pharmaceutical division. McGraw outlined the options available. "He said they would give me time to put together a group to buy it. Or if I wanted to help them sell the company, they would put me on a management-incentive contract. If the company were sold and I decided not to stay with the new ownership, they would have a place for me at Marion," Mahoney remembered. He jumped at the chance to acquire the company. Drawing on local investment counsel, as well as legal and accounting services, he obtained the necessary financing. "We started about the first part of January of 1980 and we actually closed the deal on November 26—about eleven months of hair-raising experience. . . ."

Although out from under Marion's corporate mantle, Mahoney continued to maintain contact with Kauffman. Both men belonged to the Indian Hills Country Club, so they often saw one another on the golf course. Mahoney admitted that years later after he owned American Stair-Glide outright, he always felt a twinge of guilt when he encountered Kauffman on the golf links on a weekday. During his initial interview with Kauffman in 1968, they had bantered about their mutual fondness for the sport. They both confessed to the school truant's guilty pleasure of slipping away from business early on a spring afternoon to play the back nine. Abruptly, the older man had said to the new hire, "But I don't expect you to be on the golf course anytime during the week for at least five years!"

On Saturday mornings when Kauffman and his gin rummy cronies gathered at Indian Hills to play cards, Mahoney and his younger friends were usually playing gin at a nearby table. On several occasions after acquiring American Stair-Glide, Mahoney returned to Kauffman for business advice. "I remember calling him. He'd ask me to send a little summary of what it was so he would be versed on it. Then we would talk for an hour or so. If you would listen carefully, you could pick up the real good things and filter out all the stuff that did not relate [to your specific situation]. He would raise questions back in terms of 'Have you thought of this? Why are you doing that?' He always gave me some challenging questions that I had to go back and think about."

Kauffman's willingness to counsel other entrepreneurs was well known among his Kansas City business associates. Barnett Helzberg, whose family owned a successful retail jewelry business in Kansas City, said, "I can't tell you the difference I think he made in my company, in my life, and everything else." Helzberg, who knew of Kauffman and Marion Laboratories, actually met the Kauffmans when attending a meeting of the Young President's Organization in Pebble Beach, California, in 1972. Both Ewing and Muriel were featured speakers. After hours, over a drink, Kauffman invited the young man to drop by Marion for a visit when he returned home. "I started going to his office, just every so often. And it was kind of like opening a curtain for me," Helzberg said. "I learned that it isn't stupid to reward people, and it isn't stupid to pay people, it isn't stupid to share. I learned it's no fun to drink champagne alone. I learned you can only wear one suit at a time. I learned it's a lot more fun sharing it than not."

Kauffman was always accessible to those who sought his counsel, but was never presumptuous. His approach was always indirect, questioning the entrepreneur to stimulate more creative responses, probing for explanations to cause the other person to reflect on his rationale for certain actions and often to rethink his entire strategy. In spite of his openness and willingness to share time from a very busy schedule to advise others, Kauffman was more of a patriarch than a pal. He was approachable and friendly, but seldom intimate. "There was always that reserve—not a wall, and I don't think it was self-imposed," Mahoney recalled. "He was somebody who had a lot to do, a lot on his mind. . . . But if you had a question, he would answer it. He always gave me the time of day, and I always respected him for that."

Once all the subsidiaries had been sold, Marion associates at all levels focused exclusively on what they knew best, the sale of pharmaceuticals. While Lowell Miller's staff in research and development worked through the clinical trials, gathering and analyzing the data necessary to complete a new-drug application for FDA, preparations to support the marketing of the new drugs were taking place throughout the company. Slaughter recalled, "I got the responsibility to bring compensation plans up to snuff." That assignment was unusually delicate. "The task really was one of finding ways to implement this very progressive, participatory, high-sounding philosophy that Mr. K continued to voice, to put that into practice because it never had been done. If you want to treat people like you want to be treated, that means something. If you want to pay people for producing, that means something. So you have got to figure out what are the kinds of systems, plans, programs, policies, and procedures that you need to put in place to make those words be true, not just hollow things that people say at the end of every year," he said.

Kauffman had always taken pride in treating Marion associates fairly and rewarding those who produced. And there was ample evidence that an associate who worked hard, stayed with the company, and took advantage of stock options could prosper. As the company's earnings grew steadily through the mid-seventies, all the associates reaped the benefits through the profit-sharing plan. But when earnings slowed, then declined in 1974, senior management recognized the need for new incentives to spur growth and help generate the cash needed to bring the anticipated new drugs to the marketplace.

Slaughter proposed a company-wide bonus plan—a rarity for the industry then as now. In the early years, Marion Laboratories had two bonus plans: one for salesmen and one for senior officers. The bonus plan for the sales force was activity-oriented. It was calculated on the number of calls made and on the amount of drugs sold. The senior executives' plan was tied to a percentage of the company's profits. Depending on the amount of profit at year's end, Kauffman would decide how much bonus each senior officer received. But the system was flawed because there was no agreed-upon target beforehand. An executive "never really knew what to shoot for. And Mr. K was also known very frequently to say, 'Well, if you're able to make the target, the target isn't high enough.' So he could adjust the payout," Slaughter recalled. In reflecting on Kauffman's generous words as contrasted with his often parsimonious actions in those early days, Slaughter admitted that he did not know if Kauffman had been consciously aware of the inconsistency. "Mr. K had an uncanny ability to be willing to promise anything as long as he didn't think—and this is a personal opinion—as long as he didn't think it was going to cost too much."

Trying to sell Kauffman on a revised and extended bonus plan was not easy. Slaughter argued that if the plan was to be truly motivational, it had to offer incentives to produce the desired behavior. The targets must be clearly stated at the year's beginning, and the payout had to be guaranteed if the targets were met. And the practice had to be consistent from year to year so the associates would get experience with it and gain confidence in the system. "Nobody really believes you'll pay that kind of bonus until you've paid that kind of bonus," Slaughter said. "But once you pay that kind of bonus, then it is real. And then it becomes motivational for years in the future." In conversations with Kauffman, Slaughter came back to the same point over and over. "If people think it's always going to be an elastic ruler or every time they jump [the hurdle] you're going to raise the bar a little higher, that becomes very demotivational."

Over a period of about two years, Kauffman's conservative position eroded and then gave way. In countless interviews and by relentless probing—"Why do you do this? Why do you do that? Why the stock options?"—Jerry Holder helped Kauffman define, and then refine, what he wanted the company to be. In response to Holder's questioning, Kauffman was able to distill a philosophy from what one associate described as a "chaos of attitudes." While his rhetoric may have seemed at odds with his actions at times, Kauffman sincerely believed he was treating the associates fairly and that he was equitably rewarding those who produced. "Jerry helped: here's the rhetoric [he would say] and here's what you're really saying. All this fits, but some of these things don't. We need to make some changes [Holder would say]. . . . Mr. K then was able to even clarify all that in his mind, and that was a good anchor for him to make decisions from," Cotterman recalled.

Giving bonuses only to senior executives and salesmen was common practice in the pharmaceutical business. To Kauffman it seemed appropriate, since they provided the leadership and generated the sales that resulted in the profits, and all associates reaped the benefits through the ever-growing profit-sharing plan. Kauffman bridled at the suggestion that he might be fudging on promises when he altered a growth target he felt had been too easily met. Had he not proven his fidelity to the associates when he made up the shortfall in the profit-sharing plan when revenues dipped in the mid-seventies?

A caring man by nature, Kauffman could be extraordinarily generous and thoughtful toward the associates. He was a sentimental man, quick to show appreciation in small, but important, ways. He would send birthday cards to associates' children with handwritten notes about how important their father or mother was to Marion Laboratories. "I always told the associates that the three most important dates in their lives were when they were born, the date of their marriage, and the day they came to work for Marion Laboratories," Kauffman recalled. Many a personal note to a salesman's wife on her wedding anniversary telling her that he understood the hardships and loneliness that a traveling man's family experienced became treasured family memorabilia.

Kauffman also remembered to acknowledge the sacrifices that a parent might have made to rear and educate a son or daughter who became a successful associate. Lou Smith, the president of Allied Signal's Kansas City division, recalled a letter Kauffman wrote to his father, George Smith, about his son's contributions as a member of the board of directors of the Kauffman Foundation. "You must be very proud of Lou," Kauffman wrote to the elder Smith. "He is not only intelligent, dedicated, and a leader, but even more—he cares for others and gives of himself. I have heard him say that you have been and are his role model—you also must be special." Smith said that it was as if his father had received a personal letter from the president of the United States, "but it was better. The sentiments of the letter made my dad feel very, very good. [Mr. K] had a knack of knowing."

Muriel Kauffman also played an important role in acknowledging the associates' importance to Marion Laboratories. On business trips to Europe and the Far East with her husband, she would spend days searching out special gift items indigenous to a country, then place large orders directly with the manufacturer. "These people couldn't believe that she was buying grosses of articles!" Kauffman said. "What we would do on an [employment] anniversary date was give this person six beautiful crystal water goblets. On the next anniversary, they would get six more. Then these might be followed by champagne glasses and so on. When our associates would be entertaining and their guests would exclaim about these beautiful things they had been given, they would say, 'My company, Marion Laboratories, gave these to me on my anniversary of employment.' Naturally, almost 100 percent of those individuals hearing this story would comment, 'My company never gives me anything.'"

Marion's founder never underestimated the importance of these gestures of recognition and appreciation. He understood the motivating effects when salesmen who met certain goals received fur jackets and world cruises for their wives. But he also came to believe that giving all the associates an opportunity to earn bonuses and making the stock option plan more generous would do two things: All associates, whether in plant maintenance or the executive suite, would pull together as a team, and the results would be increased revenues, which the company needed.

Kauffman's initial resistance to some of the ideas for improving benefits and compensation did not surprise the senior executives. "There was always a confrontation with Mr. K over improvements in the compensation systems and . . . the benefit plans," Slaughter recalled. When Holder and other executives met to try to persuade Kauffman of the merits of their proposals, he usually took the offensive. "He challenged us personally [about] what we were going to get out of this. [He said] we were being much too generous, we wanted to give away the store. 'You don't need that. People are willing to work here for less than anywhere else because it's such a great place to work.'"

Kauffman's reluctance to agree to the enhanced compensation plans was not difficult to understand. The company already had bonuses for salesmen and senior executives, as well as stock options, medical benefits, and profit sharing for all associates. But with the challenges to Marion's biggest products such as PAVABID and NITROBID, revenues had slowed at the very moment that extensive new resources were needed to prepare the launch of several new products. Once the new products were successful and earnings had improved, Kauffman said he would be willing to consider enriching the rewards system. But they were asking him to agree to spend money that had not yet been earned. However, senior management was united in the belief that, "in order to promote teamwork and cooperation and the 'we're-all-in-this-boat-together' kind of mentality, everybody needed to be on the bonus plan regardless of what function they performed," Slaughter said. There were to be no second-class citizens at Marion Laboratories. Everyone would get the chance to participate through a complex formula that determined bonus levels and amounts based on specific responsibilities. "For example, people in the product management and marketing group had a higher percentage of their compensation based on bonus than the people in accounting," Slaughter explained. Senior management was totally committed to the notion that an enhanced comprehensive package was a crucial element in the strategy to turn the company around.

And there were also reasons other than inherent fiscal conservatism for Kauffman's caution. Some associates thought that as the founder of Marion Laboratories, he was naturally a control-oriented individual. He considered finances and employee relations the areas of his greatest expertise. The salary schedules, limited bonus opportunities, and stock options seemed to be working just fine. So he saw no need to turn loose of additional scarce dollars that would be required for expansion as new drugs were readied for market. Yet his insistence on control in these two areas did not prevent him from relinquishing control in other arenas where he thought others could do a better job. His reluctance to accept the new compensation plans may also have stemmed, in part, from a lingering fear of being taken advantage of as he had been at Lincoln Laboratories.

There was also the issue of how he perceived people. Kauffman thought of people as individuals and people as employees within organizations in two very different ways. Slaughter noted that there was such a contrast between his views, "that you've just got to hold them in two different parts of your mind. [The differing approaches] are balanced by seeing him do a lot of things, really warm, caring, generous, personal things for people. He really did care about people. When it was a one-on-one kind of a situation, he really cared about them. But when he started thinking about people in general, people in an organization, he was very different."

The breakthrough finally came when James Gardner, a relatively new Marion board member, assumed the role as mediator on compensation. Gardner's election to the board in 1975 came as a result of Kauffman's decision that additional management talent from the outside was needed. Up to this point, Nat Robertson, senior vice president of Air Products and Chemicals, Inc., was the only board member who had experience in another industry. Yet as a long-time Kansas City resident and a member of the Marion board since 1963, he was really an insider. Kauffman also recognized that Lyons, as chief executive officer, should have a major role in identifying and selecting any new members. "Fred, you select them," he said.

Robertson had known Gardner since the early fifties when they both worked for an entrepreneur named Dick Morse, the founder of National Research. When Robertson learned that his former colleague was preparing to retire from the presidency of Armak, a specialty chemical company with extensive international interests, to become dean of the school of business at the University of Utah in Salt Lake City, he decided to take the initiative. He suggested to Lyons that Gardner would be a good prospect for the Marion board, and they flew to Chicago so the two men could get acquainted. Lyons and Gardner quickly found much common ground. "I think Fred was looking for people who had quite a bit of management experience, diverse management experience, and a strong sense of the importance of technology in business. But it was more, I think— a human chemistry issue," Gardner remembered. "I liked him very much when we met, and I think he liked me. We got acquainted and Fred asked me to join the Marion board without my ever having met Mr. Kauffman."

One of Gardner's initial board assignments was to serve on a newly established compensation committee. Kauffman, with Nat Robertson's encouragement, was convinced there should be a compensation committee of the board. Gardner thought, "It was a good idea because a lot of different things were done sort of randomly on rewards [at Marion Laboratories]." Kauffman, Gardner, and Hughes made up the committee. "And strictly, we were supposed to be dealing with senior management salary levels, bonus awards, and conceptual kinds of compensation. But it got into more broadly based compensation-oriented issues in the company and various kinds of programs," Gardner recalled.

While Kauffman finally agreed to the revised and more generous compensation and bonus schedules for the sales force and senior executives, he remained skeptical about the relative benefits of extending the same kind of package to everyone throughout the company. But as business began to improve a bit in the late seventies, the senior management team renewed its efforts. "Fred pressed very hard for a lot more money, not just for himself, but for everybody," Gardner said. "He wanted a very, very tight set of financial incentives." Whenever Lyons would advance more generous compensation and bonus proposals, they would be too rich for Kauffman. Lyons was proposing to reward staff people as well as line people, and this was foreign to Kauffman's experience and his inclinations. "Ewing was very generous. . . . He never had a problem with anybody in the sales organization or people in the technical organization or people in the manufacturing organization," Gardner recalled. "But he was less sure there were other people really contributing anything like that even though all the surveys showed other companies were doing it. And he also was more anxious to pay a lot after things were accomplished." As the argument dragged on, Kauffman conceded that everyone should get a bonus and that the bonuses should be larger. The sticking point became timing. He wanted to see results first and pay afterward. Lyons was saying, "We will lose all these people, and we're making awfully good progress and it should be much richer."

While Gardner worked to find a middle ground between the two positions, McGraw and the operating officers who reported to him sat down with Kauffman to plead the case from their perspective. Even though he acknowledged that by their method of restructuring the compensation schedules that bonuses for all the associates could be implemented without costing any new money, he continued to resist. Then McGraw cut to the heart of the issue. He reminded Kauffman of the key principles of doing business at Marion Laboratories: treat people the way you want to be treated and share the rewards with those who produce. "We're saying all this stuff, and we're doing all these other bonus plans for salespeople and managers. Here's a group over here that really makes a contribution to the company. Now we're not talking about big dollars. But we think it will do a lot toward getting everybody to pull together."

The arguments from the operations people were no different from what Lyons and Holder had been saying from their perspective in the executive suite. But hearing it from the men who were in daily contact with associates throughout the company penetrated Kauffman's defenses. Once Kauffman accepted the new compensation and bonus schedules for all Marion associates, he made the concepts his own. He not only embraced these ideas, he ingested them. They became a natural part of his conversation. From the podium, they blended seamlessly into his traditional rhetoric. For in his own mind, Marion Laboratories had always treated all associates fairly. Everyone had always shared in the rewards. For Kauffman, all that was different was that the new plan enhanced and enriched long-established practices—and there would be even more rewards for everyone when they met the goals.

Lyons and his executives had achieved their purpose. Kauffman was now the most eloquent advocate of this new approach. Now they had the incentive to induce the behavior they believed crucial to success as they struggled to keep the company alive and prepared to launch new products. Almost overnight Kauffman was at work taking the message into every corner of the company. Gardner recalled that Kauffman was in close touch with Marion associates all the time. "He was going through the rituals and the realities of the culture of the company. He was on the phone with the salespeople. And he and Muriel were still entertaining in their home and attending the annual sales training. He was out on the factory floor with the suggestion awards, so he was playing the symbolic role, but he was also very much in touch people-wise."

Marion Laboratories' senior executives knew that to motivate the associates to work harder and smarter and more efficiently, they had to believe that tangible rewards lay in store. Trust in management's word was key, and the associates, to a person, trusted Ewing Kauffman. They saw him as the grand, caring, generous chairman. "People in that organization would have pushed their mother off the side of a ship if they thought Mr. K wanted them to do that to make the organization succeed," Slaughter said, only partly in jest.

From that fateful day in 1977 when Kauffman endorsed the plan to accelerate the development of a group of four newly licensed drugs, two of which were CARDIZEM and CARAFATE, all energies were bent to keeping Marion afloat until the new products were approved for market. And by 1980, the company's thirtieth anniversary, most of the components of the complex "turn-around strategy" were in place. All of the associated businesses had been sold, thus freeing capital as well as management to concentrate on the pharmaceutical business. The company aggressively recruited sales personnel educated in science and gave them intensive training to sell the sophisticated products about to emerge through the pipeline. As professionalism increased within the sales force, turnover slowed to an acceptable level. And as all of the associates began to understand the new compensation package and how their individual actions could push earnings upward, they unified into a cohesive team.

Harley Tennison, who was recruited from G.D. Searle & Company in 1976 as vice president of product management, credited McGraw's influence for the success of the survival strategy that helped sustain the company through the late seventies. "He brought an incredible intellect and charisma and a warmth and a natural problem-solving ability to cut through the morass of opinions and see the track ahead. And then he just kept us moving." Tennison also remarked on the amazing similarity between Kauffman's permissive management style and McGraw's. "Like Mr. K, Jim gave us the license to go out and do some pretty crazy things that hadn't been done before in the industry. And certainly had never been done before inside of Marion."

From the mid- to late seventies, Marion Laboratories changed from selling old compounds to marketing sophisticated, scientific pharmaceutical products. "And we hired strange kinds of people, too," Tennison said. Youthful computer geniuses designed in-house intelligence systems to monitor customer demand down to the zip code level. The marketing team tied everything from professional education for physicians to direct-mail advertising into a logical sequence of events that stepped with ever-increasing momentum to the actual product launch.

While adopting new technologies and developing total learning systems for physicians and salespeople, the company also remembered to do the basic things to enhance earnings. Every possible new approach was employed to update the image of older products and to beef up their sales. Graphic artists redesigned packaging while wordsmiths rewrote the sales literature to be sure that every product benefited from the advanced scientific knowledge of the day. Salesmen were trained to communicate the nuances of a given product in order to hone Marion's competitive edge in the marketplace. "And all those things helped turn [all] the products around," Tennison remembered. "Even PAVABID turned!" They applied all the new marketing approaches to GAVISCON and SILVADENE and old standbys like OS-CAL, and sales began to climb. Because most of their products were mature and they were waiting for the growth products to come on line, they began using "pricing strategies" to get more revenue out of each unit. Stu Gold noted that "in those days, the drug price increases were well below the increases in inflation. So . . . we determined price increases that would be certainly fair, wouldn't be gouging, but would enable us, in those years, to . . . survive. And interestingly, those price increases did not halt the demand for the products. . . . It was an important strategy and helped a great deal." They launched line extensions such as PAVABID HP, and introduced new cough syrups and wound-care applications. With Merle Wood's deft guidance, Marion Laboratories built a government sales organization in those years to tap into growing third-party reimbursement trends and became the number one company in government sales in the 1980s.

The late 1970s at Marion Laboratories was a time of struggle, turmoil, and immense challenges. "We did every trick in the book to stay alive," Tennison remembered. "The result was that as things began to come in place and we began to change the system, you're in a ballistic situation. We bottomed and then started to climb out. So we were already coming past $100 million in sales before we ever launched the big new products, CARDIZEM and CARAFATE!"

The associates who survived the seventies acknowledged the pivotal role McGraw played in keeping the momentum building. Fred Lyons, as chief executive officer, was the architect of the strategic plan that identified the core business and focused all the resources there. He brought discipline, methodology, and order to the process, and it was he who won Kauffman's allegiance to the plan. But his reserved demeanor precluded his crucial contributions from becoming a part of the company folklore. "Fred had the title," Gardner observed, "but there has always been somebody else that everybody knew was the luck." Lowell Miller recalled, "Mr. Kauffman and Jim McGraw were the two spirits, in effect. Jim McGraw personified and carried Mr. K's message through people like Michie and Jerry Holder. . . . Jim is . . . one of those rare individuals who will carry the burden for operations but also has the warmth and personality. He got people to follow him more so than even Mr. K could."

The Merger 10

Marion Laboratories celebrated its thirtieth anniversary in 1980. It marked both a milestone and a turning point in the company's history. In his message to the shareholders that year, Kauffman predicted, "Marion in the eighties will be a dramatically different company from Marion in the seventies." He reminded them that a sound company was one that adapted to the environment in which it operated and to the circumstances that affected its performance. Kauffman liked to use the analogy of a road map rather than the management term, *strategic plan*, when he talked about redirecting Marion Laboratories. "And the fuel for the journey will come from new products," he always said. New products, moving steadily through the developmental pipeline and into the market, were essential to survival and growth.

During the decade of the 1970s, Marion's sales had grown from $29 million to $116 million. However, a significant percentage of sales was from one product, PAVABID. Although the product mix was substantially broader by the end of the decade, there was also a never-ending need to search out and license compounds already invented that were not available to patients in the United States. In the summer and early fall of 1979, Marion's research scientists filed two new-drug applications with the Food and Drug Administration. CARAFATE, a drug for the treatment of duodenal ulcers, was a Japanese medication developed by Chugai. Marion and Nordic Labs, Inc., received marketing rights in the United States and Canada respectively, while E. Merck was licensed for sales in West Germany. The three companies cooperated in developing and sharing information, both clinical and preclinical. CARAFATE seemed to have great market potential, since three to four million people in the United States alone saw their physicians for ulcer disease each year, constituting about twelve to fourteen million patient visits annually.

The second application was for the newly acquired drug, dothiepin, which had been licensed from Boots, a British pharmaceutical house. It was a tricyclic antidepressant which showed potential in relieving symptoms of anxiety accompanying depression. With more than 20 percent of the United States population experiencing at least one major episode of depression in its lifetime, and with patterns of recurrent episodes commonplace, that market also looked promising.

The annual report also alerted shareholders to diltiazem, "a third important product to watch." Tanabe Osaka Seiyaku Company, Ltd., of Japan had developed the drug and marketed it there since 1974 as HERBESSER. Diltiazem inhibited the flow of calcium to the smooth muscles of the coronary arteries and permitted blood to flow more easily. Between two and three million Americans were known to suffer from symptoms of heart disease, particularly angina pectoris, because of impaired circulation. This represented more than six hundred million days a year of therapy. Preliminary clinical data indicated that diltiazem might offer the cardiologist a new therapeutic option in treating a range of symptoms involved in cardiovascular disease. Kauffman announced that Marion planned to file a new-drug application for diltiazem in 1981, with the hope of bringing it to the marketplace sometime the following year.

As the company geared up to introduce and market these new drugs, it hired a considerable number of new associates. The members of the executive management team anticipated that FDA approval to market CARAFATE would be obtained by summer 1980. They wanted to be in a position to move quickly. They expanded the sales force and intensified its training. They built complex intelligence systems which required additional personnel to run the data programs and interpret the information. They added new staff in manufacturing so they could respond quickly to the demand they hoped to create. And, of course, there were other additional personnel needed to support growth throughout the organization. But the 1980 schedule proved far too optimistic, since the new-drug application for CARAFATE was not ready to be filed until July 1979. When it became clear that approval might not come until as late as 1982, all these new associates suddenly seemed like a huge liability.

"I have never laid off anyone in my life," Kauffman was proud of saying. So when the crunch came in 1980, he challenged the senior executives to find alternative ways of getting through the crisis. Slaughter recalled that the strategy was to take the problem directly to the associates and ask them, "What kinds of things can you think of that would keep us from having to lay people off?" The result was a range of tactics to keep everyone, new hires and old, on the job. "We didn't replace people who retired. We didn't replace people who went on sick leave. We didn't replace people who got fired for performance. We didn't replace people who quit to go back to school or quit for other reasons," Slaughter said. Knowing that their jobs were safe, the associates responded positively to the crisis.

When approval to market CARAFATE finally came on October 30, 1981, the atmosphere at Marion Laboratories was one of celebration for everyone. They had gone through a trying time together, a period of sacrifice that had enabled the company to keep everyone employed and to hang on until the approval came through. Kauffman believed that the experience had a profound effect on the way people worked once approval was in hand. Associates felt the company had treated them fairly, and they reciprocated in kind. Instead of taking well-earned leave, they were now working extra shifts just to keep even with the enormous demand Tennison's marketing strategy produced. "So it was a victory not just for the company. It was a victory for everybody in the process," Kauffman recalled with pride.

In spite of their confidence in the marketing strategy and the persuasive talents of the sales force, Marion Laboratories' executives seriously underestimated the success of CARAFATE, and later CARDIZEM. The only comparative experience with CARAFATE was in the Japanese market, which had completely different market dynamics than the United States. Tennison speculated that in much of the rest of the world, "CARAFATE had just been introduced directly into the market and had died. They didn't [properly] 'step through' the launch process," he noted. But when Marion Laboratories introduced CARAFATE, the launch process employed was a model marketing plan. Bringing CARAFATE to the market was like the out-of-town tryouts for a Broadway play. By the time CARDIZEM received approval late in 1982, the script, the players, and all the bits of complicated action required to launch a new product had been rehearsed and perfected: all the work of restructuring, refocusing, and retraining, all the new data systems, and all the new financial incentives combined with a new product of the highest quality to generate record sales and record growth.

Harley Tennison developed the "launch process," which was a tactical strategy to position a drug completely differently from anything else that existed in the market. It was a totally different world from the days when Kauffman dreamed up the product, wrote the sales literature, and then made the rounds calling on doctors. Instead of beginning with the general practitioner, Tennison started with the academic research scientists, asking them to tell him as much as possible about the compound. "They get excited and they write in the technical journals," he said. "Their papers are read and discussed at symposia across the country, and high-level clinical researchers as well as academic are added to the process. As these scientists begin to report their findings about the drug's effects on animals and then humans, the interest and awareness builds. And the more they write, the more others want to get involved," Tennison recalled. "By the time you're at the actual launch phase, you've got the academic community in a high degree of excitement and . . . the thing just kind of explodes. . . ."

The sales representatives became the major actors once the product was ready for distribution. And their movements were choreographed like an opening-night ballet. In the past, Marion sales representatives had directed most of their energies toward general practitioners because of the relative lack of sophistication of the products in the company's line. Although neurologists had been targeted for PAVABID sales and cardiologists had been identified as major prescribers of NITROBID prior to the 1980s, the sales force had concentrated primarily on the general practitioner. That strategy was now outmoded. The launch of both CARAFATE and CARDIZEM was a total reversal of earlier practice. Instead of sending everyone out armed with samples and instructions to sell to general practitioners, a select group of sales representatives was trained to work strictly with the respective specialists—gastroenterologists for CARAFATE and cardiologists for CARDIZEM. "We didn't even train the people who would handle the GPs until some weeks, actually months, later and then let them go to the GPs," Tennison recalled. The reasoning was straightforward. If the general practitioner used the product incorrectly and encountered problems, he would inevitably consult with a specialist. If the specialist did not know the drug in question, he would inevitably change the prescription to a medication with which he was familiar. "So what he's now done is reinforce for the GP that he did it wrong, so the GP never uses that drug again," Tennison explained. "However, when the process was reversed, the influence builds as it rolls. So, when the GP writes the drug and gets into trouble and calls the specialist, the specialist now knows the drug, understands the drug, knows how it should be used, and then reinforces it. Instead of killing the drug, he reinforces it."

Tennison characterized the entire launch process, which began with technical studies and ended with the general practitioner writing a prescription, as stepping through an influence pyramid. "The very top of that pyramid is academic medicine. Then you get to what I call academic clinicians," he explained. "And then from there you get down into the high-level board-certified specialists. The next level are specialists who really aren't board certified, and then finally you're at the general level." The products, the people and the process were a blend of the best thinking and practice in the pharmaceutical industry in the early 1980s.

Regardless of how much change had taken place within Marion Laboratories, one aspect of the process remained constant—Ewing Kauffman. When CARAFATE and CARDIZEM were introduced into the market, Kauffman focused his formidable energies on their launch. Pharmaceutical sales would always be his first love, and he relished the excitement always associated with new products. But instead of trudging the streets with his detail bag as in the 1950s, he was on the telephone every evening with sales representatives all over the country learning about their day. He wanted to know the questions the doctors had asked; which brochures and pamphlets seemed the most persuasive; had the prelaunch mailings been read and understood; were they encountering any unanticipated responses or problems; and, of course—how many orders had been generated.

When Kauffman was not talking with sales representatives, he was visiting the manufacturing plant to pep up the associates who were swamped with demands for more and more product. He was dropping into the Communications Department to preview the latest print ads and television commercials being readied for release. He seemed to be everywhere asking for suggestions, listening, cajoling, and encouraging. Cotterman recalled that while Kauffman had a special feeling for the sales associates, he also was very close to the hourly associates. He made it a regular practice to ask Cotterman's secretary to arrange a meeting with six or eight associates at a time. Over donuts and coffee, he might banter with them about the ball club and their families, how work was progressing on the line, and what their ideas and suggestions were for doing things better, faster, or less expensively. "He might be there for half an hour or he might be there for two hours," Cotterman said. "Then he'd go out wandering around to talk to all the people. They all knew him and loved him. And when he came through, work almost stopped. It was really something to see. He really had their deep respect." If Kauffman noticed that something was amiss, he would be sure to tell Cotterman in private what he had heard or observed. He was always very sensitive to the associates' feelings. It might be something as seemingly minor as not having had the favorite barbecue caterer for the company picnic. Always mindful that he had handed the reins to others, Kauffman fulfilled his role as company cheerleader, beloved founder, patriarch, and visionary.

By the end of fiscal 1983, Marion Laboratories had crossed another threshold in its corporate life. Since the mid-1970s, management had been planning for the introduction of two new, dynamic products and the rapid growth they expected to follow. But even McGraw, the chief operating officer, was astonished at the speed and ease with which the final stages of the launch process were implemented. Within three days following the notification of the FDA's approval, supplies of CARAFATE were on the shelves of all of Marion's U.S. wholesalers. By the end of two weeks, initial stocking of 90 percent of the retail trade had been accomplished. The National Wholesale Druggists Association recognized this remarkable race to market by presenting the 1982 award for "Best New Product Introduction" to Marion Laboratories for the CARAFATE launch. Within a year, CARDIZEM was approved and a successful parallel launch was accomplished within an even shorter time span.

As expected, both drugs sold well from the very beginning. Sales for CARAFATE, introduced late in 1981, increased steadily even against such well-established competitors as Glaxo's ZANTAC and SmithKline's

TAGAMET. However, when Marion executives redeployed marketing resources to launch CARDIZEM in late 1982, CARAFATE's sales naturally slowed for a time. But by the end of fiscal 1984, CARAFATE had captured 5 percent of the market for antiulcer medications.

With CARDIZEM, Marion's growth exploded. The drug quickly surpassed two of its three competitors in the calcium slow-channel blocker market in terms of new prescriptions written. In the first eight months on the market, sales totaled almost $17 million, with more than one hundred thousand new prescriptions being written every month. By the end of the first year, sales climbed to $35 million, and surpassed $65 million during the second year. And doctors were writing more than three hundred thousand new prescriptions for CARDIZEM every month.

During the same time period that CARAFATE and CARDIZEM sales were taking off, Marion executives worked hard to extend the life of their older, proven products. They kept the NITROBID family of nitroglycerin products growing with the introduction of an intravenous application of the drug. The resulting spurt and then steady climb in sales indicated that they had predicted the market with accuracy. Instead of the new calcium slow-channel blockers like CARDIZEM preempting traditional nitroglycerin therapy for angina patients, concomitant use of both types of products became the predominant therapy. In spite of limited manpower support because of the heavy dedication of sales and marketing efforts to CARAFATE and CARDIZEM, other products held their own. Some even increased their sales volume. DITROPAN, an old standby for treating bladder dysfunction, had been marketed almost exclusively to urologists. Using a refinement of the "pyramid of influence" strategy that worked so well for CARAFATE and CARDIZEM, special-sales personnel began directing their efforts toward nonspecialist physicians, and the product's market share began to grow again.

Strategies for the various product groups depended on the circumstances. When Lederle Laboratories unveiled CALTRATE 600 in 1984 and priced the product just below Marion's market-dominating OS-CAL, the gauntlet was thrown down. Marion executives responded quickly and decisively to defend their thirty-year-old product. Historically, OS-CAL had been sold only in drugstores, with Marion relying on physicians to recommend that patients take calcium supplements. With its sales force concentrating on the newer products, the marketing approach for OS-CAL had to change. Soon OS-CAL was available on grocery store shelves, at health food emporiums, and in the health and beauty aid sections of general merchandisers like K mart, Wal-Mart, Target, and Gibsons. There was a multimillion-dollar blitz of sophisticated newspaper, magazine, radio, and television advertisements that made the blitzes of an earlier era seem quaint by comparison. Where Marion had once focused marketing efforts for OS-CAL on the prenatal market, the new campaign reflected changing national demographics. Bone loss, beginning in midlife and extending into old age, became the new thrust as Marion educated the nation about the dangerous possibility that one woman in four would develop osteoporosis after menopause. The television promotion campaign made OS-CAL a familiar household brand name, and the introduction of pleasantly flavored, chewable calcium tablets helped the company hold on to its market share and increase sales further.

GAVISCON tablets for heartburn, Marion's first licensed product on the market since 1970, also became the subject of a national consumer advertising campaign using the mellifluous voice of the actor Vincent Price. Within less than six months, there was substantial growth in what had been a static market. Images of dyspeptic overeaters who suffered "nighttime heartburn" after indulging in spicy meals soon had consumers quaffing GAVISCON tablets and then wolfing down the liquid version when it became available. Some of Marion's products such as SILVADENE slipped in sales temporarily when the patent rights expired in 1982. But from a position of commanding more than 80 percent of the burn-treatment market, sales soon stabilized and began to grow again. Although a number of companies producing generic drugs attempted to duplicate the SILVADENE formula, they were never completely successful. SILVADENE, as manufactured by Marion Laboratories, was simply a superior product, and McGraw's concept of "empathetic marketing," implemented in the 1970s, had created unshakable loyalty among burn specialists and patients across the country.

The planning process initiated in the mid-seventies had called for enhancing and strengthening the product mix, and that is exactly what was done. By the end of fiscal year 1985, there was no question about Marion Laboratories' mortality. The leadership team of Lyons, McGraw, Herman, and Holder that Kauffman assembled in the mid-seventies had proven its mettle. Beginning with the introduction of CARAFATE, Marion Laboratories had experienced three consecutive years of earnings growth of more than 50 percent. And for the first time in the history of the company, one product, CARDIZEM, had exceeded $100 million in sales in a single fiscal year. How ironic this phenomenal single product must have seemed to Kauffman, who had dreamed of the day when the entire product line would generate total sales of $100 million. An additional one hundred million would be produced from the combined sales of four other major products, CARAFATE, OS-CAL, GAVISCON, and NITROBID.

But the financial results, the excellent products, the thorough and thoughtful planning were only part of the success story. The team of two-thousand-plus Marion associates and the working philosophy which directly tied the company's productivity to the individual productivity of each associate was the engine propelling the success. Quarterly "Marion on the Move" meetings kept the associates informed about company activities and focused on company goals. And the Marion Spirit Suggestion Program translated philosophy into dollars by rewarding associates for suggestions that contributed to productivity through cost savings and increased efficiencies. Kit Truex-Mair, who administered the Suggestion Program, recalled, "The whole reason Mr. Kauffman started the program was that he was smart enough to realize that he didn't know everything that happened at Marion Laboratories. He realized the people who worked with the machine or somebody who did each piece of work every day really had a better knowledge base than anybody else. Mr. K wanted to make sure that if they thought of a better way to do it then they had a voice through a formal process." When Kauffman first began talking about doing such a program, he met with lukewarm resistance, but resistance nonetheless. In 1980, Lyons and McGraw wanted all resources focused on the pending CARAFATE launch. But as the CARAFATE new-drug application languished at the FDA and concern spread about how the company would hold on until the drug could begin to generate the projected new revenues, Kauffman sensed the importance of an additional way to keep everyone involved and committed to larger goals. "Since senior management really didn't want to do [it], so Mr. K just announced a suggestion program to all associates at the July 1980

Marion on the Move meeting! Then as he was going off stage he asked rhetorically, 'Do you think you can run it?'" Truex-Mair recalled.

The flood of suggestions and the cost savings that resulted more than justified Kauffman's uncharacteristic disregard for his executives' wishes. And later, even he acknowledged rather sheepishly that their resistance had been understandable. But it was his intuitive genius that prompted him to override their objections. Started as a two-year trial, the program generated more suggestions during those initial years than there were people employed at Marion Laboratories. "The associates made it successful," Truex-Mair said. Within two years, the program had become a permanent part of the Marion structure with its own staff and a process that guaranteed a full and fair evaluation of each idea. Although Kauffman did not interfere with the evaluation process, once the selections were made he would scrutinize every award. "We would argue and he would challenge me. He would ask me to justify every idea, but he really never vetoed an approved suggestion. He trusted the process," Truex-Mair said. No matter whether the suggestion was a minor one which earned the associate dinner for two or twenty dollars or five hundred dollars in cash, Kauffman personally announced each one as if it were the Academy Award, the Pulitzer Prize, and the Nobel Peace Prize all rolled into one.

One of the suggestions that Kauffman always mentioned when talking about the program had come from a forklift operator who had less than a high school education. The problem the associate solved was a space shortage both for manufacturing and storing finished product. For a time, it looked as if the only solution was to spend millions on a new building. The driver's winning suggestion involved the manufacturer delaying delivery of material that was not critical until three days before it was needed. In addition, he proposed a way to use empty space near the top of the warehouse. Products not in immediate demand could be moved up and down by a series of belts and pulleys. "Our associates may be only high school graduates and they may have a mechanical or menial job, yet they may have creative minds," Kauffman boasted.

He loved to recount examples from the long list of award-winning suggestions and never failed to mention the grand prize of them all. It went to two scientists who came up with a way to recover part of the active ingredient of CARDIZEM which was being wasted as tablet dust created during the manufacturing process. They shared $200,053. Their suggestion had to go all the way through the exhaustive FDA approval process, which took years, but it resulted in annual savings of eight million dollars—much of that being the import tax on the raw material—in producing a single product. By the time of the merger with Merrell Dow in 1989, the Suggestion Program had become a profit center returning seven dollars for every dollar spent.

And there was one more indispensable ingredient in this heady elixir for success—that elusive something Kauffman called "The Marion Spirit." In trying to explain the effect that this had on associates, Kauffman liked to tell the story of a heavy winter snowstorm in Kansas City. Speaking on television and radio, the mayor asked citizens to help keep the roads and bridges clear of traffic until the cleanup could be completed. "Only those people who are critical to their companies should go to work in the morning," the mayor advised. "Of course, everybody at Marion showed up for work as usual," Kauffman recalled with a smile. Every Marion associate knew that he or she was an essential member of a successful team. When Fred Lyons was asked once about how many people were on the "productivity committee," he responded by saying that Marion Laboratories had 2,148 associates. "I don't know how you can capture that or write about it, but of all the things, [the people] are what make us different, not the products," Lyons said. "The products are good, of course. But Marion is the spirit of its people. If we ever lose that spirit, you'd better sell [Marion's] stock fast!"

Buy, not sell, was the order of the day where Marion stock was concerned. In 1985, profits grew by 59 percent—almost six times the industry average—according to the *Value Line Investment Survey,* a New York investment research publication. The explosive growth combined with optimism about continued development of other therapeutic applications for CARDIZEM, such as for treatment of hypertension and prevention of second heart attacks, lifted the company's stock price into the sixty-three-dollar range by March 1986. The anticipation that FDA approval of CARDIZEM for treatment of high blood pressure was imminent had the investment community abuzz with hyperbole. David H. MacCallum of Hambrecht & Quist Inc. in New York decreed, "CARDIZEM is a one-in-a-million drug."

Richard Stover, a pharmaceutical industry analyst at Smith, Barney, pointed out that while four million Americans had problems with angina, hypertension affected about sixty million. "The implications of these numbers are awesome," he concluded. "Only a few drugs are likely to be as big as CARDIZEM."

With a reservoir of cash, Marion executives moved aggressively to keep the momentum alive. In November 1987, Kauffman announced that Marion Laboratories would spend thirty million dollars to enlarge facilities and hire an additional four hundred people in the Kansas City area over the next three years. This investment would be to expand the research-and-development division in order to strengthen the company's ability to develop ways to use its existing drugs as well as to bring new products to market. He also announced a budget increase for the research-and-development division from its then $100 million a year to $150 million over three years. This was clearly an offensive move to allay the risk of becoming increasingly stagnant as products lost their patent protection, generic competition increased, and the competition to license new drugs became more intensive. Once again, Wall Street nodded in approval. "They've got to do this if they want to grow."

The strong sales and earnings growth continued into 1988, with CARDIZEM contributing almost 60 percent to the company's total sales. Kauffman could now boast that Marion had the largest-selling cardiovascular drug in the United States, with prescription volume of one million per month for the single product. Yet within a few months of being the pharmaceutical darling of Wall Street, Kauffman began to feel the sting of rumors about weakness at the company. The *Wall Street Journal* compared his role as a winning ball club owner to his position as major stockholder at Marion Laboratories. "Ewing Kauffman is no stranger to superstars. His baseball team, the Kansas City Royals, won the World Series in 1985 led by superstar third baseman George Brett. And the pharmaceutical company of which he holds 23 percent, Marion Laboratories, has posted sales growth of 800 percent since 1980, propelled by its superstar drug, CARDIZEM. But Mr. Kauffman is learning that dependence on a superstar can be tricky." The writer concluded that the stock had fallen to near a fifty-two-week low of nineteen dollars precisely because of growing concerns about Marion's dependence on one or two products. Although the company had exclusive rights to market CARDIZEM until 1992, as the product aged and the possibility of generic competition loomed, the ardor of both investors and analysts cooled somewhat.

And there also was the nagging question of when the FDA would approve an enhanced version of CARDIZEM for treating hypertension. The application had been pending for three years. Optimistic that approval would be forthcoming in 1988, Marion began stockpiling supplies of the CARDIZEM hypertension capsules at its Kansas City distribution center in March. While company officials insisted that approval was imminent, several bearish analysts lowered their estimates of Marion's earnings for fiscal 1988. With only one more quarter remaining in the fiscal year, earlier predictions which had assumed FDA approval were whittled downward. Yet in the midst of all these rumors swirling around, Kauffman remained undaunted. He assured shareholders and the investment community that another superstar was not necessary to keep growth steady. "There may not be another CARDIZEM," he said philosophically. "But we don't need to hit another grand slam home run."

Kauffman's response was neither ingenuous nor duplicitous. He knew that a blockbuster product like CARDIZEM was rare, and that to have two highly successful products at the same time was even more exceptional. He knew the company had a range of good products, and the board had recently approved a substantial increase in funds for research and development. The acquisition of Nordic Laboratories in 1982 had given them access to the large Canadian market as well. And, of course, he had great confidence in Lyons and the other members of the executive management team. They had relished the challenge of redirecting the company in the late 1970s. They had taken major risks by concentrating so many resources on CARDIZEM, but they had not gambled blindly. And that calculated risk had literally paid enormous dividends for everyone involved. The data systems, the sales training, the new compensation plans and bonus schedules, the sale of the subsidiary businesses, the development of government sales, and all the other strategies designed to support the launch and develop the market for CARDIZEM and CARAFATE had also enhanced the sales of other products. All boats had been lifted in the wake of CARDIZEM's rising tide. Kauffman understood that these executives were daring, but not reckless. They were professional managers who believed in planning for broad-based success with potential for future growth. And he also knew that they shared his belief that they must be responsible stewards of the shareholders' assets and interests.

Nat Robertson recalled that beginning in the mid-eighties there had been some general discussion within the board about the company's future. CARDIZEM and CARAFATE would both be faced with the potential of generic competition in the early 1990s. Without good, new products to fuel continued growth, Marion Laboratories could be back in the same position as in the late seventies—only worse. In 1987, about a year before the stock market began to reflect investor unease regarding Marion Laboratories' dependence on CARDIZEM, the executives with operational responsibilities—the so-called Six-Pack—began to focus on the company's future. At their annual planning session at Brush Creek Ranch just outside of Kansas City, McGraw posed the dreaded question, "Is there life after 1992?" Then they began struggling with the numbers. They could see that sales were going to peak in 1992. "We need more new products to maintain our growth. We knew we had to keep building the company forward. . . . We had quite a meeting. And it became clear at that meeting that we needed to get married," Tennison recalled. After the meeting, McGraw shared the discussion with Lyons, who was skeptical that anything as drastic as a merger was necessary.

Later in the year when the executives in the office of the president met in Arizona for their annual planning session, the subject of combining with another firm cropped up again. The first part of the meeting was devoted to planning the licensing activities where specific companies, compounds, and therapeutic areas were identified as targets. For the second phase, the members of the office of the president—Lyons, McGraw, Holder, and Herman—with Gold from strategic planning and Tennison from marketing joining them, met to thrash out major policy issues. Among the many strategies that were discussed to keep Marion Laboratories growing and profitable, various types of alliances were examined. McGraw recalled there had been a number of opportunities. "We had been spurning any offers as far as merger, consolidation, or what have you because Mr. K wanted to remain a separate entity. And we felt that all the associates wanted to remain a separate entity."

Although Kauffman was aware of the potential problems for Marion in the 1990s, he was reluctant to think of merger. Throughout the seventies and early eighties, he had rejected a number of offers from other companies who were eager to purchase Marion because of the sales force. "We would have been a natural fit for many companies because we didn't have the research investment that they did," he recalled. Yet without a partner, he feared Marion Laboratories would have to cut back and lay off people while intensifying the search for new products. Marion was also finding the licensing alternative to research much more competitive. "When we started licensing, the other pharmaceutical companies laughed at us," Kauffman recalled. "They said, 'Marion Laboratories doesn't even produce their own products. They have to go chase products down and license them.' But it wasn't long, five or six years [before other pharmaceutical companies] started doing the same thing." But by the 1980s, Marion Laboratories was at a competitive disadvantage in signing licensees because larger companies, such as Merck and Lilly, were in a position to trade products. "They could say, 'if you give us your products for leukemia, we'll give you our products for allergies. You can sell [them abroad] and we have the United States market for your products.' Marion just didn't have the products to trade," Kauffman said.

While Kauffman still had hopes that Marion might repeat the dramatic revitalization of the late seventies, he realized that such a scenario was probably unlikely. He recognized the need to plan for future contingencies, and initially he participated in some of the sessions which ultimately culminated in the merger with Dow Chemical Co. As was natural, the senior executives deferred to Kauffman, the founder and chairman, when they all talked about the future. "I participated to start with," Kauffman remembered. "And they said, 'What do you want us to do? Where do you want us to go?' I responded, 'I don't think that's my job. I may not even be here. It's your job to decide that.'" But he did have one request of the planners. "I would like for you all to see to it that this company, Marion Laboratories, is always a company for which everybody wants to work. If you do that, you will be highly successful."

Given Kauffman's hope to avoid a merger and the probable loss of Marion's distinctive corporate culture, senior management had been looking at likely candidates for joint ventures. On October 9,

1987, Marion Laboratories and Squibb Corporation of Princeton, New Jersey, had announced a tentative agreement to combine CARDIZEM with CAPOTEN to produce a hybrid medication to treat heart attack victims and help prevent a recurrence. The two drugs treated heart ailments in different ways, and it was common practice for physicians to prescribe both drugs for a patient. It seemed logical that a combination of the two could provide a more potent and convenient drug. Both drugs were their company's leading products based on sales. Although Marion Laboratories was David and Squibb was Goliath, a successful collaboration seemed to offer great promise for future revenues.

The news of this pending alliance nudged Marion's stock price upward a bit, but the market chaos in mid-October 1987 swamped any progress that had been made. Drug shares in general fell almost 28 percent in price, "behaving no better than volatile airline and manufacturing stocks," according to Salomon Brothers. By December 10, the *Wall Street Journal* was telling its readers that "professional investors in recent months have been casting off drug stocks after a long love affair with them. This group's laggardly performance since the fall shows how quickly—even irrationally—stock market sentiment about industry prospects can change." The bogies of generic competition, competing brand-name drugs, and legislative rumblings about prescription drugs being too costly began to worry industry giants like Merck, Lilly, and Pfizer—and Marion was no exception.

When Lyons and his senior executives met in Arizona early in 1988 for their annual planning session, the outward signs seemed a bit more encouraging: Earnings for the first half of the fiscal year were at a new high; the company had landed a very large contract to supply CARDIZEM to an agency of the Department of Defense; a final agreement had been signed for the joint venture with Squibb; and a new series of wound-care products was poised to come on the market to complement SILVADENE. McGraw recalled that much of the discussion was about how the pharmaceutical industry was changing. "It was starting to consolidate. Regulatory challenge was longer, more arduous, more expensive. When we began doing licensing in the 1970s, we were doing that because we had no other course of action. In the 1980s, Merck announced that 50 percent of their compounds would not be through internal development but through licensing. We had formed a joint venture with Tanabe to develop new compounds and that had proved disappointing."

After several days of discussing a range of strategies, the issue of fiduciary responsibility emerged. "A number of us felt that we had to act responsibly [on behalf of] the shareholders, that we were a very, very attractive company, and that no, we did not want to put a 'for sale' sign on the front lawn. That was not our objective," Mc-Graw recalled. A member of the board of directors and chief operating officer, McGraw was uncomfortable with the company policy of continuing to rebuff inquiries about possible mergers with other firms. "If indeed in 1992 or 1993 when some of our exclusivities had ended, like on CARDIZEM, and the stock was down and somebody asked, 'Well, where were you if you had an opportunity to consolidate with such and such a firm? You were probably more interested in your own job than you were in the shareholders' [interests].' You can fill that scenario out in spades," he said. "So I suggested that we should address this issue." The group that finally wrestled with the question of what was in the shareholders' best interest was small—Lyons, Herman, McGraw, Gold, and Tennison. After several days of discussion and analysis, they were in agreement. "We felt that to act in the shareholders' best interests, we should go to Mr. Kauffman, and to the board if necessary, saying that . . . if somebody knocks on our door and says, 'Hey, I'd like to talk,' we'd better listen."

The meeting with Kauffman was one that neither he nor any executive in the office of the president would ever forget. Lyons, as chief executive officer, spoke first when they were all gathered around the boardroom table. He reviewed the discussions that had taken place in Arizona and the groups' consensus that opportunities for any potential consolidation or merger should be explored. The office of the president also recommended that an investment banker be retained to help management professionally evaluate any prospects. Finally, they recommended that Stu Gold be assigned the responsibility of surveying every company in the industry to determine if they might be a suitable fit with Marion and to determine if they had any interest in a possible merger.

As was his habit in meetings with the senior executives, Kauffman listened carefully and seldom interrupted. On that particular day he was unusually quiet except for occasionally tamping more

tobacco into his pipe. His bright blue eyes indicated his full attention was focused on the discussion. First one executive and then
another would speak about some aspect of a potential merger.
Kauffman sat silently and continued to puff on his pipe until the
smoke nearly enveloped him. When everyone had finished, Mike
Herman recalled that Kauffman carefully laid the pipe aside and
replied in a soft voice. "I have no desire to sell. I don't need the
money. I will not sell this company." Then as the executive team sat
in numbed silence, he continued quietly. "But if you are saying it's
in the best interest of the shareholders and associates that we have
to do this, I'll do whatever you people want to do. But, there's one
condition: I want to be treated the same as everyone else." When
McGraw spoke of that meeting more than four years later, he recalled the resignation in Kauffman's demeanor and the sadness in
his voice. Herman, in recalling Kauffman's acceptance of the recommendation and the condition he placed on the sales of his own
stock, saw the response as irrefutable evidence of Ewing Kauffman's integrity as a businessman and as a human being. "It's very
rare to get an entrepreneur who, in his lifetime, lets his company
be combined for the right reasons and not hold on or torpedo it. . . .
He could have sold his stock at a way high price to give control to
someone. He didn't do it. He wanted to be treated the same. That's
why the man was so great!"

As wrenching as the decision to sell was for Kauffman personally,
the professional in him immediately surfaced. He asked that Fred
Frank of Shearson Lehman, the investment banker he had worked
so closely with in taking the company public, be engaged to handle
overtures from potential partners. Also at his behest, everyone who
had any knowledge of the discussions took an oath of secrecy. "All
right. We'll do it," he announced. "Everyone in here, from this moment forward is sworn to secrecy. You may not even discuss this
with your wives. Nobody does any work with your secretaries. Any
work we do as a team, you do at home—you do on your own." Tennison's response to the secrecy mandate was immediate and practical. "That's when I went out and bought a computer. And I started
living in my basement, doing my own secretarial work." To keep
the number of Marion associates involved to an absolute minimum, they agreed to retain outside legal counsel. All the associates
working on the search for a partner froze on any investment activ-

ity that had anything to do with the company. "It was the most difficult year and a half of my life," McGraw said. "Unless you've gone through one of these things you just can't believe how difficult it is. It was a million-dollar experience I wouldn't give a dime to repeat!"

To maintain secrecy, the working group met at the Alameda Plaza Hotel, a few miles from Marion headquarters. The first order of business was to develop a list of potential partners. Stu Gold began by identifying the best companies and then placing them on a list of A, B, and C candidates according to how they met certain criteria. The desired partner must have a strong research capacity and a global market in order to recoup the expensive investment in research. The ideal prospect should also enjoy consumer confidence and have a similar or compatible corporate culture. Several of the likely candidates were foreign companies. Kauffman recalled being "kind of worried about the foreign companies because their [business] culture was so different." Herman noted that Japanese and German companies would be the most eager to obtain a company like Marion who could assure them of good U.S. distribution. However, he and others felt that Marion's Midwestern heritage of individualism would not blend well with a more authoritarian society's corporate behavior. Just coming to terms with the need to combine with another company, much less a foreign one, was a cultural leap of faith for management. And it would be even greater for the associates when the time came.

The first company to approach Marion was a foreign concern which had already tried to purchase another U.S. pharmaceutical company. The encounter confirmed all the reservations about trying to blend two distinctly different business cultures. Lyons and McGraw met with the firm's chief executive officer and the financial officer. When Lyons suggested that other key people from both firms needed to be involved, his counterpart demurred. "He sort of grinned and said, 'No, they'll just do whatever I tell them,'" McGraw recalled. "Typical Swiss approach!"

The Marion board had agreed that management should listen to all overtures from other companies, and they did. There were several proposals that faltered quickly and a rather protracted negotiation between Lyons and the chairman of another company. But that proposal was totally unacceptable. Then early in 1989, Lyons received a call from the chief executive officer of Merrell Dow. He said they had completed their strategic planning and thought that the two companies would fit very well together. The Merrell Dow people indicated they were very serious about exploring the possibility of a merger and pressed for a meeting. The overture came while the senior executives were in Arizona for their annual strategic planning meetings. So instead of returning to Kansas City, Lyons, McGraw, Herman, Tennison, and Gold flew immediately to Chicago to confer with the Merrell Dow principals. "It always amazed me that nobody ever figured out that we didn't have any receipts from Arizona for that day," Tennison recalled. "And no one ever called us on it. For all practical purposes in the records, you won't find any record of any expenses or anything. We weren't anywhere."

The initial session with Merrell Dow went well, and a series of meetings followed. Yet even after those discussions were well under way, an alternative plan began to take shape within the board. "The management thought they [had given] us a big surprise [with the merger recommendation]," Gardner recalled. However, for some time he and Nat Robertson had been talking regularly about finding just the right partner for Marion Laboratories. Gardner recalled that Nat Robertson used to call him on Saturday mornings and they would talk for hours, reviewing the assets that Marion Laboratories had to offer in a potential partnership. "There were a lot of people that didn't have the things Marion had: a really powerful sales force; Fred [Lyons]; some products that had some life or were really kind of still quite good; and we could make a list of them." The more they conferred, the more the same idea kept occurring to both men. Rather than make a hasty marriage with the wrong partner, why not wait until the right fit came along? As Gardner saw things, "We'd have to sweat through a trough and that was kind of . . . the idea—sweating through a trough—that it had been done once before. I felt it might be worth it."

Gardner decided to lay the idea before Kauffman, sensing that he might warm to the competitive challenge of a second turnaround. The two men had a private meeting one evening at Kauffman's Mission Hills home. Gardner assured him of his support of the search for a merger partner. "I thought what we were doing was absolutely right—to materialize our future . . . with Dow," he recalled.

But, if there were a possibility of persuading Jim McGraw to lead an effort to revitalize the company without a partner, Gardner said he wanted to keep the management and try to repeat the 1970s. ". . . I thought it was a long shot, but if McGraw were in, I was for it. We'd maybe license some more products . . . we'd done it all before. I didn't have a concrete plan," he admitted. Gardner and Kauffman both recognized that the Marion management team had no reason to want to do what Gardner was suggesting. They had worked backbreaking hours through the seventies; they had reaped the rewards of the eighties; they were all young enough to have other careers and or to relax and pursue other activities with complete financial security. Gardner admitted it would be an enormous gamble. "But the whole thing [in the seventies] had been a gamble. Oh, I would have loved it too! I almost joined the company to help out," he said, recalling the excitement of that evening.

Kauffman was no stranger to gambling, and he found the idea exhilarating. He agreed with Gardner that if they could get Jim Mc-Graw to buy into the idea, it might work. They might even try to persuade Mike Herman to stay on and do his financial wizardry again despite the announcement that he would be leaving the company to assume the full-time presidency of the Ewing Marion Kauffman Foundation. "And it didn't occur to us that Fred would [stay with the organization after the merger], to be quite frank . . ." Gardner admitted. "I think only McGraw could have done it. I really [thought] McGraw could get a group of people to do it."

Gardner recalled that Kauffman told him he put the idea to Mc-Graw, but it was not to be. McGraw remembered the story differently. After, not before, the merger was announced he said Kauffman talked to him because he was concerned about the leadership for the new company. McGraw, hoping to reassure Kauffman, said he would stay as long as Kauffman wanted him. "But no, neither [Kauffman nor Gardner] had ever spoken to me about that idea in any tangible form." With the excellent prospect of an agreement with Dow that would strengthen both partners and result in substantial financial gains for Marion shareholders, McGraw would not have been willing to tempt fate. Furthermore, he had been the director who had initially raised the issue of their fiduciary responsibility: to do what was best for the shareholders. Regardless of whether he might have relished the challenge personally, he believed they should proceed with the negotiations with Dow. If Dow's research capability could be combined with Marion's sales prowess, that partnership offered substantial potential benefits to all the stockholders. Gardner agreed. "Once it was clear that the management wasn't inclined to try it, [the merger] was exactly the right thing to do. We made the best deal we could, and we didn't see it in terms of Ewing cashing in or anything else. We saw it as the right thing for the company," Gardner said.

There were three months of secret, intensive negotiations before the deal was consummated. "It was just unbelievable!" McGraw said. "We were still negotiating up to the point of Monday, July 17, when it was announced!" What happened was that the attorneys found some unresolved details at the last minute. Everyone worked until about one on Monday morning and then returned at six. They were hoping to make the public announcement Monday morning. So when Marion associates arrived for work and saw the television monitors and the chairs arranged for a meeting, they knew something big was about to happen. "The feeding frenzy occurred then," McGraw said. "And at eleven that morning the price of the stock jumped, so Fred was forced to make a public announcement at that time. But we had not merged!" Even though the final documents had not been signed, both parties were fully committed. So the Marion officials raced back for a series of "Marion on the Move" meetings held simultaneously at various sites. A videotape had been prepared with Kauffman and Lyons reassuring the associates and explaining what they could expect. Following the announcement, the Marion and Merrell Dow executives huddled again. Finally at 7:30 P.M., more than six hours after the public announcement, all the papers were signed. Now it was official. The new company, Marion Merrell Dow, would be officially merged on the final day of November.

The long days and late nights of negotiations and the strain of secrecy had been exhausting for everyone involved, especially Kauffman. Although he was spared the tedium of actual negotiations, the entire process was like a lingering deathwatch for him. In the final hours of the negotiations, as all the parties were still trying to keep everything under wraps for fear of triggering a reaction in the stock market, the Kauffmans were whisked in and out to sign papers. That weekend was not a good one. On Saturday morning, the press had announced that Kauffman's partner in the Kansas City Royals baseball team, Avron Fogelman, was experiencing serious financial reverses. Then Kauffman suffered a painful attack of kidney stones. McGraw recalled how small and drawn and fragile Kauffman had appeared when he arrived to sign the final papers. "I felt so sorry for him. He was in absolute pain, suffering from a kidney stone. Finally about eleven Sunday night he said, 'Gentlemen, I've got to leave. Fred's in charge. This kidney stone is killing me.' Plus Fogelman was killing him too," McGraw remarked. The only redeeming thing about the Fogelman debacle coming when it did during the merger negotiations was that the local press thought that all the meetings and the arrival of the Kauffmans concerned the ball club and not Marion Laboratories. "In fact, it was rather humorous when you think back on it," McGraw said. "It's something you want to go through once but never want to do again."

Kauffman had consented to make the videotape which was shown to all the associates when the merger agreement was announced that Monday at noon. There he was on the big screen reassuring everyone about the wisdom of the decision and the safety of their jobs. But he did not take part in any of the briefings because they would have been too emotional for him. Linda Constantine, Kauffman's personal assistant for many years, told McGraw that for months after the agreement had been signed he would literally cry about it every day. "If anybody brought it up, tears would come to his eyes."

Kauffman admitted, without any embarrassment, how painful the merger was for him. "This was a very emotional decision for me. It really ruptured me." Truex-Mair recalled seeing Mr. Kauffman on the day of the merger. "It was so painful for me to see him cry," she said with emotion coloring her voice, "to know the pain he was going through." Groping for words to help ease the sense of loss, she reminded him that intellectually he had made the right choice, although emotionally it could not help but hurt. The associates who had worked closely with him over the years knew he looked upon Marion Laboratories as his family, his flock. He genuinely believed Marion stock was the most valuable asset a person could own, and he fretted when any associate sold shares, no matter how few. Every month or more often he would send McGraw a list of the salesmen who sold their stock. "He'd ask, 'Jim, why are they selling their stock? They should hang on to it.'" When Mc-

Graw would point out that one salesman needed new tires for the family car and another needed money for a child's college tuition, Kauffman would frown and lament that they should try any expedient but selling their stock. "He took it personally," McGraw said. "And even when we gave the awards [for suggestions], he would then permit them to take cash only if they really needed it. This was a tremendous intellectual, emotional, and personal change for him."

With the merger, Kauffman assumed the title of chairman emeritus. Joe Temple of Merrell Dow became chairman of the board and chief executive officer. Fred Lyons became president with the understanding that he would become CEO the second year. And within a year, all the other key Marion executives who had stayed to help implement the merger had retired. Kauffman continued going to the office every day to confer with Marion Merrell Dow executives, and he paid special attention to trying to bring the two business cultures together. Nat Robertson, who retired from the Marion board at the merger, remarked that both he and Jim Gardner were surprised that Kauffman took such a great interest in the new company. "Of course, he had a hell of a block of stock." But Robertson thought most men in Kauffman's circumstances "would have washed their hands of the whole thing. The power passed." And then he seemed to remember, "But, of course, Marion was his first love."

Take Me Out to the Ball Game 11

Many of Kauffman's family and business associates worried that Marion's founder might be at loose ends after the 1989 merger with Merrell Dow. They need not have been concerned. The man who often said, "I don't even enjoy vacations. I've got to have something to do," was immediately swept up in protecting his beloved Kansas City Royals from becoming intertwined in the complex negotiations surrounding Avron Fogelman's restructuring of his vast financial holdings.

The story of how Kauffman came to buy the Kansas City ball club and built it into a world-class competitor in a relatively short time in many ways paralleled the building of Marion Laboratories. Just as he entered the pharmaceutical business indirectly—because he liked taking aptitude tests—he did not deliberately set out to own a major league baseball team. "My involvement in baseball in Kansas City was purely a happenstance," he always said, his inflection and facial expression telling the listener that it had, in the main, been a pleasurable one.

Kansas City had enjoyed professional baseball as early as 1884, fielding teams in the minor league competitions of the Union Association, the National League, and later, the American Association. The Blues won seven pennants in the class AAA American Association between the end of World War I and 1957. But the best known team was the Kansas City Monarchs, a formidable power in the Negro American League. The legendary pitcher Satchel Paige and major league baseball's first black coach, Buck O'Neil, were among the Monarch's alumni. By the early 1950s, Ernest Mehl, the *Kansas City Star*'s sports editor, headed a group of businessmen who began talking about going after a major league team. With the Philadelphia Athletics going broke, Mehl recommended pursuing the possibility of moving them to the heartland. All he needed was a group of affluent sports fans willing to take the risk of underwriting the enterprise. When no local Kansas Citians stepped forward, Mehl persuaded Arnold Johnson, a Chicago vending machine millionaire, to purchase the Athletics and move them to Kansas City to begin the 1955 season. Unfortunately, Johnson died suddenly during spring training in 1960. Johnson's will, written in 1953 before he acquired a controlling interest in the Athletics, made no mention of the disposition of the ball club. Once again, Mehl tried to organize local backing to acquire the team, but events moved too slowly. Charles O. Finley, an insurance tycoon from Gary, Indiana, won control of the franchise.

Although there were high expectations that Finley would use his wealth to transform the losing Athletics into a pennant winner, the team never experienced a victorious season in Kansas City. Not only did he field a losing team, Finley was personally unpopular. He offended the baseball world and humiliated Kansas City fans with silly antics such as trying to check the team mascot—a brown mule named Charlie O.—into hotels along with the ball players. Charlie O.—the owner—possessed a volatile temper and feuded constantly with either city officials, the press, or other businessmen. He complained about the lack of local support and threatened to move the team first to Louisville, then to Dallas, to Milwaukee, and finally to Peculiar, a Missouri suburb of Kansas City. "Mr. Finley was a very innovative thinker," Kauffman recalled with characteristic generosity, "but not very good at public relations. He was constantly in trouble with the fans of Kansas City." Finally in October 1967, the American League owners gave in to Finley's constant badgering and voted to allow the controversial owner to move the team to Oakland, California.

There was a collective sigh of relief in Kansas City that the querulous Finley was gone, but so was major league baseball. However, a delegation of civic and business leaders had anticipated the loss and was present at the American League owners' meeting in Chicago to petition for a new franchise immediately. The owners quickly agreed to consider awarding Kansas City an expansion franchise, "as soon as practical and not later than 1971." Mayor Illus Davis saw the delay as a deliberate slap at his hometown. Through the years Kansas

City fans had demonstrated their support for major league baseball through ticket purchases and, most recently, they had approved $43 million in bonds to construct a state-of-the-art sports complex. The owners' response was insulting, and Davis was determined to revise the timetable.

Stuart Symington, a United States senator from Missouri who had accompanied the Kansas City delegation to Chicago, was not pleased with this brush-off either. He called Joe Cronin, the president of the American League, with the suggestion that the owners reassemble. "If you don't, you are going to hear from me on the Senate floor Monday morning!" Baseball owners had always zealously guarded their freedom from antitrust action, and were not eager to have a powerful member of the Senate's inner circle raise the specter of regulation. Less than twenty minutes following Symington's thinly veiled threat, the owners reconvened. They unanimously agreed that Kansas City could have an expansion franchise in 1969 on the condition that sufficient financial backing could be secured.

Kauffman had been so busy building Marion Laboratories into a successful company that he had not taken an active role in Kansas City's civic affairs. He supported the United Way through the company and occasionally attended Chamber of Commerce meetings, but he was not well known and certainly not a member of the community power structure. He was also not keenly interested in baseball. He had played pickup games on many a sandlot as a boy, but had never succumbed to that mysterious power that transforms otherwise normal individuals into fanatics who live only for baseball season and mumble about batting averages and win/loss records in their sleep. However, he was interested enough in Kansas City's future to attend a Chamber of Commerce luncheon where Gabe Paul, the general manager and president of the Cleveland Indians, talked about the value of a major league club to a city. When Paul finished speaking, Kauffman responded to a plea for backers to form a group to underwrite a team. "I raised my hand and said I would be willing to put in a million dollars, not really doing it from anything but a civic standpoint," Kauffman recalled.

In spite of Kauffman's generous and unexpected offer, no one else came forward. With another meeting of the American League owners just a few weeks away, Mehl and Earl Smith, a strong baseball booster and an owner of Smith-Grieves Printing Company, called on Kauffman at his office at Marion Park. They came straight to the point. "We need to show the American League there is somebody in Kansas City that is somewhat interested in baseball and financially can afford it," Mehl and Smith told Kauffman. "Could we use your name and tell them that we do deserve a team and that you would probably be willing to look into it?" They assured Kauffman that he did not have to buy the franchise, but they needed proof that someone in Kansas City had the resources to do it. Flattered, Kauffman agreed to help. "Commerce Trust gave me a letter of credit for four million dollars which they took with them to show the [American League owners] that I could financially own a team." He also submitted a second letter of credit from a New York financial firm for six million dollars. The second letter was to demonstrate that he could absorb large pending contributions to the league pension fund and operate until the new owner's share of national television and radio fees came on-line in 1972.

Up to this point, Kauffman had never thought seriously about owning a baseball club. But Kansas City was his hometown, and he felt an obligation to share some of his good fortune with the community that had nurtured him and Marion Laboratories. As he pondered the challenges, he could not help recalling the excitement of building Marion Laboratories. He loved a challenge; he thrilled to competition. His interest was piqued, and, at Smith's suggestion, Kauffman decided to talk with several baseball owners to find out more about the advantages and disadvantages of owning a major league franchise. There was no question that he had the money to do it now that Marion was a public company. He had the time as well. He had been augmenting the Marion management team with people experienced in the pharmaceutical business, so he did have more time to devote to leisure or a new enterprise. Why not explore it more fully, he asked himself?

Kauffman decided first to visit Gene Autry and Bob Reynolds, owners of the California Angels. Not only were the Angels a successful and well-managed franchise, they were also in the process of building a new stadium in Anaheim. In Kansas City, Jackson County voters had approved a multimillion-dollar bond issue to construct a new sports complex in an effort to shore up their case to the American League. And Kauffman recognized that he would need seasoned help should he decide to undertake the twin tasks of building a major league team and a baseball stadium at the same time.

When the Kauffmans flew to the west coast, Mehl and Smith accompanied them. During talks with Autry and Reynolds, they met Cedric Tallis, the Angels' vice president and business manager. "[Tallis] had a lot to do with the building and operating of Anaheim Stadium and was assigned to show us around," Kauffman said. Before the visit ended, Kauffman was impressed with Tallis's extensive knowledge of baseball. If he should decide to buy the franchise, Kauffman concluded that Tallis might be just the kind of executive he would need.

On the flight back to Kansas City, Kauffman seemed unusually quiet. It was clear to everyone on board that he was deep in thought, weighing the options. Anxious to end the suspense, Mrs. Kauffman seized the initiative. "She said she thought I should do it because maybe I wouldn't work so hard at Marion. She thought baseball would give me a secondary interest and enjoyment and that possibly I might live longer." Before the plane landed in Kansas City, Kauffman told Mehl and Smith that he planned to be an active contender for the franchise.

Kauffman had been the only person in Kansas City sufficiently sympathetic to the baseball issue to submit a letter of credit to the American League. But once the owners announced their decision to award Kansas City a franchise for 1969 and opened the process to bids, a number of contenders surfaced. And by the time the American League met in Mexico City in November 1967, there were four principal groups, plus Kauffman, angling for ownership. There were several other groups vying for the franchise, yet none of the potential investors asked Kauffman to join with them. Although he had never sought admission into Kansas City's inner circle of social or business elites, Kauffman was now stung at being ignored. He also knew that the city's wealthy businessmen, under the influence of conservative local banking interests, had twice dallied and lost ownership of a major league team to outsiders. His civic pride was too great to let that happen again. "Here I, who started it all, was going to be left out in the cold. Well, my salesmanship rose up! Although I hadn't wanted the team originally, I didn't want somebody to steal what I felt was possibly my team now. I had spent time and money, so I took the attitude there were other groups trying to take something away from me," he recalled.

Confident of his prowess as a salesman, Kauffman decided to sell himself to the American League owners. He boarded his private jet and flew to all the American League cities to talk with owners and executives of the clubs. Because he was known to enjoy casino gambling in Las Vegas, there was some concern among several owners that he might attract an unsavory element to baseball. But he quickly laid that issue to rest. He said he gambled for fun in Las Vegas, on the golf course, and when playing cards with friends. And, yes, he owned racehorses and loved to play the ponies. However, he told the owners that he had never bet on baseball or football, and he had no intention to do so. He gave his word, and that closed the subject.

Kauffman was very adroit at making his case with the owners. He used his experience as the owner of a winning racing stable of twenty-four horses and as founder and principal stockholder of Marion Laboratories to illustrate how he planned to run the team. "If I get the ball team," he said, "I'll do what I did with the stable—hire professionals and turn the operation over to them. I'll lay down the financial policy. The baseball end, I'll leave to the baseball men." To reiterate his willingness to resist the temptation to try to run the ball club, Kauffman cited his experience at Marion. "When I replaced myself as sales manager of Marion Laboratories, I saw a lot of things that the man I had put in was doing wrong. But I didn't interfere. I let him learn by his own mistakes. I know sales management. So if I could resist the temptation to tell my sales manager what to do, I'm sure I'll be able to resist interfering in baseball, about which I know nothing." Kauffman also wanted to assure the American League owners that his pockets were deep. In an interview he gave while making the rounds to press his case, he said if he were to be the successful bidder, the team would be a personal commitment. It was to have no connection to Marion Laboratories. "I want no one else to risk his money with me. . . . Does this mean that I expect to lose the money? It does not. I hope to make money on the team by developing a winner."

Once Kauffman made up his mind that he actually wanted the ball club franchise, the contest was over. He had the money, the self-confidence, and his wife's enthusiastic support to stay the course.

While waiting for a decision from the American League owners, he told a reporter that he was planning his future around owning and enjoying the ball team. "I've set up trust funds for my three children. I've got sixty million dollars and I'm going to enjoy it. I'm counting on baseball to provide one of the means of enjoying it. I'm not sure I'll get the franchise, but if I were the league owners, I'd award it to me."

All the bidders gathered at the Muehlebach Hotel on January 11, 1968, to await word of the decision, although there was little doubt about who would be the victor. The announcement of Kauffman's unanimous selection came less than two hours after the American League club owners and officials convened. Joe Cronin, the league president, said, "Mr. Kauffman was chosen because of his fine business background, his connections in the public relations field, and his unending desire to own a major league franchise." Reynolds, the president of the California Angels, stressed that his fellow owners believed that Kauffman would be a continuing member of the American League. "We had the feeling there was none better than Ewing." As the crowd cheered and the other bidders graciously promised their support, Kauffman stepped to the podium to make a pledge that would cost millions more than he could ever have anticipated. In a voice full of excitement and confidence he vowed, "In my lifetime, this team will never be moved. If there is a financial loss, I can stand it. But I hope we can develop a successful organization." So that there could be no doubt about his sincerity or determination, Kauffman also revealed that he had filed a letter with the city stating that in the event of his death his estate would be bound to offer the club for sale locally. He was entering into a binding covenant with his hometown, a place he genuinely loved. He had returned to Kansas City after World War II to raise a family and build a business in familiar neighborhoods surrounded by close friends. In the weeks leading up to the announcement of the franchise award, he had often remarked, "Kansas City has been good to me and I want to show I can return the favor." This was a pledge and a commitment that he would maintain with absolute fidelity.

Kauffman paid $5,300,000 for the expansion franchise, which was scheduled to become operational in 1969 along with another one awarded in Seattle. The two new franchises increased the number of teams in the American League to twelve. In addition to the franchise purchase, he also had to pay an additional $600,000 into the major league pension system over the next three years. In an interview with Joe McGuff, sports editor of the *Kansas City Star*, Kauffman said he estimated that operating expenses would run between $300,000 and $400,000 without any compensating income at the start. He also estimated that there would be tax losses of about $1,500,000 the first four years. However, once the new stadium was completed, he believed revenues would begin to grow. "I will take no salary or draw any money from the club. All of our cash will be used to build a better team."

Kauffman wanted to field a team for the 1969 baseball season, so he lost no time in putting an organization in place. In fact, he had been mentally selecting board members, scouting for an executive vice president, and toying with various names for the team from the day he decided to become a serious contender for the franchise. On January 16, he announced that he and Mrs. Kauffman had asked five prominent Kansas Citians to join them as directors of the new baseball team: Earl Smith, vice chairman of Smith-Grieves Printing Company; Les Milgram, president of Milgram Food Stores; Charles Truitt, senior vice president of the Commerce Trust Company; Ernest Mehl, retired sports editor of the *Kansas City Star*; and Charles Hughes, corporate secretary of Marion Laboratories. Kauffman graciously singled out Smith and Mehl as the men who made it possible for him to acquire the team. Their encouragement and commitment to the sport had indeed influenced him in his decision to try to win the franchise, but his own reputation and resources had carried the day. In choosing the other board members, Kauffman turned to close friends. Truitt was his banker and longtime business associate, and Hughes his oldest and closest friend. In every undertaking, whether it was the pharmaceutical business, the ball club and later the private foundation, Hughes was always present to safeguard his friend's best interests. Kauffman had implicit trust in his old roommate's judgment and knew him to be of impeccable integrity.

The fifth board member, Les Milgram, had been one of Kauffman's chums at Faxon Elementary School. The two had played baseball in neighborhood games after Kauffman finished his duties as a carryout clerk at Milgram's father's grocery store number three. Milgram's family had been closely identified with sports in Kansas

City and he had been president of the Ban Johnson League, one of the pioneer amateur sports leagues in the nation. For years, Milgram had worked alongside Mehl and Smith to persuade civic leaders to keep major league baseball in Kansas City. Kauffman was especially delighted with the way Milgram had announced the directorship to the grocery store employees. The headline in the food store monthly newsletter proclaimed in bold type, "FORMER MILGRAM CARRY-OUT BOY BUYS K.C.'S NEW MAJOR LEAGUE BALL TEAM." The subhead read: "Old School Chum and Ex–Bat Boy Named to Board of Directors."

The day following the announcement of the board, Kauffman surprised the sports world when he released the name of the baseball organization's executive vice president and general manager. It was Cedric Tallis, the veteran baseball executive who had impressed him so much on his visit to the California Angels several months before. While Tallis worked quickly hiring office staff, coaches, and scouts, he also had to institute a minor league system and prepare for the expansion draft. Kauffman turned his attention to the public-relations aspects of launching a new ball club. First, the club had to have a name, and what better way to choose a name than to have a citywide contest, he decided. The public loved being involved, and more than seventeen thousand entries flooded into the ball team's makeshift offices in the Continental Hotel. The sports press reported the entries by alphabetical category and ran cartoons of players in uniforms and hats that reflected the names. The animal kingdom was the source of a great many names, as were various Indian tribes. Word plays on Kauffman's occupation and name inspired others. "Caps" and "Capsules" were suggested, "both of which were better than 'Pills,'" opined a sportswriter in the *Kansas City Star*. The suggestions which tried to use some form of Kauffman's name were even worse: "Kauffs," "Kauffies," "Kauffers," and "Kawsmonats." After weeks of speculation, Kauffman made the announcement, "The name 'Kansas City Royals' is definitely the winner." His personal preferences had been either "Kings," "Stars," or "Eagles," but the other board members convinced him of the appropriate tie to the city's great parade and pageant honoring the billion-dollar livestock industry known widely as the American Royal. Soon blue and white, the Kauffmans' racing colors, became the baseball team's colors as well. Kauffman jokingly suggested that he had a racehorse he would be willing to loan as a mascot since he was not winning at the track. And what more fitting emblem for the Royals than a magnificent crown?

Kauffman moved quickly and easily to create visibility for the new team. In mid-February when questioned about the possibility of televising games, he replied that he had already signed a contract with the Schlitz Brewing Company for sponsorship of sixteen road games and at least twelve home games. He added, in a matter-of-fact way, that the arrangement had been concluded "for twice as much money as had ever been offered Charlie Finley." If anyone had doubted that Kauffman's salesmanship was transferable from pills to players, they kept silent.

As Kauffman worked to make the Royals' name familiar to every Kansas City household, Tallis concentrated on building the team. To assist him, he hired Charley Metro, who had an excellent reputation for scouting new talent. For fifteen years Metro had managed in the minor leagues, with one season as a head coach for the Chicago Cubs. Less than a month after the franchise was awarded, Metro joined the Royals as director of personnel. Lou Gorman, a thirty-eight-year-old who had been serving as director of minor league clubs for the Baltimore Orioles, was hired as director of player development. With a skeleton crew in place, Tallis announced the Royals' philosophy for the major league expansion draft scheduled to begin in October. "We won't take players just because they have names," he said. "We have to build with young players; we're going for prospects." Kauffman echoed that view, noting that "Washington went for older players in 1961 and finished in a tie for last place." If he were going to spend $175,000 for each player in the expansion draft, he was determined to be ready to make good choices and to get his money's worth. He also wanted players on which he could build a team. "We don't expect to finish last in the American League in 1969," he boasted.

There were scores of decisions to make in the short time before the fall draft. In June, the Royals selected Fort Myers, Florida, as their base for spring training. The same month, Kauffman signed a four-year lease for Municipal Stadium in Kansas City, which would be the Royals' home until the new stadium was completed in 1973. With Kauffman's go-ahead and an infusion of $400,000, Tallis began building the Royals' minor league system. He also hired scouts to search out the prospective players he hoped to acquire.

To jump-start the sale of season tickets, Ewing and Muriel Kauffman got in their cars and went all over Kansas City buttonholing old friends and making new ones. Kauffman personally sold more than two thousand tickets, and Mrs. Kauffman sold almost one thousand that first season. "Kansas City was so thrilled that we had a major league team that it was very easy for me to sell [tickets]," Kauffman recalled. "This is the first time these CEOs would meet me. I'd just walk in . . . and say, 'I'd like to speak to Mr. So-and-so, the CEO,' and give my name. He would meet me just because I was the new owner and he [had] read about me. And I'd end up selling him season tickets." For a man who had never been a recognized member of the Kansas City business and civic elite, this was a heady experience.

But Kauffman knew he and his wife could not sell all the season tickets alone, so he borrowed an idea from Marion Laboratories and created the Royal Lancers. Similar to membership in the elite Marion M Club, admission to the Royal Lancers was reserved for boosters who sold at least seventy-five season tickets the first year. By early September, thirty-six persons had qualified. They had already sold more than two thousand tickets. Jean Sperry and Bob Pruitt were among the first individuals to qualify, proving that a Marion-trained salesman could outsell anyone else, no matter what the product. Membership in the Royal Lancers entitled the person to admission to any American League stadium in the United States and jet fare to the Royals' spring training headquarters in Fort Myers, Florida. In announcing the ticket bonanza, Earl Smith urged the members of the Greater Kansas City Sports Commission to redouble their efforts. "There's no reason in the world why we can't make this Lancer Club an expensive thing for Ewing Kauffman," he said.

Season ticket sales got another push upward with the announcement in September that the Royals had raided the California Angels again. This time it was to hire Joe Gordon as the new manager. Gordon had played second base for the New York Yankees and the Cleveland Indians before managing the Indians and later the Detroit Tigers. In 1960, Charlie Finley had hired him to manage the troubled Athletics. Although Finley fired him after only fifty-nine games, Gordon had become popular with Kansas City fans. Word of his hiring quickly pushed ticket sales up to 4,654. By the end of September, the Royals Lancers claimed an all-time American League record for advance season ticket sales—6,441 season tickets had been purchased. With the American League draft just a few days away, the *Kansas City Times* reported that the franchise now had a local owner, a staff of proven front-office talent, a name, a manager, a record of season ticket sales, and an emblem to decorate pennants, caps, and uniforms. All that was missing, of course, were the players.

The Seattle Pilots were the other expansion team scheduled to compete in the draft. They had announced their intention to draft "established players," a strategy designed to attract fans to their antiquated ballpark, while the Royals were primarily interested in youth and potential. Tension mounted as the draft date drew nearer. On Friday, October 11, the American League released the list of players the established clubs planned to protect. For the next three days, the Royals' management was engrossed in a hypothetical chess game of plotting moves and alternatives depending on who won the toss, which players Seattle selected, and which additional players were protected as the draft progressed.

When the player selection process opened in the main ballroom of the Boston Sheraton Hotel on October 15, Ewing and Muriel Kauffman were on hand. The evening before, they had sat with Tallis and his team as they went through a dry run of possible draft choices. The excitement was palpable because the choices made over the next hours would determine how successful Kauffman's multimillion-dollar investment would be. After almost seven tension-filled hours, the Royals had their thirty players: sixteen pitchers, seven infielders, five outfielders, and two catchers. Tallis had stuck to his commitment to select young talent. With the exception of three players, the remaining twenty-seven draftees averaged twenty-three years of age. The news of the successful draft pushed season ticket sales in Kansas City past the seven-thousand barrier. With the Kauffmans playing hosts, it was champagne all around, both in Boston and back in Kansas City. "Your Royal organization went in there prepared," Kauffman said upon his return home. "And I can tell you this, inside of five years, we'll have a crackerjack team for you."

When Earl Smith first talked to Kauffman about becoming the owner of a baseball team, one of his most intriguing arguments was that it would give Kauffman the opportunity to employ in sports some of the principles he had used so successfully in the pharmaceutical business. Shortly after the new year, Kauffman announced that he was including profit sharing in the Royals' benefit package. Major league players had their own retirement system through the players' union, so Kauffman's innovations were directed toward nonplayer personnel. In explaining the plan, Kauffman noted, "There usually is not much profit in baseball, but the Royals will make a fixed contribution of 7.5 percent of the compensation paid to each participant. This figure will be increased if the club makes money." The participant would become vested on an incremental schedule over ten years. "This plan will enable us to hire the best people for the Royals. We're going to work harder and longer and I'm sure that everyone will give more of himself." The Marion practice of sharing with those who produced was in place.

When April 8, 1969, arrived, opening day of the first season, the old Municipal Stadium was crowded with dignitaries and cheering fans. Joe McGuff wrote, "It was one of the most emotional scenes in the history of the old ballpark." When Kauffman was introduced, the crowd was on its feet cheering. Smiling broadly and with his blue eyes betraying a tear or two, he responded to the ovation. "If you do not believe I've been repaid in full for buying the Kansas City Royals baseball team by your wonderful applause, then you are sadly mistaken. As long as I live, this will be your team, forever and forever." After the turbulent, rancorous years with Finley and the Athletics, here was an owner who fairly radiated goodwill, good humor, and clearly liked a good time. The great love match between Kauffman and the fans had begun.

The Royals won their opening game against the Minnesota Twins and finished the season with a 45–45 record against clubs in the Western Division. It was a much better season than anyone had expected, topped off when their Omaha farm club won the pennant in the American Association. Kauffman had committed an additional $400,000 to the Royals' farm clubs during the summer of 1968, and the results were clearly visible. Kauffman was prepared to spend money for good coaches and good managers in the farm system because he was committed to developing talented young players. But he was not averse to the opportunity to sign an established ball player at a high figure if the management thought it a good investment. One such opportunity arose that first season when Kauffman and the other owners met in Miami Beach to elect Bowie Kuhn commissioner of baseball. After the meeting, Kauffman and Tallis were relaxing with some of the other owners and club officials. As they talked, the conversation turned to the price the National League had put on its expansion franchises. "Charlie Finley was asked how much he would sell his franchise for," Kauffman said. "He said fifteen million dollars. It was then that I asked him how much he would sell one player for." Finley thought about Kauffman's question for a moment and then said he would sell any player in his club for one million dollars. Turning to Tallis, Kauffman said, "Cedric, if you really feel it will help us that much, I'll scrape up the million dollars somewhere."

Kauffman and Tallis continued to discuss the matter and finally decided it would be a good move for the Royals. Then Kauffman turned to Finley and said he was ready to do business. "He gulped a little and said no, we had waited too long and the deal was off," Kauffman remembered. "Well, we talked a little more and then he wanted to know if he could have the money in cash if we went through with the deal. I told him, 'Charlie, you can have the money in ten-dollar bills if you want it that way.' He said he had always promised his wife a million dollars. We were there about another hour and you could tell he was still thinking about it, but he wound up turning it down." When the story finally appeared in the sports press months later, Kauffman said the two players he and Tallis had discussed were Rick Monday and Reggie Jackson. "I'll tell you this," he said in an interview with McGuff, "if we had Jackson, we'd be in first place in our division right now. All we need is a big bat like that in the middle of our order and we'd be competitive with anyone." There was no doubt that Kauffman was intent on having a winning team and prepared to invest the dollars needed to get it.

Kauffman wanted to win, to be number one, to be the best. Before the second season opened, he was boasting to a reporter for the *Kansas City Star Magazine*, "We'll win a World Series within the next six years." When the interviewer asked how he could possibly hope for a world championship so soon, Kauffman responded that there were three reasons. First, the Royals were recruiting and signing good players. Second, with more coaches and managers in their farm system than any other team, their young players received plenty of personal instruction. "And three," he said, "we'll have the

Baseball Academy, which will supply us with players we would not have had otherwise. In the next four to six years, the Academy will supply us with three to six major leaguers."

The Baseball Academy was Kauffman's entrepreneurial approach to creating a championship ball club. "It was the only additional thing I could think of to build a winning team faster," he acknowledged. No matter how much money he might spend for scouts to identify potential talent, or how many trades the Royals might initiate, it was still a slow process to acquire the right mix of men, talent, and desire to produce consistent winners. "I just didn't want to wait that long," Kauffman said. As he pondered the slow method of developing baseball players, Kauffman was struck with how conservative and resistant to innovation the sport was. He had made his fortune in a business where the search for new ideas, better ways of doing things, and new products were the lifeblood of the industry—the only way to survive, much less succeed. He began to chafe at what he considered the hidebound practices and almost total ignorance of how technology might inform and improve the training process. Just as he studied any card or dice game he might play, Kauffman began to study baseball. "I kind of look at baseball from a statistical side—the law of averages. And sometimes I wonder if things that have been done for years are really best. For instance, statistically, it doesn't improve your chances if the hitter bunts with a runner on first and no outs," he noted.

Kauffman understood statistics, but he was not content to use the normal baseball records as his only source of statistical information about his players. He went to the extra expense of having new categories of information kept on the Royals. All games were carefully charted and analyzed. At his request, the Royals began to keep statistics on the success or failure of each player in advancing runners; how many times each player got on base; and how they hit with no one on base in the first through sixth innings as compared with the last third of the game. Utilizing computers to manage all this data, the team began to come up with certain innovations. They could now make an intelligent decision about whether a given player should concentrate on home runs or focus more on raising his average.

Once the team had some additional information, Kauffman was hungry for even more. He wanted someone to invent an instrument that could mathematically measure the correct weight of a bat for a batter. "We should be able to tell a hitter that he should swing a thirty-three inch bat and hold it at the handle—or tell another that his correct choice should be a thirty-six-inch bat." He worried that a manager really could not know which pitcher had the fastest fastball. "How does he really know?" he asked rhetorically. "He doesn't. Why don't we measure the speed to be able to know that one pitcher has an eighty-five-mile-per-hour fastball, while another has a ninety-five-mile-per-hour fastball. Then, we could stop guessing." In the pharmaceutical business, Kauffman knew what the therapeutic effect of a given drug was and what its potential side effects might be. But in baseball, millions were invested based on judgment calls, impressions, predictions, and imprecise information. "We guess too much," he concluded. "You can talk to baseball people and ask them what part of the body is the most important in hitting and come up with all sorts of answers. One says the wrists, another the shoulders. . . . But all we have to do is put sensors on the body like you do with the astronauts and tell right away where a batter gets his power. When we know that, we can give the players exercises to develop those muscles."

Kauffman's impatience with the slow pace of developing a baseball team and his belief in utilizing sophisticated scientific technology to identify and nurture potential talent culminated in the Baseball Academy. The idea occurred to him during one of his nightly work sessions. "Every evening from eight until about ten P.M. I just sit, smoking my pipe, trying to think of new ideas. How to increase sales in a certain product, how to work out a finance problem, how to get fans more involved in baseball. It was during one of those sessions that the idea for the Academy came to me."

The Royals owner studied baseball with the same care he studied a new development in the pharmaceutical business or an unfamiliar card game. He knew that if his fellow Kansas Citians were to buy tickets and attend games, he would have to field a winning team— or at least a team with good prospects to grow into a champion. "I wanted to bring Kansas City a winner in the quickest way possible. It soon became apparent to me that there were only four ways in which we could get better players, and not one of them was going to do us much good."

The four methods Kauffman deemed wanting were the free agent draft, the minor league draft, trades with other major league teams, and buying players from other teams. A wily student of the law of averages, Kauffman saw no advantage in the free agent draft where "just about every club has the same chance." The minor leagues did not seem to provide many prospects since only eight players out of fifteen hundred were selected in 1970. "To trade well you have to be either lucky or have a lot of players other teams want. And money," he concluded "doesn't do that much for you." He had already offered Charlie Finley a million for Reggie Jackson, and Finley had spurned the deal. "The only thing I could do was go outside the normal baseball avenues open to us and try to find better players," he said. "So I came up with the idea that you didn't have to play baseball all your life to be a good baseball player. That's what the old-timers in baseball thought. I thought that if you had the physical attributes necessary to be a baseball star, you could be taught baseball."

The Royals Baseball Academy, which began operation in Sarasota, Florida, in August 1970, was based on the notion that the baseball draft equalized team talent to the extent that an ambitious club had to look for innovative factors to pull ahead of the others. And with Kauffman as the owner, the Royals were an ambitious, aggressive, self-confident expansion club with a vision to be a world champion as soon as possible.

To establish the physical attributes necessary to be a baseball star, Kauffman hired Dr. Raymond Reilly, a young research psychologist who had worked with NASA and the Office of Naval Research. His task was to test one hundred and fifty major league players. Kauffman instructed him to concentrate particularly on the Cincinnati Reds, who were considered the best team in baseball at that time. "Dr. Reilly came up with these requirements: first, speed of foot. Second, good eyesight. I don't mean twenty/twenty. I mean twenty/fifteen or twenty/ten where he could see a fly over there twenty-five feet away on the wall. Third, fast reflex actions. The ability to move like that is God-given. You cannot improve it more than 10 percent with repetitive action. And fourth was body balance—the ability to move around on your feet."

Reilly's earlier research had also interested Kauffman because he identified personality traits that he believed were predictors of success. He advised the Royals to look for young athletes "with a strong need to achieve something of significance . . . who are well above average in intelligence . . . and have a good memory for facts and figures." These were the same traits Kauffman had learned made successful pharmaceutical salesmen, so why not pennant-winning ball players?

In picking the thirty-five athletes who made up the Academy's first class, Kauffman established tryout camps in forty-one states. More than seventy-six hundred high school athletes tried out. These were young men who had shown skill in swimming, tennis, wrestling, basketball, and baseball. The Academy's scouts were searching for the five-foot, eight-inch high school basketball star who was too short for college or professional ball but possessed the attributes they had identified. Or they hoped to find a young man with all the necessary physical attributes but who had never played high school baseball or any other sport because he had to work to help meet family expenses.

While the Academy's emphasis was to be on developing potential star baseball players, Kauffman insisted that every "cadet" be a high school graduate. He provided free college instruction for them in the mornings at nearby Manatee Junior College. Among other things, he wanted them to learn enough about business and public relations to be able to manage the money he expected them to make in baseball. He also believed it was important that they have skills to support themselves when their professional sports careers ended.

The Baseball Academy was designed as a two-year program. In addition to two years of junior college education, including tuition, room, board, and books, each boy received $100 a month for the first ninety days. The stipend increased to $150 for the next ninety days and then $200 up to the time the Gulf Coast League opened. Mornings were for academic studies, but the afternoons and evenings were reserved for baseball. The New Mexico high school wrestling champion, a Missouri high school sprinter, a pole vaulter from Wichita, a boy who excelled in bowling and weight lifting but had never played baseball, and a Topeka quarterback who set records in the javelin throw added variety to the first class. "All they did was eat, sleep, and talk baseball," Kauffman remembered fondly.

Kauffman encountered a lot of critics who thought the Academy would never get off the ground, much less succeed, but he never doubted that the idea had merit. "I was laughed at," he recalled. "Even my own people at the Royals felt that it was a mistake. [They were] afraid we would show ourselves up when we started playing our team against the other teams of the major league clubs who had drafted qualified baseball players. But I told them, 'You worry about the Royals and I will take care of the Baseball Academy.'" And he did. He spent more than $1,500,000 to put the campus in shape. In addition to classrooms and dormitories, he built five new baseball diamonds. Each was constructed to the exact specifications of the playing field in the new stadium that was scheduled to open in Kansas City in 1972. In addition to the best facilities, Kauffman invested in talented people just as he had done at Marion Laboratories. Sid Thrift, a former Pittsburgh Pirates scout, became the Academy director. He assembled a staff consisting of two former major league managers, a catcher from the Washington Senators, the one-time University of Kansas track coach, and a former major league player. When Walter Shannon, the Baltimore Orioles director of scouting, visited the Academy during its first year, he was very complimentary. "I'm excited about it," he told *Sports Illustrated*. "It's the type of forward thinking in player development that has been needed. The ideas and results that will come out of there are things that could change many of the ideas people have held on to for perhaps too long a period."

When the Baseball Academy opened, one sportswriter noted that "not since Bill Veeck signed a midget had baseball produced such a laugh." But by the end of their first season in the Gulf Coast rookie league, Kauffman's experiment had achieved the best record in all of professional baseball—a staggering .813 winning percentage. None of the young ball players had even been considered seriously by any other major league team during the draft period, and eight of them had never played even one inning of high school baseball. Yet after a year of intensive training and individual coaching, these novices were hammering the top draft choices of the Minnesota Twins, the Pittsburgh Pirates, the St. Louis Cardinals, the Cincinnati Reds, the Chicago White Sox, and the Cleveland Indians.

Critics tried to discount their achievements by saying that the Academy Royals were winning because they had played together for a year. But Academy Director Thrift dismissed that reasoning as nonsense. "People say that we can execute better than teams that have been together only six weeks. Heck, you can execute all day and never win if you have players who have weak arms or are slow runners. Our players have good arms and speed." The Academy's strengths were the result of thinking about the game differently, recruiting players by a different criteria, and then working with them more intensively, employing the latest technology and theory about physical training. There were videotaped replay sessions, body building exercises, classroom lectures, and individual coaching. Every day every boy practiced batting a minimum of twenty minutes against live pitching. In the major leagues, many players failed to get that much hitting time in a week—and even less against live pitching.

The Academy faculty specialized in turning old practices on their heads. For example, the coaches used automatic pitching machines for regular batting practice, then turned the machines around and aimed them at the infielders. Since the pitching machines threw a ball at exactly the same spot every time, an infielder could move closer or farther away to perfect his technique with various bounces. Then to make the practice more challenging, the coach would switch to a curve-ball pitching machine. When the season closed that first year, Kauffman's belief that "baseball players can be made if the mental and muscular sciences are put to work," began to earn respect among serious students of the game. And the Academy's critics were no longer laughing. "After all," reported *Sports Illustrated*, "it gets tiresome being beaten by football players. In fact, it's no laughing matter unless you are Ewing Kauffman. Then it's hilarious."

The Twenty-Million-   12
Dollar Fan

It was fortunate that Kauffman had not acquired the Royals' franchise with the intention of making money, because it did not. And it was equally fortunate that Marion Laboratories continued to become more profitable in the early 1970s as the Royals' owner invested more and more of his personal wealth in developing the ball club and its facilities. In a speech to the Kansas City Advertising and Sales Executives Club in early 1971, Kauffman remarked that he had had a lot of fun the last two years since buying the Royals, "but I've never lost so much money." A year later, as the new stadium neared completion, he disclosed that his personal investment was almost twenty million dollars—"enough to discourage anyone from going into the baseball business," he liked to say.

In addition to the initial outlay of approximately seven-and-a-half million dollars required to purchase the franchise and players, plus developing the farm operations and the beloved Baseball Academy, Kauffman had sustained cash losses of almost five million dollars. Then when Jackson County ran low on funds to complete the sports complex, he put almost seven million dollars more of his own money into making the new stadium a showplace to attract maximum attendance. And there was more to come. Kauffman planned a mammoth scoreboard and a "dancing water spectacle." Major league baseball was big-time entertainment, and the showman in Kauffman loved an extravaganza. The water spectacle, Muriel Kauffman's idea originally, was designed with a series of waterfalls which contained one hundred fifty combinations of spray and color effects. Kauffman proudly announced that the "dancing water spectacular" would put on shows before and after games. He predicted that many persons who would not otherwise attend a ball game would buy tickets just to see the fountain. "When the crowd yells, the water shoots up. The louder they yell, the higher it will go. If they yell loud enough, five jet streams of water will go seven stories high," he exclaimed.

His own pet project in the new stadium was an informative and entertaining twelve-story-high, state-of-the-art scoreboard. A huge matrix containing more than sixteen thousand light bulbs, the scoreboard had the capability to produce intricate and elaborate animated displays. The one accompanying the national anthem used more than eight hundred drawings. Like the gigantic fountain, the scoreboard interacted with the spectators. As the volume of cheering mounted, the board's perimeter lights would rise in response. Between light shows and special displays, the two-million-dollar scoreboard also displayed out-of-town scores on a minute-to-minute basis—a must for many dyed-in-the-wool fans.

When completed, the Harry S Truman Sports Complex, which included the Chiefs' Arrowhead Stadium along with the Royals' home, cost seventy million dollars—thirty-seven million more than the bonds approved. A significant portion of those additional dollars had come from the respective teams' owners, Kauffman and Lamar Hunt of the Texas oil-rich Hunt clan. Now the challenge was to see if they could field teams worthy of this setting. The Royals had planned to be in their new stadium in 1972, but a huge construction strike delayed the completion for more than a year and severely strained club finances. Kauffman had projected significant increases in income for 1972 based on the drawing power of a new and attractive stadium. The delay proved to be expensive, costing him an additional two million dollars.

As the costs associated with building a major league baseball team continued to mount, Kauffman reluctantly began to rethink the Baseball Academy. While it was still too early to deem the experiment an unqualified success or failure, he did yield to Tallis's request to integrate the farm operation into the Academy. Players who were signed through normal channels should be able to benefit from the intensive instruction being offered raw recruits, Tallis had argued. Beginning in August 1972, the Academy's entering class was cut to twenty boys between ages seventeen and nineteen to accommodate the minor league players. Sid Thrift returned to his former position as the Royals' eastern scouting supervisor. Lou

Gorman, head of the Royals' scouting effort and the farm system and Tallis's ally in scoffing at the Baseball Academy, replaced Thrift as director in Florida. This was a clear signal that more changes were to come.

By the spring of 1973, the Baseball Academy could boast that its first graduate, Frank White, had reported to the major leagues. White, who grew up within walking distance of the old Municipal Stadium, had attended Lincoln High School, which had no baseball team. But he played on local teams and collected a batch of city-wide honors. Yet in spite of his obvious ability, not a single baseball club contacted him about a future in the sport. With a wife and a baby son by his nineteenth birthday, White seemed destined for a blue-collar future stacking sheet metal at one-hundred dollars a week. But his wife, Gladys, persuaded him to attend the Royals' first tryout camp, and shortly he was on his way to Sarasota. As he approached his major league debut with his hometown team, White seemed uneasy with the notion that he was a scientifically developed baseball player. When he was reminded how well he had tested in the tryout camp and that those results had prescribed the training he received at the Academy, he would throw up his hands and protest through a big smile, "Stop! I feel like I've been through a test tube and rolled into a capsule." Then he would add, "Of course, if it wasn't for the Academy, I'd probably still be working in that sheet metal plant around the corner from the old stadium."

By spring 1974, other cost-cutting moves surfaced at the Academy. First, the Royals announced that the fringes would be curtailed, most notably the subsidized, supplemental college education plan. This was a difficult decision for Kauffman, who felt a responsibility to provide the young players with some academic training to fall back on when their sports careers ended. But neither the athletes nor the Royals' management valued the junior college experience, so he reluctantly acquiesced. At the same time, two farm clubs, from Billings, Montana, and Kingsport, Tennessee, were moved to the Academy and combined with two Gulf Coast League teams, the Sarasota Royals and the Academy Royals.

Although a few major league teams picked up some of the Academy's training techniques—the Cincinnati Reds had begun testing new recruits' vision and the New York Mets experimented with optometherapy, a visualization program to improve a player's batting average or pitching—no other baseball academies were established. In an interview with Joe McGuff in early April, Kauffman hinted that he might have to abandon his dream. "I don't want to give up the Academy," he said, "because we're starting to get results, but it's costing us about $600,000 a year." But by the end of April, it was all over. Gorman, not Kauffman, made the announcement. He said the decision was extremely difficult, particularly since the Academy concept was working. "The Academy has accomplished what it was intended to do, namely to develop inexperienced, raw talent into major league prospects." Gorman pointed to Frank White as proof of the experiment's success, and there would be others. He attempted to skirt the finality of the decision with euphemistic phrases about the Academy being "revamped," but in truth, it was already dead. The facility would continue to be used for instructing and developing the Royals' minor league players until 1979, when the Kauffmans gave the property to the Kansas City YMCA.

Closing the Academy was a painful decision, but Kauffman kept his own counsel for the time being. It was true that his investment in the club was much greater than he originally anticipated it would be. Still, he was always willing to spend the dollars needed to hasten the development of a championship team. But he was first a good businessman and then a sports owner. As Marion stock began to drift downward and PAVABID's future clouded in 1974, he recognized the need to be more prudent in his personal spending on the Royals. There was some reshuffling in the ball club's front office, stricter internal financial controls, and cutbacks in the scouting operations, but in the end the academy had to go.

The decision had as much to do with the internal resistance within the Royals' management as it did with finances. In an interview a year after the closing, Kauffman vented his frustration with the baseball world's inflexibility. "They're not receptive to novel, new ideas," he complained. In reflecting on his zeal for the Academy and his efforts to introduce new approaches to preparation for the game, he admitted that he had probably been fighting a losing battle from the start. "When it came to visualization and concentration tests, I *ordered* the players to take them and they *did*. But if a coach says, 'Oh, that doesn't mean anything!' it hurts the program. [When you have] a coach who has been in baseball for forty years and runs the program down, then the players are not going to work at it. And it takes work to make *anything* succeed. So this is what I mean by saying they are hidebound traditionalists in baseball."

It was clear that Kauffman, the hardheaded, pragmatic business-man was at war with Kauffman, the optimistic, visionary entrepreneur. To reduce losses further, he cut back the farm operation and eliminated the twenty full-time and fifty part-time scouts. The Royals would share a centralized scouting bureau with nineteen other teams. While he acknowledged that he had experienced some tax savings, he still had a twenty-million-dollar investment that had not earned 1 percent in interest in seven years. "In fact," he told an interviewer, "we still haven't as yet broken even. Not a single year."

Like a wealthy father who provided his favorite daughter with a lavish, extravagant wedding then fumed over the bills, Kauffman's irritation with the costs of owning a major league team was beginning to show. "I never dreamed I'd be worth a million dollars! And it's a good thing I am, because the ball club has taken a good part of it!" As the interview progressed, Kauffman actually seemed to be rethinking the wisdom of ever having gotten into baseball at all. He had been motivated by the desire to do something for his home-town, and now it was beginning to look at if he might have erred in his choice. "I'll never get the twenty million back!" he lamented. "I'll just leave that to Kansas City, the stadium and all its beautiful surroundings. But this is my only regret about having baseball . . . I would have done so much more with twenty million dollars for Kansas City."

But issues other than the huge financial investment were also worrying Kauffman. He was disillusioned with baseball players. Like Peter Pan, they seemed to have no interest in growing up. He was especially concerned about how the players typically handled their finances. "They make big money, but they spend it. They blow it or people take advantage of them. They just don't realize that they may only be up here four or five years or eight years." He worried about how they and their families would live when these young men could no longer command huge salaries on the ball diamond. He had offered everyone associated with the Royals free financial counseling and special training to learn a second career during their playing days. Yet to his amazement and obvious chagrin, few players had taken advantage of the offer. Players were naturally distrustful of owners, an attitude that had its roots in the era when owners treated athletes as little better than chattel goods. When players organized their own union and began the practice of using agents to negotiate on their behalf, the relationships between owners and players were no better—some said they were even worse. The agents reinforced the commonly held view that "you can't trust an owner. He'll just try to take your money."

A true child of the Depression, Kauffman could never comprehend this cavalier approach to the future. Once again he was trying to operate in the world of baseball as he did at Marion Laboratories—he wanted to treat people as he would wish to be treated, and he was willing to share the rewards, should there ever be any—but neither the players nor the sport as a whole seemed receptive to his overtures. "It just isn't possible to put in an incentive program for motivation," he said with obvious disappointment. "The rules are against it." This world of major league baseball was baffling and disheartening to a man like Kauffman. At times he felt like an intruder in alien territory.

But he was essentially an optimist, so the glum mood passed rather quickly. Soon he was tossing around new ideas about player compensation, incentive pay calculated on bases stolen and the number of runners batted in. He was thinking about bonuses for players who lost weight or achieved some other mutually agreed-upon goal. "I'm proposing to the major league owners that we change our contracts so that we can provide incentives," he announced, apparently forgetting that these were the men he had just characterized as hidebound traditionalists.

The best tonic for Kauffman's flagging enthusiasm was the Royals' first American League Western Division championship in 1976. That victory started a chain reaction of six division wins and two American League pennants within a decade, culminating in the World Series championship over the St. Louis Cardinals in 1985. That first division championship was tinged with irony, because to win it the Royals had to defeat Charlie Finley's Oakland Athletics. One sportswriter recalled how Finley and his infamous mule had once been the symbols of Kansas City's baseball failure. Now the seven-year-old expansion team of the city Finley fled had soundly trounced his west coast dynasty. "How could success taste any sweeter?" the reporter asked, tongue in cheek.

For the Kauffmans, 1976 was a banner year. The Kansas City sportswriters hailed them as "Mr. and Mrs. Baseball" even before the division win. The award acknowledged Muriel Kauffman's important role in the team's ownership. She had encouraged Kauffman to buy the franchise, and she worked tirelessly to make the team successful. From selling season tickets to decorating the stadium's executive offices to cheering from the owner's box, she was an effective and visible partner. And with as competitive a temperament as her husband, Mrs. Kauffman was happiest when the Royals were winning.

In making the presentation, Joe McGuff, the *Star*'s sports editor, lauded the Kauffmans' leadership, saying, "They [came] forward when others were hanging back." He likened their purchase of the expansion franchise to "an act of philanthropy" on a par with the contributions that had made the Nelson Gallery, the Philharmonic, the fountains of the Country Club Plaza, and the area's colleges and universities a reality. "Admittedly life would have gone on in Kansas City without baseball. . . . But who would want to live in a city without a soul?" he concluded.

There was another significant honor that same evening, although no one could have known at the time how accurate a predictor of success it was to be. George Brett, the Royals' young third baseman, received the Les Milgram Award as the local player of the year. In accepting the award, Brett acknowledged that Kansas City had been very good to him. "In return, I hope in '76 I will be a part of a team that wins the Western Division and American League championship, and possibly the World Series." Although another nine years would elapse before all Brett's wishes came true, he would be on the team when they did. And he would become the undisputed star in the Royals' crown. In addition to the accolades and awards for baseball that evening, Muriel Kauffman captured the spotlight when she announced to her husband and the seven hundred sports fans attending the banquet that she would become a United States citizen on February 10. When the big day arrived, Kauffman surprised her when he appeared at the naturalization ceremonies as the featured speaker. Afterward as the couple posed for photographs, Kauffman jokingly announced to the others, "It's the duty of every [new] American citizen to become a baseball fan."

Kauffman's response to winning the division title that year confirmed the nature of his character. He wrote an unprecedented letter to the *Kansas City Star*, "a fervent thank you," to all the fans, the reporters, the regional sports commentators, and the Royal Lancers. He downplayed his financial investment in the franchise. "I cannot forget that it was the faith of the residents of Jackson County that made possible the bond issue and the most beautiful sports complex in the world," he wrote. He praised the fans for their continued attendance "even in the darkest of those days . . . those . . . nervous days in mid-September when the team experienced a severe hitting slump." He likened the season to a "beautiful coming together of . . . loyalties and affections, a response typical of a community rightfully called the Heart of America. A show of love? Yes!" he proclaimed. With that letter, written in the flush of victory, Kauffman revealed himself again as a sentimental, affectionate, and emotional man. That instinctive gesture and the willingness to give others credit secured his place in the affections of his fellow Kansas Citians, whether baseball enthusiasts or not. But lest anyone think that this outpouring of genuine thankfulness had dulled his competitive edge, he concluded the letter, "I say, on to the World Series title!"

As the Royals began to pile up victories, Kauffman again became impatient for more success. He felt that given the money he was investing, the team still was not progressing as rapidly as it should. And he frankly admitted that his own lack of knowledge of baseball, coupled with the game's stultifying traditions, had hampered progress. Then he let it slip that he was still toying with the idea of starting up the Baseball Academy again. Unfortunately, the Baseball Academy was destined to become a lingering memory. In the final years of his life, Kauffman conceded that he wished he had pursued that dream. Yet, he felt no bitterness. "That's a disappointment in myself because I wasn't smart enough to see [the long-term value]. And I let the finances of it bother me too much. And, of course, at the time I didn't have as much money as I did later on."

When the Royals captured the division championship a second time in 1977, the club's financial picture began to change "from unrosy red to blissful black." In reporting the healthier balance sheet, Kauffman noted, "My financial people tell me if we do it eight more years, I'll get all of my money back." But as he had said before, he earned his money at Marion Laboratories and his pleasure in owning the ball club lay in what it could do for Kansas City. A study which attempted to gauge the Royals' economic impact on the city in the mid-1970s concluded that spending by the club, the visiting teams, and the fans generated more than twenty million dollars a year. There were other benefits too that pleased Kauffman. The ball club generated publicity for the city as well as dollars. "When you are trying to hire people from other areas, they want to know what the city has to offer in museums, music, entertainment, parks, and other things," he said. "That Kansas City has a major league ball club is a big plus."

The following year brought the Royals another division title. Once again they were pitted against the New York Yankees in the struggle for the American League pennant. And for the third straight season, New York proved to be their nemesis. The Royals dropped to second place in their division in 1979, but 1980 was the turning point. They battled the Yankees for the American League championship again and won. For the fourth time in five seasons, the Royals had won a division title, now a league pennant. Sportswriters across the country consulted the record books and all agreed this was the best record for an expansion team in the history of baseball. Now they were to play in the World Series just as Kauffman had promised they would.

As the Royals prepared to meet the Philadelphia Phillies, Kauffman reflected on the years it had taken to win a berth in the national championship playoffs. Cedric Tallis and the early management team had laid the foundation for an outstanding core group of players. Their emphasis on scouting and the farm system had given the Royals the depth that permitted them to bring most of their talent up through their own minor league system. As they approached the World Series, the Royals had no highly paid free agents on their roster. A majority of the players were products of the team's farm system, and several had come out of the Baseball Academy experiment. Kauffman boasted about the team's relative youth. "Amos Otis is one of our older players at thirty-three," he noted, "and he still is a beautiful center fielder."

Those early years had not been without rumblings from the fans occasionally. Although it was uncharacteristic of Kauffman to defend personnel decisions—he had declined to explain Tallis's dismissal in 1974, and he was tight-lipped when the fans roared their disapproval over shifts in general managers in the 1970s—he felt that the Royals' pennant-winning performance vindicated Whitey Herzog's dismissal as manager in 1979. And he said so. Unlike many other major league owners, Kauffman did not dabble in day-to-day team management. He had decided early in his involvement with baseball that he would either have to trust the executives he hired or he would have to fire them. That had been his policy at Marion Laboratories, where he understood the pharmaceutical business. That was to be his policy in the baseball world, where he knew much less.

He also reminded those who had urged him to spend major dollars to secure big-name free agents in the late 1970s that the Royals had achieved national prominence and still been fiscally prudent. Even in a winning season, the fiscal conservative in Kauffman chafed at the financial losses he incurred with the Royals. By 1980, after a string of division titles and unprecedented attendance at the ball park, he admitted he was almost ten million dollars in the red. Although he could write off some of the losses after an initial seven years as an owner, Internal Revenue Service regulations penalized him severely because baseball was not his primary source of income. His greatest expenses with the Royals had come during the mid-seventies, when Marion Laboratories was experiencing difficulties and his own income was reduced. Later, when the Royals did begin to generate some profits, he had to declare those funds as unearned income, which was taxed at 70 percent. Although he always said the Royals had provided him with great pleasure and a sense of community involvement, he reminded his listeners, "You'd be foolish to invest in baseball."

Kauffman and the Royals would have benefited significantly had the major league owners agreed to share local television and radio revenue—a total of almost $39 million in 1980—as they shared the national media package. The Royals' television and radio revenues of $500,000 for 1980 were the smallest in the major leagues according to *Broadcasting* magazine. The Philadelphia Phillies, their 1980 World Series opponent, had a package worth three and a half million, second only to the New York Yankees. Yet Kauffman never pressed for that concession. "It's always brought up by the have-nots," he admitted. And he did not blame owners in the major markets for their refusal to share the lucrative local media contracts.

"It's the same thing as if they asked the gate receipts be shared equally. I would say 'no' because I have good gate receipts. I would also say, 'You don't work as hard to get the fans in, you don't spend the money I do.'"

Gate receipts were, in fact, a place where Kauffman could easily have increased revenue, but he was adamant about making it possible for as many fans as possible to attend Royals' games. In the middle of the 1980 World Series, season ticket sales soared above the previous year's record of 12,200. Kauffman telephoned from Philadelphia instructing the Royal Lancers to limit their sales to fifteen thousand. The baseball world was startled. This was reportedly the first time a major league owner had issued such a directive. He had always kept 12 percent of the seats at $1.50. "We've done that so those baseball fans who are not in good financial circumstances can still attend. As long as I can, I will keep those . . . seats at $1.50." It was not surprising that Royals' fans had a special sense of ownership about the team and great affection for Kauffman.

Although he delivered on his promise to bring the World Series to Kansas City, the Royals would not win the world championship until 1985. But when asked about his greatest thrill in baseball, Kauffman never cited either World Series encounter. The magic moment for him came during the playoffs for the American League pennant in 1980. "When we beat them three straight in the playoffs, that was the ultimate," he said. The last hit of the last game was the one that would remain vivid and fresh in his memory. "We're behind something like one to nothing, and in the eighth inning, George Brett comes up with a man on base, only because it was U.L. Washington, one of the academy boys, who hit a grounder to the shortstop. But he ran it out as hard as he could and just barely beat the throw. So, here we have a runner on first base with two out and George Brett up. And they bring in 'Goose' Gossage, who is the best relief pitcher in baseball." Every time Kauffman told the story, his voice would rise in excitement and the listener could almost smell the pungent mix of sweat, hot dogs, and popcorn in the air. "Gossage threw that ball at ninety-seven to ninety-nine miles an hour," Kauffman said, savoring every detail of the confrontation. "He faced Brett and threw a strike in there at ninety-seven; threw another pitch in there at probably the same speed, and George Brett hit it into the grandstand for a home run. And now we were the

American League champions and got to go to the World Series. That to me was my greatest thrill in baseball. And the moment was all the more memorable because it had come at the expense of the New York Yankees."

After the euphoria of the first American League pennant victory and of playing in the World Series, the 1981 season was bound to be a letdown for both Kauffman and the players. Then physical problems put a damper on Kauffman's spirits. In May, he had surgery to remove a tumor from his chest wall and part of one rib. Although the tumor was benign, Kauffman was sixty-five years old. This brush with mortality caused him to give serious thought to the long-term future of the baseball franchise. Just as he was beginning to feel the return of his old vigor, the players bolted in a dispute with the owners over compensation and free agency. Play was suspended in midseason. And Kauffman, who loved to win, seemed to lose some of his enthusiasm for the game. He characterized the strike issues as rather silly and certainly negotiable. Then in a voice that sounded like someone who was tired and a little apprehensive that baseball would never again excite him as it once had, he admitted, "It isn't as much fun as it used to be."

News of Kauffman's surgery gave rise to rumors about the Royals' future. When asked directly about his plans, he responded, "If I sell the team, it would be more from the standpoint of preparing for the future. I might sell half of it four or five years from now if I could find someone who is qualified and can do a good job for Kansas City." The fans breathed a sign of relief, as did the city fathers. Rumors of a sale being imminent were just that, rumors. Kauffman was just being prudent. Surely there was no need to worry. The rest of the summer was taken up with settling the strike. A compromise was reached between players and owners after seven weeks of often bitter wrangling and just five days before the owners' sixty-million-dollar strike insurance policy was to expire. Although he had sounded rather militant during the strike talks, Kauffman was in good humor when the players returned to the field that August. Before the first game, he was in the clubhouse and the dugout, shaking hands. He welcomed the team's new players to Kansas City and assured everyone of his good humor and goodwill. "I wanted everyone to know there are no hard feelings and how happy I am to be back watching baseball," he said.

As the interrupted season dragged on into the fall, rumors that Kauffman might sell bubbled up again. He admitted that the lengthy and rancorous strike had lessened his enthusiasm temporarily, "but with our team rejuvenated and going toward another possible pennant and World Series participation, my optimism and enthusiasm [have] returned." But if he were to find the right person, he announced he would still consider selling 49 percent of the club. This time, there was no mention of waiting four or five years; he was ready to listen to offers, if approached. His willingness to sell an interest in the franchise was with the proviso that he would run it for the next five or ten years, at which time the minority investor would have an option to buy the remaining half.

Kauffman's reasons for seeking a partner were understandable. "I'm sixty-five years old," he said. "I've enjoyed baseball, and I would like possibly to get back some of my investment. There are other things I would like to do." Among the other things, he mentioned using his time and resources to publicize the life-saving technique of cardiopulmonary resuscitation on a national basis. Marion Laboratories and the Royals had worked with city officials in the late 1970s to train more than one hundred thousand people in the Kansas City area in this life-saving technique. Hardly a week went by that Kauffman did not receive a letter from some person telling him how they had used the CPR training to save a life. When he became troubled about the Royals finances, he often mused that he could probably have done more to benefit his hometown through extending CPR training than with baseball.

He also indicated he was thinking of using some part of his fortune to train doctors, nurses, and pharmacists. Perhaps he might help minorities prepare for those professions, he said. Marion had been providing research funds to a number of universities over the years, and it was natural that, having made his fortune in the health care field, that he would think about philanthropic activities there. But nothing was formulated. He was unsettled in his thinking and merely exploring a range of possible actions.

Kauffman hoped that the announcement that he was willing to listen to proposals for a partner in the franchise would elicit support from someone in Kansas City. "There are people in Kansas City who have the wealth to be in baseball," he said, "but unfortunately their interest is in other fields." He ruled out a syndicate-type ownership, characterizing it "as the worst thing in the world. I think I wouldn't want more than three or four people involved at the most." But any prospective purchaser would not only have to have enough money to buy in, but would have to have the financial capacity to withstand possible operating losses. Given this scenario, the field was definitely limited.

Over the next few months, Kauffman had discussions with several prospective purchasers, but nothing more. A year after first announcing his intention to sell a minority interest in the franchise, he was patiently waiting for the right candidate. "I haven't pushed it," he told a reporter from the *Star*. "I've had several inquiries, but I haven't gotten serious with any of them except possibly for one and even there we haven't talked facts and figures. There's no doubt I could make a deal if I wanted to, but I'm not rushing." That fall, a six-member group of investors approached Kauffman expressing interest in purchasing the Royals. Although he declined the offer, he continued to negotiate with one of the group, Michael Shapiro, a thirty-five-year-old former Kansas Citian living in Los Angeles. When asked why he had continued talks with Shapiro, Kauffman responded, "He's a good salesman. I'm impressed with him."

By February 1983, it looked as if Kauffman and Shapiro had reached an agreement. The *Kansas City Star* reported that Kauffman had signed a letter of intent to sell 49 percent of the ball club stock for ten million dollars. In addition, there was another rumored deal regarding the sale of cable television rights to Royals' games. Now public curiosity about Shapiro was piqued. Kansas Citians were asking "Who is Michael Shapiro?" His press releases portrayed him as a businessman, entrepreneur, and investor in the entertainment industry. Lee W. Huddleston, president of Country Club Bank who had been associated with Shapiro in business for five or six years, admitted, "I don't know what he is, [but he is] backed by investors who are some pretty heavy hitters. He's been successful at whatever he has been doing because he has some money. He travels a lot."

Although Shapiro eluded the local press, they began to ferret out fragments of his background. He had attended Southwest High School in the mid-1960s before his family moved to California. At twenty-five, he had been an unsuccessful candidate for a Democratic nomination to Congress from Los Angeles. Somewhere along the way he had organized an unsuccessful professional rodeo league and was

part of a group of investors who tried to purchase the Cleveland Indians. One of his business associates told the press Shapiro was a
businessman with ties to the movie and television industries. Another said he was an independent movie producer who had once
been associate director of business affairs in television for Twentieth Century–Fox. Even Kauffman seemed unable to shed much
light on Shapiro other than to say he knew he had ties to the Johnny
Carson organization. In spite of a rather mysterious personal history, it did appear that he was keenly interested in professional
baseball. Michael Fernandez, an attorney representing Shapiro's investor group, described him as "an absolute baseball fan, complete
and total and [who] knows baseball very, very well."

Kauffman and Shapiro struck a deal. Then, less than a week after
the letter of agreement was reported in the press, the negotiations
were off. Kauffman made the announcement personally in a press
conference at Royals Stadium. "Michael Shapiro did not meet the
terms and conditions of our agreement, one of which was the delivery of funds by five P.M., Central Standard time. . . . We were
waiting in our lawyers' office at five o'clock. . . . They very well may
have [the money], I don't know. I didn't see it. I don't know. . . .
And as a result, our negotiations have been canceled." Shapiro had
agreed to deliver eleven million dollars cash and a letter of credit
for an additional twelve million. When he failed to do so, Kauffman
and his advisers realized that it had all been smoke and mirrors. Although Shapiro sputtered that "the deal hasn't fallen through," he
was quickly hinting at possible legal action.

Everyone seemed relieved to have the shadowy Shapiro out of
the picture, especially Kauffman. In an interview with Jonathan
Rand of the *Kansas City Times,* he likened the experience to giving
away a daughter in marriage: The closer it got, the less eager he was
to go through with it. But the question remained: How could a
businessman as successful as Kauffman enter into serious negotiations with a person of such a murky background? And how could
he have signed an agreement for so much money when, by his own
admission, he did not know Shapiro's source of cash? The answer
was simple and believable to anyone who knew Kauffman well. He
was too trusting. With the best legal and financial advice available,
Kauffman still relied on his personal judgment about an individual's merits. He trusted another's handshake and word until he had

concrete reasons to do otherwise. He had liked young Shapiro and had been impressed with his salesmanship. He probably saw himself reflected in this young man from his own hometown who appeared to have become a person of substance and influence. Although Shapiro was somewhat brash, a rather flashy dresser, and even a bit pushy, Kauffman freely admitted to having been characterized with those same words in his palmier days. And Shapiro's claims to ties with the television and entertainment industry appealed to Kauffman, who believed that the future revenues for baseball would be heavily dependent on television.

But when Shapiro failed to deliver the money on schedule, Kauffman knew he had misjudged the situation. He admitted that he had had a narrow escape and was prepared to drop the subject and move on to winning another division title, maybe a pennant. Perhaps this would be the year for the World Series victory. Like the fan in the $1.50 seats, he was capable of making a mistake—a fact that endeared him even more to Kansas Citians. For as one reporter commented, "Ewing Kauffman is just a fan who struck it rich."

The Kauffman-Fogelman Dynasty

The collapse of the Shapiro negotiations in mid-February 1983 seemed to sour Kauffman on looking for a partner. His trust had been abused and he was weary of the constant speculation in the press. He told close associates that he would probably take a break from such negotiations for a year or so. But suddenly on May 17, he announced he had sold 49 percent of the Royals for ten million dollars in cash to Avron B. Fogelman of Memphis, Tennessee. For an additional million dollars, Fogelman also secured an option to buy the remaining 51 percent at any time from 1988 to 1991. Kauffman would become legally obligated to sell Fogelman the rest of the club in 1991.

Although the sale seemed to appear out of thin air, the negotiations had begun in February shortly after the Shapiro debacle became public. "I read in the newspaper that Mr. K was ill and interested in selling 49 percent of the team. I picked up the phone to call him," Fogelman said. "My discussions were only with him." Following the aborted Shapiro agreement, Fogelman flew to Kansas City for face-to-face talks. Both men said that there were no negotiations and no bargaining, as such. Kauffman told McGuff that he asked Fogelman to name a fair price, and, in response, Fogelman asked him to set the figure. "We decided twenty-two million was fair and we agreed on that," Kauffman said. "I've been offered more, but he is the first gentleman who I felt I can get along with and who desires to be in baseball and has the spirit to be in it."

Unlike the mysterious Shapiro, Avron Fogelman was a well known, forty-three-year-old real estate developer and investor in professional sports clubs from Memphis, Tennessee. In partnership with his brother Robert, Fogelman controlled more than fifteen thousand apartment units throughout the South as well as other commercial real estate. Highly regarded in Memphis for his philanthropy and civic involvement, he was the owner of the Memphis Chicks baseball team of the Southern League, a minor league franchise which he had acquired in 1978.

In announcing the partnership, Kauffman beamed, saying, "When I found this man, I knew I'd found what I was looking for. He can afford it, he has the personality, and he loves baseball." Like Kauffman, he was also a skilled salesman. "I think I started out selling, and he finished up selling," Fogelman recalled. "I didn't push him; I didn't give him any dates or ultimatums." But Fogelman did mention he was looking seriously at another ball club which turned out to be the Cleveland Indians. Fogelman's intimation that he might deal elsewhere was probably unnecessary to spur an agreement, because Kauffman instinctively liked the younger man. "He has the enthusiasm I had fifteen years ago," Kauffman announced.

Kauffman had every reason to believe that with a trusted, vigorous, young partner he could now relax a bit and really enjoy life. "[Fogelman is] going to do the running, but I'm going to help him. I'm going to have fun for eight more years," he said. With the completion of the transaction, the Royals were in excellent financial condition. Kauffman had always conducted his business affairs with a minimum of debt, and the loan he incurred to complete the stadium had always nagged at him. With the infusion of Fogelman's cash, he retired the debt. Now he had the added comfort of knowing he would be able to share whatever financial losses might come with a wealthy partner. "For the first time since Mrs. Kauffman and I purchased the club . . . we have no debt," he boasted. "Few clubs can say that."

For Fogelman, becoming an owner of a major league baseball team was the fulfillment of a life's ambition. Shortly after the purchase agreement was announced he said, "I kind of feel that every red-blooded American boy would love the opportunity to own a baseball team. . . . I'm a guy that had nothing fifteen years ago, and here I am having all this." Both men were genuinely pleased about their new partnership. The arrangement permitted Fogelman to share ownership that he described as a "good situation." He believed that the Royals were a good investment because of the potential millions television would eventually bring if local media revenues were ever shared among the owners. Although he admitted that he had never considered taking a partner other than his own brother, and he never thought he would put up so much capital without acquiring control, he said, "This is a special situation. If Kauffman was not the kind of owner I respected, I doubt we could have come to the kind of decision we did. He has accepted me as a co-owner with all the flexibility I wanted. I have done nothing to infringe on his territory. I am just a successor. He is the mentor." Fogelman was respectful, almost deferential, toward the older man in his public statements, and Kauffman seemed to have regained his youthful zest for the game. An ebullient, optimistic person by nature, he made comments to the press that bordered on hyperbole. "We can have a dynasty here," he proclaimed, "if he's willing to put the money in. You've heard of the Habsburg Dynasty? Well, this is the Kauffman-Fogelman Dynasty!"

The spurned Shapiro, upon learning of the sale, threatened legal action against Kauffman on the grounds that the letter of agreement he had signed was a binding, enforceable contract. He accused Kauffman of acting in a cavalier fashion. "Our ages are much different," he said, "but we both can learn a lot about life. We just might learn about it in court." It would be 1987 before Shapiro made good on his threat. By then, his reputation as a successful, young entrepreneur was sullied. An investigative reporter for the *Kansas City Star* learned from Dana Collins, president of the business affairs department at Twentieth Century–Fox, that Shapiro had held "the lowest position in business affairs" in the company. And as president of the Championship Sport Enterprises of Los Angeles, he had led a two-year, abortive attempt to establish a professional rodeo circuit. Under cross examination, Shapiro finally acknowledged that his résumé inflated his education and the importance of past positions. He also conceded that he had been adjudged bankrupt in 1980 and that his October 1981 financial statement listed money, stocks, and other assets—including a thirty-million-dollar trust fund—that did not exist. Kauffman found the trial distasteful and depressing. "The first day I felt pretty low because I heard so many bad things about me," he admitted. "But once the jury got it, I didn't worry a bit. We had done our best. I never worry about what I can't do anything about." A federal court jury found in Kauffman's favor because "we didn't believe [Shapiro] at all. He misrepresented himself time after time."

Within a month of purchasing a minority interest in the Royals, Fogelman was hinting at the possibility of changes to come. In a speech accepting the key to Kansas City from the Chamber of Commerce, he said he and Kauffman shared similar philosophies about operating the Royals. But Fogelman was anxious to establish his own identity. "It's not right to think I'm going to be a stereotype of him," he cautioned. "I don't think he would want that and I wouldn't want that." Then he responded to the unspoken question of where differences might arise. "Let me say that free agency is something we've got to consider. Four or five years ago that might not have been the approach. Today, it might be the approach."

During Kauffman's fifteen years as sole owner, the Royals had signed only two free agents, although management acknowledged making serious bids for several others. The team had been brought to contending status largely through trades made in the 1970s—Hal McRae, Amos Otis, Larry Gura, Fred Patek, Cookie Rojas—and the development of younger players like George Brett, Frank White, Al Cowens, Dennis Leonard, and Paul Splittorff through the farm system and the Baseball Academy. Just as he had developed executives internally in the early years of Marion Laboratories, Kauffman had favored that same practice with the Royals. Fogelman did not take issue with Kauffman's past approach to free agency, and he assured his listeners that "If Kauffman hasn't signed free agents before, it hasn't been because of money . . . that man could not have let money be the reason for not signing free agents. But," he argued, "free agency is now the way of baseball. He and I both want to win, but not at the sake of disrupting an extremely successful organization."

In response to Fogelman's public reference about a possible change in operating philosophy, General Manager John Schuerholz said he thought the two approaches could be blended. In his mind, free agency was no end-all to a team's problems. At best it was useful for the short term. Like Kauffman, he believed strongly in nurturing talent though the farm system. And Kauffman, not wishing to rebuff his new partner so early in their relationship, conceded that he was willing to go after free agents, "but I don't want to be foolish." He also reaffirmed that the Royals' players would still come first in the free agent era. However, now that he had Fogelman to share half the losses, he could take more risk. "Last year we lost two million dollars in cold cash," he said. "That's a lot of money for one person to lose. It's a lot easier to lose it if somebody else is putting up half. We might be more aggressive in the future . . . for the right [player]."

In spite of the excitement over the new partnership, the Royals' 1983 season was a lackluster one. Kauffman denied that it was the start of a long-term decline. He characterized it as a short-term difficulty, although discouraging. "It's a combination of one or two players getting to the point where they are older, and injuries certainly have been a factor," he told the press. The solution, in his view, was to bring up some young pitchers from the farm clubs in September. He also acknowledged that an earlier decision of his might have contributed to the Royals' declining performance. "That occurred eight years ago when I had them cut down the scouting staff because we were losing money and [we] got into the major league scouting bureau. That has not been as successful as the [American League] owners hoped it would be," he said. But the Royals were in a three-year process of rebuilding their own scouting staff and were also adding two additional minor league teams. And, he admitted, he was seriously weighing the option of bidding aggressively in the free agent market. "I think there comes a time when any club can use a free agent, and this may be the year." Kauffman's name had just appeared on the *Forbes* 1983 list of the four hundred richest Americans. It estimated his worth at $160 million. Profits at Marion Laboratories were rising since the introduction of CARAFATE and CARDIZEM, so his prospects for even greater wealth seemed secure. Perhaps this was the right moment to become more aggressive with the ball club.

When asked if he and Fogelman would be able to agree on a strategy to strengthen the Royals, Kauffman responded affirmatively. But he reminded the questioner that decisions at the Royals were made in full consultation with the team's general manager. "I will not dictatorially say this is the way things are going to be because I respect [Fogelman's] business judgment. And if John Schuerholz says, 'No, we shouldn't do it, Mr. K,' then we sure aren't going to do it. So it's going to be agreement between John Schuerholz, Mr. Fogelman, and myself."

As the 1983 baseball season moved into the late summer, everything seemed to go wrong for the Royals. A knee injury took Dennis Leonard out of play in late May. In early June when he was beginning to hit his stride, George Brett broke a toe and was lost to the game for more than three weeks. In late summer, two one-time stars—pitcher Vida Blue and outfielder Otis Amos—were dropped from the Royals' roster. Then left fielder Willie Wilson broke a knuckle. Although they had been favored to win the Western Division at the beginning of the season, the Royals slumped into second place, a full twenty games behind the champion Chicago White Sox. At the tail end of this dispirited season, rumors began to circulate that a federal drug probe was focusing on as many as ten Royals players. When questioned about the reports that three players in particular were being investigated, Kauffman acknowledged that the news was distressing. However, he reminded the press that "there is no evidence any of our players are involved, only that they were questioned. So we'll have to wait and see." A few weeks later, Jerry Martin, Willie Aikens, Willie Wilson, and Vida Blue pleaded guilty to misdemeanor cocaine charges. They received ninety-day terms in a federal penitentiary, and Baseball Commissioner Bowie Kuhn suspended them for the entire 1984 season.

Kauffman was stunned. He had worked so hard to build a winning team in a sport that he considered wholesome, all-American, family entertainment. He was confused that this kind of activity could have occurred among his players without his knowledge. He also felt a twinge of betrayal. "The thing that bothered me is that I always wanted to associate with the best people. These are associates of mine—I don't like the word 'employees'—and I was hurt that my associates like Willie Wilson would do these things. It was just a tremendous hurt. It was heartache to me." Schuerholz expressed the sense of profound shock that everyone in management felt. "[Drugs were] an enemy that we'd never confronted before. It wasn't a pennant race we had to win, or a shortstop who got hurt, or a manager making a bad decision. This was something new and scary to all of us, and the entire organization had to regroup and win back the confidence of the public."

Willie Wilson, the only one of the convicted Royals who returned to the team after serving the sentence and the suspension from baseball, tried to explain the pressures that led to drugs.

"Everything I did was spotlighted," he said. "Before I played base-ball, I never smoked or drank or took drugs. People think the game is glamorous, but I never wanted the attention—good or bad. I felt a lot of pressure trying to satisfy the club, the public, my parents. People wanted me to be a role model; even the judge said so when he sentenced me. I always felt your parents should be your role models."

In an extensive interview that winter, Kauffman agreed with the judge that baseball players had a special responsibility to the public with regard to their behavior off the playing field. He admitted that he had struggled in his own mind with the question of how society should treat sports figures accused of wrongdoing. "Should their standing as stars be a part of the calculation of punishment?" he asked himself. Kauffman reasoned that successful baseball players have a unique relationship with their fans—one in which public support becomes a vital source of inspiration in their performances on the playing field. And their performances, in turn, bind the play-ers to the public with a loyalty that causes fans to emulate the play-ers' actions both on and off the field. "The greater the player's rep-utation, the sadder the consequences of his misdeeds," he wrote. He acknowledged that the situation was both sensitive and complex. "A player [is] punished in part for something that is separate from his misdeed, something that involves an ancient loyalty between fan and player and the deep pleasure the public experiences in its em-brace of the player. In such circumstances, it may take a Solomon to render a judgment that honors all the equities. Perhaps there is one that must be acknowledged: The player-hero is held to a higher [standard] of behavior."

As always when confronted with a problem or a new subject that he did not fully comprehend, Kauffman tried to learn as much as he could. He quickly turned his attention to the search for a solu-tion. He was astonished to learn that many youngsters began using addictive drugs in elementary school. Treatment programs for drug users showed such poor success rates that he concluded education and prevention held far greater promise. "If we could stop the usage so they don't need to go through the treatment, we [would be] far, far ahead," he said. He recognized that the more effective avenue for attacking the drug problem would be through the pub-lic school system, not the ball club. Yet he hoped that professional athletes would participate to help stimulate attendance and the participation of young people. In his capacity as CEO of Marion Laboratories and through his private foundation, Kauffman committed substantial resources to research, develop, and implement a drug education and prevention program in the Kansas City public schools which would be called STAR, the acronym for "Students Taught Awareness and Resistance."

In announcing the drug awareness program in the wake of the Royals' scandal, Kauffman was sensitive to the fact that the public might perceive it as nothing more than a public-relations ploy. But it was not. While he had been shaken and bitterly disappointed that Royals players were involved, he was far more profoundly disturbed as he began to learn of the magnitude of the problem from his personal reading and the research he commissioned. It was incomprehensible to him that children in elementary school could be prey to the drug trade. He felt it was imperative that those with the resources to affect this problem do so and do so quickly. "Anyone concerned about the vitality of the community must recognize the pressures and dangers that youth face today," he said.

Kauffman's commitment to drug prevention did not fade when the stories ceased in the press. He had said in the beginning that he was in for the long haul—five years, ten, perhaps for the rest of his life and beyond, if necessary. In 1992, five years after the scandal, he happily announced, "Some good did come out of what happened with the Royals. This last year [1991] we taught over one hundred thousand kids the principles of self-management and social skills to resist cigarettes, alcohol, and drugs. So yes, there was some good from the things our players did, but at the time, it hurt me a great deal."

Kauffman's response to the 1983–84 drug scandals was felt within the team as well as in the community at large. He began to press management even more than in the past to recruit a certain type of player. He wanted men of integrity, responsible citizens who were capable of playing baseball and who recognized the responsibilities a sports hero faced. He was weary of recruiting athletes and hoping for the best. "We've even tried to trade players that are not our type of players," he admitted. The Royals had always focused on developing their own talent, and their internal concern over the drug scandal, as well as the excessive cost of free agents, intensified that policy. In his first year as minority owner, Fogelman began to worry more and more that free agency was robbing the smaller franchises of their key players. He believed that stability within the team was important for players and helped maintain the support of fans. In 1984, he persuaded Kauffman that they should sign George Brett to an eight-year contract having a value in excess of fourteen million dollars, with the Royals holding options through 1993 and various incentives, including a five-million-dollar loan. Brett emerged from the negotiations as the fourth-highest-paid player in baseball, and the best-paid American Leaguer.

The following year, 1985, Fogelman pushed for similar arrangements for relief pitcher Dan Quisenberry, outfielder Willie Wilson, and infielder Frank White. Fogelman's New York advertising agency announced that these players' contracts would be similar to Brett's, and would include association with Fogelman's real estate business. There was speculation in the sports press that the total value of Brett's contract, when combined with those expected to be signed, created as much as a $250 million obligation over forty years. The final totals were not made public, but the other contracts did not approach the lucrative terms Brett received. Fogelman said the reason he could not speak about the worth of the players' financial packages was because of clauses which permitted ties to investments. "The amount of investments will be what the players' druthers are," he said. Quisenberry and Wilson both received extended contracts to 1990 and 1989, respectively. In each case, the Royals held options to renew. This was a coup for Wilson, who had come to spring training just a year before in limbo. He had spent three winter months in prison because of a drug conviction and then served an additional suspension which the baseball commissioner imposed at the start of the 1984 season.

In Frank White's case, the *Kansas City Times'* writer Mike Fish reported, "A lifetime contract it isn't." Acting upon advice from his agent, Steve Fehr, White declined Fogelman's initial package. It featured the opportunity to invest in the Tennessean's real estate holdings but offered only a one-year extension beyond his existing contract, which would expire in 1987. He finally signed for a two-year extension, which was what he had sought at the beginning of negotiations. When Kauffman announced White's contract, he could not conceal his special feelings. "Frank . . . has always been a favorite player of mine because he came through the Royals Baseball Academy."

Kauffman was sincere in his wish to see Fogelman take a strong role in the overall operation of the Royals. He had deferred to the younger man first in the spring of 1984 on the matter of a new contract for George Brett. Joe McGuff reported, "Kauffman thought it would be prudent to wait before offering Brett a new contract. Fogelman, [general manager John] Schuerholz, and Royals president Joe Burke favored immediate action. Kauffman listened to their arguments and conceded the point." Fogelman had argued that lifetime contracts were a logical extension of the Royals' established corporate strategy of committing themselves to long-term contracts after free agency came to baseball. They were an extension and refinement of Kauffman's original strategy. He predicted they would bring stability to the organization by helping stabilize the payroll and would enable the Royals, as a team in a small market, to retain their stars.

Fogelman defended the expenditures, saying there was "no other alternative but to sign them to a guaranteed long-term contract." Although Kauffman had always believed in building from within, he remained lukewarm about Fogelman's approach, which seemed to involve stakes as high as the free agency market. But his partner was young and eager to make his mark with the team. And, of course, he had the resources to sustain such commitments. "[Kauffman's] position was never clearly enunciated," Fogelman recalled. "He left it up to me since he never felt the responsibility was going to be his, since our agreement stated that he possibly might not be an owner when the guaranteed payments were due to be paid . . . he left it up to me. Parenthetically, I wish he hadn't." By 1989, Kauffman and those closest to him would share that sentiment.

The 1984 Royals managed to put the drug scandals behind them and slugged their way to a fifth Western Division championship in nine years. This was the first time they had had to battle a team other than the New York Yankees in the playoffs, and they lost to the Detroit Tigers. In spite of the pennant loss, the outstanding pitching from three young players—Bret Saberhagen, Mark Gubicza, and Charlie Leibrandt—justifiably excited the fans, who were predicting a World Series victory in 1985 before the 1984 season had closed.

Winning the World Series in 1985 was not as easy as many had thought it would be at the start of the season. As late as mid-July, the team was in a tie for third place in the American League West, finally beating the California Angels. Then came the playoffs against the Toronto Blue Jays. This was the first time that two expansion clubs had contested the American League championship, and it was a grueling best-of-seven format. The Royals lost the first three games, then rallied to win the right to play the St. Louis Cardinals in the World Series. The pennant was undecided until the sixth inning of the seventh game, when Jim Sundberg's three-run triple pushed the score to 6–2 in the Royals' favor.

The Royals' 1985 season was their most mercurial to date. No team in the history of baseball up to that point had ever lost the first two games of a World Series at home and then rebounded to win. Bret Saberhagen pitched a five-hitter, and the Royals defeated the St. Louis Cardinals 11–0 in the seventh game of what the sports-writers dubbed as the "Show Me Series." Six times during post-season play the Royals faced elimination, yet each time they emerged victorious. Quisenberry, the Royals' relief pitcher who seemed more skillful at turning a phrase than Yogi Berra, summed up the season. "The sword of Damocles kept swinging down and giving us haircuts, but we kept ducking."

Kansas City baseball fans celebrated the victory with a gusto that revealed that the sweetest part of the triumph may have been in toppling their "snooty and sophisticated" sister city. There was a huge parade with fireworks, balloons, shredded paper and George Brett making a "mournful noise" on a baritone saxophone which he had borrowed momentarily from a student in the Turner High School band. Several days after the victory, the Kauffmans, Fogel-man, and the team assembled in the White House Rose Garden to receive congratulations from a former sports broadcaster, Ronald Reagan. A local Washington, D.C., disk jockey, hoping to deflate the celebrants, commented that when "Washington's 'in people' talked about the arrival of the Royals, they meant Prince Charles and Princess Diana." That may have been true inside the beltway, but the rest of American knew who the true Royals were.

It was natural that the year after winning the World Series would be a letdown for Kauffman and the Royals. In the middle of the season in which the Royals would finish in a tie for third place in the Western Division, Kauffman gave an interview in which he reflected on his involvement in the sport. The game was not as much fun as it had once been, the sixty-nine-year-old admitted. But it gave him an outlet for his nervous energy and kept him from being "the richest man in the cemetery," he joked. Two strikes during his tenure had altered his relations with the team. He blamed the owners for the distrust that had soured relations. "There wouldn't have been a union if [the owners] would have treated the players right. Their [former] leader, Marvin Miller, was so capable and the owners were so dumb. They were the older owners. They lived through the era when they had 100 percent control over the lives of the players and they weren't going to give that up, and eventually they were forced to." What Kauffman found so astonishing was that the very owners he criticized had been highly successful businessmen. But they were not good businessmen when it came to baseball. Of course, he defined a good businessman as one who treated people fairly and shared the rewards. Others may have chosen a different yardstick.

When asked to comment on the Royals' slump in 1986, Kauffman acknowledged that winning sometimes blunted the appetite for competition. "I'm sure that winning the World Series had an effect on our players, that they weren't as hungry. They had achieved the ultimate, climbed the mountain top and surveyed the world at their feet. . . . I'm sure the endorsements they've been making, the commercials they've cut, the dinners they've attended, and that type of thing, had an effect on them, and maybe it's a good thing they're getting knocked down. Maybe they'll learn something," he mused philosophically.

When asked if there was anything he wished he had done differently as an owner, Kauffman said yes. It was not the millions he had spent on the stadium that he would never recoup, or the losses he had to withstand before he sold a minority interest to Fogelman. He regretted the money he had been too timid to spend. "The one regret I have is that I closed the Baseball Academy. If I had kept it going, the Royals would have dominated baseball for the past ten years." This regret was all the more poignant because earlier that year the Academy's land and facilities in Sarasota, Florida, had been sold. In 1979, Kauffman had given the Kansas City YMCA title to the property which they later sold for $2,500,000. The proceeds went into an endowment to fund innovative new programs. An editorial in the *Kansas City Star* lauded "the generosity of Mr. Kauffman . . . as a mark of how good civic leaders invest in their community." While Kauffman appreciated the recognition and the kind words from his fellow Kansas Citians, he remained nostalgic for the Baseball Academy. He believed there had been enough results in four years to justify having pressed on. And in fact, the money had been there. All he had really lacked, he commented with a sigh, was the nerve.

Although the Royals did not play pennant-winning baseball the year following their World Series victory, they did grab sports headlines with Kauffman's rather startling decision to sign Bo Jackson, the Auburn University Heisman Trophy winner. Just when everyone thought Jackson would be signing with the Tampa Bay Buccaneers to play professional football, he announced he was taking less money to play the game he preferred. He declined Tampa's seven-million-dollar, five-year offer to accept what the Royals called a "comparable" contract for a first-round baseball choice even though Jackson was selected in round four. A "comparable" contract meant that Jackson was guaranteed one year, with the Royals holding a two-year option. He would earn $100,000, and he received a $100,000 signing bonus. When asked how he could turn down the chance to be an instant millionaire, he shrugged, saying he liked to take chances. "The key was, Bo wants to play baseball," Jackson said, referring to himself in the third person. "I've won my trophy in football."

The original strategy was for Bo Jackson to start the 1987 season playing with the Royals' Class AAA affiliate in Omaha, Nebraska. He was very talented, but he lacked experience in the field. During spring training John Schuerholz had advised Kauffman, "Bo should go to Omaha and get 150 at-bats and then we'll bring him [to Kansas City]." Kauffman agreed. But a day later, he reversed the decision, saying, "Mr. Fogelman asked me if I'd reconsider. He said, psychologically, it would hurt Bo." After thinking about the conversation, Kauffman called the general manager and asked his advice. Schuerholz, too, had changed his mind. But Kauffman was still cautious. "Let's give Bo the decision," he told Schuerholz. Jackson, to no one's surprise, chose the possibility of instant celebrity status in Kansas City over six more weeks with a farm club. He went directly from Memphis, where he was training with Fogelman's minor league team, the Chicks, to Kansas City and major league competition. A reporter for the *Kansas City Times* concluded that the whole affair was "like asking a six-year-old whether he'd like to spend the afternoon in the candy store or the library."

On the first day at Royals' batting practice shortly after being drafted, Jackson had hit a ball that landed near the bottom of the Royals Stadium's huge, crown-shaped scoreboard beyond the four-hundred-and-ten-foot mark in center field. Dick Howser, the Royals' manager, seemed stunned. "Potentially, I've never seen anybody with the batting strength this kid has," he said, his enthusiasm spilling over. "For sheer power, he's like Mickey Mantle, Harmon Killebrew, and Frank Howard were." When Jackson came to Kansas City, he proved to be a power hitter. By the middle of the season he was leading the Royals in home runs with eighteen to his credit. Then to the chagrin of his teammates, he announced he had agreed to a contract with the Los Angeles Raiders that would enable him to fulfill his dream of playing both professional football and baseball. Fogelman, speaking for the Royals, said that Jackson's contract would be restructured to protect the team should he be injured in football.

Jackson combined a knack for appearing in the headlines with an unerring ability to offend almost everyone. His announcement that he wanted to play professional football alienated many of his Royals teammates, who questioned his dedication to baseball. Then when he attempted to recover with the comment that he would treat professional football as a "hobby . . . like hunting and fishing," he alienated future teammates with the Los Angeles Raiders. To make matters worse, men who had played their hearts out for the Royals felt devalued as both management and the owners scrambled to keep Jackson happy. Everyone knew that whatever his antics or however erratic his performance might be, he was the Royals' biggest attraction. In a market that depended heavily on gate receipts, Bo Jackson had the drawing power of a rock star.

As the furor over the Jackson contract mounted, Kauffman, who had kept a low profile up to this point, stepped forward to accept responsibility for the decision. "Just remember," he said, "I am the majority owner . . . I make the final decision." Kauffman denied that the club was showing favoritism to Jackson. He said that some players had reacted vehemently because the decision had not been explained to them. He accepted full responsibility for that mistake and then explained how the problem had developed. Schuerholz, the general manager, had been on his way to Oakland and Kauffman was preparing to leave for speeches in Joplin and Columbia when the Jackson issue surfaced. Knowing that Fogelman had a private plane and a more flexible schedule, Kauffman asked him to fly to Toronto and work something out with Bo. He acknowledged that he had misjudged the situation. "We shouldn't have sent an owner because it made it look bigger in the eyes of the players. We should have sent Schuerholz." The second mistake had been in failing to explain to the players that the owners were not playing favorites. He announced that any Royals player could have his contract changed so he could play any other sport from "road racing to sky diving," but they would have to accept the same qualifications that Jackson had—namely, that if they were injured and could not play baseball, they would not get paid. "That's our deal with Bo." When asked for his assessment of what Jackson would face with the Raiders, Kauffman quipped, "I think he's going to get the devil knocked out of him!"

Bo Jackson was an unending source of irritation and a spectacular draw from 1986 until his departure in 1991. George Brett, a shoo-in for the Hall of Fame, shared the same dugout but good-naturedly retreated into relative obscurity when Jackson was in the game. "I actually kind of liked it," Brett admitted. "In one way, there was a lot less pressure on everybody else when Bo was around." Brett also acknowledged that he was as fascinated as anyone else when Jackson stepped up to bat. "You never knew when you might see something that would be remembered for a hundred years."

Early in January 1991, Jackson injured a hip playing football for the Raiders. In March, Dr. Steve Joyce, the Royals' team physician, said that Jackson might play baseball again, but it would be nine to twelve months before he could be certain. Two days after receiving the doctor's report, Herk Robinson, the Royals' general manager, telephoned Kauffman at his home to say that he and Royals' president Joe Burke recommended releasing the superstar. Kauffman concurred. Jackson retaliated. He created a firestorm in the media, claiming he had been treated unfairly. He alleged that Kauffman had used the injury as an "excuse" to get rid of him because of a long-held vendetta. Kauffman was calm and deliberate as he explained how the decision had been made. "The doctors gave their findings to our baseball people, Mr. Burke and Mr. Robinson. They, in turn, made their recommendations to me, and I simply agreed they should go ahead." When asked about his personal feelings on learning that Jackson was so badly injured, Kauffman permitted the public a glimpse of his paternal feelings toward the ball players. "In some ways, I feel we failed to do what we could have done with Bo, as far as insisting he just play baseball. He would have been so much better off if he hadn't played football. Not that I blame him. His family needed his help, and he got a big signing bonus for football. If I'd been in Bo's position, I'd have done exactly the same thing, personally."

But, Kauffman said, he wished the Royals had tried harder to push Jackson toward baseball. However, once Jackson and his agent discovered the endorsement value of playing two sports, it was too late. Playing football, Kauffman maintained, had been unwise. "It destroyed, potentially, the best talent ever to put on a baseball uniform. Being young, you always think you can't get hurt. But as we've seen, you can. It's a sad thing for him and for us." The lure of big money and the intoxicating roar of the crowd obscured a gifted athlete's ability to see ahead to the time when he would no longer be perfectly healthy, agile, and young. Kauffman had witnessed this scenario time and again, and it troubled him deeply.

Exit Fogelman   14

In January 1988, Avron Fogelman exercised the option in his contract with Kauffman and purchased an additional one percent of
the Royals for $220,000. In exchange, Kauffman acquired the right
to remain a partner until the year 2012, at which time he would be
ninety-five years old. They now shared equal ownership. If either
partner were to die before year 2021, provisions called for the remaining partner to buy the balance of the team. Fogelman was
elated with the new arrangement. "Mr. K's contributions to the
club and his knowledge just cannot be replaced. It would be less
than prudent for a man with his expertise not to own the Royals."
Within a year, those words would prove prophetic.

Just as the two men now shared ownership equally, they shared
frustration and disappointment with the Royals' performance. The
year had started on such a high note, but by July, things were looking grim. At midseason, Fogelman commented, "In my five years,
this has been the most difficult period for me because I know we
have a great team on paper. But I'm not going to criticize anyone,
and there's no one to blame. . . . It'd be easy to second-guess a few
decisions, but ball players are like a stock. Sometimes you're going
to miss, and sometimes you hit. Things just haven't worked out like
we thought so far." Kauffman, too, appeared restless and somewhat
irritable as he always did when the team was not winning. "It's
hard to be optimistic at this point," he confessed. Less tolerant of
poor performance than his younger partner, he lashed out. "You've
got to place the blame on everybody. The pitching . . . certainly
hasn't come through. That's our greatest weakness."

Even though he now had a full partner with whom to share the
costs, Kauffman continued to fret aloud about finances. When the

team played poorly, gate receipts suffered; in turn, sales of concessions dropped off. The Royals' share of the national radio and television revenue was only about five or six million dollars, and local broadcast revenues still were not shared as they were in some other sports. Where the Royals might earn approximately three million dollars annually in local television and radio receipts, cities like New York, Los Angeles, and Chicago were earning from forty to sixty million a year. Yet Kauffman and Fogelman had to pay the same high salaries in the Midwest as did Autry and Steinbrenner in Los Angeles and New York.

Kauffman had not purchased the Royals to make money. He was sincere when he said, "It was something I could do for Kansas City to give back some of the good I've received here." He never considered the baseball franchise as a part of his financial portfolio. It was a part of his civic philanthropy akin to his support of CPR training, only on a much larger scale. For that reason, he was always somewhat irritated when someone tried to determine the value of the Royals as an investment in light of other financial opportunities. Early in 1987, a professor in the accounting department at Rockhurst College had calculated that Kauffman's initial franchise investment of six million dollars in 1968 would be worth more than $111 million if it had been invested in Marion Laboratories stock. In 1983, Kauffman had sold Fogelman 49 percent of the team for $11 million with an option to purchase the remaining stock by 1991 for a total of $22 million. While the team was undoubtedly worth more than $22 million in 1987, its value was nowhere near $100 million. To make the scenario even more depressing, the professor had calculated that the same amount of money, invested in tax-free, low-risk government securities, would have earned $26 million over the last eighteen years. "I don't know how many wealthy people would accept the kind of losses that Kauffman and Fogelman do," he concluded. Within a year, rumors began to circulate that perhaps Fogelman might no longer be able to finance his part of the operation.

The Royals finished the 1988 season in third place, but Kansas Citians were forgiving. That fall, the Jackson County legislature unanimously passed a resolution renaming the ballpark Kauffman Stadium in honor of Ewing and Muriel Kauffman. Kansas City Mayor Richard L. Berkley heralded the name change as long overdue. "I think the Kauffmans have done so much for the community. It's most appropriate that it be done." But Kauffman, who usually basked in the crowd's applause and affection, demurred. Through Dean Vogelaar, the Royals' spokesman, he said he wanted to review the idea next year. Until then, the team would continue to use the name Royals Stadium. Kauffman was deeply honored and touched and expressed his appreciation to the county legislature. "However, I believe if the name . . . is to be changed, it should represent the feelings of the vast majority of the citizens of our community."

In March 1989, Kauffman revealed that he was growing more concerned about the team's finances. Salaries in major league baseball were continuing to escalate as some players received lucrative settlements through arbitration and others bargained their price up through free agency. "It's ridiculous!" he exclaimed. "You'd think it has to stop somewhere. But maybe it doesn't." As players' salaries rose everywhere, the Royals had to find ways to keep pace yet remain financially viable. Kauffman acknowledged that he had given Fogelman the go-ahead to negotiate the long-term, high-dollar contracts with Brett, Wilson, and Quisenberry. "[Those] were Mr. Fogelman's idea. I thought it was one way he could learn. I did get in at the last and put a lid on it," he said.

To generate additional revenue, he revealed that the Royals would probably have to raise ticket prices and parking prices in the coming year. When asked about the possibility of adding more seats to the stadium, Kauffman said, "I don't think it will really make that much difference. Those would be general admission seats at low prices." Kauffman reluctantly admitted that without a sharing of local broadcast revenues and some help from the city, county, and state, the Royals could be in a bad way financially in a few years. While baseball had an economic impact of about $120 million on the Kansas City area economy, owning a team would probably never be a profitable venture. "The truth is that Kansas City is really too small to have a baseball team," he said. "But we're going to stay here one way or another. I would never [move the team]," Kauffman vowed again as he had so often before. "And Mr. Fogelman won't, either."

Nineteen eighty-nine was a difficult year for Kauffman. Senior executives at Marion Laboratories, with his concurrence, were seeking a merger partner and were traveling constantly or locked away

in confidential meetings. Although his heart was not in it, Kauffman had agreed to the merger efforts because he believed such a
move was in the best interests of Marion Laboratories' shareholders. Nevertheless, the atmosphere produced tensions that could not
be voiced, and this was emotionally draining. His health was none
too good either. Because of bad knees and painful arthritis, he had
given up golf several years earlier. He missed those long afternoons
on the course at Indian Hills in the company of old friends. Playing
cards with his cronies at the Kansas City Club or an afternoon swim
and watching the Royals play were the few diversions he enjoyed.
At home he loved to match wits with the studio contestants on
"Jeopardy" and "Wheel of Fortune," play a match or two of computer chess, and read. He slowed his pace physically, but never
mentally. Even in the last months of his life, he would engage in
mental gymnastics with his driver by multiplying numbers on car
license plates while driving to the office or the club. In the late
1980s, he had begun to experience intermittent, brief ischemic attacks which resulted in temporary facial paralysis or numbness in
his feet. But he was never incapacitated for more than for a day or
two. And he adamantly refused to have the surgery which might
have lessened or alleviated the blockage. But it was inevitable that
he would begin to show his seventy-four years, and he was sometimes a bit querulous as if he sensed some impending disaster.

In June, the first tangible signs of trouble appeared. The *Kansas
City Times'* business writers reported that Fogelman was considering
selling or reorganizing the investment finance division of his enterprises. This was the arm of the Memphis-based Fogelman Properties which sold real estate limited partnerships. Most of the partnerships were private arrangements similar to the Hilton Head
Golf Limited Partnership, which was an effort to raise $37 million
through the sale of shares in golf course and tennis club properties
at Hilton Head Island Resort in South Carolina. Of Fogelman's public partnerships, one, known as Prudential Bache/Fogelman Strategic Mortgage Series, was struggling to raise $200 million to buy first
and second mortgages on office buildings, apartment complexes,
hotels, and shopping centers. There were rumors of trouble as the
partnership stalled after raising only $12 million. Most of Fogel-
man's twenty-three partnerships were tax oriented, providing
write-offs for wealthy investors. In a statement issued through Vo-

gelaar, Kauffman responded to questions about Fogelman's plans. "There is really nothing I can add to the story," he replied. "To my knowledge, Mr. Fogelman is in excellent financial shape."

Neither Kauffman nor Fogelman could recall precisely when they first discussed Fogelman's troubled financial affairs. "I don't recall how it was communicated," Fogelman said, "except that he and I had a couple of conversations and he inquired of the nature of the debacle. He seemed interested and was kind of low-keyed about it whenever we discussed it." Kauffman deliberately downplayed speculation about how Fogelman's chaotic finances might affect the Royals, and the local press stressed in virtually every article on the subject that Kauffman had ample resources to protect the team from any fallout that might occur. Fogelman's Memphis business associate Scott Ledbetter, president of a local real estate brokerage and management firm, dismissed the speculation that his friend might be experiencing financial difficulties. "Avron's the kind of guy who, when things aren't living up to his expectations, isn't afraid to make a change. He's a trader. If someone's making an offer, he'll consider selling."

Those observers who believed that Fogelman's interest in selling the financing division of his real estate empire was a signal of serious trouble found additional evidence in the report in the *Commercial Appeal* of Memphis that he was also selling five of the older, local apartment complexes in his portfolio. By early July, Fogelman's financial picture seemed to worsen daily. As the beleaguered developer attempted to relieve the stress on his empire, former employees, accountants, and bank analysts leaked information from which the press pieced together a fairly detailed picture of his situation. Although he was thought to have a personal net worth of more than $120 million, most of it was in illiquid real estate holdings. He had $60 million in unsecured loans that lenders were watching with growing concern. And some observers thought he may have had as much as $290 million in contingent liabilities and guarantees used to sweeten various investment partnerships. The *Kansas City Star* reported, "Bank analysts say news about Fogelman's finances is more likely to get worse than better." In his own hometown, where he had a high profile as an investor in local sports franchises and as a generous contributor to Memphis State University, there seemed to be interest in his plight, but little sympathy. The visibility associated with his local philanthropy and the public fascination with him as a major league baseball owner had caused some resentment—and perhaps jealousy—among other Memphis civic stalwarts who thought their contributions deserved greater recognition. "He never played team ball with the mainstream of the business community," said Barney DuBois, editor of the *Memphis Business Journal*.

As Marion Laboratories moved into the final stages of negotiations with Dow Chemical and the press continued to report on new complications in Fogelman's troubled finances, Kauffman began to show the strain of both situations. He was on the brink of relinquishing the controlling interest in the pharmaceutical house he had founded almost forty years earlier. For a man who still reveled in work of the company he had founded and who loved the personal contact with his associates, assuming an emeritus role in a merged company would inevitably be different. This scenario was not a happy prospect. He was already enormously wealthy. *Forbes* magazine had estimated his worth at $740 million in 1988. When the proposed merger which called for the sale of 30 percent of his stock was completed, he would have an estimated additional $500 million in cash. The prospect that he might have to shoulder the total financial burden of the Royals was not as disconcerting as was the possibility that the team might somehow become a pawn in Fogelman's widely rumored impending financial collapse.

On July 16 when Kauffman and his wife entered their lawyers' offices to sign documents related to the merger, he looked very tired, very old, and as if he was unwell. In fact, he had suffered an attack of kidney stones in the night and was in excruciating pain. That same day, he had learned that the bank group that held Fogelman's unsecured debt was pressing the developer to pledge his half interest in the Royals as collateral for the sixty million in loans. Based on recent sales of other major league teams, Fogelman's 50 percent stake could be valued from thirty to fifty million dollars. There was even talk that some of the bankers had suggested they would finance his acquisition of Kauffman's interest, if he would then agree to pledge the entire team as collateral.

For a time, it appeared that the Royals might become a pawn in the negotiations to resolve Fogelman's troubled affairs. But in reality that was probably never a viable, and certainly never a wise, strategy. R. Pete Smith, a bankruptcy lawyer and partner in the Mc-Dowell Rice and Smith law firm in Kansas City, noted that using the ball team as collateral "would be feasible. But you have to watch for creditors who do not get anything." Fogelman could pledge his stake in the Royals as collateral for unsecured creditors as an entire group. But if he devoted his stake to just a few major banks, that could spark a petition for involuntary bankruptcy from other creditors. Since Fogelman could pledge only his 50 percent stake in the team and not Kauffman's, and because Kauffman could refuse to sell his 50 percent until well into the twenty-first century, new rumors erupted. Was Kauffman positioning himself to bail out Fogelman? Was the timing of the sale of Marion Labs just coincidental with news of Fogelman's troubles? Although these questions may seem rather farfetched in retrospect, there were enough bits of information to provide the seedbed from which these rumors sprouted. The Kauffman-Fogelman partnership had been very cordial; some said it was like a father-son relationship. Fogelman had been the diligent pupil, Kauffman the seasoned mentor. It was well known that Kauffman was dedicated to keeping the Royals in Kansas City, so it was logical that he might choose to use his enormous wealth to protect and insure the team's future. When Dale Rohr, the Royals' vice president of finance, told the press that the "Marion Labs sale will not affect the Royals at all," he was forced to concede that Kauffman "will have more cash available to spend on the Royals if he chooses to do so."

In order to quiet all the rumors, Kauffman agreed to an interview with Charles R.T. Crumpley, a senior business reporter for the *Kansas City Times*, just two days after the merger was announced. He said he welcomed the opportunity to clarify what his future role with the Royals would be given the changes taking place at Marion Laboratories. "It won't change much," he remarked. "Rather than giving it a few hours a month, I will be giving it days." When asked if he knew whether Fogelman had any plans to sell the Royals, he shot back, "No, sir." Then he explained that Fogelman could not sell without giving him the right of first refusal and that he had promised to give Kauffman plenty of notice should the need to sell arise.

When the questions turned to Fogelman's financial difficulties, Kauffman brushed them aside. "The speculation on his financial status is all speculation as far as I'm concerned. He has not indicated to me that he's in bad shape. He's just retrenching and consolidating as far as I'm concerned." Then Kauffman changed the subject to his plans for improving the Royals. He spoke of the need to make better decisions in drafting players and of training the team's scouts to analyze personal characteristics of individuals as well as physical talents. He acknowledged that at times he may have been too conservative in his spending for talent and hinted that the Royals might move aggressively into the free agent market. This was the confident, enthusiastic, optimistic Kauffman of old.

In spite of Kauffman's efforts to quash rumors about the Royals changing hands, the speculation continued. In early August, the two partners met at Royals Stadium for discussions with baseball executives. Later, they conferred privately about Fogelman's situation. Kauffman was smiling when he left the meeting. He told the waiting press that he was "98 percent positive" that Fogelman would work through his financial problems. "He's been honest, a good partner," Kauffman said with genuine warmth in his voice. But when asked whether he would try to block any effort by Fogelman in the near future to buy the rest of the Royals, Kauffman replied thoughtfully, "I don't know where I would stand, legally, on that." Then he acknowledged that he had not proposed to buy out Fogelman.

If Fogelman had tried to raise cash by forcing Kauffman to sell his half interest, the most likely strategy would then have been to find investors willing to pay between sixty and seventy million dollars, the team's estimated worth. The only investors likely to do so would probably want to move the Royals to a larger, more lucrative market. A group in Tampa, Florida, had recently tried to buy and move the Chicago White Sox, but were thwarted when the American League owners refused their request to relocate the team. Even if Fogelman were to acquire Kauffman's half interest and could find new investors, what he might realize from the sale would still not be sufficient to settle all his debts. Furthermore, it was doubtful that the American League would favor moving the franchise. "You are talking about [moving] a team that is drawing two million fans a year!" said Donald M. Fehr, executive director and general counsel of the Major League Baseball Players Association. The American League president, Dr. Robert W. Brown, attempted to close off any further talk about the team being moved with a statement which he released at Royals Stadium just before the Royals-Boston game on August 9. "It is inconceivable that the American League or major league baseball would even consider [the Royals'] franchise being moved. The Royals remain well run, well financed, and well regarded. They will remain in Kansas City." And there were many who believed that, beyond the official difficulties of moving a franchise, the Kansas City community would not allow it. Clark G. Redick, chairman of the Chamber of Commerce of Greater Kansas City, predicted, "If the need is for additional money, it will be done by donations from the business community. The Royals' franchise is part of the heart and soul of this community."

In response to all the speculation, Fogelman hastily issued a statement designed to allay fears that his financial problems might, in a worst-case scenario, cost Kansas City its major league baseball team. He said that the restructuring of Fogelman Properties would have no adverse effects on the financial or policy decisions of the Royals. "I want to emphasize that the Royals will not be moved from Kansas City and it is my desire to continue my partnership with Mr. K into the next century." Kauffman chose to remain silent.

All through the fall, Fogelman's financial picture dimmed. But the ball team's fortunes brightened. The Royals played better than they had since the 1985 World Series, finishing second in the division. Attendance at home games remained well above the two million mark, which meant that revenues were good as well. By mid-December, Kauffman appeared to have made up his mind about any future course of action involving the Royals. But he continued to decline politely to respond to any questions about whether he would regain full control over the franchise. His actions, however, spoke for him. Just prior to baseball's winter meetings, Royals' general manager John Schuerholz told reporters, "Mr. Kauffman reminded me the other day: 'In case anybody's wondering whether we have the money or aggressiveness to sign free agents, we do and we will.'" Before Christmas, the Royals signed long-term contracts totaling nineteen million dollars with free agent pitchers Mark Davis and Storm Davis. "Fogelman apparently was not a factor in the signings," reported the *Kansas City Times.*

Kauffman, weary of the rumors and speculation and conscious of how painful all this clamor must be for his young partner, let it be known that he wished to avoid any public statements regarding the

Royals' ownership until Fogelman's financial difficulties were resolved. But he was more than willing to talk about his new point of
view on free agents and to use the press as a way to win concessions
from the county in the negotiations over a new lease for Royals Stadium. Kauffman said his negative attitude toward free agency had
been "because I value loyalty very highly." He was proud that the
Royals had never lost a player to free agency, with the possible exception of Darrell Porter. And he boasted that Mark Davis, who
could have signed for more money with another team, "chose us for
reasons other than money."

Kauffman had always been a demanding taskmaster both in the
pharmaceutical business and in baseball. He would negotiate, but
only to a point. He had always believed that being associated with
his people and his organization gave a person significant intangible
benefits that outweighed mere dollars. And he could recount many
examples from Marion Laboratories in which new associates had
settled for less money initially in exchange for potential growth
through stock options, profit sharing, and other benefits. Although
signing with the Royals was not analogous to going on the Marion
payroll, Kauffman was generous in offering benefits such as loans,
educational training, and financial counseling and planning. He
had offered Marion stock to George Brett instead of a cash signing
bonus when he joined the Royals, but Brett admitted years later
that he was too green and too young to understand the value.
Kansas City was also an attractive asset. It was a good place to raise
a young family where baseball fans were supportive and loyal in
good years and bad. And just as there was a "Marion Spirit," the
Royals was a congenial organization where the superstars were an
integral part of the team.

What had turned Kauffman against free agency was the relentless bidding war in which players and their agents goaded owners
into higher and higher salary contracts. A particular episode typified the whole experience for Kauffman. In the early days of free
agency, the Royals made Tommy John of the New York Yankees a
good offer. The following Saturday night, his agent called Kauffman at home to tell him they were about to make a decision. But
they had received a larger offer in the interim and wanted to know
if Kauffman would top it. Kauffman recalled that he had trouble
hearing the agent because there was a great deal of background

noise. When Kauffman asked about the noise, John told him he was with George Steinbrenner at Club 21 in New York City. He knew instantly that the ball player was engaged in a ploy to escalate his salary. "No, we're not interested," Kauffman said, replacing the receiver. He then instructed the Royals' general manager, "From now on, make them an offer, take it or leave it." Kauffman held to that position until the end of the 1980s. But the ball club's strained finances finally caused him to change his mind. In the early years of the Royals, "I couldn't stand to lose the amount of money we'll lose next year," he admitted in an interview in January 1990. But since the sale of Marion Laboratories the previous year, his personal financial situation had changed materially. "Before [the sale of Marion], people said I was a multi-multi-multi-millionaire, but it was paper, stock certificates. Now it's hard cash. Some of my money is still paper, but 33 percent of my total value is now cash. Before, it was 5 percent."

Kauffman anticipated that the Royals would sustain a three-million-dollar cash loss in their operating income in 1990. That amount, coupled with interest of about one million dollars ball players owed on loans, plus two million in depreciation, added to another two million required to pay Storm Davis's contract, made the projected total loss for 1990 about eight million dollars. The Royals were projecting that two million, two hundred thousand fans would pass through the turnstile, with gate receipts providing about one-fourth of the team's total expenses. If by adding a couple of powerhouse players they would push the attendance up to at least two and a half million, Kauffman reckoned the Royals could reduce their cash loss by $1,800,000. "In order for us to be competitive, it was necessary to [get into the free agent market]. With Oakland as powerful as they were, California getting better, and Minnesota and Texas, I couldn't see making up the ground in any way, shape, or form aside from free agents." Kauffman had reached that decision by weighing one type of loss against another. He was resigned to losing money in baseball, but he was not blind to any strategy that might help reduce the drain somewhat. What he was unwilling to accept was a losing team. "If the Royals cannot have a chance to win more than their fair share, then I don't want to be in baseball." Then with the assurance of a man who knew he could last a long time even with that amount of negative cash flow, he said, "It's more fun to lose when [you're a winner] than to lose when you're a loser!"

When Kauffman overcame his resistance to the free agent market and began talking more openly and in greater detail about the Royals' finances, rumors about the team's ownership naturally emerged again. Unidentified individuals close to the situation told the sports press in late January 1990 that he and Fogelman were close to an agreement in which he could eventually regain 100 percent ownership of the Royals. The purported agreement was that Kauffman would lend Fogelman as much as $34 million in return for all his stock as collateral and the immediate surrender of his option to buy the other half of the team. In buying back the option, Kauffman's ownership position would be greatly strengthened. And, if Fogelman were unable to repay the loan, Kauffman could repossess the stock, regaining 100 percent of the Royals.

The scenario seemed plausible. On January 19, 1990, the Royals signed a new twenty-five-year stadium lease with the Jackson County Sports Complex Authority. Kauffman had used the concerns about Fogelman's financial problems and the resulting sense of uncertainty to negotiate a favorable lease. Any sale to an outside investor looked more unlikely now, as the new lease would make it unreasonably expensive to move the baseball team. With a loan rather than a sale, Fogelman could avoid income taxes and use the total amount to pay down the debt to banks and other creditors. If he were to forgo bankruptcy and retain some assets, the creditors would have the possibility of getting more money eventually. Although the sources said all parties had agreed in principle to the loan and related matters, they cautioned that the agreement was very complex and it could come unraveled. However, the rumor was, especially among the financial institutions involved, that a final agreement could be consummated by March 1.

Halfway into February, the talks between Kauffman and Fogelman turned chilly. "I felt as if there was acrimony in the air," Fogelman recalled later, saying he regretted "that anything was done that infringed upon a remarkable partnership." Negotiations appeared to have stalled as rumors appeared in the press regarding Fogelman's role in the future of the Royals. There was speculation that he might want to continue attending baseball owners' meetings and be active as well as highly visible. Yet that was the last thing Fogelman desired. "At that time, I did not want a prominent or high-profile role in any public endeavor!" he recalled. When Kauffman heard the rumors, he indicated he was strongly opposed to such a scenario. He might agree to the loan, but he did not intend to agree to continue the relationship as if nothing had changed. As he told reporters just after the new year, "I'm not going to be a goose that's plucked."

The March deadline passed without an agreement, but a threatened players' strike, or alternatively, an owners' lockout loomed during spring training as major league owners tangled with the Players Association. Kauffman was uncharacteristically irascible. When the players refused to reach a compromise with the owners, Kauffman growled, "In my viewpoint, we owners have given and given and given. If I was running things and they didn't settle the thing very quickly, it would be my nature to withdraw everything that's been offered and close the season down." Royals' president Joe Burke was as surprised as everyone else at Kauffman's outburst. "I can't recall when I saw him like this. He was speaking more as a fan than an owner. He loves this game and he wants to get on with it." The strain and tension of the Fogelman debacle were clearly beginning to show.

By the first of April, all observers agreed that Fogelman was out of the picture. When a reporter asked Kauffman what role his partner had played during the spring training lockout, he answered tersely, "None." And Fogelman's office had announced that he would not attend opening day of the baseball season, commenting that Passover began that evening. Then there was the matter of the disappearing portrait. The *Topeka Capital-Journal* had reported that "Avron Fogelman is officially out as co-owner of the Kansas City Royals." The article quoted an unidentified Royals' official as saying Fogelman's portrait "would have never come down if he were still involved with the club." Both co-owners denied the report, and Vogelaar said the picture was taken down temporarily, dusted off, and would be back on the wall. The atmosphere was so tense that every action and occurrence, no matter how minor or ordinary, seemed symbolic and laden with hidden meanings.

In early May, Fogelman added a new wrinkle to the negotiations. In return for the earlier proposed loan of $34 million, Kauffman would receive Fogelman's stock in the team together with Fogelman's option to buy the remainder of the team. The loan funds would be used to partially satisfy Fogelman's creditors. In addition to the loan, he proposed that the Royals be offered for sale to the highest bidder acceptable to major league baseball to satisfy creditors that Fogelman was getting the fair market value for his share of the team. Kauffman would have the final bid. An investment banker would be hired to market the team with bids accepted until October 15. Kauffman would have the right of a final look at the bids and he could retain the team by matching the highest bid. The auction strategy would produce three possible scenarios. If no bids were forthcoming, Kauffman could cancel the loan, keep the stock, and regain total control of the Royals. If a reasonably low bid was received, he could match the bid. If a very high bid was submitted, and Kauffman was unable or unwilling to match it, the Royals would have a new owner. However, a new owner would have to honor the twenty-five-year stadium lease as well as the long-term contracts with the players.

Kauffman's response to questions about the proposal was measured but not without compassion. He acknowledged that his personal relationship with Fogelman was drastically changed. He said they had not talked in months. When asked if he really cared if his co-owner ended up as he had started, managing apartments, Kauffman revealed he had personally offered financial help when he first learned of Fogelman's business reverses. Acknowledging that he felt sorry for Fogelman and knew that he was deeply embarrassed, Kauffman continued, "I don't blame him. . . . What he's doing is logical because he's drowning. He's trying to stay alive. So this is the only thing he can do and [the baseball team] is the only asset he has that has some dollars in it."

Mike Herman, who advised Kauffman on finances relating to the Royals as well as his personal and other business investments, cautioned everyone, saying, "This thing is not all wrapped up." But public attention had already leaped ahead of the facts to gossip about who in Kansas City might bid for the Royals. Philip Pistilli, president of the Raphael Hotel Group, remarked there were a lot of people with the money but nobody with the inclination to buy. Because of the baseball league rule that required teams to maintain assets worth a certain amount more than their liabilities, any serious bidder would have to have personal net worth measured in the hundreds of millions of dollars. Although he declined to identify any-one, Kauffman told the press that he had received two inquiries. One was from a local banker who said he had five million dollars he could invest in the Royals. The other caller listened politely while Kauffman explained the financing necessary to maintain and field a team and then he begged off, saying he could not participate as he had only $200 million to spend. Then with a flicker of the old competitive light in his eyes, he quipped, "Tell the Kansas City fans not to worry . . . the club's going to stay here."

Throughout May and into mid-June, Kauffman continued to pick at the proposal. "Mr. Fogelman's proposal is very onerous to me personally," he told a reporter for *Sporting News*, "but I am giving full consideration to his wishes." Kauffman objected to earning no interest on the proposed $34 million loan, a loss he calculated at two million dollars. Then he found fault in the details of the bid process and he argued that the seller, not the buyer, should be liable for the investment banker's fee. But the real sticking point was buried in the details of the lifetime contracts Fogelman had given to Brett, Wilson, and Quisenberry in 1984. Those contracts included real estate deals with Fogelman personally. Kauffman was adamant that Fogelman—not the club, and certainly not he—was obligated to meet any shortfall arising from those contracts.

The negotiations dragged on. And if Fogelman's financial collapse was not enough to put Kauffman in a foul mood, the Royals' win/loss record that season definitely was. "Never have I entered a year with such great expectations and had such great disappointments," Kauffman confessed. He had committed nineteen million dollars in multiyear contracts for two free agent pitchers. The Royals now had the highest payroll in baseball. Yet all this money was not producing a winning team. Kauffman had watched the Royals, who were projected to finish first in the American League West, settle into last place by mid-June. "It doesn't necessarily mean adding free agents is the wrong thing to do, but it may mean that . . . it takes awhile for the team to gel," he said. When asked, "How do you remain so patient in the face of great disappointment?" he responded, "Maybe age."

The following day, Royals' president Joe Burke announced that Kauffman had decided to proceed with the loan to Fogelman. Beyond the agreement to lend Fogelman $34 million, Kauffman also agreed to assume responsibility to pay the shortfalls from Fogelman's real estate deals with Royals players. Picking up those costs alone could entail another $20 million. In addition, he said he would be willing to pay $5 million into the Royals' coffers to cover the yearly asset contribution that his partner had failed to make the previous December. And finally, he would pay all of the estimated $7 million in operating losses anticipated for the Royals in 1990.

There was a collective sigh of relief from baseball fans and civic leaders alike. "This is terrific news," Mayor Richard L. Berkley proclaimed. "Ewing Kauffman is there when you need him. He's been fabulous for Kansas City. From CPR to the STAR program to the employees of Marion, he has an extensive commitment to Kansas City." Berkley was correct. It was Kauffman's sense of civic responsibility, his recognition of the economic stimulus of baseball, and his determination to keep the team at home that finally persuaded him to accept the agreement. Once again, when Kansas City needed help, he alone stepped forward. When he had purchased the franchise in 1968 he had been younger, bristling with a competitiveness that fueled his personal campaign with the major league owners to win their votes. He had spent freely to provide the city with a spectacular stadium and to build a World Series championship team. And he had had a marvelous time doing it all. But now he was seventy-four years old and sadly disappointed in the young man he had taken as his full partner and co-owner in the Royals. He was tired of the negotiations, the haggling, the tedium of dealing with platoons of lawyers, bankers, and accountants. So he decided to accept the agreement and shoulder the enormous costs by himself just as he had started with the team more than two decades earlier. The last two years had been emotionally and physically draining. There had been the gut-wrenching decision to sell his controlling interest in Marion Laboratories and now this financial crisis with the Royals. Fogelman had violated his trust and his friendship. Kauffman had been resigned to appearing at the press conference to lay the nightmare of the Royals' ownership crisis to rest once and for all. When the last of the intricate financial details had been explained and he had responded to questions, one reporter asked him how he felt now that it was all over. In a low voice he said, "I feel like I have been taken advantage of. . . ." Then he turned and walked slowly from the room.

The Succession Plan   15

Ewing Kauffman may have made some harsh statements about his partner and the nightmare of the ownership crisis as the loan negotiations dragged on for almost a year, but Muriel Kauffman never lost her sense of humor. When someone complimented her on a hat or a new outfit that summer she would say, "I'm glad you like it. With all the money we've spent, I won't be able to afford another one." But a few days after the agreement was announced, Kauffman began to sound like his old self—he was trying to be fair, to view the situation from the other person's perspective. He was attempting to understand while coming to forgive. "Mr. Fogelman had the best of intentions," he said. "He had the idea of always keeping the ball club in Kansas City. I talked to him about expanding too much and working too hard. I guess there comes a time when you get older, you don't take chances."

But Kauffman was still taking chances. He was making a calculated assessment of the situation and betting that Fogelman could not repay the loan. In that event, Fogelman's interest would revert to Kauffman and he would then own 100 percent of the team again. He was also betting that no bidder would appear in the auction phase willing to offer a price high enough to entice him to sell. "I don't see how anybody could be stupid enough to want [the ball club]," he had said many times. "If you don't have someone with a personal income of millions of dollars annually, they're not going to be able to make up the loss." When asked what he would do if a bidder offered $200 million cash for the Royals, Kauffman responded, "I'd laugh at him and say '[I] take it.'" Because of the Royals' new twenty-five-year stadium lease, it seemed unlikely that a successful bidder would come from outside of Kansas City. Within the city,

there were a number of individuals with the personal wealth to acquire the team. Donald J. Hall of Hallmark Cards and Louis Ward of
Russell Stover Candies quickly came to mind. Both had assets estimated at greater than $500 million, but neither had indicated any
interest in acquiring the ball club.

The Royals retained J.P. Morgan of New York to handle the bidding process, which occupied the rest of the summer and fall. Finally on December 19, 1990, the Kauffmans called a news conference at Royals Stadium to announce their decision concerning the
team's future. Seated at a dais draped with the symbol of the Royals' 1985 World Series championship, they both seemed relaxed.
When Kauffman rose at precisely one P.M., he began to talk about
the history of the couple's involvement with the club, the quality of
executive leadership, the record of play. He clearly intended to in-
ject some additional drama into the already-electrified environment
as he paused and said that the auction process was complete. Then
he paused. "And the news is . . ." He paused once more, milking the
moment. "The Kauffmans will remain as owners of the Royals."

Once again, he had studied the situation carefully, calculated the
odds, wagered, and won. Kauffman revealed that about two hundred people had indicated an interest in the team, although all but
a handful were eliminated. The final list of potential bidders was
pared to three, with each submitting a range of nonbinding offers
with high and low figures. But none of the three came up with even
a tentative offer that would equal the amount of money Kauffman
had already invested in the team. In making the announcement
that he would again become the sole owner, he said the minimum
bid he would have considered was $91 million. He cited the na-
tional economic downturn and the specific realities of operating a
club in the major leagues' smallest market as probable reasons why
no binding bids were received.

In closing, Kauffman was unequivocal about the direction the
team would continue to choose. "Both [Mrs. Kauffman] and I have
agreed . . . that we want a winning team." That meant continuing
to spend major dollars to attract and keep good players. In response
to the predictable questions about whether he would seek another
partner or what the plans might be for the team after his death, he
replied good naturedly, "That's a decision Mrs. K and I have to
make—what happens when the *event* occurs—the *event* being my

kicking the bucket. Hopefully, I'll live for many, many years. As long as I'm living and Mrs. K's willing, we'll still own the Royals. I will continue to be active as long as I have my health." Mrs. K, never one to be upstaged, walked over to one of the attorneys representing her husband and said in a loud stage whisper, "I'm working on keeping the old man alive." Then she sighed for effect and added, "Not that it's easy." Kansas City fans were euphoric, and editorial comment reflected their feelings. "Tuesday was a happy day for Kansas City inasmuch as the Royals again were fully under the wing of an owner who pays his players more and charges his customers less than his balance sheet prudently should allow," wrote Jonathan Rand in the *Kansas City Star*. "For his announcement Kauffman should have donned a red suit and beard."

Everyone was relieved that the "Fogelman crisis" had been resolved, but in reality Kauffman was back to where he had started in 1983. Only now he was older and faced with all the issues surrounding his own mortality. He knew he did not want to go through the search for a partner again. And he had said that because of the tax laws, it would be foolish to consider having the Kauffman Foundation assume operation and ownership of the team after his death. He also downplayed the likelihood that either his children or his wife would assume ownership because the ball club would be strictly a money-losing proposition for them. As far as he was concerned, the idea that local government might become involved in ownership, such as Montreal did with the Expos, was ludicrous. "They're having trouble now even coming up with the two million dollars they've pledged for stadium upkeep," he said, dismissing that suggestion.

Shortly after the New Year, Kauffman told Mike Herman that he would like to have a definitive plan to submit to baseball's ownership committee and Commissioner Fay Vincent. Herman, who had recently stepped down as president of the Kauffman Foundation, was devoting a large part of his time to the Kauffmans' personal finances as well as trying to help resolve the Royals' ownership dilemma. "We are not in the process of trying to find another owner," he told the press in April. "We're trying to think of an innovative idea that is compatible with the community, the spirit of baseball and keeping local ownership." And there was no arguing with his conclusion: "It is really a hard problem."

While trying to craft a succession plan, Kauffman was eager to resolve a number of issues now that he had regained ownership. Before January was gone, he announced that he had paid off the Quisenberry and Wilson "lifetime" contracts and was near agreement with first baseman George Brett. He declined to reveal the details, beyond saying that he had taken over the real estate Fogelman had given the players as investments in return for a lump-sum settlement. "I bought them out," he said. "I'd prefer not to announce any figures because they're ridiculous."

The agreement with Brett took longer. And it was also more complicated. In addition to trying to get compensation for the Fogelman real estate—which had never produced a positive cash flow—Brett was also pressing for a renegotiated contract. He was complaining because the Royals had signed free agent Mark Davis at a salary substantially higher than his own. At the start of spring training, Brett retained Dennis Gilbert of Los Angeles, a well-known sports agent, to help resolve the matter. But Kauffman stood firm on the issue of renegotiating Brett's contract. As one sportswriter put it, "The obstacle in . . . negotiations between George Brett and Ewing Kauffman is a matter of principle, not principal." As a matter of principle, Kauffman never renegotiated a contract.

He was adamant. "I do not renegotiate contracts, period!" he reiterated. But he did agree—as he had told Brett when he complained about his salary after the 1989 season—that he was willing to compensate him with appreciation bonuses beyond the salary stipulated for the three remaining years of his contract. The issue for negotiation then became one of when and in what form to make the payments. Although the Royals' owner refused to reveal the substance of the negotiations, he responded to press inquiries by praising the venerable ballplayer. "[I] couldn't think more highly of any player," Kauffman said. "George never slacked off because he had a guaranteed five-year contract, and he's had three of them. He knew he'd get paid regardless of what he did. But he always delivered 100 percent." There seemed to be little doubt that Kauffman was more than willing to work out a deal: to restructure, if not renegotiate. When the press asked Brett how the discussions were going, his response was ambiguous. "Kauffman's offered us some money," he admitted. "We're just trying to figure out the best way to get it. We're not asking for a penny more than he offered."

By mid-May 1991, Kauffman and Brett had agreed upon the "restructured" contract. It guaranteed the ballplayer at least seven million dollars. The old contract had guaranteed his salary though the 1991 season and gave the Royals options for 1992 and 1993. The new agreement extended the salary guarantee through the 1992 season with the Royals retaining an option for 1993. It also promised appreciation bonuses of up to three million dollars upon retirement. Kauffman agreed to take over the Fogelman real estate in exchange for one million dollars. And finally, the agreement authorized Brett to receive an additional half million dollars of previously deferred income whenever he chose.

The restructured contract was generous. Kauffman had made every effort to reach an accommodation with Brett. But he had refused to accede to the ballplayer's wishes on one issue: He would not guarantee the contract for 1993. If Brett played the 1991 and 1992 seasons, he was to receive a two-million-dollar appreciation bonus. If the Royals chose not to exercise their option for 1993, the buyout was to be an additional one million dollars. Should the Royals pick up Brett's option for the 1993 season, the appreciation bonus would rise to three million, and his base salary for the final year would be $2,500,000. That was all Kauffman was willing to do. He balked at the request to guarantee through 1993. "It seemed that was a major stumbling block in the negotiations," Brett said. "We tried to get '93 guaranteed and they said, 'No.'"

Kauffman had to draw the line somewhere. His wealth was such that he could withstand the Royals' losses, but he had to think about the time when he would not be around to pick up the tab. With Brett's restructured contract, the Royals moved into the number eight position among major league teams with players making one million dollars. Eleven players were paid more than a million dollars a season. And three of the eleven earned more than three million dollars each. The Royals' average salary for 1991 was a little more than $1,100,000. No one was surprised that the Oakland Athletics led the majors with sixteen players making more than one million and five players making in excess of three million dollars. These inflated salaries were the order of the day with the California Angels, the Los Angeles Dodgers, the New York Mets, and the San Francisco Giants. Those teams were located in huge population centers and enjoyed lucrative television and radio revenues. But in

Kansas City, circumstances were markedly different. As the team continued to play below its usual standards, attendance at home games declined, dragging revenues from ticket sales and concessions downward while the Royals' payroll remained one of the highest in baseball. Dale Rohr, the Royals' vice president of finance, said that since regaining full ownership in January 1991, Kauffman had contributed nearly thirty million dollars to make up for the Royals' cash shortfalls. As his health continued to deteriorate and his energy level declined, Kauffman believed it was imperative that he find a solution to prevent the team from being sold and moved after his death.

As Kauffman reestablished full control of the ball club, his usual good humor began to return. When asked how he was faring without a partner, he said, "I like it better . . . after all, now I can make a decision and not have to worry about somebody else having to agree with it." While he acknowledged that he still was not happy that the team had ended up sixth in their division in 1990, that year, even with the Fogelman debacle, had not been the worst. "No, the drug year was the worst," he confirmed. Now his overarching concern was to devise a plan to keep the Royals in Kansas City after his death. Working closely with Herman, Kauffman explored various financial strategies, talked with fellow owners to keep them informed as their concurrence would be needed, and visited with Kansas City's civic and business leaders to ensure their continuing support. Finally the day to reveal the plan arrived. The succession strategy that was announced on April 19, 1993, at Royals Stadium was as imaginative as it was complex. One local sports commentator, after looking at the diagram prepared illustrating how the plan would work, remarked, "I have seen diagrams depicting the mysteries of life in DNA that looked simpler."

The succession plan was essentially a process for keeping the team in local hands until a suitable buyer could be found. Kauffman was to own the Royals throughout his lifetime. At his death, the team would be turned over to a limited partnership of five Kauffman-designated individuals who would manage the finances, operate the team, and seek a new owner. Kauffman's estate would donate money sufficient to pay the Royals' projected yearly losses—in excess of three million dollars a year—for three years. Local philanthropists would be asked to contribute fifty million dollars to the

Greater Kansas City Community Foundation, which in turn would purchase nonvoting stock in the Royals. The limited partnership would invest those funds, and the interest earned would be used to pay the Royals' operating deficits. Kauffman hoped that the economics of baseball would improve during the period when the Greater Kansas City Community Foundation would, in effect, own the team, with the limited partnership, the Royals Baseball Corporation, operating the team. He believed if major league baseball was to adopt a plan to share local broadcast revenues or if owners and players could agree on a salary cap, the Royals might become, at most, a profitable sports franchise or, at least, a break-even operation. At a future time when a new owner purchased the team, the original fifty million dollars in charitable contributions would be returned to the Community Foundation. The original contributors then would have the right to direct their contributions and gains to qualified charities of their choosing.

The succession plan was a strategy to buy time in the hope that baseball's economics would improve sufficiently to make the team attractive enough that a local buyer, who would agree to keep the Royals in Kansas City, would come forward. If, after eight years, no hometown owner had appeared, the management group could look for a nonresident buyer with the purchase proceeds going into the Community Foundation. "Everything's going to be taken care of," Kauffman reassured the crowd at the press conference, "and you won't miss me."

In spite of Kauffman's assurances, there were still several hurdles to overcome before the plan could become a reality. First, owners in both leagues had to approve, although it seemed likely that they would. Seattle and Montreal had gotten the owners' go-ahead for less creative plans to retain local ownership. And baseball owners usually liked for teams to stay put. But the most worrisome obstacle was the Internal Revenue Service. Would the IRS agree that Kauffman's effort to keep the Royals in Kansas City constituted a charitable contribution? If so, the complicated succession plan could be implemented tax-free. If not, the plan would almost certainly trigger ruinously expensive taxation. Stanley P. Weiner, a tax lawyer who had been working with Kauffman and Herman, admitted, "If the IRS says no, we'll have to regroup."

Since at best it could take three to six months before the IRS ruled, and because of the plan's complexity the review might drag on more than a year, an alternate strategy was being considered. Kauffman's advisers had talked with two of Missouri's influential members of Congress, Senator John Danforth, a member of the powerful Senate Finance Committee, and Representative Alan Wheat about the possibility of amending the tax law, if necessary, so the succession plan could become legal. Both men agreed to help should it become necessary to seek a change in the law. Some individuals close to Kauffman hinted that the Internal Revenue Service might move more quickly to issue a private ruling rather than risk having the tax code amended to enlarge the scope of the meaning of "charitable contribution."

Not everyone praised the succession plan as "altruistic." There were some detractors who saw it and the hint of possible congressional action to amend the tax code as nothing more than another way for a man who was already a billionaire to escape inheritance taxes. Even with annual operating losses in the millions, the Royals were valued at $117 million according to *Financial World* magazine. Because taxes for Kauffman's estate would be 55 percent, the heirs would be forced to pay $64 million to inherit a money-losing team. But if avoiding additional inheritance taxes had been Kauffman's goal, the law already provided an avenue to accomplish that. And, until the succession plan was developed, his estate plan had provided that the Ewing Marion Kauffman Foundation would inherit the ball club. By giving the Royals to a charitable foundation, the estate would pay no taxes on the value of the sports franchise. But Kauffman's goal was larger than escaping taxation. He was seeking a way to keep the team in Kansas City until a local buyer would be found. If the Kauffman Foundation was to acquire the Royals after Kauffman's death, it would not be able to use money intended for charitable purposes to pay the losses of a noncharitable enterprise. Worse still, the foundation might be required to sell the baseball team quickly to the highest bidder—including an out-of-town buyer intent on moving the team elsewhere.

In the judgment of most tax specialists, the succession plan was tax neutral—it did not seek to reduce Kauffman's taxes nor did it create a financial gain for the heirs. Daniel J. Haake, a former IRS revenue agent who had examined the plan, predicted, "I think it's going to fly." He reasoned that the IRS would be sensitive to the public-relations aspect of all this money ultimately going to charity and that a favorable ruling for something so all-American as a baseball team could reflect well of an agency that seldom received favorable press attention. He concluded, "Something like this creates a lot of goodwill."

The civic and business leaders who attended the private meeting where Kauffman revealed the complex succession plan were saddened by his appearance. He seemed frail and shrunken, with dark circles under his eyes, and he sat during the announcement to conserve his waning strength. Everyone knew he had been in poor health, but no one knew that he was suffering from bone cancer which had spread to the vertebrae, causing him great pain. Yet when he talked about the plan, he spoke optimistically of its success. His voice was strong, his blue eyes filled with the hope of keeping the team in his beloved hometown. As Kauffman invited his peers to join in this effort to preserve major league baseball in Kansas City, Muriel Kauffman spoke up and said she would give the first five million toward the goal of fifty million if her husband would match it. Grinning, Kauffman responded, "I'd look like a shortstop if I didn't." Later as the meeting was breaking up, Henry Bloch, the founder of H&R Block, teased Muriel, asking if Ewing had put her up to making the challenge. "Kauffman doesn't tell me what to do," she said playfully. It was the famous couple at their best—kidding, challenging, and supporting one another in public. And for a few seconds it seemed like the early years when they had just purchased the team and every day in baseball was colorful, fun-filled, and exhilarating. The *Kansas City Star* writer who commented on the succession plan seemed to speak for thousands in the community when he wrote, "Just when you begin to think Ewing and Muriel Kauffman could not possibly top their generosity to this community, they come along and redefine selflessness."

Business and civic leaders lauded the Kauffmans' generosity and began lining up their own contributions to the plan. The Hall Family Foundations, created from the wealth of Hallmark Cards, led the way with the first pledge of ten million dollars. The H&R Block Foundation pledged $1,500,000, the largest donation in its history. Then pledges for two million dollars more arrived. Each was a gift of one million from the Kansas City Star Co. and Capital Cities/ABC Foundation, the *Star*'s parent company. "The fact that this is the single largest charitable commitment [we have] ever made is some measure of how important we feel the Royals are to Kansas City's status as a major league city," said Robert C. Woodworth, president and publisher of the *Kansas City Star*. There were other significant pledges from such companies as Sprint, Kansas City Southern Industries, Twentieth Century Co., and Stauffer Communication of Topeka, although they preferred not to disclose the amounts.

Ordinary working people and schoolchildren made pledges too, although there was no formal appeal outside of the philanthropic and corporate communities. Janice C. Kreamer, president of the Greater Kansas City Community Foundation, said the foundation had received so many unsolicited small pledges from schoolchildren as well as retired people that a special fund would have to be created to receive the donations. "That's an unbelievable testament to Mr. K and the Royals," she noted. Kauffman had always said that the Royals really belonged to the fans; he had kept ticket prices low so families on limited budgets could attend the games. Now they were paying him back with small bills and small change, trying to help keep their team in place when he was gone. These were the gifts that touched him most; the gifts that confirmed his life's experience that a man could truly grow richer by giving his wealth away.

In appreciation for all of his contributions to Kansas City, and the plan to keep the ball team in particular, the *Kansas City Star* urged the Jackson County Sports Authority to revisit the issue of naming the baseball stadium after Kauffman. When this had been considered several years earlier, Kauffman had brushed aside the idea. More editorials followed, and letters flooded into the paper agreeing with the suggestion. An out-of-state reader summed up the general feeling when he wrote, "I can think of no more appropriate way to recognize the generosity that Mr. Kauffman has continued to display for Kansas City." It was signed, "Avron Fogelman, President and Chief Executive Officer, Fogelman Properties, Memphis, Tennessee."

Before the question of renaming the stadium could be settled, Kauffman was inducted into the Royals' Hall of Fame. He was the eleventh member and the only inductee in 1993. The ten men who preceded him—eight ballplayers, former Royals president Joe Burke, and former manager Dick Howser—all owed their induction to him.

As the day grew near, there was some concern that Kauffman would be unable to accept the award in person at the ceremonies before the game with the Seattle Mariners. The general public was now aware that he was terminally ill. "Hopefully I can put up with the pain for the fifteen to twenty minutes of the ceremony," he said, for he wanted to accept the honor in person. To everyone's delight, and his own, he was able to attend. Driven onto the field, Kauffman stepped from the car clad in the owner's "uniform"—a Royal blue polyester suit with matching blue socks and blue patent leather loafers, a pale blue shirt, and the Royals' necktie. Smiling and waving as if he felt no pain, he accepted the honor with a pep talk urging all the fans to write their congressmen and senators to keep major league baseball in Kansas City. Even as he acknowledged the accolades, he declined the credit, saying, "You are well aware that the associates of the Royals earned all the awards that I will ever receive." Just before the Hall of Fame event, a reporter asked Kauffman if he had ever had any regrets over bringing baseball back to Kansas City. "Never, never, never," he replied. On that fine evening in May before thousands of baseball fans and admirers, it was clear that he really meant it.

By the second week in June, Kauffman had selected the five individuals who would form the limited partnership to take control of the baseball team at his death. The five named were David D. Glass, the head of the world's largest retailer, Wal-Mart Stores; Gene A. Budig, chancellor of the University of Kansas; Larry Kauffman, Kauffman's son; Louis W. Smith, president of the Kansas City Division of Allied Signal Inc.; and Michael E. Herman, Kauffman's financial adviser, longtime associate at Marion Laboratories and the Kauffman Foundation and his closest aide. Muriel Kauffman and Charlie Hughes were to serve on the board of directors.

Kauffman was to select one of the five to be the managing general partner, or designated representative, and the betting was that it would be either Glass or Herman. Glass got the nod. Glass had met Kauffman years earlier when he owned a chain of stores in Springfield that purchased pharmaceuticals from Marion Laboratories. Although they lost touch personally, over the years Glass said he had admired Kauffman's business success and followed the fortunes of the baseball team. Glass was a confirmed baseball enthusiast and J.P. Morgan and Company had contacted him when seeking possible bidders during the 1990 auction. While he had expressed some interest, nothing ever materialized. In naming the five men, Kauffman said, "While these gentlemen have varied backgrounds, they share in my general philosophies and have special qualifications and interests to the Kansas City area and the Royals. I am confident they will provide the type of leadership to the organization consistent with what has made the Royals one of the top franchises in professional sports."

The daily papers were filled with news regarding the succession plan, which fueled public sentiment to name the stadium for Kauffman. In early June, the Jackson County Sports Authority approved a resolution supporting the name change. Shortly thereafter the Jackson County legislature, the body with the authority to rename Royals Stadium, concurred. When Marsha Murphy, the county executive, sent word to Kauffman that she would not proceed if he objected, he said he wanted to consider it for a few weeks. But Muriel Kauffman finally prevailed, persuading him that he should accept the tribute. "[Muriel's] the one who put the pressure on and persuaded me to change my mind, which she's highly capable of doing, and so I acquiesced," he revealed.

When the day for renaming the stadium finally arrived, more than eleven years after the initial campaign started, Kauffman was too ill to attend. In acknowledging the honor on her husband's behalf, Muriel Kauffman said, "He thought about coming and sitting in his box, but he's just too exhausted." Then she assured the crowd, "His spirit is here." Kauffman had said on many occasions that he did not want his name emblazoned on hospitals, universities, libraries, and museums. He had an enormous ego and an unshakable belief in himself and his abilities, but he was neither vain nor arrogant. In spite of his aversion to "bricks and mortar," he came to understand that having his name on the baseball stadium was a fitting tribute indeed. As Jeff Gordon wrote in the *Kansas City Star*, "Among the extremely rich, Kauffman remains an anomaly . . . He is everyman who hit it big. . . ." And that was exactly how Kauffman thought of himself. "To think that a little farm boy, eight years old, came to Kansas City, and who would imagine that years later they would name the baseball stadium after him?"

Outside of Kansas City critical developments needed to support the succession plan were moving much more slowly. The major league baseball's owners committee approved the plan in concept in mid-June with the understanding that it would take final action depending on the IRS ruling. And there was no indication when the IRS might act. The succession plan contained a number of issues that required IRS approval, the most crucial of which was a determination that gifts to the Community Foundation on behalf of the Royals would be treated as tax-deductible charitable contributions. "We're asking the IRS to give us the opportunity to save what is a vital economic-development vehicle for our community, which means jobs for our city," Kreamer said. "That is very charitable."

Another potentially sticky issue involved how the IRS would treat the return on the limited partners' investment when the team was sold to a new owner. The plan provided that when the sale was complete, the first fifty million would go to the Community Foundation. The limited partners would then be permitted to recoup their initial investments, plus an amount not to exceed 15 percent annual return on the original investment. The IRS would have to determine if such an arrangement constituted an improper benefit to private individuals. Put another way, if the succession plan was to be considered a charitable endeavor, could individuals make money or receive other gains through their investment and work as limited partners? To get over this hurdle, the limited partners agreed to donate any gains to charity.

As speculation regarding possible IRS interpretations continued, the campaign to raise the fifty million attracted additional donations. And as it became widely know that corporations and foundations were making record pledges to the effort, the inevitable backbiting began. Bill Hall, the president of the Hall Family Foundations and coordinator of the fund-raising effort, acknowledged the concerns among some local charity leaders that money donated to keep the Royals in Kansas City might make grant money for other community needs scarcer. "I think we would be naive if we didn't believe that in the short run this wouldn't have some negative impact on giving," Hall said. But he stressed that in the long run the community would be adding to the pool of philanthropic assets.

The concern was understandable, but it probably reflected more accurately the not-for-profit agencies' ambivalence about the Kauffman Foundation than it did the effect of the succession plan. Kauffman's private foundation, the Ewing Marion Kauffman Foundation, was not, at that time, a grant-making foundation. Instead, it initiated and operated its own programs in the areas of entrepreneurship, youth development, and substance abuse. Community agencies who tried to obtain grants from the Kauffman Foundation sometimes felt threatened when they learned that the foundation engaged in well-funded programs similar to their own, but in apparent isolation from their colleagues, unaware of the daily struggles these agencies confronted just to keep programs afloat. And rumors that the foundation would have assets in excess of one billion dollars after Kauffman's death did nothing to ease the tense situation. Kauffman heard these rumblings as if in the distance, but by July he was struggling so against pain and exhaustion that he possessed neither the will nor the time to respond.

The Philanthropist Emerges 16

Marion Laboratories brought Ewing Kauffman immense wealth; baseball brought him great pleasure; but philanthropy—the opportunity to give back—brought him genuine happiness. "When you've accumulated a certain amount of money, you have an obligation to spend it wisely," he said. "I personally believe in giving your money away while you're alive . . . so you can enjoy it. I like to invest my money in people . . . [and] I'm seeing results in the smiles on kids' faces."

When the press tried to portray him as a benevolent patriarch lavishing his wealth on the needy and less fortunate, Kauffman would shrug off the rhetoric, saying, "I don't impress people; my actions impress them." Then, leaning back in his chair, he would light his pipe, the signal that he was ready for a bit of reflective talk. As he exhaled clouds of smoke, he would remind the listener of his simple tastes for such things as twenty-nine-cent Briggs straight tobacco. Then leaning across the massive desk in his office, he would continue, his voice betraying a kind of quiet passion. "You may say I'm generous, but I'll tell you what many people don't realize. They hear it, but they really don't understand it. The more you give, the more you get. It's just that simple. The more you give to any association in life, the more you will get in return. It's not altruistic either. I don't consider myself an altruist. It's just a simple formula that is very practical. It works in all aspects of life."

Kauffman became a philanthropist relatively late in life. As with most self-made individuals, he spent the early years earning the financial independence that would permit him to have the millions to give away. But as he began to underwrite various community endeavors through Marion Laboratories in the late 1970s and early

1980s, he was suddenly struck by how much joy he had missed. The money, he realized, was less important than a caring spirit and the giving of one's self and time. To illustrate that point, he often told the story of receiving a letter from a widower in Kansas. The man was financially comfortable, but by no means wealthy. He wrote that he had read of Kauffman's work with school children in PROJ-ECT CHOICE and wondered what he might do with his limited re-sources. "I wrote him right back," Kauffman recalled. "[I told him] if he just took one or two young people in that town and worked with them, told them that if they would do what was right, would graduate [from high school], that he would help them go through college or a university." More than a year passed and Kauffman as-sumed that nothing had come of his suggestion. "Then . . . I got an-other letter telling me how much fun he had had mentoring two young people and helping them!" In the last months of his life, when he suffered agonizing pain from bone cancer, Kauffman was still responding to letters, telling correspondents how they could use small amounts of money to enrich the lives of others, and, in turn, enrich their own.

After Marion Laboratories became a publicly traded company in 1965, the Kauffmans were much more visible among the wealthy in Kansas City. As a result, they were asked to contribute to nu-merous causes, serve on prestigious boards—in short, to become a part of the Kansas City elite. But Kauffman, who had never been interested in the social scene and who had always felt excluded from the inner circles of business and civic affairs, was not inter-ested in bartering his wealth for position. While he had not yet fo-cused on his long-term path of charitable giving, he was adamant about what he would not do in the present. Nat Robertson, who served on Marion's board for almost a quarter century, recalled that Kauffman was wary of fund-raisers and suspicious of grant-seekers in those early days. "He was a man of great generosity . . . but he was not a philanthropist," Robertson said. He remembered Kauff-man saying, "Miller Nichols was in to hit me up for some money [for the art museum]. But he's not going to get any out of me. I don't give a damn about the art museum! I create jobs for the com-munity!" He was equally resistant to colleges and universities which wanted him to accept honorary degrees. "No," he told Robertson, "they're just after my money." When Jerry Holder and Robertson approached Kauffman about creating a corporate program to match associates' donations to colleges, he turned them down, saying, "No, I never went to [a university]. We don't need a matching gift program." But as the requests kept coming, especially from nearby colleges and universities, Kauffman developed an ingenious response. When asked to contribute to an endowment campaign, he would decline, but then offered the solicitor an option. "You buy Marion stock, and I'll give you a letter personally guaranteeing you against any loss." Robertson said he did not know how many college presidents followed through, "but I never heard of him covering any losses."

When Marion Laboratories became a public company, Kauffman had hard cash, "real money, not just paper," he liked to say. His attorneys advised him to take advantage of the favorable tax laws at the time, and in 1967 he established the Ewing and Muriel Kauffman Foundation. He, Muriel, and Charlie Hughes were the founding directors and trustees. Kauffman had no plans for what the foundation might someday become. At the time, he was using it as tool to reduce his personal tax liability and as a conduit for personal giving. But as his fortune increased dramatically during the 1980s, Mike Herman began urging him to formulate a philosophy and direction for the foundation. Since he had made his money in the health care field, he initially thought about continuing to support health care–related activities. But nothing substantive was decided; the time was not right. The foundation remained little more than a legal entity with minimal endowment which Kauffman used as "a pass-through vehicle" for fairly small charitable contributions to the symphony, the public library, and other worthy causes. The vision and the mission were still to come.

During the fifties and sixties while he was consumed with building Marion Laboratories, Kauffman had little time for personal involvement in civic or charitable activities. In Kauffman's mind, Marion Laboratories fulfilled its corporate citizenship responsibilities through the annual contribution to the United Way. And senior executives were discouraged from serving on more than two community organizations' boards, lest volunteer service impinge on their responsibilities at work. "As a matter of fact, Marion was not involved at all with the community," Herman recalled. Kauffman believed that creating jobs and meeting an ever-expanding payroll were the most important contributions he and his associates could make to their community. Later, that policy changed dramatically as Marion's executives were loaned throughout Kansas City to participate in and lead all types of civic and charitable undertakings.

The events that transformed Kauffman into a committed philanthropist began in the late 1960s. His purchase of the American League baseball franchise in 1968 was the opening wedge—a decision that was part emotion, part ego. Kauffman felt a sentimental gratitude toward his hometown. The Kansas City of his youth had provided a gentle safety net of school, scouting, church activities, friendly neighbors, and odd jobs for Ewing when his parents divorced. He had gone abroad in World War II, but he never thought of settling anywhere else when the hostilities ended. When he decided to start his own pharmaceutical business, neighborhood physicians and pharmacists had been among his first and most loyal customers. Once he became successful, he liked the idea of helping the town that had helped him. And he quickly recognized the potential economic benefits associated with being a "major league city." But ego played a large role in that purchase, too. The farm boy from Cass County had built a successful company with little or no help from the financial powers in Kansas City. They had not invited him to join the Kansas City Country Club and they never sought his counsel on civic matters. And he relished his victory over the various local syndicates and partnerships which vied for the franchise because not one of them had invited him to participate. As he warmed to the celebrity status that owning a major league team automatically conferred, he demonstrated a sense of responsibility toward the fans and the community at large "to do it right." His sudden fame in the community created in him a greater sense of involvement and responsibility for his fellow Kansas Citians that meant more than building a winning baseball franchise. In a curious way, the competitive sports world opened his eyes to the needs of the those around him. He had always been kind and caring in the workplace. Over the next two decades, he would grow into a compassionate benefactor within his own community.

Unlike his overnight celebrity as a baseball owner, Kauffman's reputation as a philanthropist and his understanding of the best use of his growing resources came more slowly. In 1969, as part of an in-house health and safety training program, Marion associates began receiving instruction in emergency cardiopulmonary resuscitation. By this time, Kauffman was beginning to realize that creating jobs was important, but it was not enough. He had been so focused on creating a profitable, yet personally caring, environment which encompassed the company, its suppliers, distributors, and customers, that he had virtually ignored his own community. If Marion Laboratories was to become a socially responsible company, he needed to find a larger way to participate in the life of the community. CPR NOW! was his first response.

The CPR NOW! program was part of a collaborative effort involving six pharmaceutical producers of coronary products. The initial goal was to teach the employees the importance of emergency paramedical care. Once the employees were trained, the companies planned to offer CPR instruction in key cities across the country. Marion's founder readily admitted that he decided to participate initially because he thought it was a good business investment. And the old Eagle Scout in him believed that every individual should be prepared to deal with life's emergencies. But when Elmer Henry, a Marion associate, told him about the thrill of saving a neighbor's life, Kauffman's enthusiasm was ignited.

Combining corporate funds with their personal money and using the allure of the Kansas City Royals, the Kauffmans set out to train one hundred thousand Kansas Citians in CPR over the next decade. Marion executives were released from corporate duties to coordinate the project. Al Mannino, Marion's vice president for corporate affairs, became president of the ACT Foundation, the national consortium of pharmaceutical companies which provided most of the funds. In a single weekend in the spring of 1981, Marion volunteers, with trainers from the American Heart Association, the American Red Cross, and local hospitals and universities, taught more than ten thousand people at Royals Stadium. Down on the AstroTurf alongside his neighbors, the Royals' owner was among those who learned the life-saving technique that Saturday afternoon.

Participating in CPR training became "the thing to do" in Kansas City. Often on weekends there would be classes meeting at fifty sites or more. There were special classes to train the visually impaired, the deaf, and persons with other physical handicaps. One project manager told of an incident in which a woman took the training as payment to her physician. "She had had a heart attack in church and someone had saved her. The only payment her doctor would take was that she [be prepared to] save somebody else's life." At another locale, the manager reported, "We had one family of ten and another of five come in to celebrate Mother's Day the best and easiest way."

"CPR is the most unselfish thing you can do," Kauffman said when elders of the Church of the Latter-day Saints honored him and Muriel in Salt Lake City. "It only takes about four hours to learn, but you're helping someone. One day you may be called upon to actually save a person's life." Muriel shared her husband's enthusiasm and commitment to the endeavor. When the couple received the Red Cross Man and Woman of the Year award in Washington, D.C., in November 1981, Mrs. Kauffman's remarks stirred the audience. "Last year there were two men who, within twenty minutes of finishing the course, both saved someone's life. What more precious gift could you give?"

During the seventies and into the early eighties, the Kauffmans' financial support and personal involvement helped train 125,000 people. They also persuaded both the National and American baseball leagues to promote CPR training in the cities where professional baseball teams played. "To this day," Kauffman said in the summer of 1991, "I still get a letter or two every month which states, 'I took your training program in CPR and last night, we— *we*—saved a life.' It can't help but give you a thrill to know something you did that many years ago is still effective today."

For Kauffman, the experiences associated with the CPR training program had been as exhilarating as seeing Marion Laboratories listed on the New York Stock Exchange. Although victory in the World Series was still a few years away, nothing he would ever do again would be as personally fulfilling as using his wealth to help others. From that point on, he was more responsive to requests for assistance from community organizations. He began encouraging Marion associates at every level to become more involved in a variety of volunteer activities. And, as always before embarking in a new direction, he began to read about philanthropy and the programs of the nation's large foundations. He was searching for a way to formulate and structure what was to be his greatest legacy.

Kauffman already had the corporate structure called a private foundation; he had sufficient funds to endow it; all he lacked was a program. But he felt there was no need to hurry. No sense of urgency compelled him to move in any particular direction. In fact, at this point, he was thinking of the foundation as a checkbook, not as an organization with a mission, goals, a definable program, a governing board, and a staff. The act of giving wisely was challenging and satisfying, and the foundation was merely a convenient means to achieve a specific end. When Mike Herman tried to prod Kauffman into defining his giving philosophy or talking about structuring the foundation in a businesslike way, he would counter, "I'm not interested in that; it's something I don't want to worry about. When I die you can worry about it!" His instincts counseled caution. He was reading, learning, and thinking; he was growing, not groping. He believed he would know when the right project came along, and he would not need a foundation bureaucracy to identify it. Then in the bitter cold winter of 1979, he thought he had found it.

That year, executives at Hallmark Cards approached Kauffman, asking that Marion Laboratories join them in funding Project Warmth, a program to assist those who could not pay their escalating gas and electricity bills. Hallmark launched the campaign with $50,000. Marion Laboratories joined with $25,000, and a local television station donated public-service time to generate smaller donations. The effort was successful. No one in Kansas City went without heat that winter. "A year later," Kauffman remembered, "the same thing occurred, a cold winter. They came back and wanted another contribution, and we told them no. Why? Because it didn't solve the problem. They just threw money at it."

The experience with Project Warmth helped clarify Kauffman's thinking. He knew he cared deeply about the plight of those who were less fortunate than he. He had been moved to tears thinking of children in Kansas City going home to unheated rooms, with no gas for cooking and no lights by which to do their homework. But he was not satisfied with relieving the symptoms when the root causes were too few jobs and insufficient wages. "This time I made the resolution that we would . . . contribute to various social problems, but we would add . . . something [extra] that we felt we had, which was executive talent." With that statement, Kauffman sketched the broad outline that his foundation would follow—he wanted to focus on solutions, and he would do so with his own people whom he believed to be the best. But it was to be another four or five years before he actually turned his full attention to implementing those vague plans.

Then in 1983, the Royals' drug scandals shook Kauffman's world. "Three of the Royals' baseball players were found guilty of trying to buy cocaine over the phone," he remembered. "They were made examples, even though there were a total of twenty-six people taped on those calls. They were the only three who were taken to court and served ninety days in the penitentiary." Horrified that this problem had occurred among players under his watchful eye, Kauffman plunged into reading everything he could find about drugs and drug-use prevention. And what he learned stunned and frightened him. "I was amazed to find out that the drug problem started in the sixth and seventh grade. [It] is unbelievable to start at such a young age. So I decided that Marion should do something on that problem." True to his own instincts, by patiently waiting yet still preparing through reading and considering possible directions, he was ready to respond when the problem that needed his help emerged.

Because of his dissatisfaction with Project Warmth, Kauffman was now resolved to work toward solutions. His extensive reading convinced him that it was more important to prevent children from ever starting to use drugs instead of focusing on treatment and rehabilitation. Having settled on the goal, the immediate challenge was to find the people who could work on the problem. The course that Kauffman followed in establishing the drug program, which was known as STAR, set the initial pattern for the function of the foundation and the development of new initiatives.

When Kauffman decided to use his wealth to fight the drug problem in Kansas City, the foundation was still little more than a shell. It had a small board, but no staff. So he naturally turned to Marion executives for advice on how to proceed. Jerry Holder suggested hiring a person knowledgeable about the public school system since that seemed to be the best route to reach elementary and junior high students. Holder, whose own two children had attended the public schools in Shawnee Mission, a Kansas suburb of Kansas City, was acquainted with several of the district's best teachers and administrators. In particular, he recalled being very impressed with Calvin Cormack, a young principal at his children's high school. He

learned that Cormack had resigned his position as associate superintendent and was interviewing for a superintendent's job in several other communities. "I just got a call out of the blue one day
from one of Mr. Kauffman's senior vice presidents . . . who knew of
me and had heard that I was leaving the community," Cormack recalled. "He . . . was calling on behalf of an idea that Mr. Kauffman
had and wanted to visit with me." As a courtesy to a district patron,
Cormack agreed to meet with Holder. He had no inkling of what
Kauffman might be planning, but Cormack had no intention of
leaving public education.

Holder and Cormack had several extended conversations about
Kauffman's general plans to fund drug-prevention education. Soon
Cormack was meeting other corporate officers, and then Holder asked
him to meet with Kauffman. "I agreed to do it because by that time
I was becoming intrigued by what . . . I was hearing," he said. As a
senior high school principal, Cormack had been involved with school
suspensions resulting from drug use. He recognized that public education's policy of expelling students using drugs was not dealing
effectively or responsibly with the problem. "What we were doing
was just pushing them out the door for the rest of the community
to deal with. All of us in education knew that was no solution."

Holder told Cormack that he was recommending that Marion hire
him to develop and implement a drug-prevention program for the
public schools—subject to Kauffman's approval, of course. But Cormack was cautious. As much as he agreed with Kauffman's general
approach, the position Holder described would be no more than a
lateral move for him economically. "Although there were certainly
some additional opportunities that sweetened that [offer] in terms
of participation [in profit sharing] and stock options—things you
don't do in public education—it wasn't . . . a lucrative kind of offer,"
he recalled. In spite of his restrained interest in the position initially,
once he met Kauffman, Cormack's fate was sealed. "I was capti-
vated by my first conversation with him," he remembered. "The di-
rectness . . . the commitment that I could see there clearly. And . . .
he wasn't fanatical about it at all. I had a sense that when he spoke I
knew I could trust what he said. I knew that he meant what he said.
He wanted to bring someone in from education and look at how we
could impact the whole system. And maybe even impact the approach that we were taking in this country to substance abuse."

In mid-April 1984, the Kauffmans held a press conference at Marion Laboratories' corporate offices to announce the launch of a drug-awareness campaign aimed at Kansas City area elementary and junior high school students. "Six months ago the problem hit home for me," Kauffman said, alluding to the Royals' drug troubles. "We made a commitment to do something about it. . . . We won't reinvent the wheel, but I will say that it can't be a program that will run for a year or three years. It may go on forever—as long as it's successful." Kauffman acknowledged that the details of the prevention effort had not been fleshed out, but he announced that Cormack would become the project's executive director. In June when his resignation from the Shawnee Mission school district became effective, Cormack went to work at Marion Laboratories. The first major initiative of the Kauffman Foundation was about to be launched.

In announcing the drug-prevention program, Kauffman did what few individual donors or foundations ever do. He promised to commit resources for the long haul, perhaps in perpetuity, if the concept proved successful. That statement was an important signal to the Kansas City area education community, which was all too familiar with foundation- and government-sponsored projects whose funding dried up about the time everyone was finally figuring out what to do. Kauffman's willingness to stick with the endeavor if it was successful, and later his initiative in picking up all the implementation costs, went a long way toward securing the cooperation that was essential to make everything and everyone work. His commitment to long-term support was also a major influence on the foundation's initial development as an operating entity—one that initiates, staffs, and delivers its own programs—rather than as a more traditional grant-making organization. The strategy that resulted in STAR (Students Taught Awareness and Resistance), was straight out of Marion Laboratories. Just as he had licensed drugs others had developed, Kauffman decided to investigate and adapt already-proven methods which addressed the social problems that concerned him.

Once on board at Marion, Cormack reported to Holder, but he met weekly with Kauffman, who followed every detail of his progress with intense interest. "What Mr. Kauffman asked me to do . . . [was] to take a look at what was happening nationally with prevention and education about substance abuse," Cormack said, describing the development process. "It was a matter of searching out the most effective strategies and then bringing those strategies back to Kansas City and helping school systems and other youth-serving agencies [and] community agencies implement those strategies here." By September, Kauffman had settled on adapting a University of Southern California program developed to help teenagers stop smoking. "The thing we liked about it [was] that they did research prior to putting in the program," Kauffman said. "They sent analysts out and found out the percentage of these teenagers smoking, and after the program, research analysts went out and found that they had reduced smoking by 50 percent. We took this program and added to it various other things to combat the alcohol and drug situation."

Using the USC concept and model, Cormack and a team of consultants developed multiple strategies. They started with a school-based curriculum designed to help middle school and junior high students understand the kinds of influences they were going to encounter as they moved into high school—influences which encouraged the use of alcohol, tobacco, and other drugs. A key part of Cormack's early work was to develop a means of measuring the program's success. Again he turned to USC for help in constructing an evaluation design. "One of the things that Mr. Kauffman was very clearly saying was that he was willing to spend a lot of money on this project," Cormack said. "But he wanted to know that what was being spent was going to make a difference in the number of kids that became involved with drugs."

Late in the summer, Kauffman hosted the fifteen Kansas City area school superintendents at a luncheon in his suite at Royals Stadium. Cormack was extremely pleased with how well his colleagues responded to Kauffman. "He met people so easily. He made you feel comfortable. He . . . had . . . a special ability, I think, to treat all people alike. It didn't make any difference whether you were the president of a bank or if you were the doorman. People felt good meeting Mr. Kauffman and felt that he was very genuine." All the superintendents enthusiastically agreed to participate. Kauffman was offering them a fully developed program, was willing to train the teachers and pay all implementation costs. He was committed to systematic evaluation. And, most important, he promised continuing support if the program proved successful. All these factors were important in securing the superintendents' cooperation, but Cormack believed that the timing was also crucial. "My sense was that it was easy for them to agree to cooperate because one of the things we pointed out was that there was an expectation developing in the country in 1984 that schools ought to be doing something about our drug problems. So, they were getting pressured to become active in this area."

The STAR program was launched in the Kansas City metropolitan area schools in 1984, and a decade later more than one hundred thousand students had participated. And at Kauffman's insistence, a statistically valid evaluation process was in place from the beginning. "We had a control group of eight hundred students who did not receive the program," he said, describing the measurement process. "We had another group of eight hundred students of comparable economic level, social strata, etc. that took the program. . . . The control group was followed for five years. . . . [In] the group of eight hundred students who had the antidrug program, smoking was reduced by 37 percent compared to ones who didn't have the program. . . . Alcohol 25 percent reduction; marijuana 43 percent reduction, which showed that the program stayed with these students."

As evidence of the STAR program's effectiveness became known, Kauffman began receiving requests from around the country for help. When the Kansas commissioner of Alcohol and Drug Abuse Services asked for assistance in taking the program statewide, Kauffman countered, "If you are willing to put up a third of the cost— you, the state—and we can get the communities, the local school districts, to put up a third of it, I'll pay for the other third." When Kansas teachers started training in the STAR methodology, Kauffman told Cormack that they needed to offer the same training in Missouri schools.

As University of Southern California faculty began to publish the evaluation results in national journals, interest in the STAR program mushroomed. Through relationships with the Eli Lilly Company in Indianapolis, Marion officers shared their enthusiasm for what STAR was accomplishing. A short time later, when one of the Lilly corporate officers joined the staff of the Lilly Endowment, he helped replicate STAR in Indianapolis. The next request for help came from a consortium of businesses in Washington, D.C., called Corporations Against Drug Abuse. This group had commissioned a national review of drug prevention programming, and STAR had been identified as the most effective program at that time. While Kauffman was pleased that STAR had been validated through evaluation and was being recognized nationally, he began to see that even with his enormous personal wealth, it would be impossible to commit funds to implement programs everywhere. But he wanted to help, so he agreed that Cormack and his small staff could act as consultants to other communities who would, in turn, generate their own funding. Impressed by the business community's determination to attack the drug problem in the nation's capital, Kauffman decided to help fund the first pilot in two District of Columbia junior high schools. His investment of $25,000 quickly multiplied as local foundations, businesses, and government accepted responsibility for on-going funding as the program quickly spread from the federal district into Maryland and northern Virginia suburbs.

In 1989, President George Bush named Kauffman to a presidential commission on drugs, an appointment he happily accepted. He saw this as an opportunity to use his influence and the proven results of STAR to achieve national implementation of drug-prevention programs. But the experience was disappointing for an activist like Kauffman. Deliberations and reports smothered any will to act. And by 1991, America's war in the Iraqi desert had overwhelmed the nation's war on drugs. But the experience was a salutary one. He learned the limits of his ability to influence public policy at the national level. He became acquainted firsthand with the vagaries of doing business in the not-for-profit world, the imprecise and shifting nature of public-private alliances, and the illusory quality of cooperation when turf battles loomed. The experience caused Kauffman to reflect on how he, through his foundation, could have the greatest influence on social problems that he wanted to effect. It also pushed him toward the decision that he would focus the foundation's activities in Kansas City and the general area. Kansas City would become the laboratory to research, develop, and pilot solutions.

Project STAR set the general pattern for how future Kauffman Foundation projects would develop. But as the activities surrounding STAR grew and new strategies were implemented to involve parents, community leaders, and the media, Kauffman recognized the need to conduct his philanthropy on a more businesslike basis. Up to this point, he had rather casually mixed company and foundation activities. STAR's staff was carried on the Marion payroll while other funds needed to implement the project were Kauffman's personal dollars paid through the foundation. In his dual capacity as Marion's chief financial officer and Kauffman's personal financial adviser, Mike Herman had become very interested in the foundation's potential and saw it as a possible second career. "I told Fred Lyons that my career path was such that I did not want to be the CEO or president of Marion. I'd really like to be involved with the foundation," Herman recalled.

Herman's interest in the foundation pleased Kauffman. The two men had developed a close and trusting relationship over the years so it was natural that Kauffman would welcome his involvement. With his financial expertise and his curiosity about using the foundation as an active problem-solver, Herman was an ideal choice to help Kauffman develop the vision and the structure for his philanthropy. From midwinter to early fall 1987, Herman worked feverishly to fulfill his huge responsibilities as Marion's chief financial officer and executive vice president while exploring myriad issues and a mass of details relating to the foundation. Kauffman had asked him to develop a series of recommendations for structuring the foundation to ensure the safety and growth of the assets, with special concern for a governance process, staff, and programs to carry on with Kauffman's interests and wishes after his death.

In mid-February, Herman wrote a memo to the files summing up a conversation with Kauffman that reflected the state of events and identified the important issues at the time. First, there was the question of selecting a CEO for the foundation. "[Kauffman] explained to me that he had discussed the situation with Fred Lyons," Herman wrote. "Fred expressed a desire to be CEO of the foundation and Mr. Kauffman advised Fred that he would like me to be the CEO of the foundation." In choosing Herman, Kauffman was not favoring one executive over another. He was simply identifying the person with the skills and talents most appropriate for the situation. Lyons had proven to be an extremely deft and adroit leader in a complex and sometimes chaotic business that pharmaceuticals had become.

He was a careful and thoughtful planner. And he had the discipline and patience to keep everyone in a large organization focused and moving toward a common goal. Knowing that Marion Laboratories would face challenges from generic competitors when the patents on CARAFATE and CARDIZEM expired, Kauffman believed Lyons was the most experienced executive to steer the company through those treacherous shoals ahead.

It was unlikely that Lyons would have been willing to relinquish his position at Marion Laboratories with the salary and perquisites involved to become the chief executive of Kauffman's private foundation. It seemed more plausible that he may have wanted to hold both positions concurrently. Herman wrote that he and Kauffman had had "a philosophical discussion about some of Fred's desires to be assured that the foundation [would] vote its stock to protect Marion." Kauffman immediately recognized the potential for conflict of interest and told Herman that "the Marion management should do a good job for the shareholders and the foundation should vote its stock accordingly."

In selecting Herman to lead the foundation, Kauffman had picked a man of eclectic talents and interests. He possessed a keen mind and a quick wit. He had a facile command of finances, a genuine curiosity about a wide range of social issues, and an enthusiasm for experimentation. He had also demonstrated a personal commitment to philanthropy by creating his own charitable fund within the Greater Kansas City Community Foundation. "Mr. Kauffman thought that Karen's and my interests in our own community foundation and Karen's and my individual interest in the foundation more fit with the position. Mr. Kauffman indicated that he had explained this to Fred and all went well."

Herman went on to outline the rest of their conversation in the memo. He had pressed Kauffman about the necessity of his being personally involved with the foundation for the next five to seven years. "I explained to him the awful burden of giving somebody a half a billion to a billion dollars to manage without having the founder set the tone and direction," Herman noted. Kauffman, the consummate delegator, seemed to be intent on giving Herman full responsibility and authority. "He expressed confidence in my ability to hire, train, and develop an organization to run such a large foundation." Kauffman's trust was complimentary, but Herman was determined to engage Kauffman fully in planning for the foundation, in determining its mission and its guidelines. Precisely how he would do that he had not yet resolved.

From Herman's memo, it was clear that Kauffman was still undecided about the foundation's programmatic direction. Although he was deeply and personally committed to substance-abuse prevention through STAR, he was still toying with ideas about using the foundation's resources to strengthen educational programs that could, in turn, benefit Marion Laboratories. He told Herman he was thinking about the possibility of putting more money into the foundation to explore improving pharmacy education. And he was contemplating how he might help Marion associates expand their opportunities for graduate training in business as well as health-related areas while still working full-time. Yet he was not ready to make a decision. He remained cautious, realizing that there were a broad range of issues yet to be explored. The enormous potential for "doing good" intrigued and excited him. At the same time, the magnitude of the responsibility of informed and effective philanthropy tempered his actions and caused him to reflect more deeply on the possible implications of his choices for the foundation's direction. Wisely, he permitted himself the flexibility of allowing his own thinking to mature.

Kauffman also gave Herman a copy of several sheets of handwritten notes with his ideas for the foundation. The older man was in the habit of jotting down his thoughts and ideas as they occurred to him. Linda Constantine, his assistant, kept those in a special foundation file so that he could review them from time to time as he formulated what he wanted to do. Those notes encompassed fundamental principles as well as administrative details. For example, he wrote, "No. 1 priority—PRINCIPLES OF MARION." He wanted the foundation to embody his philosophy of treating people right and sharing the rewards. Then he noted that the foundation should not award grants to colleges and universities that the staff or trustees had attended. He did not want the foundation's resources to be used to take care of board members' personal philanthropic responsibilities, and he was sensitive about appearances of conflict of interest. He had even thought about details such as limiting the CEO's discretionary authority to $250,000. This seemed to indicate he saw an active role for the foundation's board in allocating funds. In the same sheaf of notes he jotted a reminder that a school for entrepreneurship might be the way to teach what had been learned in building Marion into a successful company. He had always enjoyed counseling with entrepreneurs, and he wanted to find a way to continue creating jobs. All his compassionate impulses about funding social-action programs for young people were tempered with his understanding that there must be jobs available for them. Beyond those issues, the discussion between Herman and Kauffman had ranged over questions about the selection of trustees and the Kauffman family's future role in the foundation.

Herman tried to stimulate the discussion about the foundation while cautioning Kauffman not to transfer any more money until they could explore more fully the tax consequences. His first recommendation was that Kauffman establish a charitable remainder trust with the Ewing Marion Kauffman Foundation as the beneficiary. With this type of trust, the donor could put in appreciated assets, avoid capital gains, enjoy the income for his lifetime, and avoid inheritance taxes by leaving the corpus to a charitable foundation. The trust would also provide Kauffman with the additional advantage that the money could grow and compound tax-free. With the charitable remainder trust, there was no requirement that a certain percentage of the funds be disbursed annually as there would be if the funds were transferred to the foundation's endowment. This arrangement afforded Kauffman access to all the income he might want during his life. He had the luxury of time to plan and develop programs and staff for the day when the foundation would be required by law to distribute tens of millions of dollars each year.

In August 1987, Kauffman responded affirmatively to press rumors that he was "quietly building a charitable foundation that promises to be by far the largest in Kansas City and possibly among the largest in the nation." He said he had committed $600 million to the charitable remainder trust which could be worth as much as one billion dollars in five years. And he revealed that the foundation would ultimately be the beneficiary of one half of his personal net worth. "Most people don't know it," he said. "I haven't talked about it a lot." Then he announced that Mrs. Kauffman would have a separate foundation "that's going to be equal in size when she dies. It will be just as great or greater." The Muriel McBrien Kauffman Foundation would probably fund the arts, he said, while educational programs would be the main emphasis of the Ewing Marion Kauffman Foundation. "But not a dime for brick and mortar," he reminded the reporters. "I don't believe in that."

Kauffman closed the interview with the announcement that Marion executives were to head up the foundation and that a small, full-time staff would be recruited. Later that year, he named Mike Herman as the foundation's first president. His instructions to Herman were to look for areas where the executive talent of Marion Laboratories could be combined with the foundation's resources to develop solutions to societal problems. "The essence of our foundation [should be] to develop programs . . . that can be emulated and duplicated in other areas of the United States," Kauffman said. Herman, who had already been reading extensively and visiting various large foundations to study their operations, retained Waldemar Nielsen, a veteran foundation observer and scholar, to advise Kauffman and himself. Nielsen and Kauffman were near the same age and developed an immediate rapport which grew into a warm and trusting relationship. Nielsen, who had worked with many donors, counseled Kauffman to take a more active role in the foundation so that his philosophies and ideas could become firmly rooted as the organization matured.

Kauffman's satisfaction with the STAR program, coupled with Herman's and Nielsen's gentle prodding, spurred him to do more and more for young people. PROJECT CHOICE, his second major philanthropic initiative, grew out of his voluminous reading. "I got to studying about the dropout situation," he said. "When these students drop out, it hurts them in their future life. But above all, it hurts the business community. Five and ten years down the road, we will not have people who can do some of the complex jobs that are necessary." Kauffman recognized that the world had changed dramatically since he attended high school. Back then, a student who quit school before graduation could usually get a job in the manufacturing sector and work up to a decent livelihood over time. "But that is not true anymore," he concluded. "You must have more than a high school education to go to work [even in a factory], because of the computers and the other [sophisticated] machines they have."

As he studied the problem, he became convinced that students must be enticed to finish high school. The bait, he decided, would be the promise to pay the cost of college or vocational training. "He [had] a very simplistic answer to the problem," Herman recalled. "He said, 'Why don't we just offer kids [the means] to go to school? We'll pay for it and that will solve the problem.'" Given Kauffman's values and his strong work ethic, if anyone had offered him the chance to go to college when he was young, he would have jumped at the opportunity, Herman explained. "As it turned out," Herman said with the help of hindsight, "that was not the answer in the 1980s."

Once Kauffman had decided that offering the means to attend college was the solution to the dropout problem, he was anxious to set a program in motion. But instead of doing the kind of research that had preceded the STAR program, he told Herman to find a good person and "delegate down." Herman thought they already had the right person inside the Marion organization, Tom Rhone, a corporate recruiter. Rhone had been a teacher and a principal at Wyandotte High School in Kansas, with an ambition to become a school superintendent. "But [at that time] black people in Kansas couldn't get ahead," Herman said. "Tom was career blocked; that's why he came to Marion. . . . And as a recruiter, he couldn't go any further." Herman and Rhone had gotten to know one another socially on the golf course, so Herman began talking with him about Kauffman's "concept of taking a school and becoming involved." He asked Rhone what he thought of the notion, and he agreed that the idea had merit. Kauffman, after a brief conversation with Rhone about his ideas for a dropout program, asked him to accept responsibility for developing what would be called PROJECT CHOICE. Rhone was to flesh out the details and was instructed to focus on a high school with a demographic mix representative of Kansas City's inner core. He found it in Kauffman's own alma mater, Westport High School. "It was 60 percent black, 20 percent white, 18 percent Hispanic and 2 percent Asian; almost 90 percent were low economic status," Kauffman said. Once the school was identified, Kauffman was impatient to launch the new program. He began at once to press both Herman and Rhone to set a date to announce PROJECT CHOICE. "Because Mr. K was so anxious to get something done, we probably started . . . too soon," Herman admitted. "We didn't do the research that we've done now." Everyone became infected with Kauffman's enthusiasm and accepted the notion that the dropout problem could be easily solved. "It turned out it was not easy," Herman recalled.

When 240 Westport eighth graders and their teachers gathered in the school's auditorium on April 7, 1988, they were excited at the prospect of hearing the school's wealthiest and most famous alumnus—Mr. K, the Royals' owner. One of the teachers later told a reporter, "I knew when I saw that it was Marion Laboratories at the assembly that it had to be something big. In my fondest dreams or prayers, I never thought it would be this big." Kauffman got right to the point. He told the students he was there to offer each one the opportunity of a lifetime, something he was sure they had only dreamed of. "You, you, and every one of you," he said, "can go to college if you choose." He told the wide-eyed students how he had sat in the same seats where they were sitting over fifty years ago. "I look back and see the importance of education in my life. The world steps aside for a person who knows where he's going. That's what this program can do for you." And yes, there was a catch. The students and their parents must each sign an agreement promising to live up to Kauffman's requirements. He spelled out the rules: "Don't abuse alcohol, and if you do, you must accept rehabilitation under our direction and payment. Second, no drugs," he emphasized. "You and your parents must sign an agreement that we can randomly drug test you any time we wish. Third, avoid parenthood. Be a good citizen. Graduate from high school, and we [will] live up to our part of the signed agreement."

As rigid as the program's requirements may have seemed, it was significant that Kauffman was not limiting the offer to those who excelled academically. His goal was to encourage all students—of all abilities—to stay in school and graduate. "You don't have to be an A student. You don't even have to be a B student. You just have to graduate." In return, Kauffman promised the foundation would pay for tuition, fees, books, and reasonable room and board at a vocational or technical school in the Kansas City area. For those who wanted to go into higher education, he promised the same benefits at a college or university in Missouri, Kansas, or another institution in the United States at the foundation's option.

When a reporter asked Rhone for an estimate of how much such an endeavor might cost, he demurred. "We didn't put a budget together because there isn't any limitation on the aspirations of these students." But Herman and Kauffman had made an attempt to project future costs. Herman was convinced that, although financially it looked like a lot of dollars, minority graduates of inner city schools would attract college scholarships from a variety of sources. His concept was that Kauffman Foundation funds would be used primarily to give students the incentive to finish high school. Then some other source might help pay part or all of the cost of college or vocational training. Although Kauffman did not speak publicly about the leveraging effect of his contribution, he estimated that the foundation would spend one million dollars helping the eighth graders through high school. Those costs would involve small stipends to the students, plus fees for tutors and drug testing. He estimated the foundation's actual costs for postsecondary education for the first Westport class to be from one to three million dollars a year.

The response from students and parents was one of wonder. Stephanie Heldstab, who dreamed of being a veterinarian, rushed home to tell her mother the news. Peggy Heldstab was a single parent who knew she could not afford to send Stephanie to college. But when she saw the letter and brochure explaining PROJECT CHOICE, she was overjoyed. "I told her, 'That's your ticket, baby.' It's like a dream come true. Like Santa Claus."

The first year was difficult, as Kauffman and Rhone encountered every conceivable obstacle to a child's success, but they persisted. When a new problem would crop up, Kauffman looked upon it as a challenge and was involved in developing the strategy to deal with it. He was learning what every successful philanthropist learns sooner or later—that money alone will not solve a problem. He was also coming to realize that any effort focused on changing individual behavior usually takes longer than anticipated, is more complex than imagined, and costs more than initially budgeted. But because he was so committed to the solution and because he believed so fervently in the human potential of Westport students, he continued to give of himself and his resources.

Kauffman soon learned that the promise of a college education four years into the future would not magically transform an inner-city eighth grader into a focused and committed college-bound scholar. He had made the mistake of thinking that his background, a poor boy without the resources to complete college, was analogous to the situation of children who were poor and lived in Kansas City in the late 1980s. But the differences were dramatic. Kauffman's mother was a college graduate—an achievement that was rare for her time. He had learned the pleasures of reading and studying at an early age in his home. As a second grader he had experienced the thrill of competition in spelling bees and math contests. He had learned the value and dignity of work as he helped his father selling fish and eggs. While Kauffman sincerely believed that PROJECT CHOICE could effect a revolution in the lives of young people, he quickly recognized that evolution was a more realistic goal. As David Griffin, principal of Westport High School, summed up the situation, "I'm dealing with kids who don't know what it means" to be promised a free college education. "It's our responsibility to help them realize the meaning of PROJECT CHOICE."

The first challenge was to get the students to school every day, for the entire day. Just getting out of bed was a hurdle for students without alarm clocks or students whose parents left for work too early to ensure that their offspring were in school rather than in bed, or worse, out on the streets. To Kauffman, this seemed a soluble problem. He knew that people responded to incentives. So he offered fifty dollars to any student with perfect attendance for a semester. Each unexcused absence cost a student a ten-dollar deduction. At the end of the first semester, forty-five students collected fifty dollars each. Lesser amounts went to sixty-four others in PROJECT CHOICE. Kauffman recognized that the money was merely an enticement, a carrot to keep the students in class until they could experience the rewards that would come through accomplishment. One student admitted that while she liked having the extra fifty dollars, she had other reasons to get out of bed and off to school on time. "Mr. Kauffman is depending on us," Maria Lugo said. "I wanted to show him our gratitude. I felt like I owed him something. And PROJECT CHOICE keeps me away from trouble."

Once students were attending school on a regular basis, PROJECT CHOICE began to focus on performance. Drawing on what he had done with Marion Laboratories' associates, Kauffman knew it was important that the students be motivated and encouraged constantly. PROJECT CHOICE offered students an extra enrichment class every day, tutors were available for most subjects, and there was a special health class. When Tom Rhone discovered that most students in the program were reading significantly below grade level, Kauffman quickly agreed to fund a Saturday school to build basic skills.

Getting parents involved with their children's education proved to be the toughest hurdle. Kauffman was somewhat startled that many parents seemed lukewarm about their responsibilities once they had signed the initial contract. And when parental attendance at monthly meetings slid that first year from a high of seventy-one in October 1988 to thirty-six the following January, he was truly baffled. His own mother had been so involved with his schooling— finding time at night to help with homework after an exhausting day of cooking a cleaning for a houseful of boarders. It was difficult for him to comprehend how a parent could fail to help and encourage a child, especially with the promise of continued education if the child graduated. But as he began to understand the difficulties of single-parent households, language barriers, and the lack of transportation, he willingly supported additional funding to help address those problems as well. With additional money from the Kauffman Foundation, Principal Griffin began sending all school memos home in Spanish and English. Spanish translation was also available at all parents' meetings. And for those parents without transportation, PROJECT CHOICE paid for taxi rides to evening meetings. As attendance and active involvement among parents began to improve, Griffin proudly reported to Kauffman that one mother had commented, "Now I don't have an excuse" not to attend.

At the end of PROJECT CHOICE's initial year, Rhone said the results were mixed. The number of students suspended from school had dropped, but the number of days spent in suspension had increased. Grades had shown an overall improvement and the number of failing grades had declined, thanks to all the tutoring, enrichment activities, and special weekend and summer programs. Kauffman was proud of the progress despite the difficulties. He was especially pleased with PROJECT CHOICE's effect on drug use. "The most startling fact . . . is the attitude on the use of drugs," he said. "The first year out of 180 students there were very few, approximately five, who were found to have drugs in their system when they were randomly drug checked." From the very beginning, Kauffman had been insistent that an independent laboratory outside of Kansas City conduct the drug tests. Hoffmann–La Roche was selected, and they reported that one student was using cocaine

while the other four were using marijuana. The student using cocaine dropped from the program because his family was selling the
drug. But the other four students and their families asked for a second chance. "We gave it to them," Kauffman said, "but we said,
'from now on you will be checked every two weeks, and [there will
be] no more chances if you are found to have drugs in your system.'" What pleased Kauffman most was not merely the low inci-
dence of drug use, but the change in the students' attitude about
drug use. He boasted to the press, "It is now the cool thing *not* to
use drugs. They even made up buttons on their own in manual arts
training which say, 'I am legit,' meaning they are not on drugs."

At the end of PROJECT CHOICE's third year, the results of drug
testing were so dramatic that even Kauffman was skeptical. In 1991,
Rhone reported to Kauffman that the seven hundred students involved had been tested and only one was found to be using drugs.
Kauffman was astonished. "Tom, I can't believe that. It is not possible," he argued. "Take two hundred of them and check them all
over again." Once again, two hundred students, randomly selected
from among the PROJECT CHOICE participants, proved to be drug-
free. "Even President Bush didn't believe this until I told him how
many we had rechecked," Kauffman recalled with a big grin on his
face. "It illustrates a fact that if you give these students hope for the
future, if they know somebody cares for them, they will knuckle
down and give you a good job."

Kauffman was gratified by the positive results that began to come
through follow-up research on the program, and he loved to rattle
off the statistics about grade improvement and drug use. But what
truly moved him and bound him to the program were the personal
experiences with the young men and women in PROJECT CHOICE.
He loved to tell the story of walking through Westport one day
when a student came running up to him waving a paper. "Mr. K,
Mr. K, I got the first B of my life!" When Kauffman stopped to con-
gratulate the boy, he learned that the student had never dreamed of
scoring so high before, but was now eager to do even better. PROJ-
ECT CHOICE had a positive effect on parents as well. When the second Westport class was selected, parents of students who had been
in the program for a year offered to tell the parents of incoming students of their experiences. A single parent stood up and told the
others, "You are looking at somebody who was an alcoholic and was

on drugs, but fortunately was able to overcome it. But I had no hope for the future for my daughter until CHOICE gave it to us." Whenever he recounted that experience, Kauffman was always quick to point out that the daughter was not just getting by, she was making A's and B's.

Just as he knew the value of strolling through the Marion manufacturing plant to chat informally with associates, Kauffman also understood that an unexpected encouraging word to a struggling CHOICE student could be a powerful incentive for that young person to stick with the program. Rhone recalled that such an incident happened early in CHOICE's first year. One Saturday afternoon as he walked past Parkway Six Hundred, a popular restaurant on the Country Club Plaza, a familiar voice hailed him. "Hey, Mr. Scholarship, where's Mr. Kauffman?" Rhone immediately recognized Andre Ross, a CHOICE student who worked part-time at the restaurant. "Mr. K and I don't shop the Plaza together on Saturdays," Rhone responded. Ross, who was sweeping the sidewalk in anticipation of the lunch crowd, asked Rhone to "tell Mr. K that I'm working here. Tell him that I'm going to finish high school and I'm going to make him pay!"

The following Monday when Rhone met with Kauffman, he recounted the story. Both men were delighted that Ross was so determined to collect on the scholarship promise. Kauffman chuckled about the student's exuberance, and then the conversation turned to other matters. That afternoon, without telling Rhone of his intentions, Kauffman asked his driver to stop at the Plaza on the way to the Kansas City Club. As he stepped through the doorway at Parkway Six Hundred, he was instantly recognized. Thinking that he had come for lunch, both the owner and the hostess rush forward to welcome him. To their astonishment, Kauffman said he had come to see his friend, Andre Ross. Then he spotted Ross hard at work clearing tables and greeted him with an outstretched hand. He told Ross that Rhone had delivered the message that he was "going to make Kauffman pay." Young Ross was speechless. Had he said the wrong thing? Here was Ewing Kauffman—Mr. Baseball— coming to see him personally! For one agonizing moment, he thought perhaps Mr. Kauffman had been offended, then he realized that he had come to offer encouragement. The older man urged the younger man to work hard. "Be the best busboy down

here, learn as much as you can, and someday you may own a restaurant," Kauffman said, his entrepreneurial instincts coming to
the fore. And with that he departed for his afternoon swim and gin
game. As brief as the visit may have been, it helped to strengthen
and reinforce Andre Ross's resolve to complete high school and attend college. The fact that a man of Kauffman's stature and wealth—
with all the burdens of Marion Laboratories and the Kansas City
Royals on his shoulders—would take time to visit a CHOICE student at his job was not only an uncommon courtesy, it was a genuine expression of Kauffman's personal commitment to each student. That single visit would say more about how much he valued
each young person than all the speeches he might give. And it also
became a part of the folklore at Parkway Six Hundred. "The owner
speaks about it to this day," Rhone said.

But Kauffman's greatest satisfaction came from the personal thanks
he received from students. "Over at one of the high schools in Kansas,
they had three of the PROJECT CHOICE students make a speech of
thanks to me," he recalled, his blue eyes brimming with tears. "This
one young girl got up and she just couldn't say a word until she
turned to me and said, 'Mr. K, we love you.' And, of course, that re-
pays you for all that you have done, or will do in the future."

By the beginning of the 1990s, Kauffman was deeply committed to the work of the foundation. This was a chance to solve problems, to test ideas, to effect change. He enjoyed most seeing the transformation in young lives. When a young black boy or a Hispanic girl grasped the possibility that their life could be more productive and more challenging than they had ever dreamed and began to behave in ways that would help them achieve those new goals, Kauffman was overjoyed. He spent many hours with the STAR and PROJECT CHOICE directors and Mike Herman poring over program-evaluation data. He was constantly asking why certain outcomes differed from what they had anticipated, probing why certain assumptions were not valid. In all of this, Kauffman was impatient for change to occur. He was always pushing, always suggesting or approving new approaches or different strategies. Yet in spite of his eagerness to move forward, he was never intolerant of mistakes or resistant to modifying a program, if necessary. Herman described Kauffman's approach best when he said, "It was okay to fail. When we were not failing, we were not on the cutting edge. If we were not making mistakes, then we were not trying enough experiments and that's a belief. It was okay to fail here."

While Kauffman relished the good feelings he had about what the foundation was accomplishing, he insisted on accurate measurement tools and the absolute integrity of data. Just as he understood progressing though the pyramid of influence when preparing to introduce a new pharmaceutical product, he was learning there was a similar strategy for affecting social change. He recognized that the data on STAR and CHOICE would have to be of such quality that leading scholars and researchers would use and comment on them in influential journals. That information would then flow to the policy makers—the representatives, senators, and professionals—who formulate legislation and develop policy regulations and guidelines. He believed that a pilot project in Kansas City, properly funded, well administered, and impartially evaluated could influence national policy. Yet even while working toward such a grandiose goal, he never lost the simple, yet powerful, belief that public policy mattered only when it was used to transform an individual life for the better.

And as always, he was reading. Once his evenings at home had been devoted to new ideas for Marion Laboratories or innovations for the Baseball Academy. Now, he would settle down to study what other foundations were doing. During his morning office hours, he was talking with acknowledged experts in a number of areas that Wally Nielsen and his colleague, Siobhan Nicolau, introduced to him. In the evening following those conversations, he would pore over the same experts' articles and books, always thinking about how to improve and extend what the foundation was already doing.

The foundation's third and fourth program initiatives grew out of Kauffman's evening reading. Through Nielsen, he had became acquainted with the work among preschool children that Irving Harris, a Chicago philanthropist, had funded. "I was reading some information on research done in Chicago at the kindergarten level in one of the poverty areas which stated that forty-some percent of the five-year-olds coming to kindergarten—forty-some percent— didn't know their first and last names. They also could not differentiate colors. Well, that [information] plus the reading inability and the math inability of our freshman class [in PROJECT CHOICE] got me to thinking that maybe we were starting too late. We should start sooner," he decided. Kauffman immediately saw the dilemma. Children of low-income, inner-city families did not arrive at school with the basic skills necessary to learn and progress. But the school system assumed that a certain level of development had already taken place in the home. As a consequence, the child started formal education with disadvantages and usually fell farther behind each year. "We didn't think we could change the public school system quickly," Herman acknowledged. "But at least [we decided] we could intervene early."

PROJECT EARLY evolved from the experience and knowledge

gained in other Kauffman Foundation projects and was enriched with the expertise of national consultants. As with the other foundation programs, Kauffman urged Herman to hire a staff person to direct and oversee the development. This time Herman looked for talent beyond Marion Laboratories. His wife, Karen, an executive at the Oppenstein Brothers Foundation, had often spoken highly of Gerard "Jerry" Kitzi, the executive director of Adolescent Resources Corporation, a Kansas City social service agency. Herman thought talking with him would certainly be a place to start.

As it happened Kitzi had been trying for months to make contact with Herman. He wanted to request funding for a new health project at his agency. Even though he knew that the Kauffman Foundation was not a grant-making organization but chose to operate its own programs, he believed if he could just talk to Herman and Kauffman, he could persuade them to fund his agency's program. When Herman finally returned his calls, Kitzi thought he was responding to a concept paper on Health Tracks, the adolescent health program he wanted to implement. But halfway through the luncheon meeting with Herman and Carl Mitchell, a Marion executive who was helping Herman part-time at the foundation, Kitzi said he realized they weren't interested in health care. "There was a second agenda and it was looking at me."

Three months after the initial interview, Kitzi met Kauffman. "He wasn't what I thought he was going to be," Kitzi recalled. He had envisioned Kauffman as a "high-society kind of gentleman, not really concerned with the plight of the poor. Although [I thought] there was probably something in him saying 'I should do good.' But he was real. And I connected to him at that level. I said, 'Wow! I can work with this guy.'"

Kitzi recalled Kauffman telling him that while he was not disappointed with PROJECT CHOICE, "he had had an 'aha' [experience] with the program. The 'aha' was [that he] had started too late to make a difference in [many of] those kids' lives. He offered them tremendous incentives, but they were so far behind." Kauffman also confided that he felt getting the students in CHOICE "up to speed" was almost an overwhelming task. But he was committed to a comprehensive, collaborative approach to the problem. He had come to the realization that there was no simple answer, no silver bullet.

Kitzi accepted the job with PROJECT EARLY late in 1989, confident that he could easily implement Kauffman's vision for the program. But when he asked Kauffman, "What do you want me to do? What is your vision?" the answer shocked him. Kauffman replied, "I want kids to have the best start possible. You decide what it is." Kitzi could not believe what he was hearing. For the first month, he kept going back and forth with Kauffman and Herman trying to get them to spell out their wishes. "I kept . . . saying, 'What do you want?' They kept saying, 'We don't know. What do you want?'" Then it finally sunk in. He had been recruited to conceptualize, design, and implement the Kauffman Foundation's initiative to see that children were ready to learn when they started school. "I went berserk," he said, recalling those heady days. "I did all the things that I always wanted to do—systems, issues, agency-capacity issues—I finally had some resources! I put together a program that was way beyond what their agenda really was. But they trusted me and they supported it."

The program Kitzi designed to fit under the PROJECT EARLY rubric was far more complex and expensive than Kauffman had envisioned, but he backed it fully. Kauffman had grasped that a child's potential was shaped from conception by the quality of prenatal care the mother received. No less in importance were those early developmental experiences that gave a child basic motor skills and stimulated the natural curiosity to learn. What Kitzi was able to show him was that a mother who was struggling to find child care so she could work, or who was worried over paying the electric bill, could not focus fully on her child's growth and development. If Kauffman was to achieve the goal of helping prepare children so they would be ready to learn when they started school, the myriad problems of health care, day care, housing, job training, employment, and family-support services would all have to be addressed. PROJECT EARLY became a collaborative effort of government entities, social service agencies, the Kauffman Foundation, and the families themselves to work toward family self-sufficiency.

PROJECT ESSENTIAL, the Foundation's fourth undertaking related to children, grew out of a conversation between Leslie Teel, a psychologist at Marion Merrell Dow, and Mike Herman. During the Marion era, Teel reported to Herman on matters relating to business intelligence and strategic planning. When she learned that the Kauffman Foundation was beginning to work in the area of early childhood, she told Herman of her mother's work helping children build self-esteem. Sue Teel, Leslie's mother, was teaching at Pembroke Hill School, a Kansas City private school that attracted the children of the area's social, civic, and business leaders. She had developed a curriculum to teach the principles of self-esteem in grades K through third. It had been successful with those children, and Teel believed it would work with inner-city children too. "If [the foundation] is going to do early childhood, you need to know, or at least be aware about things like moral and ethical development, how schools are affecting kids and their self-esteem," Teel said. Herman became intrigued with the notion that the schools could provide a systematic approach to a child's moral development. He began reading the literature in the field and was soon aware of the sharp divisions among educators and scholars regarding the validity of self-esteem education.

In the late 1980s, the Kauffman Foundation was still housed at the Marion Merrell Dow corporate headquarters, so Teel would run into Herman quite often during the daily course of business. And each time she did, she would refer to some aspect of the self-esteem debate. As each conversation wound down she would find herself saying, "Now Mike, do take these things into account as you [and the foundation] go forward with your work." One day when he responded, "You come take them into account for us," she fired back, "I will pack my office in an hour." In his capacity as president of the Kauffman Foundation, Herman hired Teel to develop programming in the area of self-esteem, which she preferred to call "ethics, integrity, and moral development." She had hardly settled in her new surroundings when Herman appeared saying, "You have convinced me that there is a need for this kind of programming. Now, you convince Mr. K."

Although Teel had worked with senior management at Marion Laboratories and in the merged company as well, she had had very little interaction with Kauffman. She found the prospect of selling him on her ideas somewhat daunting. And the Marion Merrell Dow boardroom setting made it even more so. They began with several informational sessions. "I simply talked to him about these issues and what we were doing and what was possible," she recalled. At one point Kauffman, who had been listening patiently, interrupted. "Okay, I understand all this. [I understand] what you're trying to do, but how do you do it? How do you talk to a kindergartner about all this?" "You don't really want to know, do you?" Teel asked. "Yes, I really do," Kauffman replied firmly. For their next session, Teel arrived with all the materials used in the program. She had a basket filled with kindergarten puppets, song sheets, and the games used to teach abstract principles such as justice and compassion to five-year-olds. ". . . I was so embarrassed," she recalled. "I thought, 'I can't do this.' But we sat in the formal boardroom and we played kindergarten card games about responsibility. It was hysterical!" To no one's surprise, Kauffman, a.k.a. "Lucky," won. His endorsement was swift. As he departed for his afternoon gin game at the Kansas City Club, Kauffman gave Teel the thumbs-up signal and said, "Go for it." And PROJECT ESSENTIAL, a program to help children earn and maintain their self-esteem, was born.

As Kauffman's interest in children and their education became widely known, requests for financial help began to pour into the foundation. Although he believed that the foundation's appropriate role was developing and running its own programs, he occasionally agreed to participate in worthwhile efforts that were already under way. One such program was URBAN PARTNERS, which the Learning Exchange, a not-for-profit organization that shared educational strategies among Kansas City teaching professionals, had developed. When he became aware that the Learning Exchange was trying to launch a program to train principals in various management skills, he decided to participate. "[The school system] takes the best teachers and promotes them to principals, and they need additional training," he recalled. "They knew nothing about budgeting, about purchasing, about personnel work and finance, they knew nothing about performance appraisals." The Kauffman Foundation, in partnership with Marion Merrell Dow and Hallmark Cards, initiated URBAN PARTNERS to provide management training for school principals. Kauffman thought the program ideal for the company and the foundation: "It was the executive talent we added to it." When Hallmark was unable to furnish enough executives to conduct the training, "Marion Merrell Dow, with their egotism, which is well founded, said 'We can do it,'" he recalled.

To Kauffman's delight, the first class was over-subscribed by 300 percent, even though school districts had to pay 20 percent of the overall tuition for each of the principals attending. He also loved to recount the anecdote of the principal who told him more than a year after the program was over, "Mr. K, the chancellor of Kansas University is mad at you." When Kauffman said that could not be true, as he and Chancellor Gene Budig were close friends, the principal said, "No, not any more." It seemed that the principal had told Chancellor Budig that he had learned more in eighteen months in URBAN PARTNERS than he had in four years at Kansas University. With the foundation just as with Marion Laboratories or the Kansas City Royals, Kauffman wanted to be recognized as the best.

In the three years prior to 1990, the Kauffman Foundation changed from being primarily a checkbook for Kauffman's giving into a structured philanthropy which initiated and operated its own programs. There was some limited grant making, primarily to supporting activities that complemented the foundation's program initiatives. When Kauffman began to devote significantly more time and dollars to the foundation in 1987 there had been three directors, himself, Hughes, and Herman. That same year, Mrs. Kauffman, who had been a director of the joint Ewing and Muriel Kauffman Foundation, formed a separate philanthropic entity to pursue her interests in the arts and other cultural activities. The following summer, Kauffman asked Carl F. Bobkowski, a Marion executive who worked closely with Herman, to join the board. The foundation was growing rapidly as staff was being added and relationships were being forged with other philanthropies as well as with governmental agencies and not-for-profit organizations. Herman, who had left Marion laboratories in 1987 to devote full-time to the foundation, still had the responsibility of handling Kauffman's personal finances. He was also Mrs. Kauffman's financial adviser and assisted Kauffman with the Royals. The workload, the frenetic travel schedule, and the details of daily management began to take their toll. In April 1990, Herman unexpectedly announced he was relinquishing the presidency to spend more time with his family and to pursue some personal goals. But he agreed to continue as a foundation director and as chair of the finance committee which was responsible for the foundation's investment activities.

Kauffman named Robert Rogers, vice president for community affairs at Marion Laboratories, to the presidency. Rogers was the natural choice. He had worked closely with Herman at Marion and had been instrumental in the collaboration between the company, the foundation, and others in URBAN PARTNERS. In fact, it seemed as if much of his earlier life had prepared him for this challenge. Rogers, who had grown up in western Massachusetts, had experienced firsthand the crucial role a caring community can play in a child's development. His father died when he was only seven years old. His mother, a maternity nurse, suffered from a debilitating illness but worked when she was well enough. Rogers and his brother both began part-time jobs at an early age. And with social security payments, the young family managed to get by. Like many fatherless boys, Rogers could have easily gotten into trouble. But he credited the small town of West Springfield with making "sure little Bobby Rogers didn't go bad. If a young man or a child like myself was in trouble or in need, [that community] really jumped in and helped out," Rogers recalled. Having grown up with a web of supporting relationships—neighbors, scout leaders, YMCA counselors, Sunday school teachers, and parents of friends—Rogers looked for ways to repay that kindness and help.

"Because of my background, I've always had something inside me that says you really need to give something back. So all through my career I was always the one in the company that was known for being active in the community," he said. Rogers joined Marion Laboratories in 1975 as corporate comptroller. He advanced rapidly, but always found time for volunteer work with United Way, the Methodist church, and several other not-for-profit programs in Kansas City. In 1986, when he had his annual career review, he told Herman he wanted a different direction for his future. He was fifty years old and realized that he had accumulated sufficient wealth to permit him to think seriously about a career change where he could focus on his desire "to give more back." He said that by his fifty-fifth birthday, he wanted to begin spending more time involved with community service work for Marion Laboratories.

The following year he began to move toward that goal. He added the responsibility for community affairs to his portfolio as vice president for financial controls. Four years later when Herman stepped down, Kauffman immediately sent for Rogers. "I went in to see Mr. K and didn't have any idea what he wanted to talk to me about. He said, 'I want you to run the foundation.' I said, 'Okay.' Then he said, 'Don't you want to talk to [your wife] Kathy about it?' And I said, 'No.' It was just an absolute dream come true to be able to do that and Kathy would see it that way, too." When Kauffman asked if he wanted to know how much the job paid, Rogers responded, "That isn't important." "Good," Kauffman retorted, "then I won't pay you anything." "Of course, he later changed his mind on that," Rogers recalled. When *Ingram's* magazine ran a profile article on the four individuals who headed Kansas City foundations in 1990, they characterized the Kauffman Foundation's new president in the following way: "His public persona: Imagine Fred MacMurray as financier and philanthropist."

Later that year, when Carl Bobkowski left Marion Laboratories, he resigned from the foundation board. Kauffman immediately called Jim McGraw and told him he wanted him to become a member of the board. When McGraw said that he wanted time to talk the offer over with his wife Ann, Kauffman responded, "It's not an offer." Kauffman was concerned that persons who knew him well and understood his wishes for the foundation be on the board. "Jim, I'll need you more after I'm dead than while I'm alive," he said. "While I'm alive, I'm going to run it." Shortly after joining the board, McGraw participated in a session to review the foundation's bylaws. A lively debate ensued over term limits for directors. Nielsen had counseled Kauffman to set time limits on a director's service. "He had advised Kauffman that sometimes when the founder is gone, the board members just run it for their own benefit," McGraw recalled. "And therefore, you've got to get rid of the scoundrels." McGraw objected on the grounds that term limits were inconsistent with Kauffman's intent. "You want us on the board now so that when you're gone we can carry on your traditions," he reminded Kauffman. Term limits would impede continuity, McGraw argued forcefully, not promote it. He raised the issue three times in the same meeting, before Kauffman finally saw the illogic of his own position and concurred. "And so, we changed the bylaws of the Kauffman Foundation. Mr. K affectionately referred to it as the 'McGraw Amendment.'"

Kauffman wanted McGraw on the foundation board not just to see that the founder's wishes were carried out. He had confidence in McGraw's judgment and believed that when the need for change in the foundation's policy arose, as it surely would at some future time, McGraw would see that the spirit of Kauffman's philosophy was preserved. Adding McGraw to the board also signaled that

Kauffman was preparing to move the foundation aggressively in a new direction—a direction where his experience, intelligence, and judgment would prove most helpful. From the earliest time that Kauffman began to write down his thoughts and ideas about the foundation, he consistently noted an interest in some aspect of entrepreneurship. Even as he began to fund substance-abuse awareness and to offer postsecondary education to those who completed high school, he was always conscious of the need to create more jobs and better paying jobs for those young people as they prepared to enter the workforce. He also wanted to institutionalize his concept of "principle-centered leadership" with young entrepreneurs because he genuinely believed that what had been done at Marion Laboratories would work in any business environment, large or small. His initial ideas ranged from funding a visiting university professorship to establishing a school of entrepreneurship where the Marion principles of treating people fairly and sharing the rewards would be the cornerstone of the curriculum. By 1990, he was satisfied that the foundation's programs relating to young people and education were sufficiently well established that it was time to begin the research on what was being done nationally with entrepreneurs.

Kauffman's desire for a program for entrepreneurs had deep roots in his experience in the pharmaceutical business. "Mr. Kauffman had always enjoyed helping entrepreneurs," Michie Slaughter recalled. "When entrepreneurs from the community would call [for advice], he'd find a way to make time for them in his schedule. And if they were wise enough to try what he suggested and come back and tell him how it worked, he'd make more time for them." Depending on the nature of the particular problem, Kauffman often involved various Marion executives in working with these entrepreneurs. "Because Mr. K had a reputation of being a great motivator, a great compensation person, and a great organization person, a lot of times that meant [he would] call me," Slaughter said. Slaughter welcomed the break from routine, and he liked learning about other businesses. "And it was a little bit of my way of giving something back, too." Slaughter decided to retire from Marion Merrell Dow in December 1989. On his last day, he went to pay his respects to Kauffman. The older man asked what he planned "to do" since he was only forty-eight. Slaughter replied that he was sure he could stay busy learning to operate his boat in the ocean, learning to play golf, and reading for pleasure. "But what are you going to do when you get tired of doing that?" Kauffman persisted. Unwilling to accept the notion that such an intelligent and vigorous young man would not tire of even constructive leisure, Kauffman urged Slaughter to "find a way to help entrepreneurs." When Slaughter asked if Kauffman had given any thought to involving the foundation in such activities, he replied that Mike Herman had suggested that might be an appropriate program for the board to consider. But before he could pursue that thought, Kauffman moved on to another subject.

A few months after his retirement to Savannah, Georgia, Slaughter got a call from Bob Rogers asking for his thoughts on the possibility of the foundation's undertaking a program to help entrepreneurs. Slaughter believed the notion was viable and consistent with Kauffman's overall philosophy for the foundation. So he agreed to do a feasibility study, which concluded, "This is a golden opportunity!" He envisioned a program to help entrepreneurs "that would fit very nicely with the overall focus of the foundation." His reasoning was straightforward. The youth-development programs— STAR, CHOICE, ESSENTIAL, and EARLY—aimed to produce better educated, motivated young people. But, if those young people found there were no jobs available to them, then the investment would have been wasted. "All we [will do] is to create a more sophisticated but a more highly frustrated part of the population. We've got to do something to help encourage the creation of jobs."

When the Kauffman Foundation board met that fall for their strategic-planning session, Slaughter presented the feasibility study and recommended further exploration of the idea of an entrepreneurial program. Rather than risk duplicating programs already under way, the board authorized a study team to identify everything being done in the field of teaching entrepreneurism. Stephen Roling, former publisher of the *Kansas City Business Journal,* coordinated the research effort with active participation from an advisory group that included Kauffman, Rogers, Herman, McGraw, and Slaughter, several well-known Kansas City executives, Paul Henson and Bert Berkley, and Professor Jeffry A. Timmons of Babson College and the Harvard Business School. The team conducted more than 250 interviews, observed scores of business incubators, and personally visited more than fifty research parks, university programs, and foundations involved in entrepreneurial efforts.

Their report identified several areas of opportunity where the foundation might productively direct its resources: training for existing entrepreneurs; sponsoring undergraduate education and applied academic research; supporting business incubators and technical park operations; and becoming involved in venture capital networks. Even though the study team felt confident of its work, they decided to invite a dozen of the best people from those interviewed to ask them to react to the identified areas of opportunity. They received the following challenge: "Come to Florida prepared to tell us how you think we should do it and—come prepared to tell us how you would spend twenty-five million a year if you had it."

The conference was creative and productive. Although ill health prevented Kauffman attending, he was pleased with the outcome. The experts blessed the concept. However, all were in agreement that there was one major gap. "We don't see you doing anything to address the needs and opportunities to teach entrepreneurism to kids in the K-through-twelve school system," they said. Several in the group of twelve conferees were college educators, but they stressed that waiting until college was too late. "[The students have] already formed attitudes and opinions. They've missed the opportunity to learn about entrepreneurial experiences." With that addition to their projected plans, the study team recommended that the Kauffman Foundation board create a Center for Entrepreneurial Leadership which Michie Slaughter would head.

Kauffman was delighted with the board's enthusiastic support for the Center for Entrepreneurial Leadership. For more than a year, he had been talking about the idea at every opportunity. He told an interviewer in 1991, "You can call it egotism or you can also call it knowing that you are good. We believe that we can establish an institute for entrepreneurism and pass on . . . some of the philosophies, principles, techniques, and leadership tactics that will enable new entrepreneurs to be successful." But his enthusiasm was tempered with concern about the costs and the long lead time for program development. Rogers recalled that Kauffman had initially balked at the conference idea because of escalating expenses. "Mr. K [was] very, very concerned about how much you spend to do what you're doing. He want[ed] every nickel to go to the ultimate recipient of the services," Rogers remembered. "Sometimes he was just so frugal that he didn't allow you the resources you needed. What I would say is sometimes he's looking at the floor for pennies when there are ten-dollar bills hanging from the ceiling." Kauffman had not agreed with Rogers's decision to host the conference at Florida's elegant and expensive Boca Raton Beach Club. But Rogers argued that it was the perfect setting to lure busy entrepreneurs from other pursuits—especially in early January. In lieu of paying the participants an honorarium, Rogers had offered to make a grant of $2,500 to the entrepreneur's charity of choice. "Mr. K was very much against that. He really chewed me out when I told him we had done it. He asked, 'Why did you have to make those grants?' He didn't see that as part of active philanthropy." The staff and consultant expenses for the entire research phase and the conference, plus the twelve grants, totaled $108,000. This was considerably less than the research costs to develop STAR and EARLY, but Kauffman remained concerned nothing had yet been spent to benefit fledgling entre-preneurs.

While he later acknowledged that PROJECT CHOICE might have been less costly in the long run had more time and money been spent at the conceptual stage, he was always impatient to launch an effort that would channel services and financial resources to the targeted population as quickly as possible. And his early habits of frugality were difficult to overcome regardless of how large the foundation's assets might be. Giving money away thoughtfully and intelligently would be for him as great, if not a greater, challenge, than earning it. "It's just [an example] of the way he looked at things." Rogers commented. "We were constantly struggling to get him to see the value that is added by the expenditure as opposed to the amount." Although Kauffman was uncomfortable with the expenses involved in developing the entrepreneurial program, he finally consented. Rogers acknowledged that because of Kauffman's tight fist and his wary eye toward expenditures, he often had to struggle over what seemed like minor dollars. "But he would eventually approve it. You know, I can only remember him turning us down once for something we recommended."

In announcing the establishment of the Center for Entrepreneurial Leadership within the foundation in March 1992, Kauffman was quick to point out that the center would train entrepreneurs, develop awareness, contribute to curriculum development, and foster strategic relationships within the national entrepreneurial networks. But it would not finance individual entrepreneurs. "We cannot finance everybody who wants to get into business," he cautioned. "But we have the capability of guiding them to the point where they can get seed money." To underscore his commitment and enthusiasm for the program, he announced that he was willing to see up to one half of the foundation's estimated annual income of fifty million dollars devoted to these activities.

The public response was staggering. The day the new center was announced, so many calls flooded into the foundation that the telephone system was overloaded. Then when a record winter snowstorm snarled traffic and virtually paralyzed Kansas City, more than seven hundred people crowded into the Allis Hotel ballroom to hear Kauffman and to learn more about the program. Although few knew it at the time, this would be one of Kauffman's last public appearances. He was suffering from bone cancer and his arthritic knees made each step very painful. Slaughter had worked out the shortest route from the car to the stage where he would speak. Kauffman refused a wheelchair, determined to make it on his own strength. The route led straight through the hotel kitchen, where every busboy, cook, waiter, and dishwasher wanted to shake his hand and talk about the Royals' season. He responded to them all as if he had time to spare and was still a vigorous executive on his way to a luncheon engagement. By the time he reached the backstage area, he was clearly exhausted. He rested for a minute, drank a cup of strong black coffee, then prepared to mount the steps up to the stage. Slaughter described the scene. "He was obviously in pain. He grabbed the rail and he got up, crawled up to the top of the stairs. He got up to the top of the stairs and Raymond Smilor, the center's vice president, introduced him. He [took a deep breath], straightened up, smile on his face, marched smartly out to the podium, grabbed onto the podium, and did eighteen minutes of enthusiastic, high-energy speech. [It was a] great reception, great applause. They enjoyed him; he enjoyed them. [It was] a really great moment. Then he turned, walked back over the same way. He go to the stairs right behind where the curtain was, and it was all he could do [to make it down]." Slaughter mused that he must have heard that speech a hundred times during his career at Marion, but he had never heard it given so well or with such conviction. After that inaugural event, Slaughter admitted saying, "I don't care what happens after this. I have fulfilled my first obligation to him which was to get the center up and running so that he could participate and enjoy it before he died." A veteran foundation executive taking note of the significant national as well as local response to the Center for Entrepreneurial Leadership predicted that it would be this initiative, above all the other programs, that would lift the Kauffman Foundation to national prominence in the philanthropic world.

As winter lingered after the official start of spring, Kauffman was preoccupied with succession plans for the foundation. In fact, planning for the Foundation's future leadership had been going on from the time he asked Rogers to accept the presidency. "Part of that plan was bringing in Lou Smith." Rogers said. "When I became president, Mr. K asked me to name someone who would work well with me when he was no longer around. So that's how we got Lou." Rogers also secured Charlie Hughes's agreement to serve beyond Kauffman's death to ensure continuity with the donor's wishes.

As he pondered the future, Kauffman decided it would be prudent to strengthen the foundation board by adding several individuals with extensive experience in the philanthropic world. He asked the directors to elect the distinguished author and his personal foundation consultant, Waldemar Nielsen, and John Gardner, former United States secretary of Health, Education, and Welfare and founder of both Common Cause and the Independent Sector, to the board. Edward A. Smith, Kauffman's personal attorney and the senior partner at Smith, Gill, Fisher & Butts, was also named to the board. Kauffman believed these men with a combined wealth of wide-ranging experience as trustees and participants in the not-for-profit arena could serve as colleagues and mentors to nurture and support his Marion colleagues. It was a thoughtful blending of age and experience, intellect and temperament; of enthusiasm, ambition, candor, and creativity. Each trustee brought a record of achievement in his chosen field to the table. Each respected the other. Kauffman had selected each of them, he said, "Because they are of good character and they have compassion for others." Together they shared an almost reverential commitment to be true to the principles Kauffman had exemplified in the business world, in the sports arena, and now in philanthropy: Treat others as you want to be treated, share the rewards, and give back to the community. It would be the board's task, after Kauffman's death, to be faithful to his principles and careful stewards of his legacy.

Epilogue

Nineteen ninety-three was to be the final year of Ewing Kauffman's life; in many respects, it was one of the busiest and most constructive. His health had been gradually deteriorating, and after the New Year he suddenly seemed shrunken and frail. Early that year he began to limit his activities more so he could rest. He was often querulous and sometimes seemed suspicious that he was in danger of "being used." When a distinguished national service organization that planned to honor him learned he would not be able to attend their evening function but would ask Mrs. Kauffman to represent him and speak on his behalf, they awkwardly withdrew the invitation. "They said that under those circumstances, they would keep my name on the pile and maybe later on I could get it. They wanted to use me as a draw for a fund-raiser!" he said with obvious pique. He also declined several honorary degrees that spring as well, recalling that Malcom Forbes "was crazy about honorary degrees. But after I had two, I understood why they were offering them. After the degree, they always come back for more. It really irritates you."

Whenever possible, he tried to follow the old schedule. He spent a few hours at his Marion Merrell Dow office each morning keeping appointments and answering correspondence with Linda Constantine. The afternoons he still reserved for the Kansas City Club. More than ever, he seemed to take special comfort and pleasure in the companionship of those old friends who gathered there each weekday. Herk Robinson telephoned him regularly to keep him current on developments with the ball club, and he still tried to attend home games. But often, if the Royals were not playing well or if he was especially weary, he might slip away early. George Brett recalled the sense of sadness he felt out on the field when he would look up and see that Kauffman's box had gone dark early.

But as his physical stamina waned, his mental vigor did not. He and Mike Herman continued working with a battery of attorneys and tax specialists to refine the details of the Royals' succession plan which was announced that spring. And although he had less daily interaction with foundation associates after they moved from Marion Merrell Dow's Ward Parkway headquarters to a building on Oak Street, he conferred regularly with Bob Rogers. He wanted to be certain that the transition from donor directed to board-guided philanthropy would be as seamless and as orderly as possible.

That winter the dream of a permanent effort to stimulate entrepreneurship through the foundation became a functioning reality. The Center for Entrepreneurial Leadership had evolved from a concept in the planning stage into a series of programs and relationships to encourage entrepreneurship at all levels, from the corporate boardroom to the kindergarten classroom. There were several occasions that winter and spring when he shared his ideas about leadership and motivation with young entrepreneurs. And even though those sessions left him exhausted for days afterward, he seemed to rise to each occasion with a vitality of spirit and a resonance of voice typical of his earlier years.

Nineteen ninety-three was also a year of reflection, assessment, and evaluation at the foundation. Just as he faced the prospect of what his death would mean for the Royals, Kauffman was equally sanguine about the consequences for the foundation. He knew the inevitable day was coming when the assets from the estate would flow into the foundation's coffers. And he feared that the task of having to distribute annually the tens of millions that the law would require could engulf and overwhelm the organization. The Ewing Marion Kauffman Foundation had been structured initially as an operating foundation because that had suited Kauffman's personal style of philanthropy. "I saw throwing money at a social problem [was] not the answer," he recalled. "You need to do more. Knowing of the tremendous amount of executive talent that we had in our company, I came to the conclusion that we could take our own money, add to it our executive talent, and run the operation ourselves . . . We had confidence that we could do it better." Operating its own programs, the foundation had expenditures during fiscal year 1992 of $12,300,000. But faced with the likelihood of a distribution requirement of up to fifty million dollars within a few years, it seemed probable that the foundation would have to become a major grant-maker.

Kauffman realized it would be impossible to staff and operate programs internally that would use funds of that magnitude in a prudent and effective manner. He urged the foundation directors and executive staff to begin to develop a grant-making strategy for the future. At Mr. K's direction, Bob Rogers convened a small group of associates and board members to talk to over 150 thought leaders in Kansas City and throughout the nation to help the foundation determine its new direction. The programs Kauffman started in the early years—STAR, CHOICE, ESSENTIAL, EARLY—were all successful, but based upon input from these experts he agreed that it was now time to change the foundation's funding strategies. He also sanctioned the board's decision to change the foundation's vision to "self-sufficient people in healthy communities." The original vision—"to bring about social and economic changes in America that will stimulate the development of youth and the free enterprise system"—would become an important strategic objective and there would be multiple strategies designed to implement the new vision. Where it had once created and staffed its own initiatives, the foundation would begin to seek partnerships and collaborative efforts with others—both grant-makers and grant-seekers—having similar interests. And Kauffman recognized, somewhat reluctantly, that it was also time to look beyond the Kansas City area for alliances and opportunities to shape the public agenda on issues that the foundation wanted to affect. Just as he had relinquished control to permit Marion Laboratories to mature and flourish, he was beginning to do the same with the foundation. Like the navigator who takes the sightings at twilight, he had determined it was time to adjust the course to avoid the shoals. And although he would not live to see the changes he had set in motion, he had the knowledge that they had begun on his last watch.

In early May, Kauffman received troubling news. Fred Lyons advised him that Marion Merrell Dow intended "to shrink the company to fit its reduced economic prospects." That meant layoffs, a hiring freeze, no bonuses, and cuts in executive compensation. Kauffman had, of course, been aware of the 20 percent decline in sales and the 56 percent plunge in profits reported at the end of the first quarter. But Lyons's latest news hit him with the force of a body blow. Throughout his thirty-nine years at the helm of Marion Laboratories, he had been spared such drastic action. Even during the most difficult days of the late 1970s, he had managed to retain all the associates through strategies like reduced workweeks, leave without pay, and not filling vacancies. Lyons and Kauffman had experienced those hard times together, so he knew that the action Lyons proposed was, in his best judgment, the only recourse. After Lyons returned to his own office, Susan Hidalgo, who was sharing secretarial duties with Linda Constantine, recalled that Kauffman told her he was not feeling well. His face looked drawn and ashen; he suddenly seemed very fragile and very old. He asked her to hold his calls. Then he closed the office door and lay down for several hours. Later that day he kept an appointment with his doctor, as he had been suffering recently with pain in his back. Within days the diagnosis confirmed that he had cancer of the vertebrae. Radiation therapy was ordered to help alleviate the pain, but the prognosis was that he probably could not live a year. At best, he could expect to live another six to nine months.

Kauffman had talked publicly about "the event," and "kicking the bucket" on many occasions over the last several years as he worked on succession plans for the ball club and the foundation. He was not afraid of death and he thought it unwise to try to deny the gravity of his condition. As Kansas City's most popular and beloved figure, he knew that as he appeared less and less in public that rumors and speculation would fill the press. He decided to acknowledge the inevitable so that everyone affected by his death could continue the preparations and planning that he had set in motion. He told his wife and his closest friends that he did not want "people praying over me" and weeping. He had never indulged in self-pity and he did not want others' pity. He seemed sad, but he was not morose. More than anything, he seemed so very tired. He wanted to rest, to be peaceful, to sleep, if possible, to escape the persistent pain.

During the last two months of his life, Kauffman continued to think of others. Several years earlier, he had drawn up specific instructions for his funeral service and burial at Marion Park. Both were to be private, simple, and brief. If he were to die on a game day or a regular workday, he wanted the Royals to play baseball.

And it "should be business as usual" at Marion Merrell Dow. He reviewed those plans now with trusted associates to reassure everyone about his wishes. On days when the pain eased a bit and his strength permitted, he answered correspondence, especially from old friends and colleagues and potential philanthropists who sought his counsel. Two weeks before his death, he reviewed the first seven chapters of his biography. He corrected several factual errors and dictated an extensive response to a number of the biographer's questions. At the end of the tape, his voice nearly extinguished by exhaustion, he promised "to help you more when I feel a bit better."

As former Marion associates learned of his illness, they began to write and telephone him to express their concern and affection. Jim McGraw wrote on the Fourth of July telling him that along with his father and Ray Brewster, an early mentor, Kauffman had been one of three men to have a major impact on his life. "You gave me an opportunity to put my skills to good use," he wrote in thanks. "You have a very special place in our lives—one that both [Ann and I] will long remember and savor." On July 8, Kauffman replied, "One of the positives that I am experiencing is hearing from old friends like you." The letter was typewritten and signed, "Mr. K." Then below the signature, in a firm and distinctive hand, Kauffman wrote, "Quit writing such poignant letters—you make me cry!!!" On July 10, McGraw telephoned. When they had finished their chat, Kauffman asked to speak to Ann McGraw. When her husband responded that she was in Kansas City to celebrate their daughter's fortieth birthday, Kauffman asked for the telephone number so he might join the well-wishers. Later that day, McGraw called his wife to ask if she had talked with Kauffman. Ann replied that he had not called. Then she noticed the light flashing on the answering machine. He had called, but they failed to hear the ring over the noisy party conversation. Kauffman had left a thoughtful message to both mother and daughter which they played over and over that evening for all the guests. "That's just the way he was," McGraw recalled. "Here he was, racked in pain, but yet he's thinking, 'Well, I can pick up the telephone and impact somebody's life.' That was the last time I spoke to him."

David Cone, a Royals' pitcher, had a similar experience to McGraw's which he related after learning he had been chosen for the 1994 All-Star game. In 1992, Kauffman had signed Cone as a free agent to a three-year, eighteen-million-dollar contract. The Royals' management had high hopes for the young pitcher, but his first year in Kansas City was a near disaster. Regardless of how hard he tried, Cone could not pitch a winning game. Midway into that dismal season, Cone got a telephone call at home from Kauffman. "He called when I was 0–5 and reassured me that they still wanted me," Cone told reporters. "He told me they weren't regretting the move. In his state of health . . . to call and know what I was going through . . . and giving me a boost, it was something I'll never forget."

Kauffman died peacefully in his sleep at home during the early morning hours on Sunday, August 1, 1993. At 1:28 P.M., following the national anthem, his death was announced at Kauffman Stadium. Most in the crowd of nearly twenty-three thousand had heard the news earlier that morning or on the radio driving to the ballpark. They all stood silently, respectfully. The only sounds came from six championship flags flapping at half staff, and from the fountains splashing near the scoreboard. Then the announcer spoke again, "And now, as Mr. K would wish, let's all sit back and enjoy the game." The following day, Marion Merrell Dow associates went quietly about their routine work as Kauffman had requested they do. Many had come to the company following the merger in 1989 and had not known Kauffman personally. But they had all experienced the benefit of his philosophies of "treating people right" and "sharing the rewards." His death was a time of genuine sadness for them all. "Mr. K and the associates of this company had a very unique relationship, one that is different from anything I have seen in industry," Fred Lyons noted in his public remarks. And at the foundation, most of the 120 associates gathered early Monday morning to share their sorrow. A number of Kauffman's closest colleagues from the Marion days were with the foundation, either as staff or on the board, and their grief was very personal. But Bob Rogers, who had worked with Kauffman for almost two decades, put matters in perspective when he noted that in the midst of a great sadness, "there was a lot of relief that Mr. Kauffman was no longer in pain."

As he had requested, the funeral and burial on August 4 were private. His old friend, the Reverend Robert Meneilly, the pastor of Village Presbyterian Church in Prairie Village, conducted the services. Meneilly had performed Kauffman's wedding in the same church more than three decades earlier when he and Muriel were married. There were only a few flower arrangements in the church because Mrs. Kauffman had suggested that those who wanted to honor her husband could do so most appropriately by helping support his work through the Ewing Marion Kauffman Foundation. "He wanted no voluminous eulogies. He wanted no tears and no regrets," Meneilly said. Julia Power, Kauffman's oldest grandchild, read from the brief college-entrance essay she had written in 1985 about how her grandfather had influenced her life. At the conclusion of the service, while the casket was being taken from the church, the organist played "Take Me Out to the Ball Game." Many who attended the funeral recalled smiling and feeling comforted as they made their way to the burial.

Although Kauffman's death had been expected, there was a profound sense of loss throughout the region. Joe McGuff wrote that "not since the death of Harry Truman has Kansas City responded so emotionally to the loss of a citizen." There were hundreds of letters and cards of condolence to the family from the great and near great, from baseball fans, stadium concessionaires, old friends, participants in STAR and CHOICE, and parents whose children he had helped. One letter which seemed to capture so much about Kauffman was from Les Wilson of Lee's Summit, Missouri. Years before as a young Internal Revenue Service agent, Wilson had been assigned to examine Marion Laboratories' and Kauffman's personal tax returns. When he arrived, company officials agreed he could use Kauffman's personal office, as the owner was scheduled to be away for several days. Then about three o'clock in the afternoon, Kauffman returned unexpectedly. Finding the young agent working in his office, Kauffman said, "'Les, I am pretty tired. Would you mind if I lay down here on the couch to take a nap? I have a speech to give at seven o'clock tonight.'" The agent was incredulous. "Can you imagine that this man that owned the company—and a little Internal Revenue agent sitting in his office—would ask [the agent's] permission to use his own office? It certainly never happened to me again in my thirty-three-year career." That incident captured Ewing Kauffman—and virtually everyone who ever met him had a story to relate about the special nature of an encounter. As Reverend Meneilly so gracefully phrased it, "He has not been one in a million, he has been one of a kind."

Less than two years after Kauffman's death, Muriel entered the Mayo Clinic in Rochester, Minnesota, for treatment of jaundice which she believed she had picked up during a European trip. Physicians at Mayo determined she had a pancreatic tumor and operated immediately. The tumor was malignant, but the doctors reported they believed they had removed all the cancer. On Thursday, March 16, the fourth day after the surgery, Mike Herman and Lou Smith, who was about to assume the position as chief operating officer at the Ewing Marion Kauffman Foundation, visited her. Herman said she was a "chatterbox," asking about the new turf at Kauffman Stadium and saying she planned to attend the Royals' home opening game on April 7. But on Friday, her condition worsened and she died that evening. The following week she was buried next to her husband on the grounds of Marion Merrell Dow.

Friends and family who gathered to mourn Muriel Kauffman spoke of her zest for living, her panache, her generosity, and her love of blue. Muriel had been a devoted supporter of the performing arts, education, and research and prevention related to health-care issues in the Kansas City area. Herman noted that the Muriel McBrien Kauffman Foundation would have roughly $225 million to continue her work.

The Reverend Robert Meneilly, who had presided over Ewing Kauffman's funeral, performed that task again for Muriel. "What she added to Ewing Kauffman's talents made them a unique team," Meneilly said. "Think of this, that today and for years and years to come a host of people will enjoy a better life because of the Kauffmans' contributions."

Within two months of Muriel Kauffman's burial, two other significant events occurred. On May 3, 1995 the *Star*'s front page announced that the Internal Revenue Service had finally approved Kauffman's complex plan designed to help keep professional baseball in Kansas City. Two days later, the lead story spelled out the details of Marion Merrell Dow's agreement to be acquired by Germany's Hoechst AG—a merger that would create the world's third-largest pharmaceutical company.

After two years in limbo over the ownership issue and a devastating strike which ruptured the national baseball season, the Kansas City Royals could finally proceed with the carefully crafted plan Kauffman had revealed just three months before his death. "I'm not sure anybody in the grave has tried to save a ball club before," Jonathan Rand wrote in his sports column in the *Star* the day the IRS ruling was made public. While no one was sure that such a post-humous feat had ever been attempted, Kauffman's admirers were not the least surprised that he had tried—and hoped for success.

The Internal Revenue Service's twenty-seven-page private letter ruling basically agreed that the gift of the team to the Greater Kansas City Community Foundation and Affiliated Trusts was a tax-deduct-ible donation for the Kauffman estate. Pending approval by the other major league team owners, the Royals could actively begin their search for a buyer who would agree to keep the team in Kansas City.

The news about the ball club brought a sense of relief, but the an-nouncement of a merger with a German pharmaceutical house un-derstandably created some anxiety in the local business community. Questions about the fate of the Kansas City headquarters location and fears about possible job losses were inevitable, given the enor-mous changes taking place in the pharmaceutical industry globally. Yet this merger, like the earlier one in 1989, was an alliance combin-ing Marion's outstanding sales and marketing network with Hoechst's product stream that needed outlets in the U.S. market. Financial analysts all along Wall Street concurred that with the acquisition, both companies should be considerably revitalized and strength-ened for the future. Kauffman, who had used his own middle name to disguise the fact that Marion Laboratories was just a one-man operation in his basement, had left a permanent legacy—as an en-trepreneur, sportsman, and philanthropist—that would not soon be equaled.

Individuals Interviewed

Although there were very few primary documents available as early company records had been lost in a flood in 1961 and later ones were restricted following Marion Laboratories' merger with Dow Chemical, a great many of Kauffman's business associates as well as family and friends were eager to help. Hours and hours of interviews formed the core of my research. These interviews were then supplemented with more than seven thousand newspaper clippings.

James H. Barickman
George Bernard
George Brett
Linda Constantine
Thomas R. Cooper
Calvin Cormack
Brant Cotterman
Charles V. (Bud) Dahner
Michael Duckett
Lester L. Duncan
Avron Fogelman
James Gardner
Rosemary Godbout
Stuart Gold
Ann Grinham
Lloyd Hanahan
Barnett Helzberg
Michael E. Herman
Dudley Hudgins

Charles L. Hughes
Byron Jennings
Ruth Kauffman Jianas
Julia Irene Kauffman
Larry A. Kauffman
Muriel McBrien Kauffman
Marion Sue Kauffman
Mike Kirby
Gerard Kitzi
Don Ludwig
Fred W. Lyons Jr.
Wallace G. McDowell
James E. McGraw
Michael E. Mahoney
Kit Truex-Mair
Al Maninno
Lowell Miller
Carl Mitchell
Waldemar A. Nielsen

Helen Pruitt
Robert F. Pruitt
Leslie S. Teel
Thomas Rhone
Nat Robertson
Spencer (Herk) Robinson
Robert B. Rogers
Rev. Thomas A. Savage, S.J.

Michie P. Slaughter
Edward A. Smith
Louis W. Smith
Don Stein
Harley Tennison
Dean Vogelaar
Merle Wood

Notes

1. The Early Years

Page   1 *metropolitan weekly newspaper. Squire,* July 20, 1989.
        biggest deals of 1989. Fortune, January 29, 1990, 32, 136.

    2 *"lived as happily afterward." Kansas City Times,* July 17, 1989.
        "if we hadn't done these things." "Ewing Kauffman Says," *New Magazine,*
        August 1976, 4–5.

    3 *"such symmetry and order."* Ibid., 6.
        "the detriment of himself." Author interview with Ewing M. Kauffman,
        December 10, 1991. Hereafter cited as Kauffman interview, December
        10, 1991.
        an opportunity to learn. Effie Mae Winders was born December 19, 1892.
        the American Civil War. John Kauffman's father emigrated at age two. His
        mother arrived some twenty years later from the Alsace-Lorraine region
        of Germany near the Swiss border. Author interview with Ruth Jianas,
        October 12, 1992. Hereafter cited as Jianas interview, October 12, 1992.

    4 *"somewhat depend on them."* Kauffman interview, December 10, 1991.
        "valuable in my business." Ibid.
        "were talking about me." Jianas interview, October 12, 1992. Kauff-
        man's parents were married July 4, 1912.

4–5 *"to have the baby."* Ibid.

    5 *"and inside toilets."* Kauffman interview, December 10, 1991.
        mother prepared supper. Jianas interview, October 12, 1992.
        "taking the fish out." Ewing M. Kauffman letter to the author, Jan-
        uary 25, 1993.
        classic children's tale. Ibid.

5–6 *"I needed help."* Ibid.

    6 *"had done previously."* Ibid.
        "know that's not true." Jianas interview, October 12, 1992.
        "my father play." Kauffman interview, December 10, 1991.

    7 *"with a pitchfork."* Phil Koury interview with Ewing M. Kauffman, Au-
        gust 15, 1967. Hereafter cited as Koury interview, August 15, 1967.
        "got up there." Jianas interview, October 12, 1992.

    8 *group of regulars.* Ibid.
        "and his friends." Ibid.

Page 8 *as "paying guests."* Kauffman interview, December 10, 1991.

    9 *Kauffman remembered fondly.* Robert Barrett interview with Ewing Kauffman, fall 1991. Hereafter cited as Barrett interview, fall 1991.
"than the grocery." Kauffman interview, December 12, 1991.
"my egg customers." Ibid.

  10 *"didn't miss anything."* Ibid.
"for the afternoon." Kauffman interview, December 10, 1991.
"out of it!" Author interview with Ewing M. Kauffman, November 20, 1992. Hereafter cited as Kauffman interview, November 20, 1992.

  11 *"No, just Larry."* Ibid.
"remember at all." Ibid.
"the rest of them." Ibid.

  12 *"she might hear it."* Jianas interview, October 12, 1992, and Kauffman letter to author, January 25, 1993.
"sat up in bed." Kauffman interview, December 10, 1991. See also Koury interview, August 15, 1967.
fatigue at bedtime. Jianas interview, October 12, 1992.
"Dr. Hudson's Secret Journal." Kauffman interview, December 10, 1992. Kauffman always told interviewers that he read these books during his illness. He said they had taught him that if you treated others fairly, things would turn out well in the end. This became one of the important principles which governed his professional as well as his personal life. However, neither book was published until after his recovery. It is more likely that he read them during his early teen years. *Magnificent Obsession* was published in 1929, two years after his illness. *Dr. Hudson's Secret Journal* was published in 1939.

12–13 *"read and read."* Jianas interview, October 12, 1992.

  13 *"part of it."* Author interview with Ewing M. Kauffman, December 12, 1991. Hereafter cited as Kauffman interview, December 12, 1991.
"in high school." Jianas interview, October 12, 1992.
"the readership badge." Kauffman interview, December 10, 1991.

  14 *phenomenal business success.* Michael E. Herman interview with Ewing M. Kauffman (videotape), March 1990. Hereafter cited as Herman interview, March 1990.
"sleep at night." Kauffman interview, December 10, 1991.

14–15 *"just different temperaments."* Koury interview, August 15, 1967.

  15 *"liked to travel."* Jianas interview, October 12, 1992.
"to think worthwhile." Kauffman interview, December 10, 1991. He received the Distinguished Eagle in 1977. *Kansas City Times*, June 22, 1977.

  16 *"aware of this."* Kauffman interview, December 12, 1991.
"pyramid my sales." Kauffman interview, November 20, 1992.
"a Boy Scout." Ibid.

  17 *"for dancing lessons."* Kauffman interview, December 10, 1991. See also Koury interview, August 15, 1967, and Kauffman letter to author, January 25, 1993.
"they will give you." Herman interview, March 1990.
"better than you are." Kauffman interview, December 12, 1991.

Page 17 *"them for granted."* Ibid. Effie Kauffman Smythe died December 20, 1979, at her home in Kansas City, Missouri. She married Charles Smythe June 29, 1950, and the marriage was a happy one. He predeceased her. See *Kansas City Times*, December 21, 1979.

18 *"the whole state."* Koury interview, August 15, 1967.
"but nothing startling." Kauffman interview, December 10, 1991.
"felt I could." Koury interview, August 15, 1967.

19 *"upon my life."* Kauffman interview, December 12, 1991.
"a discerning mind." Ibid.

20 *"that game with me."* Ibid.
"gave up and quit." Ibid.

21 *"[Kansas City Junior] college."* Kauffman letter to author, January 25, 1993.
"And he did." Jianas interview, October 12, 1992.

22 *"get a good grade."* Kauffman letter to author, January 25, 1993.
recalled somewhat sheepishly. Kauffman interview, December 12, 1991.
"my sales ability." Ibid.

23 *"your physical activity."* Ibid.
"lifelong friendship." Kauffman interview, December 12, 1991.

24 *"all about it."* Barrett interview, fall 1991.
"you were better off." Kauffman interview, December 10, 1991.
"go to her place." Kauffman interview, December 12, 1991.

25 *"Sun Life of Canada."* Kauffman interview, December 10, 1991.

26 *the insurance business.* Ibid.
"and pick them up." Ibid.
"had to win." Ibid.
"a trial lawyer." Ibid.

27 *"things that are wrong."* Ibid.
"is very important." Ibid.
"and me together." Ibid.

2. Going to War

Page 29 *Hughes agreed.* Kauffman interview, December 10, 1991.

30 *"at the bars."* Ibid.
for sea duty. Ibid.
went to sea. Ewing M. Kauffman letter to Effie and Ruth Kauffman, Monday, 8 P.M., undated, from W. 29, Barracks 304, Naval Service School, Great Lakes, Illinois.

31 *"from other factors."* Author interview with Ewing M. Kauffman, March 5, 1993. Hereafter cited as Kauffman interview, March 5, 1993.
"Christmas of 1941." Author's conversation with Charles L. Hughes, May 26, 1994.
"as your own." Ewing M. Kauffman letter to Effie Kauffman, undated, from Group II Barracks 304, Naval Service School, Great Lakes, Illinois.
"a possible miscarriage." Ibid.

32 *"and help him."* Kauffman interview, December 10, 1991.
remembered with relief. Ibid.

32–33 *"wasn't very smart."* Ibid.

Page 33 *"never forget it."* Kauffman interview, March 5, 1993.

"English-speaking signalman." Ibid.

33–34 *"our entire meal!"* Ibid.

34 *unset emerald.* Ibid.

"of [that engineer]." Ibid.

"have known it." Ibid.

34–35 *"ship at that time."* Ibid.

35 *through the Panama Canal.* Ibid.

"but not much." Ibid.

troops in invasions. Kauffman interview, December 12, 1991.

36 *"receiving [the message]."* Kauffman interview, December 10, 1991.

"outside that star." Ibid.

37 *"if you're accurate."* Kauffman interview, December 12, 1991.

"more accurate than his." Barrett interview, fall 1991.

"across the front." Ibid. Kauffman's service record shows that he "accepted temporary appointment as Ensign July 18, 1944." National Personnel Records Center, St. Louis.

38 *"an enlisted man."* Barrett interview, fall 1991.

"would run aground!" Ibid.

"his navigation officer." Ibid.

39 *"that certainly did."* Ibid.

United States until armistice. Ewing M. Kauffman letter to Effie and Ruth Kauffman, February 2, 1944.

"I do feel it." Ewing M. Kauffman letter to Effie and Ruth Kauffman, February 14, 1944.

"first husband's insurance." Kauffman interview, December 12, 1991.

41 *"Quite unconventional."* Ibid.

"give them away." Ibid.

42 *"him see me!"* Ibid.

"person he was." Ibid.

recalled years later. Ibid.

43 *"we were concerned."* Ibid.

in November 1944. Ewing M. Kauffman letter to Effie Kauffman, November 8, 1944.

"children so much." Ewing M. Kauffman letter to Effie and Ruth Kauffman, January 6, 1945.

Pacific was over. Ibid.

44 *"at Marion Laboratories."* Koury interview, August 15, 1967.

45 *"on his part."* Ibid.

November 16, 1945. Ibid.

46 *never have imagined.* Kauffman was released from active duty in an officer status on November 16, 1945, with the rank of ensign navigational officer. His release was accelerated because "I had built up a lot of points because I had spent well over two-and-a-half years at sea duty." See Kauffman interview, December 10, 1991. From November 17, 1945, to January 21, 1950, Kauffman was in service in an enlisted status on inactive duty. See David L. Petree to Howard Vander Clute Jr., May 11, 1993. This letter contains Kauffman's complete military record.

Page 46 *"name to 'Lucky.'"* Kauffman interview, December 10, 1991. See also Koury interview, August 15, 1967.

"has me beat." Ibid.

"in Kansas City." Koury interview, August 15, 1967.

47 *could be arranged.* Kauffman interview, December 10, 1991.

"extra coming in." Ibid.

"spending [the savings]." Kauffman interview, December 12, 1991.

48 *"occurred to me."* Kauffman interview, March 5, 1993.

"I'll pay it." Ibid.

"life insurance salesman." Kauffman interview, December 10, 1991.

48–49 *"enjoy taking tests."* Barrett interview, fall 1991.

49 *"close to it."* Ibid.

"money on them." Kauffman interview, December 12, 1991. See also Kauffman, "Remarks at the Strategic Planning Meeting," January 21, 1991. Hereafter cited as Kauffman, "Remarks," January 21, 1991.

50 *"to get anything."* Ibid.

"six straight weeks." Barrett interview, fall 1991.

51 *"still hire him!"* Ibid.

51–52 *"of my home."* Ibid. See also Koury interview, August 15, 1967.

52 *"much scientific education."* Kauffman interview, December 10, 1991.

53 *"all our money."* Kauffman interview, December 12, 1991.

3. Launching Marion Laboratories

Page 55 *and fifteen cents.* Robert F. Pruitt. "A History of Marion Laboratories." typescript. Hereafter cited as Pruitt, "History."

56 *"country business first."* Author interview with Ewing M. Kauffman, December 9, 1991. Hereafter cited as Kauffman interview, December 9, 1991.

"already eaten earlier." Ibid.

57 *would ride along.* Ibid.

"retail drug business." *Kansas City Star*, April 18, 1953.

"gave me, was extra." Kauffman interview, December 9, 1991.

57–58 *"on new accounts."* Barrett interview, fall 1991.

58 *"or a thousand."* Ibid.

on sales calls. Ibid. See also Koury interview, August 15, 1967.

59 *"Ewing Kauffman."* Ibid.

"not very prepossessing." Ibid.

"in the future." Koury interview, August 15, 1967. See also Barrett interview, fall 1991.

60 *"in that order."* Kauffman interview, December 9, 1991.

"that I made." Kauffman, "Remarks," January 21, 1991.

61 *"So he did!"* Author interview with Charles Hughes, April 17, 1992. Hereafter cited as Hughes interview, April 17, 1992.

"they said 'Go!'" Ibid.

"and I will." Kauffman interview, December 9, 1991.

62 *"successful at selling."* Hughes interview, April 17, 1992.

"'such a product.'" Kauffman interview, December 9, 1991.

Page 62 *"bigger and bigger."* Ibid.

"I wanted to." Ibid.

"products and research." Ibid.

63 *"which hurt him."* Barrett interview, fall 1991.

"second selling career." Kauffman interview, December 9, 1991.

"on his stock." Ibid.

"we hired Pruitt." Hughes interview, April 17, 1992.

65 *"of those obstacles."* Kauffman interview, December 9, 1991.

"a beautiful job." Ibid.

"mind on selling." Barrett interview, fall 1991.

security and stability. Author interview with Helen Pruitt, February 12, 1992. Hereafter cited as H. Pruitt interview, February 12, 1992.

"'to interview with?'" Ibid.

66–67 *"people we were."* Ibid.

67 *"to be there.'"* Ibid.

"into the stock." Ibid.

"on [the husbands]." Barrett interview, fall 1991.

68 *"money to them."* Ibid.

"of her husband." Author interview with Robert F. Pruitt, February 10, 1992. Hereafter cited as Pruitt interview, February 10, 1992.

o'clock Monday morning. Ibid.

68–69 *"to get warm."* Ibid.

69 *"rue the day."* Ibid.

"to do it." Barrett interview, fall 1991.

"the next year!" Ibid.

70 *"pay back $1,250."* Ibid. See also Kauffman interview, December 12, 1991.

"That was five." Ibid.

"we became profitable." Koury interview, April 15, 1967.

71 *"leave it there."* Kauffman interview, December 12, 1991.

"needed the help." Barrett interview, fall 1991.

"of the business." Kauffman interview, December 9, 1991.

"his sales presentation." Ibid.

72 *"my own mind."* Ibid.

"starting VICAM therapy." Pruitt, "History."

"to the restroom." Barrett interview, fall 1991.

"to scientific proceedings." Ibid.

73 *"we later developed."* Kauffman interview, December 9, 1991.

"and so forth." Ibid.

74 *"talk to him."* Ibid.

"or four days." Pruitt, "History."

"in that area." Pruitt interview, February 10, 1992.

75 *"to the literature."* Ibid.

76 *of the company.* Pruitt, "History."

shell calling cards. Ibid.

"or ten minutes." Ibid.

"as a whole." Ibid.

77 *"their name badges."* Ibid.

Page 77–78 *"ready to go."* Ibid.
 78 *"for their rooms."* Ibid.
 "had finally arrived!" Ibid.

4. The Company Grows

Page 79 *of its products.* See Joseph A. Hardy, *Obstetrics and Gynecology: Journal of the American College of Obstetricians and Gynecologists,* November 1956, 561-68. Pruitt noted that at this time, 95 percent of all calcium products were phosphorus bearing. By 1959 all major pharmaceutical companies had changed their calcium products to "phophorus free." Pruitt conversation with the author, November 3, 1994.
79–80 *"in the company."* Barrett interview, fall 1991.
 80 *"with their future."* Kauffman interview, March 5, 1993.
 "ever really succeeded." Kauffman interview, December 2, 1991.
 "two thousand dollars." Ibid.
80–81 *"to help you."* Barrett interview, fall, 1991.
 81 *a profitable concern.* Marion Laboratories Chronology, prepared for the 1989 merger with Merrell Dow. Hereafter cited as Marion Chronology.
 this "improved" process. Pruitt, "History."
 82 *"first manufacturing plant."* Hughes interview, April 17, 1992.
 "the home office." Pruitt, "History."
 "we didn't overspend." Barrett interview, fall 1991.
 83 *"regulating drug prices."* For an excellent summary of the Kefauver drug industry hearings see Joseph Bruce Gorman, *Kefauver: A Political Biography* (New York: Oxford University Press, 1971), 340–42; 358–59.
 "lend it to you." Barrett interview, fall 1991.
 "part of the family." Ibid.
83–84 *loan officer responded.* Ibid.
 84 *"lend it to you."* Ibid.
 85 *"called me collect!"* Hughes interview, April 17, 1992.
 "of losing it." Author interview with Ewing M. Kauffman, April 16, 1992. Hereafter cited as Kauffman interview, April 16, 1992.
 discoveries of others. Kauffman always credited Malcolm Dalbey with developing this strategy, but it was being used at Marion as early as 1955. Dalbey's contribution was to extend Marion's search for new products beyond the geographical boundaries of the United States. See Kauffman interview, March 5, 1993.
 86 *"to sell quality."* Kauffman quoted in Pruitt, "History."
 87 *"for his practice."* Pruitt, "History."
 "blitz Washington, D.C." Ibid.
 "on subsequent calls." Ibid.
 88 *salesman to return.* Ibid.
 "certified public accountants." *Kansas City Star,* October 6, 1958.
 89 *"you need more."* Pruitt, "History."
 "start writing ANASORB." Ibid. See also *Enid* (Oklahoma) *Eagle,* December 19, 1958.
 91 *"on increased sales."* Kauffman interview, April 16, 1992.

Page 91 *"will be made."* Kauffman memo to Haskell, Sperry, Grinham, Danielson, Seifering, and Hughes, February 16, 1960.

   92 *"more quality control."* Kauffman interview, April 16, 1992.

     "spend the night." Author interview with Sue Kauffman, September 6,
1992. Hereafter cited as Sue Kauffman interview, September 6, 1992.

   93 *"there that night."* Author interview with Larry Kauffman, December
12, 1992. Hereafter cited as Larry Kauffman interview, December 12,
1992.

     "an active father." Sue Kauffman interview, September 6, 1992.

     "'with no money?'" Ibid. See also Larry Kauffman interview, December
12, 1992.

93–94 *benefit of hindsight.* Ibid.

   94 *"seemed so happy."* Author's telephone conversation with Sue Kauffman,
May 2, 1994.

     was accidental death. Kansas City Star, December 15, 1960.

     "as a private." Kauffman interview, December 9, 1991.

     "became my family." Sue Kauffman interview, September 6, 1992.

   95 *"doubt in my mind."* Ibid.

     "coming up fast." Kauffman interview, April 16, 1992.

   96 *"wouldn't be destroyed."* Ibid.

     "Danielson had found." Ibid.

     "snakes in there." Ibid.

     "on that product." Hughes memo, October 1961.

   97 *"to do anyway!"* Kauffman interview, April 16, 1992.

5. Changing with the Times

Page 99 *"good things happen."* Kauffman, "Remarks," January 21, 1991.

     "started driving Cadillacs." Pruitt interview, February 10, 1992.

  101 *"couldn't do that!"* Ibid.

     "my suite immediately!" Ibid.

     "for Jean Sperry." Ibid.

  102 *national sales manager.* Ibid.

     sales records again. Ibid.

  103 *their research programs.* Midwest Research Institute developed a new
method of using a plastic coating instead of the sugary coating on vitamin tablets and other pills. The process reduced manufacturing costs
and helped significantly in quality control. *Kansas City Times,* January
28, 1960. Marion Laboratories made a three-year grant to the University of Tennessee School of Pharmacy to support graduate students and
others doing research on specific industrial problems. The grant included a profit-sharing plan whereby products developed in the pharmacy college and brought to market would provide profits to the university. *Kansas City Times,* June 1, 1962.

  104 *relations and export.* See Kauffman memo, February 16, 1960.

     "I'll resign." Sperry quoted in Pruitt interview, February 10, 1992.

  105 *"'We'll introduce papavarine.'"* Kauffman interview, April 16, 1992.

  106 *"have afforded it."* Barrett interview, fall 1991.

Page 106 *"we went public."* Ibid.

"hot button was." Pruitt interview, February 10, 1992.

107 *"to my prayers."* Pruitt, "History."

"prescribe PAVABID!'" Ibid.

108 *"need women's lib."* *Kansas City Star,* January 15, 1986.

"my [older] brother," *Kansas City Star,* April 5, 1981.

from McMaster University. In 1985, McMaster University granted her an honorary doctor of law degree in recognition of her distinguished business career and her humanitarian contributions. See Muriel I. Kauffman, Biography.

109 *"from a gentleman."* Author interview with Muriel Kauffman, November 19, 1992. Hereafter cited as Muriel Kauffman interview, November 19, 1992.

"That intrigued me." *Ingram's,* February 1991, 29.

"dining room table." Muriel Kauffman interview, November 19, 1992.

the offer completely. Ibid.

110 *in future years.* See *Ingram's,* February 1991, 9.

"our granddaughter, too!" Irene McBrien quoted in Muriel Kauffman interview, November 19, 1992. Kauffman adopted Julia Irene in 1990, three years before his death.

"about it to me." Author interview with Julia Irene Kauffman, November 19, 1992. Hereafter cited as Julia Irene Kauffman interview.

111 *"to be sixteen."* Kauffman interview, November 20, 1992.

"in those days." Julia Irene Kauffman interview.

"me the experiences." Ibid.

112 *"You can't win!"* Muriel Kauffman interview, November 19, 1992.

"have that anymore." Ewing Kauffman quoted in *Squire,* September 1975, 34.

"makes you happy." Muriel Kauffman interview, November 19, 1992.

"sympathetic to others." Ibid. See also Muriel Kauffman quoted in *Kansas City Star,* April 5, 1981.

her husband recalled. Muriel Kauffman interview, November 19, 1992.

113 *"the only woman."* Ibid.

"but he'd go." Ibid.

"wherever I go!" Quoted in *Ingram's,* February 1991, 29.

"need the arts." Muriel Kauffman interview, November 19, 1992.

114 *the early 1970s.* *Squire,* May 1971, 19.

said with pride. Ibid.

"big-city girl." Muriel Kauffman interview, November 19, 1992.

"I'm not moving!" Ibid.

115 *in Marion Laboratories.* Ewing Kauffman quoted in *Squire,* May 1971, 19.

"a little research." Kauffman interview, December 12, 1991.

115–16 *"care for them."* Barrett interview, fall 1991.

116 *"to those expectations."* Ibid.

"hundreds of them." Author interview with Rosemary Godbout, November 19, 1992. Hereafter cited as Godbout interview, November 19, 1992.

117 *"other's best friend."* Kauffman interview, April 16, 1992.

"leading the clapping!" Godbout interview, November 19, 1992.

Page 118 *"meet his expectations."* Ibid.

> *"enough for Charlie."* Hughes interview, April 17, 1992.
> *the IRS permitted.* Kauffman interview, April 16, 1992.
> *the IRS allowed.* Michie Slaughter noted that the 15 percent plus gains in the stock price might have resulted in gains of 30 to 40 percent in an associate's fund value, but the individuals were never "credited" with 30 to 40 percent in contributions. See Michie P. Slaughter to author, October 9, 1994.

119 *"eleven and fifteen."* Kauffman interview, April 16, 1992.

6. Marion Goes Public

Page 121 *"do uncommon things."* Marion Laboratories Inc., *Annual Report,* 1966.

122 *"we have been."* Ibid.

123 *"lake there today."* Kauffman interview, April 16, 1992. Kauffman grew to love that site so much that he secured special permission from the appropriate authorities to be buried there.

> *"we have been."* Ibid.
> *"would increase benefits."* Hughes interview, April 17, 1992.
> *"lived on faith."* Allan T. Demaree, "Ewing Kauffman Sold Himself Rich in Kansas City," *Fortune,* October 1972, 101.
> *"business was run."* Hughes interview, April 17, 1992.

124 *"to go public."* Kauffman interview, April 16, 1993.

> *"need to do."* Ibid.

124–25 *"going to earn."* Ibid.

125 *"I told them."* Ibid.

> *"else next year."* Ibid.

126 *profit-sharing plan.* Wall Street Journal, July 29, 1965.

> *"at twenty-one."* Frank quoted in Kauffman interview, April 16, 1992.
> *"that bought it."* Kauffman interview, April 16, 1992.

127 *"at twenty-one!"* Ibid.

> *"big celebration dinner."* Ibid.
> *"profit-sharing plan!"* Pruitt, "History."

129 *"to tell them."* Pruitt interview, February 10, 1992.

> *any professional meeting.* Ibid.
> *for those responsibilities.* Kansas City Star, March 16, 1966.

130 *"was through salesmen."* Author interview with Ewing M. Kauffman, May 6, 1992. Hereafter cited as Kauffman interview, May 6, 1992.

> *"to give him."* Ibid.

131 *rather than research.* Ibid.

> *British Medical Association.* Ibid.

132 *"average competitive counterpart."* Marion Laboratories, *Annual Report,* 1970.

133 *managers did not.* Kauffman interview, May 6, 1992.

> *of their wives.* Brant Cotterman conversation with the author, October 14, 1994.

134 *"And he did!"* Kauffman interview, May 6, 1992.

> *reached that accomplishment.* Ibid.

Page 135 *chief operating officer.* Ibid.

> *with visible pride.* Ibid. The Marion board of directors authorized three stock distributions during this period. In 1966 and 1968 the split was 100 percent. In 1967, the split was 50 percent. See *Annual Report*, 1966, 1967, and 1968. Marion stock started trading on August 15, 1965, at $28.00. By June 30, 1966, the price had increased to $64.86 per share. See Marion Laboratories, *Annual Report*, 1966.

136 *"at a time now!"* Pruitt, "History."

> *to the shareholders.* Marion Laboratories, *Annual Report*, 1970.
>
> *osteoarthritis and osteoporosis.* OS-CAL-GESIC was developed in 1963 for the relief of symptoms of osetoarthritis. OS-CAL-MONE, a combination of calcium and certain hormones, was introduced in 1965.

137 *time in 1966.* See Marion Laboratories, *Annual Report*, 1966.

> *"of Marion's people."* Ibid.
>
> *"very good rapport."* Kauffman interview, May 6, 1992.

139 *"event would occur."* Ibid.

> *"Missouri, backwards."* Ibid.

7. Changing the Corporate Culture

Page 141 *"the research program?"* See "Wall Street Transcript," presentation by Ewing M. Kauffman before the Kansas City Society of Financial Analysts, November 14, 1967. According to the *FDC Reports*, Marion was number one in percentage increase in sales every year for the previous three years; number one in increase percentage of earnings; number one in return on equity.

142 *"don't know yet."* Ibid. In speaking about the research association with the University of Tennessee, Kauffman said that Dr. Haskell, Marion's technical director in 1966, was a graduate of Tennessee's pharmacy program. "He felt they might be able to help. They were willing, and the deal was made. It was a three-year cooperative effort. Nothing came from it and we did not develop any products from our association with private labs or universities in those days." See Kauffman interview, May 6, 1992.

> *"our fair share."* Ibid.
>
> *"magic still works."* *New York Times*, July 13, 1967. The agreement with Syntex was finalized in 1968. Marion obtained the right to market four Syntex-developed products. As a consideration, Syntex received stock options for 60,000 shares per product, or a total of 240,000 shares. If Marion were to sell $27 million in one year of these products, an escalating clause provided that Marion deliver up to an additional 240,000 shares. See Smith, Barney & Company, "Marion Laboratories," *Special Research Report*, June 24, 1968.
>
> *"regarded research organization."* Ibid.
>
> *"make $400 million."* "Wall Street Transcript," November 14, 1968.
>
> *its introductory year.* Marion Laboratories, *Annual Report*, 1969.

143 *"Coca-Cola was handy!"* Pruitt, "History."

144 *next two decades.* Marion Laboratories, *Annual Report*, 1971.

Page 144 *the original agreement.* Pruitt, "History."

145 *"from other businesses."* Kauffman interview, Mary 6, 1992. See also Marion Laboratories, *Annual Report,* 1966.

1968 annual report. In addition to Kauffman, the other members of the acquisitions committee were Charles A. Truitt, vice president for finance; Malcom M. Dalbey, executive vice president; and William T. Doyle, vice president for corporate affairs. See Marion Laboratories, *Annual Report,* 1968.

146 *"from other sources."* Kauffman interview, May 6, 1992.

to manage steps. Marion Laboratories acquired the following companies during its diversification program: Medical Supply Company, Rockford, Illinois (1968), sold first-aid equipment of the health care industry; Kalo Inoculant Company, Quincy, Illinois (1968), a leading manufacturer of legume inoculants used in farming; American Stair-Glide Corporation, Kansas City, Missouri (1968), which was the only company in the home-elevator field with access to the medical profession through a medical sales force; International Pharmaceutical Corporation, Warrenton, Pennsylvania (1970), produced over-the-counter proprietary products for ear and oral hygiene; Mi-Con Laboratories, Wauconda, Illinois (1970), was a maker of sterile ophthalmic solutions for persons wearing contact lenses; Pioneer Laboratories, Pleasantville, New Jersey (Marion purchased a 50 percent interest in 1970), manufactured sterile impregnated dressings and was the only U.S. company to meet the standards of the Department of Defense for use in field hospitals and Veterans Administration facilities; Rose Manufacturing Company, Denver, Colorado (1969), produced a line of high-elevation safety products to prevent injury from falls; Optico Industries, Inc., Phoenix, Arizona (1972), was engaged in the wholesale and retail sales of eyeglasses and frames; Newport Scientific, Inc., Kansas City, Missouri (1973), later renamed Marion Scientific Corporation, acquired, developed, and marketed disposables and equipment for hospitals; Signet Laboratories, Inc., Burbank, California (1973), manufactured and marketed health food supplements, vitamins, minerals, and cosmetics; Indo Laboratories, Santa Monica, California (1973), produced industrial protective creams.

Time magazine interviewer. Time, December 1, 1967, 110, 113.

147 *had become millionaires.* Kauffman quoted in *Cleveland Plain Dealer,* January 24, 1968.

million-dollar mark. See *Kansas City Star,* November n.d., 1968. Stock appreciation was the major contributor to the pension fund growth, along with employee turnover, which meant that the fund retained and redistributed those benefits to others and an IRS-approved limit of one million dollars on the fund of any single participant. With a vesting period of twenty-two years required, Kauffman noted, "the earnings in both interest and capital growth of these million-dollar funds will go to replace the company's contributions."

"anything I've got." *Cleveland Plain Dealer,* January 24, 1968.

148 *"done, that counts."* Kauffman, "Creation of Change," a speech to the Junior Chamber of Commerce, September 8, 1970.

Page 149 *"Mr. K needed him."* Author interview with Al Mannino, September 8, 1992. Hereafter cited as Mannino interview, September 8, 1992.

150 *plans for growth.* Ibid. Mannino came to Marion Laboratories from Purdue Frederick and Company, where he was vice president for marketing. Prior to his service with McKesson & Robbins, he had been in a management position with Geigy Pharmaceuticals. Marion Laboratories, *Annual Report,* 1968.
"that intrigued me." Ibid.
"me for it!" Ibid.

151 *"in that area."* Ibid.
"sort of antiwholesaler." Ibid.

152 *treat other people.* Ibid.
" 'tell them something.' " Ibid.

153 *in his voice.* Ibid.
"before that time." Ibid.

154 *"these different states?"* Ibid.
"cared about them." Ibid.
"finally came out." Ibid.

155 *a logjam there.* Kauffman interviews, December 12, 1991, and April 16, 1992. Kauffman and Wood developed a warm and affectionate relationship during the years Wood worked for Marion Laboratories. After his retirement, he continued to be associated with Kauffman through the Kansas City Royals and he remained a trusted intimate until Kauffman's death.
"our life easier." Mannino interview, September 8, 1992.

156 *"good, didn't it?"* Ibid.

157 *"know them all."* Russ Mannino quoted in ibid.
"check the inventory." Pruitt quoted in ibid. Pruitt's memory of the episode is different. He recalls that Dalbey talked to his training manager about the incident. "I called Dalbey and told him never to chew out my people—any chewing was on was to be on me!" Pruitt to author, November 2, 1994.
"and 50 percent." Ibid. Pruitt recalls that the turnover was more in the 20 percent range. Pruitt to author, ibid.

158 *"were pharmaceutical people."* Mannino interview, September 8, 1992.
"Well, change it." Ibid.
"it was money." Ibid.

159 *"that professional background."* Ibid.
"this thing work." Ibid.

160 *"in the ring."* Author interview with Stuart Gold, October 12, 1992. Hereafter cited as Gold interview, October 12, 1992.
"was . . . eccentric." Ibid.

161 *"recently departed Athletics."* See "M is for Money," *Time,* December 1, 1967, 112–13.
"what Dalbey said." Gold interview, October 12, 1992.
"in the salary." Ibid.
"at my stage." Ibid.

162 *"life was secondary."* Ibid.

Page 162 *"here is smart!"* Kauffman quoted in ibid.
  "to be there." Ibid.
163 *"answers your question."* Ibid. In the matter of the Kansas City Club, Kauffman was speaking of his friend, Don Stein. "Don, in one sense, is probably my closest friend among [my golfing buddies and card playing friends]. The only other person I might put ahead of Don in the matter of friendship would be Charlie Hughes. Don is Jewish. I belong to his Jewish Country Club. He was the first Jew to be taken into Club 822, which is an inner club at the Kansas City Club." Kauffman to author, June 4, 1992. See also author interview with Don Stein, August 9, 1993.
  with a sigh. Mannino interview, September 8, 1992.
164 *a hollow one.* Marion Laboratories, *Annual Report*, 1969.

8. Surviving the Seventies

Page 165 *and development activities.* See Marion Laboratories, *Annual Report*, 1970.
166 *after the event.* Kauffman interview, December 12, 1991.
167 *"me run it."* Lyons quoted in Mannino interview, September 8, 1992.
  to centralized control. Marion Laboratories, *Annual Report*, 1973.
167–68 *"executive staff generally."* Kauffman interview, December 12, 1991.
168 *"work as hard."* Ibid.
  "all of them." Marion Laboratories, *Annual Report*, 1973, and Kauffman interview, May 6, 1992.
169 *City to investigate.* Author interview with Michie P. Slaughter, November 18, 1992. Hereafter cited as Slaughter interview, November 18, 1992.
  "as an individual." Ibid.
  "is Kansas City?" Ibid.
  "executive recruiting." Ibid.
170 *"nearly trusting enough."* Ibid.
  serious problems. Ibid.
171 *"to fire somebody."* Ibid.
  "that could happen." Ibid.
173 *venture capital projects.* Author interview with Michael E. Herman, December 11, 1991. Hereafter cited as Herman interview, December 11, 1991.
  "people that way." Ibid.
174 *"should never exist."* Ibid.
  "bunch of things." Ibid.
  "couldn't afford me." Ibid.
175 *risk their future.* Ibid.
  "Marion from afar." Author interview with Jim McGraw, February 20, 1992. Hereafter cited as McGraw interview, February 20, 1992.
  six months later. Ibid.
176 *"committed to excellence."* Marion Laboratories, *Annual Report*, 1975.
  "with these products." *Kansas City Times,* July n.d., 1973.
  "dollars a share." Slaughter interview, November 18, 1992. For additional background on the controversy see *Kansas City Times,* April 1, 1973.

Page 177 *"effect on earnings."* FDC Reports, November 25, 1974.
    178 *marketing as well.* Ibid.
      "the pharmaceutical area." Kansas City Times, July 18, 1973.
    179 *"look forward to."* Gold interview, October 12, 1992.
      "for the company." McGraw interview, February 20, 1992.
    180 *as a result.* Ibid.
      "doesn't happen again." Kauffman quoted in McGraw interview, ibid.
      and remarkably resilient. Ibid.
      "a strong demotivator." Slaughter interview, November 18, 1992.
    181 *"stock turned around."* Kauffman quoted in ibid.
      "was becoming reality." Ibid.
    182 *"to that growth."* Marion Laboratories, Annual Report, 1975.
      " 'every six weeks.' " Slaughter interview, November 18, 1992.
    183 *"Laboratories was no."* Ibid.
      "you really leave?" Ibid.
      "the sales force." Ibid.
    184 *to be started.* Author interview with Jim McGraw, June 1, 1994. Hereafter cited as McGraw interview, June 1, 1994.
    185 *"just outgrew Jean."* Kauffman interview, April 16, 1992.
      new international division. Ibid.
    186 *"as I could."* Ibid.
      "worth of product! . . ." Slaughter interview, November 18, 1992.
      " 'a burn ward?' " McGraw interview, February 20, 1992.
    187 *"could afford it."* Kauffman interview March 5, 1993.
      "in our products." Kauffman interview, May 6, 1992.
      " 'so much better.' " McGraw interview, February 20, 1992.
      "things to see." Ibid.
    188 *for senior management.* Ibid.
      "two years earlier!" Ibid.
      "with the customer." Ibid.
    189 *in the 1980s.* CARAFATE received FDA market approval in October 1981, and CARDIZEM received FDA market approval in November 1982. CARDIZEM was approved for marketing in Canada by Marion's subsidiary, Nordic Laboratories, in March 1983. See *Marion Laboratories Chronology.*
      "a captive audience." McGraw interview, February 20, 1992.
      "City to California." Martini quoted in ibid.
      " 'No problem.' " Ibid.
    190 *" 'that's your business.' "* Ibid.
      "every wholesaler benefited." Ibid.
      to the wholesaler. Quoted in ibid.

9. Turning the Company Around

Page 193 *"month of July."* Slaughter interview, November 18, 1992.
      "with a rope." McGraw interview, June 1, 1994.
      "having clean books." Ibid.
    194 *"to happen again."* Ibid.
      " 'technology-intensive line.' " Slaughter interview, November 18, 1992.

Page 194 *small and growing.* Author interview with Lowell Miller, November 18, 1993. Hereafter cited as Miller interview, November 18, 1993. Miller became vice president for research and development in 1977.

195 *telling his colleagues.* Slaughter interview, November 18, 1992.

"some new products!" McGraw quoted in Slaughter, ibid.

"bet the company." Ibid.

196 *to flourish again.* Kauffman interview, May 6, 1992.

"done with Signet!" Author interview with Brant Cotterman, November 13, 1993. Hereafter cited as Cotterman interview, November 13, 1993.

197 *"Kauffman [to hear]."* Ibid.

"a signed contract." Ibid.

198 *to be plundered.* Herman interview, December 11, 1991.

in the buyouts. Slaughter interview, November 18, 1992.

199 *"me at Marion."* Author interview with Michael Mahoney, February 10, 1992. Hereafter cited as Mahoney interview, February 10, 1992. American Stair-Glide was a money maker for Marion Laboratories, having had thirteen years of consecutive increases in sales and profits at the time of divestiture.

"hair-raising experience." Ibid.

200 *"least five years!"* Ibid.

"and think about." Ibid.

"it than not." Author interview with Barnett Helzberg, April 17, 1992. Hereafter cited as Helzberg interview, April 17, 1992.

201 *"him for that."* Mahoney interview, February 10, 1992.

"of every year." Slaughter interview, November 18, 1992.

202 *"adjust the payout."* Ibid.

"cost too much." Ibid.

"becomes very demotivational." Ibid.

203 *"make decisions from."* Cotterman interview, November 13, 1992.

"must be special." Ewing M. Kauffman to George S. Smith, February 2, 1993.

"knack of knowing." Author interview with Louis W. Smith, November 18, 1993. Hereafter cited as Smith interview, November 18, 1993.

204 *"'gives me anything.'"* Kauffman letter to the author, December 8, 1992. *the company needed.* Prior to the late seventies, all associates had stock options, but they were fairly small. "If you were a chemist making twenty thousand dollars a year in those days, and that's what chemists made, you might get an option for fifty shares. You were not going to educate your kids on fifty shares." Slaughter interview, November 18, 1992.

"'place to work.'" Ibid.

205 *"people in accounting."* Ibid.

206 *"was very different."* Ibid.

"you select them." Author interview with James A. Gardner, February 17, 1993. Hereafter cited as Gardner interview, February 17, 1993.

"met Mr. Kauffman." Ibid.

207 *"kinds of programs."* Ibid.

Page 207 *"of financial incentives."* Ibid.
　　　　　"things were accomplished." Ibid.
　　　　　"be much richer." Lyons quoted in ibid.
　　　208 *"to pull together."* McGraw quoted in Slaughter interview, November 18, 1992.
　　　　　"touch people-wise." Gardner interview, February 17, 1993.
　　　　　partly in jest. Slaughter interview, November 18, 1992.
　　　209 *"inside of Marion."* Author interview with Harley Tennison, September 2, 1993. Hereafter cited as Tennison interview, September 2, 1993.
　　　　　actual product launch. Ibid.
　　　210 *"a great deal."* Gold interview, October 12, 1992.
　　　　　"CARDIZEM and CARAFATE!" Tennison interview, September 2, 1993.
　210–11 *"was the luck."* Gardner interview, February 17, 1994.
　　　211 *"Mr. K could."* Miller interview, November 18, 1993.

10. The Merger

Page 213 *"in the seventies."* Marion Laboratories, *Annual Report*, 1980.
　　　214 *"product to watch."* Ibid.
　　　215 *to the crisis.* Slaughter interview, November 18, 1992.
　　　　　recalled with pride. Kauffman interview, November 20, 1992.
　　　　　"the launch process." Tennison interview, September 2, 1993. See also Tennison letter to author, October 24, 1994.
　　　216 *"kind of explodes."* Ibid.
　　　217 *"he reinforces it."* Ibid.
　　　　　"the general level." Ibid.
　　　218 *patriarch, and visionary.* Cotterman interview, November 13, 1993.
　　　　　shorter time span. CARAFATE received FDA approval October 30, 1981, and CARDIZEM was approved on November 5, 1982. See *Marion Laboratories Chronology.*
　218–19 *and SmithKline's TAGAMET.* It is interesting to note the difference in sales volume between Marion Laboratories and its competitor, SmithKline, at the introduction of CARAFATE. "Marion's total sales for its entire line of pharmaceutical and health-care products during the latest fiscal year were $118.6 million. SmithKline, in contrast, reported 1980 sales of more than $7 billion, with a research and development alone of $132 million." *Kansas City Star*, November 17, 1981.
　　　221 *GLAVISCON and NITRODID.* Marion Laboratories, *Annual Report*, 1984.
　　　222 *"can run it?'"* Author interview with Kit Truex-Mair, December 5, 1992. Hereafter cited as Truex-Mair interview, December 5, 1992.
　　　　　"trusted the process." Ibid.
　　　　　"have creative minds." Kauffman interview, April 16, 1992.
　　　　　a successful team. Ibid.
　　　223 *"[Marion's] stock fast!"* Fred Lyons quoted in *Kansas City Times*, October 4, 1983, and August 13, 1985.
　　　　　research publication. Kansas City Times, April 8, 1986.
　　　224 *"big as CARDIZEM."* Ibid.
　　　　　"want to grow." Kansas City Times, November 14, 1987.

Page 224 *the single product. Kansas City Times,* January 23, 1988.
"can be tricky." Wall Street Journal, April 1, 1988.
225 *were whittled downward.* Ibid.
"slam home run." Ibid.
226 *the company's future.* Jim McGraw (chief operating officer), Harley Tennison (marketing), Lowell Miller (research and development), Brant Cotterman (manufacturing), Michie Slaughter (human resources), and Lloyd Hanahan (project management) were the members of the so-called "Six-Pack." McGraw said the group got its name from his predilection for beer. When he invited Fred Lyons to their meetings once a year with the spouses, "then I sort of referred to us as the Seven-up group," McGraw said. See McGraw interview, June 1, 1994.
"to get married." Tennison interview, September 2, 1993.
"a separate entity." McGraw interview, February 20, 1992.
227 *"products to trade."* Kauffman interview, December 12, 1991.
"highly successful." Ibid.
228 *for future revenues.* CARDIZEM sales reached $350 million for Marion's fiscal 1987 and represented 59 percent of Marion's total sales of $597 million. CAPOTEN generated $522 million in sales for Squibb's fiscal 1986 and contributed 29 percent of Squibb's $1.8 billion total sales. *Kansas City Times,* October 9, 1987.
"manufacturing stocks." Wall Street Journal, December 10, 1987.
"prospects can change." Ibid.
229 *"proved disappointing."* McGraw interview, February 20, 1992.
"we'd better listen." Ibid.
230 *"as everyone else."* Kauffman quoted in Herman interview, December 11, 1991.
"was so great!" Herman interview, December 11, 1991.
"on your own." Kauffman quoted in Tennison interview, September 2, 1993.
"secretarial work." Ibid.
231 *"dime to repeat!"* McGraw interview, February 20, 1992.
"was so different." Kauffman interview, December 12, 1991.
the time came. Herman interview, December 11, 1991.
"Swiss approach!" McGraw interview, February 20, 1992.
232 *"We weren't anywhere."* Tennison interview, September 2, 1993.
"be worth it." Gardner interview, February 17, 1993.
233 *of that evening.* Ibid.
"to do it." Ibid.
"any tangible form." McGraw interview, June 1, 1994.
234 *"for the company."* Gardner interview, February 17, 1994.
"had not merged!" McGraw interview, February 20, 1992.
235 *"to do again."* Ibid.
"to his eyes." Linda Constantine quoted in McGraw interview, February 20, 1993. See also Linda Constantine interview, September 20, 1993.
"ruptured me." Kauffman interview, December 12, 1991.
help but hurt. Kit Truex-Mair conversation with the author, November 11, 1994.

Page 236 *"change for him."* McGraw interview, February 20, 1992.
"his first love." Robertson interview, November 11, 1993.

11. Take Me Out to the Ball Game

Page 237 *vast financial holdings.* Kauffman interview, December 12, 1991.
a pleasurable one. Barrett interview, fall 1991.
Monarch's alumni. For information on the Kansas City Monarchs see *Kansas City Star Magazine*, April 13, 1980, and *Kansas City Star*, September 21, 1994. See also, *Kansas City View*, November 11, 1990, and the nine-part PBS documentary "Baseball" produced by Ken Burns. On Satchel Paige, see *Kansas City Star*, May 30, 1982, and June 9, 1982. On Buck O'Neil, see *Kansas City Star*, March 15, 1981, and September 22, 1994.

238 *the ball club. Kansas City Times*, March 10, 1960. For additional background on Johnson, see *Kansas City Star*, November 14, 1954.
"of Kansas City." Barrett interview, fall 1991.
Oakland, California. Kansas City Times, October 19, 1967.
"later than 1971." Sid Bordman, *Expansion to Excellence: An Intimate Portrait of the Kansas City Royals* (Kansas City, Missouri: n.d.), 4.

239 *"Monday morning!"* Symington quoted in Barrett interview, fall 1991.
could be secured. Barrett interview, fall 1991.
civic standpoint. Ibid.

240 *on-line in 1972.* Ibid. See also *Sports Illustrated*, January 8, 1968, 42.

241 *he would need.* Bordman, *Expansion to Excellence*, 6. Kauffman interview, December 20, 1992.
for the franchise. Bordman, *Expansion to Excellence*, 7.
join with them. Kansas City Star, November 29, 1967. Also see *Kansas City Star*, November 27, 1967. The strongest group was the partnership of Stern and Kemper. Richard J. Stern was a fifty-four-year-old investment banker and Crosby Kemper Sr. was the retired chairman of the City National Bank of Kansas City. While both men had substantial personal financial resources, they announced their intention to make 75 percent of the stock available for public sale. John Latshaw, a forty-five-year-old regional vice president of E.F. Hutton & Co., headed another group of investors. He organized a syndicate of eighteen backers to try to win the franchise. The two other groups were headed by Alexander J. Barrett, founder of the Civic Plaza National Bank and Metropolitan Construction Company, and Paul Hamilton, president of Interstate Securities Company. See *Kansas City Star*, November 29, 1967.

242 *"away from me."* Barrett interview, fall 1991. See also Bordman, *Expansion to Excellence*, p. 8.
closed the subject. Kansas City Times, December 2, 1967. Kauffman interview, December 20, 1992.
"the baseball men." Sports Illustrated, January 8, 1968, 42.
"I know nothing." Ibid.
"developing a winner." Kauffman quoted in *Kansas Citian*, February 1968, 18.

Page 243 *"it to me."* Ibid., 42.

"league franchise." New York Times, January 12, 1968.

"better than Ewing." Kansas City Times, January 12, 1968.

for sale locally. Ibid.

"return the favor." Kansas City Downtown Shopper, January 25, 1968, 2.

244 *"a better team."* Kansas City Times, January 12, 1968.

Marion Laboratories. Kansas City Star, January 16, 1968.

carried the day. Kansas City Times, January 12, 1968.

245 *"Board of Directors."* Milgram News, February 1968.

246 *magnificent crown?* Kansas City Star, March 24, 1968, and March 21, 1968.

"Charlie Finley." See Jackson County Advocate, February 22, 1968.

"League in 1969." Bordman, *Expansion to Excellence,* pp. 12–13.

247 *"season tickets."* Kauffman interview, August 25, 1992.

the first year. The second year to remain in the Lancers, the individual had to sell a hundred season tickets. The idea was to renew the original seventy-five and add twenty-five new buyers. By 1992 ,Kauffman said that one member of the Lancers was selling six hundred tickets a year and more than a dozen Lancers were selling over two hundred. See Ibid.

"for Ewing Kauffman." Kansas City Star, September 25, 1968.

248 *were the players.* On Gordon's hiring see *Kansas City Star,* September 9, 1968, and Bordman, *Expansion to Excellence,* 19. See also *Kansas City Times,* October 3, 1968.

"team for you." Kansas City Times, November 4, 1968.

249 *"more of himself."* Kansas City Star, March 15, 1969.

"forever and forever." Kansas City Star, April 9, 1969.

250 *"million dollars somewhere."* Kansas City Star, July 16, 1969.

"competitive with anyone." Ibid.

251 *"six major leaguers."* Kansas City Star Magazine, March 11, 1970, 12.

"wait that long." Barrett interview, fall 1991.

"and no outs." Bordman, *Expansion to Excellence,* 12.

on the Royals. Author interview with Dean Vogelaar, August 26, 1992. Hereafter cited as Vogelaar interview, August 26, 1992.

"stop guessing." TWA Ambassador, June 1974, 23.

252 *"develop those muscles."* Ibid.

"came to me." Ibid.

"us much good." Sports Illustrated, January 4, 1971, 51.

253 *"be taught baseball."* Ibid.

"on your feet." Ibid., 130.

253–54 *"facts and figures."* Ibid.

254 *"and talk baseball."* Ibid.

"the Baseball Academy.'" Barrett interview, fall 1991.

255 *"long a period."* Sports Illustrated, January 4, 1971, 51.

"such a laugh." Sports Illustrated, August 23, 1971, 38.

255–56 *"arms and speed."* Ibid.

256 *of the game.* Kauffman quoted in *Rx Sports and Travel,* May–June 1972, 98.

"Then it's hilarious." Sports Illustrated, Op. cit.

12. The Twenty-Million-Dollar Fan

Page 257 *"so much money."* Kansas City Times, February 10, 1971.
"baseball business." Kansas City Star, February 25, 1972.
258 *"seven stories high."* Kansas City Times, October 2, 1971.
of this setting. For details on the stadium see Kansas City Royals Official American League Source Book, 2nd edition, 1973.
two million dollars. Five construction unions walked out on April 2, 1970, idling more than four thousand workers. The strike halted construction on the sports facility, the Crown Center, the international airport, and scores of smaller projects. See Kansas City Star, April 2, 1970.
259 *were to come.* Kansas City Star, July 19, 1972.
"the old stadium." TWA Ambassador, June 1974, 24. See also Kansas City Star, October 26, 1990, and September 5, 1992.
260 *"$600,000 a year."* Kansas City Star, April 7, 1974.
"major league prospects." Kansas City Times, April 30, 1974.
261 *"traditionalists in baseball."* Squire, September 1975, 35.
"a single year." Ibid., 17.
"for Kansas City." Ibid., 18.
262 *"take your money."* See Vogelaar interview, August 26, 1992, and author interview with Spencer Robinson, August 26, 1992, hereafter cited as Robinson interview, August 26, 1992.
to the future. Author interview with Ewing M. Kauffman, August 25, 1992. Hereafter cited as Kauffman interview, August 25, 1992.
"are against it." Squire, May 1971, 14.
hidebound traditionalists. Ibid., 16.
Cardinals in 1985. The Royals won the American League Western Division title in 1976, 1977, 1978, 1980, 1984, and 1985. In 1980 and 1985 they also won the American League pennant. See Steve Cameron, *Moments, Miracles, Memories: A Quarter Century with the Kansas City Royals* (Taylor Publishing Co.: Kansas City, 1992), 234. Hereafter cited as Cameron, *Moments, Miracles, Memories.*
tongue in cheek. Ibid., 12.
263 *Royals were winning.* See Vogelaar interview, August 26, 1992.
"without a soul?" Kansas City Times, January 24, 1976.
"the World Series." Kansas City Star, January 26, 1976.
"a baseball fan." Kansas City Times, February 11, 1976.
264 *"World Series title!"* Kansas City Star, October 4, 1976.
Baseball Academy again. Kansas City Star, April 11, 1976.
"did later on." Kauffman interview, August 25, 1992. See also Cameron, *Moments, Memories, Miracles,* 103.
265 *"a big plus."* Kansas City Times, October 4, 1977, and Kansas City Star, April 10, 1977.
"their nemesis." For a complete summary see Cameron, *Moments, Memories, Miracles,* 232.
"center fielder." Kansas City Times, October 15, 1980.
266 *fiscally prudent.* Ibid.
"invest in baseball." Kansas City Times, May 31, 1980.

Page 267 *"money I do.'"* Ibid.
　　　　"seats at $1.50." Kansas City Star, October 19, 1980.
　　268 *"New York Yankees."* Barrett interview, fall 1991. Kauffman told this story often and well, but the facts were a bit different. The Royals were behind two to one in the top of the seventh inning with two outs and no runners on base. Willie Wilson hit a double and U.L. Washington beat out an infield single, moving Wilson to third base. When Brett came to bat, the Royals had two outs and runners on first and third bases. Brett hit a three-run homer to win the American League championship over the Yankees and secure a berth at the World Series. See Dean Vogelaar to author, November 8, 1994.
　　　　"used to be." Kansas City Star, June 17, 1981.
　　　　"for Kansas City." Ibid.
　　　　"back watching baseball." Kansas City Times, August 18, 1981.
　　270 *"at the most."* Kansas City Star, October 2, 1981.
　　　　"I'm not rushing." Kansas City Star, June 4, 1982.
　　　　"impressed with him." Kansas City Star, February 13, 1983.
　　　　"travels a lot." Ibid.
　　271 *Carson organization.* Ibid.
　　　　"very, very well." Ibid.
　　　　"have been canceled." Kansas City Times, February 17, 1983.
　　　　through with it. Ibid.
　　272 *"struck it rich."* Kansas City Times, February 18, 1983.

13. The Kauffman-Fogelman Dynasty

Page 273 *club in 1991.* Kansas City Times, May 18, 1983.
　　　　"only with him." Fogelman written response to author's questions, February 20, 1993. Hereafter cited as Fogelman letter, February 20, 1993.
　　　　"be in it." Kansas City Star, May 17, 1983.
　　274 *"dates or ultimatums."* Ibid.
　　　　"fifteen years ago." Kansas City Times, May 18, 1983.
　　　　"eight more years." Ibid.
　　　　"can say that." Kansas City Star, May 17, 1983.
　　　　"having all this." Kansas City Star, October 22, 1983.
　　275 *"is the mentor."* Kansas City Times, May 18, 1983.
　　　　"Kauffman-Fogelman Dynasty!" Ibid.
　　　　"it in court." Ibid.
　　　　rodeo circuit. Kansas City Star, August 13, 1983.
　　　　"do anything about." Kansas City Times, March 4, 11, 1987.
　　276 *"time after time."* Ibid.
　　　　"be the approach." Kansas City Times, June 23, 1983.
　　　　for several others. Ibid. Jerry Terrell and Steve Renko were the two free agents signed. The Royals bid for Floyd Bannister, Ron Guidry, and Tommy John but lost out to bigger purses.
　　　　"successful organization." Ibid.
　　　　the farm system. Ibid.
　　277 *"the right [player]."* Ibid.

Page 277 *"be the year."* *Kansas City Times,* August 26, 1983.
 "Fogelman, and myself." Ibid.
 278 *"wait and see."* Ibid.
 entire 1984 season. See *Kansas City Star,* August 26; October 13, 14, 17, 18, 23; December 16, 1983. See also *Kansas City Times,* October 14, 15, 19, 22; November 18; and December 16, 1983.
 "heartache to me." Cameron, *Moments, Memories, Miracles,* 163.
 "of the public." Ibid., 151.
 279 *"your role models."* *Sports Illustrated,* March 12, 1984, 23.
 "[standard] of behavior." *Kansas City Star,* December 18, 1983.
 "far, far ahead." Barrett interview, fall 1991.
 280 *"youth face today."* *Kansas City Star,* April 18, 1984.
 "a great deal." Cameron, *Moments, Memories, Miracles,* 163.
 "type of players." Ibid.
 281 *million-dollar loan.* New York Times, April 3, 1985. See also author interview with George Brett, May 26, 1994. Hereafter cited as Brett interview, May 26, 1994.
 over forty years. See *New York Times,* April 3, 1985.
 options to renew. In Quinsenberry's case, the Royals held options to renew for five years beyond 1990. Wilson boasted that beyond 1989, the Royals could have "as many options as they want." See *Kansas City Times,* March 15, 1985.
 282 *"Baseball Academy."* Ibid.
 "conceded the point." *Kansas City Star,* May 12, 1985.
 "long-term contract." Fogelman letter, February 20, 1993.
 "wish he hadn't." Ibid.
 283 *"we kept ducking."* Cameron, *Moments, Memories, Miracles,* p 25
 High School band. The high school student who loaned Brett the saxophone told reporters that he planned to have the reed bronzed in memory of the occasion. See *Kansas City Times,* October 29, 1985.
 "Princess Diana." *Kansas City Star,* October 31, 1985.
 284 *"were forced to."* *Kansas City Times,* July 12, 1986.
 "learn something." Ibid.
 "past ten years." Kauffman interview, August 25, 1992.
 "in their community." *Kansas City Star,* April 27, 1986.
 285 *was the nerve.* Kauffman interview, August 25, 1992.
 to take chances. Kansas City Times, June 24, 1986.
 "trophy in football." New York Times, June 23, 1986.
 286 *"or the library."* *Kansas City Times,* April 18, 1987.
 "Frank Howard were." Ibid.
 injured in football. New York Times, July 15, 1987.
 "final decision." *Kansas City Times,* July 15, 1987.
 287 *"sent Schuerholz."* Ibid.
 "out of him!" Ibid.
 "hundred years." Cameron, *Moments, Memories, Miracles,* 201.
 "should go ahead." *Kansas City Star,* March 21, 1991.
 288 *"same thing, personally."* *Kansas City Star,* May 23, 1991.
 "and for us." Ibid.

14. Exit Fogelman

Page 289 *"own the Royals." Kansas City Star,* January 11, 1988. Under the old contract, Fogelman owned 49 percent of the Royals. He had paid eleven
million dollars for this minority position. Kauffman had the option to
sell the remaining 51 percent to Fogelman at any time from 1988 to
1991 for an additional eleven million dollars. In 1991, Kauffman would
be obligated to sell.

"thought so far." Kansas City Star, July 21, 1988.

"greatest weakness." Ibid.

290 *"received here." CityScape,* July 1987, 15.

Laboratories stock. Kansas City Star, April 26, 1987.

"and Fogelman do." Ibid.

291 *"it be done." Kansas City Times,* September 27, 1988.

"of our community." Ibid.

"lid on it." Other Paper, March 9, 1989.

"at low prices." Ibid.

"Fogelman won't, either." Ibid.

for wealthy investors. Kansas City Times, June 9, 1989.

293 *"financial shape." Kansas City Times,* June 10, 1989.

"discussed it." Fogelman letter, February 20, 1993.

"consider selling." Commercial Appeal, June 22, 1989.

in his portfolio. Ibid.

"worse than better." Kansas City Star, July 10, 1989.

294 *"Memphis Business Journal."* Ibid.

team as collateral. Kansas City Star, July 18, 1989.

295 *"not get anything."* Quoted in ibid.

"to do so." Ibid.

to sell arise. Kansas City Times, July 19, 1989.

296 *"as I'm concerned."* Ibid.

free agent market. Ibid.

buy out Fogelman. Kansas City Times, August 5, 1989.

Players Association. Ibid.

297 *"in Kansas City." Kansas City Times,* August 9, 1989.

"of this community." Kansas City Times, August 5, 1989.

"the next century." Ibid.

"'and we will.'" Kansas City Times, December 20, 1989.

"in the signings." Ibid.

298 *"other than money." Kansas City Star,* January 7, 1990.

understand the value. Brett interview, May 26, 1994.

299 *"or leave it." Kansas City Star,* January 7, 1990.

"5 percent." Ibid.

"from free agents." Ibid.

300 *"you're a loser!"* Ibid.

of the Royals. Kansas City Times, January 27, 1990.

favorable lease. Under the new arrangement, Jackson County would pay
the Royals and the Chiefs about two million dollars a year each for
daily operations, undertake about thirty-five million-dollar projects

over ten years, and there was the likelihood that the Royals might get more seats in left field. For details on the lease see *Kansas City Times,* January 20, 1990, and *Sporting News,* January 22, 1990.

Page 300 *by March 1. Kansas City Times,* January 27, 1990.

"remarkable partnership." Fogelman letter, February 20, 1993.

301 *"any public endeavor!"* Fogelman letter to the author, October 14, 1994.

"that's plucked." Kansas City Star, January 7, 1990.

"on with it." Kansas City Star, March 15, 1990.

on the wall. Kansas City Star, March 19, 1990, and April 7, 1990.

302 *with the players. Kansas City Star,* May 3, 1990.

"dollars in it." Kansas City Star, May 4, 1990. In an interview with the author August 25, 1992, Kauffman revealed that he made the offer to Fogelman's wife because "I worried about him killing himself." As his financial empire began to crumble, Fogelman had called Kauffman one day after meeting with his bank creditors. "I could just tell how desperate he was from the phone conversation," Kauffman said. He called Mrs. Fogelman and urged her to meet her husband personally at the airport, "because he is real upset. And you tell him that regardless of what happens, if he goes bankrupt, I'll start him out again in whatever business he wants, with a million dollars because I think he is desperate." Later that evening, Fogelman called Kauffman to thank him for the generous offer and to reassure his partner that he would not harm himself. The older man responded, "Well, don't you be foolish. You've got too fine a family." See Kauffman interview, August 25, 1992.

303 *"to stay here." Kansas City Star,* May 4, 1990.

"to his wishes." Sporting News, May 14, 1990.

from those contracts. The troublesome contracts were with two active Royals, Willie Wilson and George Brett, and former pitcher Dan Quisenberry, who had just retired from the San Francisco Giants. The three players had entered into real estate deals with Fogelman as part of their contracts. Under the contracts, if Fogelman's real estate failed to produce the promised income for the player, the team would pay the difference. Fogelman guaranteed that he would personally reimburse the team. Fogelman was now unable to pay and his creditors wanted him removed from the obligation, mainly to head off any legal problems as he restructured financially. Kauffman was unwilling to replace Fogelman as the guarantor. He realized that he might not own the team in the future and did not want to end up reimbursing millions of dollars to someone else's ball players. See *Kansas City Star,* May 7, 9, 1990. See also Brett interview, May 26, 1994.

"Maybe age." Kansas City Star, June 22, 1990.

304 *Royals in 1990.* Ibid.

from the room. Kansas City Star, June 23, 1990.

15. The Succession Plan

Page 305 *"afford another one." Sports News,* July 30, 1990.

"don't take chances." MCA, August 5, 1990.

Page 305 *"[I] take it.'"* Kansas City Star, May 7, 1990, and August 1, 1990.
  306 *the ball club.* Kansas City Star, May 4, 1990.
      "of the Royals." Kansas City Star, December 19, 1990.
      "that it's easy." Ibid.
  307 *"suit and beard."* Ibid.
      "for stadium upkeep." Kansas City Star, April 7, 1991.
      "a hard problem." Kansas City Star, April 5, 1991.
  308 *"they're ridiculous."* Kansas City Star, January 24, 1991.
      "not principal." Kansas City Star, March 29, 1991.
      "100 percent." Kansas City Star, January 24, 1991.
      "than he offered." Kansas City Star, March 29, 1991.
  309 *whenever he chose.* Brett had deferred $500,000 on the first long-term
      contract he signed with the Royals for the 1976–81 seasons. Under the
      old contract, he was to receive ten payments of fifty thousand dollars
      when he retired. The new agreement stipulated he could receive the
      entire sum or any part of it at his discretion. See *Kansas City Star*, May
      22, 1991. See also Brett interview, May 26, 1994.
      "they said 'No.'" The provision that Brett would become a Royals vice
      president for seven years after the end of his playing career remained
      intact. Ibid.
      more than $1,100,000. New York Times compiled the figures that were
      quoted in *Kansas City Star*, November 22, 1991.
  310 *"was the worst."* Kansas City Star, April 7, 1991.
      "that looked simpler." Kansas City Star, April 20, 1993.
  311 *"won't miss me."* Ibid.
      "have to regroup." Kansas City Star, April 21, 1993.
  312 Financial World *magazine.* Ibid.
  313 *"lot of goodwill."* Ibid.
      "what to do." Kansas City Star, April 20, 1993.
      "redefine selflessness." Ibid.
  314 *his wealth away.* Kauffman telephone conversation with the author, July
      20, 1993.
      aside the idea. Kansas City Star, April 21, 1993.
      Memphis, Tennessee. Kansas City Star, April 23, 1993.
  315 *really meant it.* See *Kansas City Star*, May 23 and May 24, 1993.
      board of directors. Budig was named president of the American League
      in 1994. Joe McGuff, former sports editor of the *Kansas City Star*, was
      named to the Budig position. Four of the limited partners would pay
      $50,000 each and the fifth, who would be known as the "designated
      partner," would pay $250,000 to buy all the Royals voting stock.
  316 *"in professional sports."* Kansas City Star, June 12, 1993.
      "so I acquiesced." Kansas City Star, June 8, 1993.
      "spirit is here." Kansas City Star, July 3, 1993.
      "hit it big." Kansas City Star, May 27, 1993.
      "stadium after him?" Kansas City Star, June 8, 1993.
  317 *"very charitable."* Chronicle of Philanthropy, July 27, 1993.
      philanthropic assets. Ibid.

16. The Philanthropist Emerges

Page 319 *"on kids' faces."* See *Topeka Capital Journal,* January 7, 1990, and *St. Louis Post Dispatch,* August 7, 1989.

"actions impress them." *St. Louis Post Dispatch,* August 7, 1989.

"aspects of life." *Kansas City Star,* October 17, 1980.

320 *"and helping them!"* Kauffman interview, August 25, 1992.

321 *"covering any losses."* Robertson interview, November 11, 1993. In the 1980s, Marion Laboratories did establish a scholarship program to help employees' children attend college. After the merger with Merrell Dow, Kauffman approved a matching-gift program and he often honored other senior executives by making philanthropic contributions to the school of their choice. See Rogers to author, September 8, 1994. For a time Kauffman considered a matching program through his own foundation, but decided against doing so after the merger.

directors and trustees. See Articles of Incorporation, Ewing M. Kauffman Foundation archives.

care–related activities. Kauffman was thinking about scholarships for pharmacists, doctors, and nurses. See author interview with Michael Herman, February 10, 1992. Hereafter cited as Herman interview, February 10, 1992.

still to come. See author interview with Carl Mitchell, December 10, 1992. See also minutes of the Ewing and Muriel Kauffman Foundation, 1967–82, foundation files.

"with the community." Herman interview, December 10, 1992.

cardiopulmonary resuscitation. Marion Laboratories, *Annual Report,* 1969.

323 *was ignited.* Barrett interview, fall 1991.

324 *and easiest way. Kansas City Star,* May 10, 1981.

"a person's life." *Kansas City Times,* September 2, 1982. See also *Kansas City Star,* May 10, 1981.

"could you give?" Kansas City Star, April 5, 1981.

"effective today." Barrett interview, fall 1991.

volunteer activities. See Marion Laboratories, *Annual Report,* 1971.

325 *"worry about it!"* Herman interview, February 10, 1992.

"money at it." Barrett interview, fall 1991.

"executive talent." Ibid.

326 *"in the penitentiary."* Ibid.

"on that problem." Ibid.

327 *public education.* Author interview with Dr. Calvin Cormack, December 10, 1991. Hereafter cited as Cormack interview, December 10, 1991.

"was no solution." Ibid.

"to substance abuse." Ibid.

328 *at Marion Laboratories. Kansas City Star,* April 18, 1984.

"those strategies here." Ibid.

329 *"and drug situation."* Barrett interview, fall 1991.

"involved with drugs." Cormack interview, December 10, 1991.

330 *"in this area."* Ibid.

"with these students." Barrett interview, fall 1991.

Page 330 *Missouri schools.* Kauffman quoted in Cormack interview, December 10, 1991.
   331 *Virginia suburbs.* Cormack interview, December 10, 1991.
   332 *"with the foundation."* Herman interview, February 10, 1992.
   333 *"its stock accordingly."* M.E. Herman memo to Ewing M. Kauffman Foundation File, February 19, 1987. Foundation files.
   "all went well." Ibid.
   "large foundation." Ibid.
   334 *conflict of interest.* In 1993, when the foundation board established a matching-gift program, Rogers, the president, commented, "Though I would agree that Mr. K did not want his foundation to cater to the particular charitable desires of the board, I believe he would have strongly supported a matching-gift program that encouraged board members to give more to the charities of their choice. The reason I think this distinction is important is that we recently implemented a matching-gift program and the Marion-based board members, who knew Mr. K well, felt he would have strongly supported it as a way of 'sharing with those who produced the results,' one of his principle values." See Rogers to author, September 8, 1994.
   allocating funds. Rogers told the author, "Although it does not surprise me that Mr. K would have wanted to limit the CEO's discretionary authority to $250,000, he never discussed this with me or other members of the board that I am aware of." When the present board established limits on the CEO's discretionary giving, they were set at higher levels, but members of the board are involved in reviewing all major grants before they are implemented. See ibid.
   335 *in the foundation.* Ibid. At one time, Kauffman had considered including his immediate family on the board of trustees. But as he studied the history of family foundations and thought about the potential for family conflicts being transferred to the foundation boardroom, he decided to separate the two entirely. See also Kauffman interview, August 25, 1992.
   336 *"believe in that."* Kansas City Times, August 21, 1987.
   "the United States." Barrett interview, fall 1991.
   organization matured. See Kauffman-Nielsen correspondence. Ewing M. Kauffman Foundation files.
   "machines they have." Ibid.
   337 *"in the 1980s."* Herman interview, February 10, 1992.
   idea had merit. Ibid.
   "low economic status." Barrett interview, fall 1991.
337–38 *"was not easy."* Herman interview, February 10, 1992.
   338 *"be this big."* Kansas City Times, April 8, 1988.
   "signed agreement." Barrett interview, fall 1991.
   foundation's option. Kansas City Times, April 8, 1988.
   339 *variety of sources.* Herman interview, February 10, 1992.
   dollars a year. Kansas City Times, April 8, 1988.
   "Like Santa Claus." Ibid.
   340 *"of PROJECT CHOICE."* Kansas City Times, February 25, 1989.
   "away from trouble." Ibid.

Page 341 *"have an excuse."* Ibid.
342 *"not on drugs."* Barrett interview, fall 1991.
"a good job." Ibid. In response to a request from the governor of Kansas, Kauffman agreed to extend the program to Kansas City, Kansas. Tom Rhone, who had worked in the public school system for nineteen years before joining Marion Laboratories, suggested using a different approach there. In Kansas, thirty freshman students from each of five high schools were randomly selected from among those who qualified for the federal school lunch program. The plan was to compare the thirty with another ninety in the same class on such measures as attendance, discipline, and grade improvement. Drug use was not compared as the ninety students who were not a part of the PROJECT CHOICE pool had not given permission. However, the Kansas PROJECT CHOICE participants could be compared to their Missouri peers on drug involvement. See *Kansas City Times,* June 7, 1989; Herman interview, February 10, 1992; and Barrett interview, fall 1991.
do even better. Barrett interview, fall 1991.
343 *A's and B's.* Ibid.
344 *"to this day."* Tom Rhone conversation with the author, November 9, 1994.
"in the future." Ibid.

17. The Foundation Matures

Page 345 *"to fail here."* Herman interview, February 10, 1992.
346 *"should start sooner."* Barrett interview, fall 1991.
"intervene early." Herman interview, February 20, 1992.
347 *"looking at me."* Author interview with Gerard Kitzi, December 10, 1992. Hereafter cited as Kitzi interview, December 10, 1992.
"with this guy.'" Ibid.
"so far behind." Ibid.
348 *"they supported it."* Ibid.
family self-sufficiency. For more detailed information on PROJECT EARLY see Kauffman Foundation annual reports, 1992 and 1993.
"their self-esteem." Author interview with Leslie Reed, December 11, 1991. Hereafter cited as Reed interview, December 11, 1991.
349 *"convince Mr. K."* Ibid.
350 *"I really do."* Ibid.
self-esteem, was born. Ibid.
"can do it.'" Barrett interview, fall 1991.
351 *as the best.* Ibid.
cultural activities. The Muriel McBrien Kauffman Foundation was incorporated in 1987. The directors were Muriel Kauffman; her daughter, Julia Irene Kauffman; and Michael E. Herman.
investment activities. Herman interview, February 20, 1992. See also *Kansas City Star,* April 18, 1990.
353 *"that way, too."* Author interview with Robert B. Rogers, February 13, 1992. Hereafter cited as Rogers interview, February 13, 1992.

Page 353 *"and philanthropist."* See *Ingram's,* November 1990.

"'McGraw Amendment.'" McGraw interview, June 1, 1994. Both Mc-Graw and Rogers were elected directors on June 7, 1990. At the September 19, 1990, board meeting by-law changes were discussed and adopted. They provided for Kauffman as the founding director and five additional directors to serve three-year terms. Each director could serve a total of three consecutive terms. The McGraw amendment specifically waived term limits for McGraw. See official minutes of the Ewing Marion Kauffman Foundation, Ewing Marion Kauffman foundation files.

354 *of the curriculum.* See "Foundation—My Thoughts," Kauffman's handwritten notes in response to a memo from Herman, February 19, 1987. Also see "Foundation Thoughts," Kauffman's handwritten notes, undated in foundation files.

"time for them." Author interview with Michie P. Slaughter, August 9, 1993. Hereafter cited as Slaughter interview, August 9, 1993.

"something back, too." Ibid.

355 *"creation of jobs."* Ibid.

356 *"you had it."* Rogers interview, February 13, 1992.

Slaughter would head. Slaughter interview, August 9, 1993.

"to be successful." Barrett interview, fall 1991.

357 *fledgling entrepreneurs.* See Rogers interview, February 13, 1992.

"something we recommended." Ibid. The funding request that Kauffman denied was ten thousand dollars to a local university's school of public administration to help community service organizations develop their capacity to reach a wider audience of potential clients and probable funders by teaching them marketing strategies. However, the project called for no active involvement of either Marion Merrell Dow or foundation personnel in teaching the marketing skills. Kauffman was firmly wed to the operating concept at that time and frowned on any grant that did not use his own executives as integral participants. Surprised at Kauffman's refusal, Rogers felt that he had an obligation to fund the program personally. He had given the university a strong indication that Kauffman would approve the request. While he learned from the experience, both in relation to working with Kauffman as well as to being a grant maker, Rogers did not regret having to provide the funds from his own trust at the Greater Kansas City Community Foundation. "That's wonderful to have the luxury to do that. And I come right back and say the only reason I can do that is because of [Mr. K and Marion Laboratories]." Rogers interview, February 13, 1992.

358 *to these activities. Kansas City Star,* March 13, 1992.

[to make it down.] Smilor joined the CEL staff as vice president in 1992. He was one of the center's original executive advisers. His primary responsibility at the foundation was to establish and direct the Entrepreneur Training Institute.

359 *"before he died."* Slaughter, August 9, 1993.

philanthropic world. Confidential conversation with the author.

Page 359 *donor's wishes.* Rogers's letter to author, September 8, 1994.

360 *in philanthropy.* At Kauffman's death there were Rogers, Gardner, Herman, Hughes, McGraw, Nielsen, Edward Smith, and Louis Smith. At the fall 1993 meeting Siobhan Nicolau and the Reverend Thomas A. Savage, S.J., were elected to the board. The following year, Gene Budig and Anthony Mayer were elected as directors. Charles Hughes resigned May 1994.

Epilogue

Page 361 *"irritates you."* Kauffman interview, March 5, 1993.

362 *"gone dark early."* Brett interview, May 26, 1994.

overwhelm the organization. Five percent of the total assets would have to be distributed annually once the foundation received part or all of the money from both the unitrust and the revocable trust. Mike Herman estimated that the foundation's corpus could exceed one billion dollars within a relatively short time.

"do it better." Barrett interview, fall 1991.

363 *1992 of $12,300,000.* See Ewing Marion Kauffman Foundation, *Annual Report,* 1992.

the only recourse. Kauffman telephone conversation with the author, May 12, 1993. For a discussion of the Marion Merrell Dow decision to cut back, see *Kansas City Star,* May 5, 1993.

364 *for several hours.* Susan Hidalgo telephone conversation with the author, May 4, 1993.

365 *"a bit better."* Kauffman taped response to questions from the author, July 18, 1993.

"make me cry!!!" McGraw to Kauffman, July 4, 1993; Kauffman to McGraw, December 8, 1993.

"spoke to him." McGraw interview, June 1, 1994.

366 *"I'll never forget."* *Daily Oklahoman,* July 6, 1994.

"enjoy the game." See *Kansas City Star,* August 2, 1993.

"longer in pain." *Kansas City Star,* August 3, 1993.

367 *"the Ball Game."* See *Kansas City Star,* August 5, 1993. On August 5 there was a memorial service for Kauffman Foundation associates, former Marion associates, and other friends. And on Kauffman's birthday that fall, September 21, the foundation hosted a luncheon to celebrate his life. At the celebration luncheon Bob Rogers reported that as of that day the foundation had received $105,000 in memorial contributions. They ranged in size from $5.00 to $25,000 and most were accompanied by anecdotes about how Kauffman had touched that individual's life.

"of a citizen." *Kansas City Star,* August 8, 1993.

"thirty-three year career." Les Wilson to Kauffman Foundation, August 5, 1993, foundation files.

"of a kind." The Reverend Robert Meneilly, remarks at Kauffman funeral service, August 4, 1993.

368 *Merrell Dow. Kansas City Star,* March 23, 1995.

"Kauffmans' contributions." Ibid.

Page 368 *third-largest pharmaceutical company.* For details on the IRS ruling see
            Kansas City Star, May 3, 1995, and *Chronicle of Philanthropy,* May 18,
            1995. On the merger with Hoechst AG see *Kansas City Star,* May 5, 1995,
            New York Times, May 5, 1995, and *Wall Street Journal,* May 5, 1995.
       369 *was made public.* See *Kansas City Star,* May 3, 1995.

INDEX